A LEVEL
Film Studies
for WJEC

Tanya Jones
Editorial Consultant: Peter Fraser

Hodder Arnold
A MEMBER OF THE HODDER HEADLINE GROUP

First published in Great Britain in 2005 by
Hodder Education, a member of the Hodder Headline Group,
338 Euston Road, London NW1 3BH

www.hoddereducation.co.uk

The advice and information in this book are believed to be true and
accurate at the date of going to press, but neither the authors nor the publisher
can accept any legal responsibility or liability for any errors or omissions.

British Library Cataloguing in Publication Data
A catalogue record for this book is available from the British Library

ISBN-10: 0 340 885 91 2
ISBN-13: 978 0 340 885 91 8

1 2 3 4 5 6 7 8 9 10

Typeset in 11/14pt Syntax by Servis Filmsetting Ltd, Longsight, Manchester
Printed and bound in Dubai

What do you think about this book? Or any other Hodder Education title?
Please send your comments to the feedback section on
www.hoddereducation.co.uk

Contents

Preface

When A level Film Studies began in the mid-1980s, it looked very similar in structure and content to the degree courses which had been set up in the previous few years and which some of its early teachers (including myself) had undertaken. It was heavily theoretical and mainly encouraged study of a canon of classic Hollywood films and European art-house directors. Of the few hundred students taking the course each year, many were adults in evening classes and all the assessment took the form of conventional academic essays.

Despite a gradual climb in numbers and some small shifts in emphasis, it was not until the major changes to A level, brought about by Curriculum 2000, that the Film Studies course underwent radical revision. Now a very popular course with several thousand students taking it each year, the specification has opened up a range of material for study, from recent popular Hollywood blockbusters to powerful challenging foreign language films, such as *La Haine* and *City of God*. A range of topics relating to British cinema, both historically and thematically, is available and there is a strong expectation that students will keep up to date with developments in the film industry itself through case studies of contemporary film releases.

The course also offers opportunities for different kinds of assessment, from essays to a dissertation-style research project to practical tasks including screenplay writing, storyboarding, and even film-making, allowing a real variety of ways of learning.

This book is a welcome addition to the growing library of material available for students of film. It is the first book to be targeted specifically at the A level Film Studies specification and is written in a style which is accessible to students taking that course. Designed as a practical companion to use while studying and revising, and for systematic use throughout the course, it summarises the main ideas and key terms and provides questions and example answers to help students prepare for exams and coursework.

Used effectively, this book should lead to a better understanding of course material which, in turn, will lead to better grades. The attraction of Tanya Jones' book is that it is 'alive'. She shows how to apply the concepts and how to get the most out of each course unit through using up-to-date examples. She also introduces material that helps to strike a balance between the familiar and the unfamiliar, which is one of the aims of the A level itself – to build upon students' existing cinemagoing and film viewing experience by introducing them to new forms of cinema. With examples ranging from *Mission Impossible II* through to *Birth of a Nation*, this book ranges widely across American cinema; it also tackles the diverse history of cinema from other cultures, from *Bicycle Thieves* to *All About My Mother*.

Every unit is covered systematically and in detail, with clear advice on how to approach assessment tasks and how to structure writing. Hopefully, taking Film Studies will have some impact upon students' film viewing outside the class – not to stop their enjoyment of what they already consume but to make them more reflective upon it and to broaden their viewing tastes. This book should help in that aim.

Some advice for students using this textbook:

- Don't leave everything to the end of the unit. Deal with course material regularly to ensure, as each unit is covered in class, that you have a sound grasp of the material. Exam preparation is much easier when you already know and understand the material.
- Prepare for classes by reading over the relevant sections of the textbook in advance.
- Use the glossary in the textbook to look up any terms you do not understand.
- Use the sample essays to help you structure your own work as a model of good essays, not as something to copy!
- Watch as many of the films discussed in the book as possible and take the opportunities suggested to find out more about film culture.
- Most importantly, allow yourself to experience the pleasure of learning more about film.

Pete Fraser

Introduction

Beginning your A level Film Studies

When asked why they want to begin a Film Studies A level, students will invariably answer that it is because they 'really enjoy films'. This is an excellent basis from which to commence a Film Studies course. It often indicates far more than you initially realise.

First, it indicates enthusiasm, which is music to the prospective teacher's ears. It shows a pre-existing engagement with the subject area, which creates an open mind to new subject matter and means that you will enjoy extending your classroom learning through independent study. If you 'really enjoy films' you will also tend to have a good passive knowledge of film language and institutions, which will be invaluable during your A level studies.

Second, you may not yet know the precise film terminology, but you will be aware that camera angles, sound and editing contribute to the impact of the film you are watching. You may not know very much about the companies and organisations behind the production and exhibition of film, but you will be aware that the films shown at an independent cinema and those on offer at the local multiplex are different, and are intended for different audiences.

If you enjoy film, regularly visit the cinema and discuss what you have seen with friends, then you already have a sense of yourself and others as part of a film audience; a group that has expectations of the viewing experience. To summarise, to 'enjoy films' makes you much better qualified to begin a Film Studies A level than you might initially think.

As with any A level study, different students will bring different levels of knowledge, experience and ability to their Film Studies course. Some students have a wide experience of mainstream cinema – others may have found themselves drawn towards a particular national cinema, or even a particular movement in cinema history. There is no hierarchy involved in A level Film Studies. The course reflects the fact that if your experience at the beginning of the A level is purely of mainstream cinema, you will be as capable of getting the most out of it as someone whose knowledge includes independent cinema products. The spectrum of cinematic experience within any film studies class is broad and this is an advantage in classroom discussions. The A level course will allow all students to fill in the gaps in their knowledge and to gain experience and understanding of a range of cinema to which they have not previously been exposed.

We live in a time when the gap between film maker and film consumer is becoming smaller. The increasing affordability of digital cameras and editing software has meant that amateur film makers can now produce films, that not only have a level of sound and image quality that was previously unimaginable, but can potentially, via internet exhibition, be seen by a much greater number of people. As film students, you can extend your activity within film studies beyond the analytical; the practical components within the syllabus units offer the potential to be a film maker as well as a film analyst. The syllabus reflects the lessening gap between producer and audience in its practical tasks; storyboard and screenplay creation in the AS year and the possibility of making a short film in the A2 year.

Whether your particular interest is analysis of film or the processes of film production, the diminishing gap between producers and audiences is a development to acknowledge; it means, ultimately, that film has become even more accessible.

You might be somebody who aspires to be a film maker or a film journalist, you might have chosen Film Studies as a fourth A level to go alongside subjects that you wish to take to degree level. Whatever your reasons for beginning A level Film Studies, the course won't disappoint.

The syllabus

The WJEC A level syllabus aims to furnish you with knowledge and skills to increase your enthusiasm for film. There are three core areas of study, which span the AS and A2 years:

- Film Language
- Producers and Audiences; and
- Messages and Values.

The relationship between the film and those who watch it is the underlying dynamic of the A level. Each of the units you complete will help extend your understanding of how the relationship between the film and its audience works.

The term 'film language' refers to the (often invisible) elements of film that help create what we see on screen. Film language encompasses camera work, lighting, editing, sound, locations, narrative structure and any other element of film that contributes to the visual and aural experience of film viewing. In order to show your understanding of film language you will need to consider how the stylistic 'ingredients' of film, such as lighting and sound, help to engage and interest the film viewer. As with any discussion of audience response, you should never forget that you are part of the audience you discuss. Your own informed and independent response to the film texts you study will provide an essential part of your essays. What established film critics say about a film will be of use within your essay discussions, but your own consideration of the impact of stylistic choices is of equal, if not more, importance. How will an examiner be able to gauge your understanding of film language without reading what your informed response is to one of the elements of film language? As your confidence with film studies grows, so will your ability to evaluate and challenge the impact of film language on the film spectator.

The core area of Producers and Audiences indicates the study of the film industry and the relationship between what is produced and how it is consumed by the film audience. Ultimately, cinema is a business and it is driven by economics. What ends up on our cinema screens is dictated more by financial concerns, than by the producer's desire to offer a message or extend the boundaries of cinema. This is not to say that what is on offer in all cinemas is purely there to create money, but industries only survive if profit is involved. Your task in discussions of producers and audiences will not just be to identify the major players in film production, but to consider the balance between economics and originality in the films we are offered in cinemas. As with your discussions of film language, your own experiences of cinema-going will be essential within any debate concerning producers and audiences. You will need to consider the relationship between what is produced and how it is received, using your own opinions regarding the products within the film market place, as well as those of established critics.

The Messages and Values of film are those which are conveyed implicitly or explicitly to the audience. To translate this further, messages and values are the ideas concerning politics, race, gender, nationality, sexuality, religion and other key areas of debate that are evident from the study of a film. Films may seem to present ideas and debates explicitly, through dialogue, character relationships or use of settings. They may seem to be deliberately and conspicuously drawing the audience towards a particular understanding of a social group, for example. Films may also seem to be using more subtle or less evident routes to present an argument – for example, through the more invisible aspects of film, such as camerawork or editing. Your consideration of messages and values will also draw upon analysis of the time in which the film was made and how the dominant ideas of that time seem to inform what is being 'said' by the film. Messages and values are not fixed, in film. They are affected by the context of the time in which the film was made, but they are also affected by the attitudes and experiences of the viewer. Your task within an analysis of messages and values will be to enter into a discussion with the ideas offered by the film, to bring your own attitudes into this debate and to consider whether this dialogue between consumer and producer helps further your understanding of the film.

The six units within the A level are designed to increase your understanding of the three core areas and, as you have probably already realised, the core areas are not completely free-standing. The choices of film language made for a film will need to be discussed in terms of how they are understood by the film audience, and how messages and values are conveyed to the audience through the language of film. Your understanding of film and success within your A level will be greatly enhanced if you remember that the three core areas of study are to a large degree interwoven and interdependent.

The six A level Film Studies units are:

- Film: Making Meaning 1 (FS1)
- Producers and Audiences: Hollywood and British Cinema (FS2)
- Messages and Values: British and Irish Cinema (FS3)
- Film: Making Meaning 2 (FS4)
- Studies in World Cinema (FS5)
- Critical Studies (FS6).

The six chapters in this book cover the six FS units.

The AS year of the WJEC Film Studies A level course seeks to give you the skills and terminology required to discuss film. In order to do this in a way that utilises your pre-existing knowledge of film, it focuses on Hollywood, British and Irish cinema. The A level course has been designed in order to make film studies accessible. There is no intellectual 'gatekeeping' involved. The AS course does not ask you to reject previous film experiences or to start thinking of certain types of film as more 'worthy' than others. What it *does* do is to ask you to bring all of your experiences and thoughts regarding film into your classroom studies and to use them in your discussions of key areas.

Information about the A2
You will find a separate section to read later, about how to approach the A2 work, immediately before Chapter 4.

Guided independent study
In order to succeed in your Film Studies course, you will need to use your own experience and opinions to give you the confidence to learn about and challenge areas of film studies that may be new to you. It is essential that you retain the enthusiasm for film with which you begin your A level course and use this enthusiasm to motivate independent study outside of the classroom. Your teachers will give you key terms and examples, but you can easily improve your potential exam and coursework grades by supplementing class-based learning with independent study. Below are some ideas for independent study tasks that could make your progress through the course and ultimate exam performance even more successful.

Film diary
Try to keep a few notes on each film you see. These notes could include details of cast and crew, narrative and genre and your critical response to the film. Keeping a film diary could help in a number of ways. It could:

- provide an easily accessible guide to films, which you could reference in your essays
- give you inspiration when completing the original storyboard/screenplay tasks in your first AS unit

- provide you with case studies of spectator response, which you could use within your studies for the British and Irish Cinema exam.

Case studies

This guide includes many case studies related to the units you will cover within your A level Film Studies. You will need to distinguish your coursework and exam essays from those of other students. One easy way to do this is to keep an ongoing resource of your own case studies. Your case studies will differ from the notes you have kept in your film diary, as they will be more detailed, but your film diary could act as a prompt for a longer case study on a particular film.

To make a case study, choose a film that you think is of particular interest and make notes on the following:

- production details; including details of director and cast
- use of genre
- narrative 'type'
- key use of elements such as camerawork, editing, sound and *mise-en-scène* (you will find all of these terms explained in Chapter 1 of this book)
- critical responses to the film
- messages and values.

A good selection of your own case studies will be extremely useful in the AS and in the A2.

Film glossary

Each unit of your Film Studies course introduces new film-related terminology. This guide includes a glossary of film terminology, which gives clear definitions for the terms you will encounter in this book. However, an ongoing film glossary of your own, which includes definitions in your own words, and your own examples for each of the terms, would be extremely useful both during the course and for revision.

How to use this book

This book has been designed as a guide to your A level Film Studies. It will give you information about key content, concepts and terminology. It also includes case studies, questions and exercises to develop your understanding and to enable you to practise applying your skills and knowledge.

There are five important ways to use this book.

1. As a guide to the meanings of key terminology and concepts.

2. As a guide to the key content you will need for your A level Film Studies course.

3. As a guide to the question types and expectations of exam and coursework components of the course.

4. As a means of practising the skills and content application you will need to show during the course.

5. As an indication of the sections into which you should organise your own notes.

Doing well in any exam is dependent on: subject knowledge; understanding how to apply that knowledge within assessed tasks; and good organisation. This textbook includes comprehensive guidance on content and skills. The rest is up to you . . .

Acknowledgement

With thanks to the A level Film Studies students at Long Road Sixth Form College, Cambridge.

Chapter 1

Film: Making Meaning 1 (FS1)

Overview of the FS1 Unit

Film: Making Meaning 1 is the first assessed unit you encounter in your AS Film Studies course. It is a coursework-based unit and there is no exam attached to it. The FS1 tasks are designed to be accessible and to use the knowledge of films that you already have, as well as introducing you to new analytical skills. The unit focuses on the kinds of films – mainstream – with which you are already familiar, then asks you to create three pieces of coursework that demonstrate your skills of textual analysis and your understanding of the shape and structure of films – film form. The FS1 unit concentrates on how a film generates meaning and how the viewer of the film responds to the meanings that are generated. You will be learning lots of new film-specific terminology during your study for this unit, and gaining experience of analysing the different elements of film in close detail. You will learn new skills of film analysis, and if you combine these with your pre-existing knowledge of cinema, then you should be able to approach the FS1 tasks with confidence.

The FS1 unit makes up 40 per cent of your AS Film Studies mark.

Two of the tasks that make up this unit are analytical essays and the third is a piece of creative work. The tasks are outlined below. (The tasks and the terminology associated with them are explained in detail in the rest of Chapter 1.)

1. Macro analysis task.
   This task asks you to analyse either one film, *or* two films in comparison. You should choose one, or two, films that could be considered part of mainstream cinema. If you decide to concentrate on one film, you will need to select a sequence of no more than 10 minutes for your analysis. The macro analysis task asks you to focus on how genre and narrative create meaning and generate a response in the viewer. If you choose to analyse sequences from two films, then these sequences should be no longer than seven minutes each.

2. Micro analysis task.
   For this piece of coursework, you will need to select one or more from the micro elements list: *mise-en-scène*, sound, cinematography and editing; and discuss how your chosen elements create meaning and generate an audience response. For the micro study you will

focus on one film and the length of your chosen sequence should be no longer than seven minutes.

3. PAL: Practical Application of Learning.
   The third piece you will need to create for your FS1 coursework portfolio is a piece of practical work, with associated analysis. Your practical work must be based on an original idea, therefore you will need to focus on your own created film, rather than an industry example. You will need to produce three pieces of writing to go with your practical work: a synopsis, cinematic ideas and a self-evaluation.

Skills required for Unit FS1

There are three main skills you will need to show in order to gain the best possible marks for the FS1 coursework.

1. An ability to show how the form and style of a film work to communicate meaning.
   The term 'film form' can be translated as the shape or structure of a film. An analysis of film form should discuss how the story of the film is organised so that it creates meaning for the viewer. You might consider what techniques are used to organise time within the whole film, or consider how the events within a particular scene are organised to create particular meanings. Analysis of film style concentrates on how the individual elements of a film, such as editing, cinematography, sound and *mise-en-scène* are used to create meaning for the viewer. Your analysis could consider how the style of a film helps the viewer to identify the genre of the film or to understand a particular character's state of mind.

2. An ability to discuss how film form and style engage the audience of a film.
   An analysis of film form and style should consider the relationship between the way in which a film is structured and presented, and the responses to this structure and presentation from the film's audience. The relationship between the film and the audience of that film is complex. Film audiences have their own expectations concerning what they see and the meanings that the film assumes it is generating are not necessarily those that are being understood by the viewer. Your essays will gain much better marks if you remember that audiences come to the viewing of a film with their own expectations and opinions. The meanings and ideas offered by a film might be accepted by the viewer, but they may also be challenged or rejected.

3. An ability to reflect on and discuss your own experience as a consumer of film.
   You have a dual role within your AS Film Studies course. First, the skills and knowledge you gain will allow you to become a sophisticated film analyst. You must not forget, however, that you are also part of the film-going community and can, therefore, discuss your own responses to a film as a member of the film's audience. Including your own

comments and reflections on the experience of viewing a film will only enhance your analytical writing. If you had certain expectations of the viewing of a particular film which were or were not met, then you should add these comments to your close textual analysis.

Macro analysis

The macro analysis task within your FS1 coursework unit requires you to study how genre and narrative work to create meaning in film. In order to be able to analyse the two macro elements, you will need to ensure that you have a clear understanding of the terms. Below are clear definitions of both terms; case studies to show you how to discuss them; plus questions and exercises in order to help you to practise your own macro analysis. At the end of the section on macro analysis in this unit there are two example essays (see pages 33–8), which you could use to check the structure and content of your own.

Genre

At some point or another in your experience of film going, you have probably stated that you would prefer to go and see a horror film, or a thriller, or a comedy. All of these are examples of genres. The word 'genre' means type, or kind, and in relation to film has become a means by which groups of films can be distinguished from one another. In order to be able to group together different films, the genre system identifies key elements that are shared within a group of films. These elements might be connected with character, props, themes, narrative or settings; and a group of films within the same genre will share a particular use of these elements. A thriller, for example, will tend to include the following elements or conventions:

- a hero with a 'flaw' or vulnerability that can be exploited by the villain of the film
- a gradual drawing in of the hero into a complex and confusing set of events
- a scene near the end of the film in which the hero is isolated and in peril
- a pre-existing connection between the hero and the villain of the film, which makes their conflict even more personal and dramatic
- themes of identity: mistaken, false or forgotten
- settings that are usually safe and secure, but where extraordinary events take place
- an enigma or secret at the heart of the narrative, which must be explained.

These conventions of the thriller genre make it recognisable to, and predictable for, the viewer; and cinema-goers who enjoy thrillers will expect to experience at least a few of these conventions in the film they have chosen to see.

EXERCISE 1

With a partner, choose one of the film genres below and list as many of the key conventions of that genre as you can:

- Western
- horror
- science fiction

- romantic comedy
- action
- fantasy.

When you and your partner have made your list, present your findings to the rest of the class. You should make notes on the conventions identified in other genres by other members of your film class and consider any similarities between the conventions.

Genre conventions act as a basic framework within a film and they offer consistency across a group of films. Conventions are not used in exactly the same way by each film within a genre, however, as this would be too predictable and ultimately unsatisfying for the film viewer. Conventions develop and mutate with time. Audiences need to experience both familiarity and difference within the films they view, and if a genre film is to be successful, then it needs to acknowledge this dual demand. The time in which a film is produced also influence the way in which the conventions of a genre are used. The changing attitudes of society and the dominant ideas within society at different points in history inform the use of generic conventions. Consider action films, for example. Do audiences today still want to see the muscle-bound hero and ineffectual heroine, or do films such as *The Long Kiss Goodnight* (Renny Harlin, 1996), *Aliens* (James Cameron, 1986) and *Terminator 2* (James Cameron, 1991) indicate a shift in audience expectations with regard to the representation of male and female characters within the action genre?

Terminator 2. **Source: British Film Institute**

EXERCISE 2

With your partner, choose a genre of film and make notes on the way in which certain conventions within that genre have changed over the years. You could concentrate on developments concerning character types, settings, or any other convention. Try to make a list of specific film examples, and identify clearly what has changed and what you think the factors were that influenced that change.

Within a main genre group, there are often smaller groups of films. These are called sub-genres. These films share the same basic conventions of the larger category, but also have their own set of very specific conventions. The horror genre, for example, includes the sub-genres of vampire films, slasher films, zombie films and demonic possession films. Sub-genres often have core audiences, who are fully aware of the conventions they expect to see. Wes Craven's *Scream* films, for example, not only discuss and use the conventions of the slasher film, but present us with characters who are slasher film buffs and are seen clearly exhibiting their detailed knowledge of this sub-genre.

Any cinema schedule today will include examples of hybrid genres. These are films that have utilised two or more sets of generic conventions in order to target the widest possible

EXERCISE 3

Look at the two stills. Which do you think is from a sub-genre and which is from an example of a hybrid genre? What evidence do you see in the stills for your conclusions?

Source: British Film Institute

Source: Strike Entertainment/New Amsterdam/
The Kobal Collection/Michael Gibson

cinema audiences. Hybrids allow the film producer to reach fans of more than one genre and thus potentially secure an even bigger film audience. David Twohy's film *Pitch Black* (2000), for example, combines the conventions of action and science fiction to attempt to secure box-office success.

As has already been indicated, the genre system can be used by the film producer in order to try to secure a good financial return on a film. One of the reasons a genre of film becomes established in the first place is due to producers' attempts to generate box-office receipts. If the very first example of a particular style or type of film were unsuccessful, then it is highly unlikely that the genre would continue to exist. The recent run of films derived from comic books for example – *Spiderman, Hulk* and *Daredevil*, to name a few – would not be in existence if the comic-book inspired super-hero genre had not already proved to be financially successful by the *Superman* and *Batman* films. Super-hero films also include the convention of spectacular special effects and action sequences, which has become a prerequisite within the blockbuster today. Blockbusters are films that have their own set of recognisable and predictable elements. They might even be considered a genre in their own right. Blockbusters have huge budgets, big-name stars, universal themes, huge set action sequences, massive publicity and usually carry a PG, 12 or possibly 15 certificate. They are incredibly expensive to make and market, but if they are successful, they can bankroll other less lucrative films.

As has already been discussed, the genre system has a key function for film audiences, not just film producers. Genre provides the viewer with a means of recognition and a pre-existing

EXERCISE 4

Before you begin your macro essay, practise your genre analysis skills by choosing a 10-minute sequence from a film and applying the knowledge you have gained from reading the first part of this section on genre. Remember to ask yourself the following key questions:

1. What are the generic conventions evident within my chosen sequence?

2. Is the film from which my sequence is taken an example of a straight genre, a sub-genre or a hybrid genre? What is my evidence for this?

3. Does the sequence I have chosen use conventions in a straightforward way? Or does it subvert the audience's expectations of these conventions?

4. How does the use of conventions in my chosen sequence (and film) differ from examples of the same genre that have gone before? What factors may have caused this development in the use of generic conventions?

5. What is the impact upon the audience of the conventions I have identified?

set of expectations, which will inform both the viewer's choice of a film and their response to it. Film audiences are demanding creatures, however, and need to see developments in the way genre elements are presented to them. Genre films thus have to adapt and develop the ways in which they use conventions. They may even use conventions self-consciously in order to acknowledge the viewer's understanding of a particular genre. Following Wes Craven's *Scream* films there have been a number of films that have sought to extend the viewer's enjoyment of genre pieces by explicitly acknowledging the conventions they are using. For example, *Scary Movie* (Keenan Ivory Wayans, 2000), presents itself unashamedly as a film about horror films, even acknowledging the film *Scream* within its spoof sequences. Films may use genre conventions in a straightforward, traditional manner; or they might parody or spoof them. They might even subvert (use in a contradictory way) the viewer's expectations of generic conventions. Your essays will not only need to identify the genre of your chosen film and the evident conventions, but discuss how and why these conventions are being used in a particular way.

You should use the two genre analysis case studies that follow to guide your practice analysis.

Case Study 1: Genre analysis

The use of generic conventions within a 10-minute sequence from Nora Ephron's *You've Got Mail* (1998)

Sequence: 10 minutes after the initial credit sequence.

You've Got Mail is a romantic comedy and adheres very closely to the typical conventions of that genre. As with any set of conventions, however, the way in which they are presented reflects the time in which the film was made. The cyber-chat between the two characters, which hides their true identities from one another and at the same time indicates the potential romance between the two characters, locates the film in its time – the late twentieth century.

Romantic comedies are built around a series of initial oppositions. The romance between the central protagonists must be hard won and their passage towards admitting their feelings for each other is often fraught with trials. *You've Got Mail* is no exception.

The initial sequences of this film provide information concerning the oppositions between the two characters. Their respective partners at the beginning of the film, along with their apartments and their jobs, provide the viewer with information concerning the hurdles and tensions that will arise in the narrative. Kathleen Kennedy (Meg Ryan) lives in a very different type of apartment to Joe Fox (Tom Hanks). Kathleen's apartment is light and comfortable. The camera pans around her apartment to reveal light wooden furniture, muted but warm colours and lots of books. This is a comfortable apartment, not overtly expensive or style obsessed, but warm and inviting. The first shots we see of Joe Fox are when he is seated in his kitchen. His apartment immediately seems different to Kathleen's. The kitchen is decorated in monochrome and the materials used it in are hard and cold, but expensive: chrome and ceramic. This is an apartment belonging to someone whose economic position is above that of Kathleen Kennedy and this is reinforced when Joe moves out of the kitchen through into the main part of his apartment. It is stylish and comfortable, yet the *mise-en-scène* of Joe's apartment includes antique Grandfather clocks and a dark, heavy, expensive wood desk. Of course, there cannot be so much contrast between the two main protagonists in a romantic comedy that their eventual union seems ridiculous, so the softer side of Joe is represented through his response to his dog (who provides the subject of the initial e-mail of the film) – not a pristine little show dog, but a big, fluffy Golden Retriever.

Fitting the expected narrative convention of romantic comedies, both Kathleen and Joe begin the film involved in relationships with other people. As is also typical of the conventions of romantic comedy, however, it quickly becomes clear that these initial partners are unsuitable for the main protagonists. Initial partners often function to indicate the core lack within the main protagonists' lives. In this film, the two central characters' e-mails are not sexual or dramatic, but express thoughts and feelings about their lives and what goes on around them. They are flirtatious, but in a way which is specific to the other character. Joe writes that if he knew where Kathleen lived he would send her a 'bouquet of pencils', thus indicating the depth to which these characters already engage with each others lives and needs. When we see Kathleen and Joe's partners, it is obvious what is lacking. Kathleen's partner wakes her not with affectionate words, but with what we can see is yet another diatribe on the state of the world. He speaks in abstracts, not human specifics and, unlike her contact with Joe via e-mail, he does not really engage with Kathleen on an emotional level. Joe's girlfriend is frantic and frenetic. She rushes into the kitchen and skims the surface of a discussion with him before rushing out to work. Having been introduced to the two partners, the audience is not surprised that the two central characters then open their laptops and immerse themselves in a much gentler and more emotional connection.

The end of this sequence sees Kathleen and Joe leaving their apartments and heading off for work. It is immediately apparent to the audience that they exist in the same city, at the same time. Their relationship might only exist at this point in the narrative in cyberspace, but dramatic irony has already been established. We know what they do not – that eventually the virtual relationship will become real. As this is the opening sequence of the film, however, the pattern of oppositions and anonymity is still being established. Joe and Kathleen are seen walking though New York to work. They are seen on the same street; both buying coffee at Starbucks; walking either side of a fence; but at this point in the narrative they have not met in person and are oblivious of each other's existence, despite the near proximity.

Characterisation, *mise-en-scène* (note: for a full explanation of the term *mise-en-scène*, see page 51) and editing have all been used during this initial sequence of the film, to provide indication of the romance to come. However, this is a romantic comedy and there has to be more of a hurdle to the relationship than the characters being in other relationships. Kathleen and Joe do not seem to be of wildly different socio-economic backgrounds and they do not differ in religion or social status. To create tension, we need more of a barrier to the development of their relationship. This is provided at the end of the sequence. Joe is seen walking into a soon to be unveiled new shop. The shop is huge and we learn that it is a superstore, selling books. When quizzed in the superstore, Joe does not seem to register (or even care about) the impact that this huge store will have on the smaller book shops in the neighbourhood. Of course, when we realise that Kathleen owns 'The shop around the corner' – a family-run, independent, small bookshop – the audience understands the main hurdle that is being set up at this point in the narrative. The two characters have wildly opposing attitudes to book-selling and the importance of books, and this will provide the basis for the major tensions to come in the narrative of *You've Got Mail*.

Case Study 2: Genre analysis

The use of generic conventions within a 10-minute sequence from Robert Zemeckis' *What Lies Beneath* (2000)

Sequence: The main character of Claire finds a mysterious key and sees the ghostly woman for the first time.

What Lies Beneath falls into the sub-genre of supernatural thriller. As such, it combines the generic conventions of the thriller, with supernatural elements. The scene this case study explores begins with a shot of Claire (the main character in the film, played by Michelle Pfeiffer), putting new glass into a photo frame that has mysteriously been smashed. The photograph is of Claire and her husband Norman. The scene is shot at night and the *mise-en-scène* is shrouded by darkness, a fitting, ominous context, in which Claire will experience both confusion and fear. The only sound at this point in the scene is diegetic (within the world of the story): that of the insects outside the house. (For more about diegetic sound and sound in general, see pages 39–45.) We know that Claire lives in a fairly isolated spot and our knowledge of this, combined with the insect sounds, generate feelings in the audience of expectation and tension.

Thrillers are often set in unremarkable locations where remarkable things happen and this one is no exception. Claire is then seen to step on a shard of glass from the smashed frame. Both her night attire and the shard of glass in her foot add to the feeling that she is vulnerable. Thrillers see their main protagonist being drawn into an ever more complex web. This scene marks the beginning of Claire's movement into the complexities of the film's narrative.

One classic convention of the thriller genre is that the main character has either a flaw or a psychological 'Achilles heel'. Many thriller protagonists have a psyche which is shrouded by guilt, regret or obsession. Many have experienced something in their pasts that makes them more susceptible to being manipulated in some way. We already know from previous scenes that Claire is in her second marriage. Her first husband was killed in a road accident and she still feels the pain and grief of this time acutely. She also clings to her daughter, as if fearful that she will lose her, too. This psychological backdrop to Clare's character makes her a classic thriller protagonist. Her fear is of loss and death, and she is 'ghosted' by the memory of her dead husband, therefore she will have a particular susceptibility to ghostly presences.

Having removed the shard of glass from her foot, Claire looks down to discover that there is a key under the small grill in the floor. At this point, the non-diegetic soundtrack (the sound outside the world of the story) begins. (For more about non-diegetic sound and sound in general, see pages 39–45.) The repeated note sequences within this music, which seem to swirl but never resolve, make it typical of the thriller genre. Thrillers keep the viewer tense, waiting for resolution until the final moments of the film: thriller soundtracks function in the same way. The viewer wants the music to build towards its climax and then offer some release, but it keeps us in a state of tension. Claire picks the key out of the vent and thus begins the mystery at the heart of this thriller. The key implies a mystery, something hidden, and Claire's confused, but intrigued, expression mirrors the audience's own response. Thrillers have an enigma at their core; something unknown and hidden that provides the motivation for the protagonist's search.

The next section of the sequence sees Claire climbing the stairs. Still shrouded by darkness and now confused, she seems more vulnerable than ever. As she reaches the top of the stairs, the camera pans round to reveal steam coming from under the door to the bathroom. The non-diegetic sound at this point in the scene takes the tension up a notch. The extended chords of the music evoke a feeling of dread and when the diegetic creaking of the bathroom door is heard, the viewer realises that the conventions of the thriller in this film have been merged with those of supernatural films. The next shot we see is a point-of-view shot from Claire into the bathroom. The obscuring *mise-en-scène* of the steam adds to the tension and our feeling that something might be lurking in the bathroom, just out of our sight. Thrillers often use fogs, mist and steam to evoke a feeling of disquiet in the viewer. What we cannot see clearly will invariably make us anxious.

Bathrooms have had much use within the thriller and horror genres. If threat enters the domestic environment, then it feels all the more intrusive and frightening. If that threat lurks in the bathroom, a place where we are often unclothed, then the sense of violation is more palpable. Claire sees that the bath is full of water. As she looks at the bath, everything seems still. The viewer can sense at this point that something is about to occur. We tend only to be given stillness in the thriller when it is about to be disturbed. Claire looks over the bath and we see her reflection in the bath water. Two thriller conventions are evoked by this image. First, the theme of mirroring or reflection. Thrillers often use mirrors or water to position us behind the protagonist, looking at their reflection with them. In this position we cannot see who is behind us and at this point in a thriller another, frightening face will often join the frame, thus making both ourselves and the protagonist feel vulnerable to attack. The second thriller convention being employed at this point is that of watching or viewing. The main characters in thrillers are often being watched, watching another character, or see something they wish they had not seen. Claire has already been seen 'spying' on her neighbours with a pair of binoculars. She sees events which she does not understand, or misinterprets. As she stands over the bath, she suddenly sees the form of a ghostly woman. At this point the non-diegetic soundtrack reaches its climax and she runs terrified from the bathroom into the arms of Norman, her husband. As with many thriller protagonists, Claire has seen something she wishes she hadn't.

Narrative

The term narrative can be most clearly understood as the means by which the story within a film is structured and organised. Your study of narrative will focus on the ways in which events are organised within a film to create meaning. Narrative and genre are often inextricably linked and, as we have already seen within the section discussing genre, narrative expectations can form part of genre expectations. An audience for a romantic comedy, for example, would be very disappointed if the end of the narrative did not include a resolution

EXERCISE 5

With a partner, choose a genre and make notes on any elements of narrative that you consider to be attached to that genre. Feed your notes back to the rest of the class.

in which the central protagonists become a couple. Try to remember the potential links between narrative and genre when you are writing your macro study.

Narrative conventions allow the different spaces and times that exist within a film to be organised in a meaningful way. A typical film lasts about two hours, but the timescale of the story of the film is often much longer. The narrative of the film will include the elements from the story that are most crucial for the viewer's understanding. Narratives often use ellipsis (where something that is not necessary is missed out) in order to edit out sections of time the audience does not need to see. A film that presents events as 'Ten years later' or 'Two weeks earlier' is using ellipsis to miss out a period of time that does not need to be seen. A particular organisation of narrative events can also indicate connections between different places, events or characters. Parallel narratives, where one set of events in a particular place is cut with another set of events within another place, suggest to the viewer that the events shown are happening at the same time and are connected. These events are obviously happening in different places, but the parallel narration of them indicates a close link between the actions of the different characters shown.

Narrative elements can also help the viewer to understand the significance of particular events to particular characters and to the story as a whole. Flashbacks, in which an event in the past is shown on screen during a present event, are often from a particular character's point of view and are used to indicate that a character is either still suffering from a past trauma, or has made a connection between a past event and a present one. Flashbacks (and the alternative flash forwards) do not stop the chronology of the film moving forward, they act to draw connections for the audience between past and present events.

In the majority of mainstream films, narrative elements help to sustain a reality effect within a film. Most narratives move forward chronologically and thus represent real time. Even the use of elements such as ellipsis, flashbacks and flash forwards do not tend to break the viewer's concentration on the story or their belief that what is happening on the screen is occurring in a realistic chronology. The viewer's suspension of disbelief, i.e. their willingness to accept the events shown on the screen as real for the length of the film, is aided and also sustained by narrative.

Your macro essay does not require you to describe or assess what theorists have to say about narrative structures or conventions. Your discussions of narrative should focus on your assessment of how narrative functions in your chosen sequence. What theorists like Propp and Todorov have to say about the function of narrative would be interesting for you in the preparation of your essay, but should not be used as the main focus within that essay.

Todorov's ideas concerned a theory of the basic structure of all narratives. He offered the theory that narratives begin with a period of 'equilibrium', a situation of relative calm and security for the main protagonists of a film. The characters within a film who could be described as anti-equilibrium (criminals, romantic interlopers etc.) or the situations that might bring about disquiet, then act to destroy the equilibrium, bringing about a period of 'disequilibrium'. The characters who have this function are called agents of disruption. The process of all stories, according to Todorov, is the (attempted) return to a new state of peace, in which all of the hurdles of the story have been overcome. He calls this the 'new equilibrium' stage, which comes about when the chaos within the story has been brought to an end. As a means of assessing narrative, Todorov's theory is a useful one, as are many others, but should not be relied upon as the only explanation of narrative structure. Here is a description of how Todorov's theory functions in the film *Scream* (Craven, 1996).

1. Equilibrium.
   Casey Becker (Drew Barrymore) is seen at home. Her house is comfortable. She is obviously from a relatively affluent background. She is relaxed and just about to settle down to watch a film.

2. Disequilibrium.
   As with any horror film, the agent of disruption is the killer. At the point where Casey's seemingly flirtatious and unthreatening telephone conversation becomes frightening, the disequilibrium begins. As she is chased, teased and then brutally killed, the viewer begins to realise that there is little motivation for this killing other than the killer's warped satisfaction. The main body of the narrative shows a succession of scenes in which the teens within the film are slaughtered. It also presents the potential agent of equilibrium in the film as Sidney Prescott (Neve Campbell). She remains alive into the last scene and eventually overcomes the killers.

3. New Equilibrium.
   The new equilibrium of *Scream*, as with any slasher film, is tainted by the killings which have made up many of the preceding scenes. The killers are dead and Sidney has found her father and remained alive. She will, however, never be the same again!

EXERCISE 6

Read the description above of how Todorov's theory of narrative sections function in *Scream*. Then choose two other films and apply the same theory. To what extent do you think audience expectations of narrative are met by the textual details you identify in each of these sections?

Source: British Film Institute

Your essays could also look at a narrative as a sequence of different sections within a film, all with their own specific and distinct function. One way of distinguishing between the different sections of a film's narrative is outlined below. In this model there are five stages through which a narrative has to progress.

1. Exposition – the exposition part of a film's narrative introduces the setting and the characters to the film audience.

2. Development – this is the stage of a film where the storyline is developed and the audience is introduced to more characters.

3. Complication – during this stage of the film's narrative, we are presented with a complicating event that will adversely affect the lives of the main protagonists within a film.

4. Climax – at this stage within a film's narrative, dramatic tension is at its height and the secrets or enigmas of the previous action are revealed. This is also the point in the film where there is often a confrontation between the two characters who represent 'good' and 'evil' in the story.

5. Resolution – the end of a film usually holds its resolution; the sequence where stability is re-established and a form of calm has been restored.

EXERCISE 7

Using the five stages of narrative described above, discuss what happens in each of these sections within a film of your choice.

As with many other theories of narrative, the application and discussion of these different sections is best suited to mainstream film, which uses the conventions of narrative form relatively traditionally. Independent or experimental films may reject the use of standard narrative structures in order to create a different effect for their audience. As with genre, audiences have an awareness of narrative and they have expectations of what they want to see happening at various stages within a (mainstream) narrative. Your discussions of your chosen film sequence should consider what expectations audiences have of narrative as a whole; the different sections within a narrative; and the use of narrative as a generic convention.

EXERCISE 8

Before you begin your macro essay, practise your narrative analysis skills by choosing a 10-minute sequence from a film and applying the knowledge you have gained from reading the first part of this section on narrative. Remember to ask yourself the following key questions:

1. In which section of the whole narrative does my sequence come? What are the general functions of this type of sequence? To what extent does my sequence exhibit these functions?

2. How does the use of narrative within my sequence help to organise time within the film?

3. How does the use of narrative within my sequence help to organise space within the film?

4. Does the sequence of narrative I have chosen help to convey information concerning genre to the audience?

5. Does the sequence of narrative I have chosen confirm or challenge the viewer's understanding of events within the film up to this point?

You should use the two narrative analysis case studies that follow to guide your practice analysis.

Case Study 3: Narrative analysis

An analysis of narrative within a 10-minute sequence from Luc Besson's *The Fifth Element* (1997)

This case study will analyse the 10-minute sequence in which LeeLoo joins the other four elements and earth is saved from attack.

The sequence from *The Fifth Element* analysed here falls into the climax section of the narrative. Dramatic tension is at its height and the enigmas, tensions and questions that have been established in the first part of the film's narrative are explained. This sequence also brings to an end the disequilibrium section of the narrative and predicts the establishment of a new equilibrium to come. The sequence focuses on the battle between those elements within the narrative which seek to disrupt and those which seek to resolve. This is a tension that provides the heart of most film narratives. The characters of Dallas and LeeLoo provide the agents of equilibrium; these are the characters, who along with their helpers, act to ward off threat and bring about a new period of safety and security within the narrative. The Dark Planet provides the role of the agent of disruption. It is about to destroy Earth and thus destroy the possibility for resolution and new equilibrium within the film.

One of the main functions of narrative structure within a film is to organise space and time, and in this sequence the narrative pattern allows the viewer to understand that each set of characters in the different locations shown is undergoing the same extreme tensions. The viewer understands that the actions of LeeLoo, Dallas and their allies will impact on the lives of the other characters seen in the other locations, and the fact that the focus of the narrative action is on the former characters indicates that it is they who will save the lives of the latter characters. There is an explicit use of cause and effect within this sequence, which again is an important element within any film narrative. The viewer fully understands what the consequences of failing to unite the five elements will be.

The action within this climactic sequence focuses on the attempts of Dallas and his group to unite the elements, thus activating a powerful weapon and stopping the Dark Planet from destroying Earth. As with any climactic narrative sequence, there are hurdles that have to be overcome in order for potential resolution to the difficulties within the narrative to take place. In this sequence, the hurdles and tension come in a number of forms. First, the agents of equilibrium are involved in a race against time. This is indicated clearly by the countdown commenced in the President's military base and sound-bridged over into the place in which Dallas and the others are attempting to unite the elements. This 'race against time' is a typical device for creating tension within the climactic sequence of a film and the tensions of the characters at this point mirror those of the viewer. The second hurdle comes in the form of LeeLoo's weakening state and her loss of faith in the ability of the human race to value the life that her actions will give them.

The thematic tensions that mark the science fiction genre: good versus evil; man versus a technological or technologically advanced alien threat; and Man versus his own propensity to destroy himself provide a backdrop of oppositions that create a further level to the tensions within this scene.

Having educated herself about mankind, LeeLoo has discovered that with technological advancement humans have invariably become empowered to destroy one another. Her comment of: 'What's the use of saving life when you see what you do with it?' provides a hurdle within this narrative sequence that is as potentially difficult to overcome as the Dark Planet's threat. The climactic sequence of a film's narrative must indicate the potential for a range of resolutions: thematic, character and narrative. On a thematic level, LeeLoo's profound disturbance at the destructive potential of mankind has to be overcome. On a characterisation level, the romantic relationship between Dallas and LeeLoo must be expressed; and on a narrative level, the Dark Planet must be stopped. As with many films, these three levels of conflict are inextricably linked. It is only when Dallas puts aside his fear of love that LeeLoo can regain some faith in the potential good of humanity and thus become strong enough to provide the power of the fifth element alongside the other four.

This sequence offers the viewer a number of met expectations:

- The Dark Planet is destroyed and thus the agents of equilibrium within the film have succeeded in their task.

- The burgeoning relationship between the central protagonists within the narrative has been expressed and is mutually felt.

- The fears the audience have of this science fiction film dissolving into a dystopian nightmare are avoided with the re-establishment of order; and thus the potential for a more harmonious, utopian world and the narrative pleasure for a resolved ending are secure.

- Even the potential fears expressed in the science fiction genre of a technology-saturated world in which the human race has lost its humanity come to nothing.

The Fifth Element evokes the fundamental need in its audience for love and truth to prevail, and for humankind to behave humanely.

Case Study 4: Narrative analysis

An analysis of narrative within a 10-minute sequence from Ridley Scott's *Gladiator* (2000)

Source: British Film Institute

This case study will analyse the 10-minute sequence in which Maximus is betrayed, taken to be executed and then escapes, to find his family murdered.

This sequence occupies the complication section of the narrative in *Gladiator*. What happens in this sequence changes Maximus' life forever and gives him his quest for revenge. Caesar has asked Maximus to act as Protector of Rome until the time when a Republic can be formed. Maximus has led his soldiers to another victory. He is an extremely popular and successful military leader. This, of course, makes Maximus a threat to Commodus, who murders his own father (Caesar), when he discovers that he is not to be made Emperor.

This sequence marks the beginning of the disequilibrium, which will only be broken when Maximus kills Commodus at the end of the film. Maximus had been heading home to enjoy a peaceful life with his family, but the murder of Caesar and the accession of Commodus disrupt these plans. Commodus takes the role of disruptor within the narrative and only his death will bring about a new equilibrium.

The sequence begins with a low-angle shot of the bust of Caesar. Commodus has just murdered his father and thus also the just rule of Caesar. The statue represents the dignified rule that has been lost with this murderous act. The sequence then cuts to a scene involving Maximus. He is awakened by his servant and told that 'Caesar' wishes to see him. Maximus wakes and immediately draws his dagger. This action indicates the fact that he senses trouble and the audience already knows he is under threat from the previous scene. Dramatic irony often plays a key role in raising tension for the audience and at this point within the sequence, the viewer knows that Maximus' fears have foundation. The candlelit *mise-en-scène* of Maximus' tent and the ominous non-diegetic soundtrack both contribute to the ominousness of the scene.

Maximus is then taken to see 'Caesar', but discovers that this 'Caesar' is Commodus. The *mise-en-scène* of the previous scene is carried through into the death chamber and the threat is further identified as originating from Commodus. Maximus leans over the dead body and whispers 'Father', thus indicating his closeness to the dead Caesar and also confirming for the audience that the benevolent father of the empire is dead. What follows in this scene is the moment where Maximus seals his fate. Commodus turns to Maximus and says: 'Your emperor asks for your loyalty.' The audience is well aware that the word loyalty can safely be attached to Maximus, but not to Commodus, and fears for the former. Maximus walks past Commodus' outstretched hand and this action signals the beginning of Commodus' attempt to destroy Maximus.

Maximus is then taken to be executed by the Pretorian guard, the leader of which is Quintus, a former friend of Maximus. As with any agent of disruption within a narrative, power is key and Commodus now has the power to corrupt even those who have been close to Maximus. The complication section within a narrative often sees the isolation of the main character. The safety and stature that the central protagonist has enjoyed up to this point is taken away and they are left to battle for what is right and good. In this sequence Maximus has been stripped of his official power and thus

becomes extremely vulnerable. His parting words to Quintus are:
'Promise me that you will look after my family' and Quintus' response of:
'You will meet them in the afterlife' creates the urgency of the remaining parts of this sequence. It is now a race against time for Maximus to reach his family before they are killed.

Maximus is taken to an isolated spot in the forest; outnumbered by six to one by the Pretorian guard. The odds are against him and the tension that is synonymous with all complication sequences builds further. As Maximus kneels to be executed he asks God to keep his family safe. His world has now shrunk in focus to his wife and child, and it is this love of his family (as well as many other important factors) that mark him as the polar opposite of Commodus. This sequence clearly defines the dynamics between Commodus and Maximus that will exist for the rest of the film. Maximus' prowess as a soldier allows him to kill the Pretorian guard and offers the viewer a prediction of the eponymous role of 'Gladiator' which he will take on later in the narrative.

What follows his escape from execution is a race against time to save his family. This section of the sequence is parallel edited to show the viewer not only Maximus' attempt to reach his family, but also their slaughter at the hands of other soldiers within the Pretorian guard. The audience sees Maximus' farm and his wife and child playing happily. The scene is idyllic but, with our knowledge of what has gone before in the scene, soon to be destroyed. Maximus' lands indicate his status and his wife and child provide an image of his loving family. In order for the protagonist's quest for justice to be centralised and made more dramatic, everything this character holds dear must be destroyed. The complication section within a family is where we see this stripping away of what is important to the protagonist. The non-diegetic sound that accompanies the shots of Maximus desperately trying to reach his family, despite being wounded, signifies the race against time and only stops when Maximus and his horse fall exhausted onto the ground on his farm. The audience has seen the barbarity with which his wife and child have been treated and knows that Maximus is too late. His farm has been burnt and his family murdered; thus setting up Maximus' quest for revenge, which occupies the remainder of the film.

How to write the macro essay

When you have completed all of your study and research into genre and narrative, you will be at the stage when you can complete your macro essay. Your macro essay should be between 1000 and 1500 words and focus on one film sequence of 10 minutes, or on two sequences of five minutes each. You should aim to choose a mainstream film, as this will make your analysis much more straightforward. Below is an essay plan you could use to organise and guide your essay writing.

Introduction to essay

Your introduction should show your understanding of the terms narrative and genre. Try to explain the function of narrative and genre conventions for the film's audience, as well as the film's producer. You could also acknowledge in your introduction that genre and narrative conventions are interlinked. Your introduction should end by identifying which film sequence you are going to discuss. Remember to give the director and date of the film.

Middle paragraphs

You could separate your discussions of narrative and genre, or discuss them together as you move through your chosen sequence. Either way, it is worth using the questions that you have already seen in the sections on narrative and genre (repeated below) to guide your arguments and ensure that the essay is systematic.

Genre questions

1. What are the generic conventions evident within my chosen sequence?

2. Is the film from which my sequence is taken an example of a straight genre, a sub-genre or a hybrid genre? What is my evidence for this?

3. Does the sequence I have chosen use conventions in a straightforward way? Does it subvert the audience's expectations of these conventions?

4. How does the use of conventions in my chosen sequence (and film) differ from examples of the same genre which have gone before? What factors may have caused this development in the use of generic conventions?

5. What is the impact of the conventions I have identified on the audience?

Narrative questions

1. In which section of the whole narrative does my sequence come? What are the general functions of this type of sequence? To what extent does my sequence exhibit these functions?

2. How does the use of narrative within my sequence help to organise time within the film?

3. How does the use of narrative within my sequence help to organise space within the film?

4. Does the sequence of narrative I have chosen help to convey information concerning genre to the audience?

5. Does the sequence of narrative I have chosen confirm or challenge the viewer's understanding of events within the film up to this point?

Overall question: How have the genre and narrative elements within my sequence contributed to the viewer's understanding of the film as a whole?

Essay conclusion

Your conclusion should summarise the main points within your essay. It should also include a comment on how effective the use of genre and narrative have been in your sequence(s) in generating meaning and creating a response from the audience.

Before you begin planning your macro essay, read the example essays that follow, to see how narrative and genre have been tackled.

Exemplar macro essay 1

Analysis of a 10-minute sequence from John Woo's *Mission Impossible II* (2000)

A film's narrative provides the structure through which the story can be told. Narrative acts to organise the events within a film into an order that helps to create meaning for the audience. Within mainstream films, narrative conventions are usually adhered to and offer a predictability of story movement that the audience for this kind of cinema expects. Genre conventions function for the audience in a similar way. Audiences might choose to see a mainstream film because of the film's star, but they may also use their knowledge of genre conventions to make decisions about which film to see. For the film producer, making sure that a film offers narrative and genre conventions in a way which will satisfy, as well as engage, the viewer is important to the film's eventual financial success. This essay will concentrate on the use of narrative and genre conventions within the first 15 minutes of John Woo's *Mission Impossible II*.

Mission Impossible II is an example of an action film. It utilises action conventions, such as: the hero's quest/mission, spectacular stunts and action set pieces, pyrotechnical displays, the physical prowess of the hero and a narrative which sees the hero increasingly isolated in the face of a powerful adversary, but eventually triumphant. John Woo is a film maker who has explored the action genre before. His action films tend to add highly choreographed and stylised action sequences, and spectacular special effects, to the viewer's expectations of the standard genre piece. *Face/Off* and *Broken Arrow* both include these extra John Woo elements.

The pre-credit sequence of *Mission Impossible II* functions as an exposition sequence. It establishes the main characters and indicates the problematic scenario that the hero will have to solve by the end of the film. This opening sequence to *Mission Impossible II* introduces the viewer to both the problematic within the narrative and to the key characters who will take part in the events. The sequence begins with a voice-over indicating the thoughts of a scientist. 'Every search for a hero must begin with something every hero requires, a villain', he says, and almost seems to be identifying the key character relationship within an action film, as well as indicating that there will be conflict ahead in this film. We see this character inject himself with 'Chimera' and when he then states that he must: 'Arrive at my destination within 20 hours of departure', we understand that what he has injected himself with is probably really dangerous. The action film convention of the 'race against time' is also established here and will provide tension and drama throughout the narrative.

The threat to safety and stability that is introduced within the exposition sequence of an action film is clearly evident within this sequence in *Mission Impossible II*.

Chimera's potential destructiveness is further indicated when the scientist sees a group of children singing 'Ring a ring of Roses', a children's rhyme which dates back to the time of the bubonic plague. This piece of diegetic sound indicates not only the threat within the narrative, but also implies the hero's quest: to eradicate chimera. The next cut within this sequence is to the character played by Tom Cruise, who is sitting next to the same scientist in a plane. The audience knows that Cruise will be playing the hero of the film and assumes that this is a meeting which will help the scientist. The series of perilous situations, which the action hero must pit himself against, is then shown via the take-over of the plane by the film's agents of disruption. The setting within the plane also provides an example of an action convention. Characters are isolated and vulnerable when flying and, if attacked, the consequences are dramatic and devastating. The passengers and real crew of the plane are drugged and the audience now expects Tom Cruise's character to save them and the scientist. However, with the aid of computer-generated imagery (CGI) it is now revealed that it is not actually Ethan Hunt (Tom Cruise's character) who has been sitting next to the scientist, but Ambrose (played by Dougray Scott), who has been wearing a prosthetic mask. The scientist is killed by Ambrose and his briefcase, which the audience assumes contains either the chimera virus or its antidote, is stolen. What has been established is twofold. The audience is now well aware of the villain's cunning and disregard for innocent human life. They are also aware that the mission of the hero must now begin.

The crashing plane then dissolves into shots of the desert, where we then see the real Ethan Hunt. Ambrose and Hunt are obviously in different geographical spaces and the progress of the narrative from this point will be to unite them in the same space in order for their conflict to be resolved. Narrative functions to organise time and space, and in this sequence the audience is presented with a distance in space between the hero and the villain which is typical of the beginning of an action film.

The shots of the desert include those that are typical of the action genre. John Woo uses a combination of long-shots and close-ups in order to present the spectacle of the place, but also the dangerous climb Ethan Hunt is undertaking. Within action films, the hero is conventionally represented as extremely physically capable. Ethan Hunt is rock climbing. He is climbing with no ropes, no help and in an environment that is isolating and extremely hazardous. The audience sees Ethan taking risks (jumping from one rock face to another and dangling from ledges) and enjoying doing so.

The exposition sequence of an action film must establish the 'credentials' of both the hero and the villain. We know that Ambrose is cunning and ruthless, and from this sequence focusing on Ethan Hunt, we know that he enjoys taking risks, is physically capable and fearless. The audience is being encouraged to trust him in his role of hero and opponent of Ambrose.

The iconography and *mise-en-scène* of this sequence of Ethan Hunt also helps establish *Mission Impossible II* as an action film. Tom Cruise's character wears a physique-revealing outfit; his mission arrives via a rocket fired from a helicopter and it is stored in a computer inside a pair of sunglasses. Spectacle and scale are important conventions within action films because they excite the viewer and engage their interest. The canyon in which Hunt is climbing is vast and the technologies attached to his message are advanced. These elements seem to promise spectacular stunts and physical displays within the rest of the film, and the fact that the viewer already knows that this is a John Woo film only serves to emphasise this promise. The non-diegetic soundtrack contributes to the high-octane action feel. It is dynamic, orchestral and dramatic.

As Ethan Hunt learns of his mission, the viewer becomes aware of two other conventions of the action genre. We learn that Hunt is a Special Agent and that if he is 'caught or killed, the secretary will disavow any knowledge' of his actions. He is a member of an elite group, and as such will have more specialised skills. His situation could also become even more precarious, because his mission is top secret. As with films such as *The Bourne Identity*, the audience understands that the hero's mission will be hazardous and isolating, but that the hero has the kind of maverick tendencies and advanced skills that will ultimately make them successful. Part of Hunt's mission is also to recruit Nyah Nordoff-Hall (Thandie Newton), and the love interest, which is again a common convention of the action genre, is established.

This opening sequence from *Mission Impossible II* clearly utilises action conventions and those narrative conventions that are typical of the action genre. As a sequel to the first (successful) *Mission Impossible* film, this one has a pre-existing audience to tap into. It can draw its audience from action film fans, fans of the first film and those of John Woo or Tom Cruise. *Mission Impossible II* is in many ways a 'perfect' example of a blockbuster. It includes many elements that could help secure the producers' financial success.

Assessment comments

This is an extremely clear and systematic analysis of both narrative and genre. The candidate acknowledges the function of these macro elements and explores how they are used within the chosen film. There is clear evidence of understanding of both the macro elements and how micro elements can be used to discuss them. This essay progresses through the chosen sequence confidently, discussing both textual and institutional implications, as well as viewer reception. The influence of the director's particular use of genre conventions is discussed and other examples of films of the same genre are used to elaborate on and to back up points. There is a very high degree of personal response within this essay and the discussions concerning the relationship between the film text and its audience are very original, with the complexities of this relationship fully acknowledged.

Exemplar macro essay 2

Analysis of a 10-minute sequence from Bryan Singer's *X-Men* (2000)

Genre and narrative conventions are important to film audiences and producers alike. Film audiences have a pre-existing knowledge of the conventions attached to different genres. This may be conscious or unconscious, but an understanding of generic conventions means that audiences have expectations of particular film genres. When these expectations are met or surpassed then viewing pleasure is guaranteed. For the industry, the production of a film which shares the same genre conventions of a previously successful film, but extends them, can help to make financial investment more secure. Narrative conventions can also be used to secure audience pleasure in the viewing experience. Within the context of mainstream film viewing, viewers will have certain expectations of the different sections within a film's narrative and if these expectations are met the audience will be satisfied. For the producer of a particular film, financial success is dependent on viewer satisfaction and delivering an absorbing film narrative that proceeds in an expected (and therefore satisfactory) way, will help secure takings at the box office. This essay will consider the use of both genre and narrative conventions within the climactic sequence of Bryan Singer's 2000 film *X-Men*.

X-Men is both a blockbuster and a super-hero film. It is a big budget production which uses big-named stars and impressive special effects to attempt to secure audience interest. Viewers of blockbuster films expect a high degree of dynamic action and impressive special effects. The climactic sequence of this film includes both. The super-hero genre has proved extremely lucrative for the film industry in recent years and *X-Men* follows films such as *Spiderman* and the *Batman* films. *X-Men* could tap into two pre-existing audiences for its own viewers: fans of comic books and those viewers who had already enjoyed previous examples of the super-hero genre. In terms of expected conventions of this genre, super-hero films include elements of the action genre, such as big, choreographed action sequences and special effects, but they also include conventions specific to themselves. Examples of the super-hero genre include conventions in order to distinguish themselves from other genres, such as: the hero as misunderstood 'other'; an ultimate goal of saving mankind; and futuristic technologies. The climactic sequence of *X-Men* provides evidence of all of these conventions.

Within a climactic sequence, audiences expect to experience dramatic tension at its height, the film's protagonist(s) will be seen in situations of extreme peril and then seen to succeed against the anti-hero of the film. Questions within the film's narrative will be answered within this sequence and the threat to the film's potential equilibrium will be vanquished. The disruptive narrative elements that the audience has watched creating havoc in the preceding sections of the film will be destroyed; and the potential for a new equilibrium, a period of new stability and calm, will be evident. This sequence from *X-Men* concludes with the defeat of Magneto and the end of his destructive plans.

The sequence begins with a fight between Wolverine and one of Magneto's 'evil' mutants. Wolverine has become the main protagonist within the film's narrative. In this sequence he has become part of the X-Men team and seems to have overcome his anxieties concerning his powers. Wolverine, as with Batman or Spiderman, has had difficulty coming to terms with his powers: all three of these characters have had to struggle not just with the villain within their narrative, but also with their concerns about their otherness and feelings of isolation from society. Wolverine's narrative quest has become twofold: to destroy Magneto and to save Rogue, a young mutant whose fear of her own powers is something with which Wolverine can identify. Within the super-hero genre of films, the protagonist's journey is always towards both the liberation of the innocents and the acceptance of their own powers. Wolverine's battle with the shape-changing mutant within this sequence is highly choreographed. Their powers make the confrontation more dynamic and exciting for the audience. The otherness of the two characters in this fight scene is evident from their make-up/prosthetics and physical abilities. Wolverine is eventually victorious within this encounter, but the series of escalating challenges which the audience expects within the climactic scene of a super-hero film has just begun.

Spectacle is an important element within the climactic sequence of a super-hero film. In this sequence from *X-Men*, we are presented with smaller scenes of increasing spectacle. Wolverine has dealt with his opponent and Storm is then seen dispatching hers with an equal level of spectacular action. She floats (on wires) across the set and then, with the aid of dramatic CGI-produced special effects, overcomes the toad-like mutant. Each disruptive element within the narrative is being dealt with one by one, which allows for escalating tensions as well as cumulative satisfaction for the viewer.

Super-hero films are set in recognisable locations, usually cities. This convention generates a sense of a world we recognise being under threat. *X-Men* is set in New York – confirmed in this sequence by the sight of the Statue of Liberty. Within super-hero films it is the 'free' world that is seen to be threatened and *X-Men* uses iconic images of New York to confirm this for the viewer. One of the myths that super-hero films ask the viewer to believe in is that of the superhuman saviour. Images of New York or Washington, which would be globally recognisable to audiences, are used in order both to represent what might be destroyed by the threat and to allow blockbusters, such as *X-Men*, to transfer into foreign cinemas and be financially successful.

As with any climactic film sequence, once the heroes of the film assume that they are winning the battle, they are presented with an even bigger hurdle. Magneto's minions may have been killed, but he is a much greater threat. The next section of this sequence shows Magneto immobilizing each of the *X-Men* and (temporarily) stripping them of their powers. It is Wolverine who escapes first, spurred on by the sound of Rogue's cries for help. The disregard for their own safety, which is a character convention within super-hero films, is evident here. Wolverine has to injure himself in order to escape his confines. Magneto is attempting to extract Rogue's powers and use them to destroy a meeting of global leaders who are planning to rid the world of mutants. Anti-heroes in super-hero films often feel ostracised from normal society and seek to destroy those who they feel are prejudiced against them. It is conventionally the role of the hero within the super-hero genre to save society, even if they are also often misunderstood and ostracised by it. Ideologically, therefore, super-hero films could be read as deeply conservative, as the films seem to suggest that a group prejudiced against should still act to save those who have misunderstood and excluded them.

With Rogue trapped in Magneto's machine, Wolverine then has to take on his last and biggest challenge: Magneto himself. The futuristic technology of Magneto's machine, plus the powers both he and Wolverine exhibit, help the viewer to clearly identify the genre of this film. The tension in this sequence is also produced by the paralleling of two narratives: Wolverine's attempts to get to Rogue and Magneto's attempts to use her powers to 'fuel' his machine. Everything conspires at this point in the film to present the drama and tension the viewer expects from a climactic sequence. The non-diegetic sound used is orchestral, dynamic and dramatic. The cuts used within the parallel events have become quicker and Wolverine is becoming increasingly weak. The end of this sequence uses a combination of long shots and close-ups to show the scale of the potential impact of Magneto's weapon and the effect of the events on the characters. Wolverine, helped by his fellow X-Men, eventually overcomes Magneto, but he still faces a final challenge. Rogue appears lifeless and he must allow her to take some of his life-force in order to survive. The self-sacrificial characteristic of super-heroes is most evident here, as Wolverine is seen falling to the ground, having saved Rogue.

This sequence offers a package of narrative and genre conventions to the audience that are both recognisable and satisfactory. As a super-hero film, *X-Men* offers predictable conventions, which have been made even more dramatic by the use of highly choreographed sequences and elaborate special effects. As a climactic sequence, this section of the film conforms to viewer's expectations. The 'package' offered by the film proved successful enough for its producers to create a sequel.

Assessment comments

This is a very confident and assured response. The candidate discusses the textual elements of genre and narrative, as well as relating these to the institutional considerations of narrative and genre choices. There is excellent use made of textual examples to substantiate points and aspects of film form are used effectively to discuss macro elements. This candidate discusses audience expectations and responses with confidence and clarity. The relationship between the film text and the film spectator is explored in detail. Film-specific terminology is used accurately and the candidate is also able to place the chosen film within a wider cinematic content, i.e. there is clear and useful reference to other examples of the same genre. There is evidence in this essay of an independent voice. The candidate debates institutional uses of genre and narrative, as well as speculating on the ideological implications of genre conventions. This essay would gain a good 'A' grade.

Micro analysis

The micro analysis task within your FS1 coursework unit requires you to study how sound, cinematography, *mise-en-scène* and editing elements within a film create meaning and generate a response from the audience. In order to be able to analyse these four micro elements, you will need to ensure that you have a clear understanding of the terms. Below are detailed definitions of the terms, case studies to show you how to discuss them, plus questions and exercises in order to help you to practise your own micro analysis. At the end of this section on micro analysis (see pages 61–8), there are two example essays, which you could use to check the structure and content of your own.

Sound

The sound elements within a film are invisible, yet provide a powerful tool for the generation of meaning. Sound is aural, rather than visual, but can provoke an equally powerful response in the viewer. The first distinction that can be made concerning sound is that between those sounds that exist within the story, and can be heard by characters, and those sounds that cannot be heard by characters, and exist on the film's soundtrack. The term used to describe the first type of sound is 'diegetic' and that used to describe the second type of sound is 'non-diegetic'. 'Diegesis' means story. An easy way of remembering the difference between the two types of sound is to define the terms as follows:

- Diegetic = Inside the story world (radio sound, speech, traffic noises, weather noises etc.).

- Non-diegetic = Outside the story world (voice-overs and music on the soundtrack).

Whether the sound you identify in a film sequence is non-diegetic or diegetic, there are many areas of potential meaning that can be generated. Often, diegetic and non-diegetic sound are used in unison to create an effect and generate a particular response in the viewer. Here are descriptions of how diegetic and non-diegetic sound are used in sequences from two films.

1. *Jaws* (Spielberg, 1975): Non-diegetic

The opening credit sequence of this film uses non-diegetic sound in order to introduce the threatening element within the film. The first shots of the film are underwater. The shark is not seen, but its presence is strongly implied by the soundtrack. The score for the film uses a series of low, repeated notes in order to illustrate the relentless and threatening nature of the shark. As the soundtrack progresses, no resolution is given. The notes continue to build tension and anxiety for the viewer and do not let that tension dissipate. The non-diegetic sound in this sequence establishes the tone, atmosphere, genre and main threat within this film.

2. *Rear Window* (Hitchcock, 1954): Diegetic

L.B. Jeffries (played by James Stewart) has broken his leg and spends the majority of his time looking out of his window, examining what is going on in the flats opposite to him. When the viewer is first introduced to Jeffries, we hear the sounds which he can hear: voices, jazz music, traffic sounds. We hear these as Jeffries would hear them and the diegetic sound here has an echoing quality, as if it is being heard across the courtyard between the apartments. Jeffries is immobile because of his broken leg; he is also bored and distant from the life going on outside his flat. The diegetic sound of the music on the radio he hears helps the viewer identify the period of time in which the film is set as the 1950s. The echoing quality of the diegetic sounds he hears helps establish his detached and bored state of mind.

EXERCISE 9

Read the descriptions of how diegetic and non-diegetic sound are used in sequences from *Jaws* and *Rear Window*. Then choose two films of your own and study the non-diegetic sound elements in one and the diegetic sound elements in the other. What kind of information is being relayed to the viewer by the sounds used?

There are four key areas of meaning that can be generated through the use of sound, whether it is diegetic or non-diegetic. These areas concern character, genre, setting and narrative.

Sound and character
As we have already seen through the example of *Jaws*, non-diegetic soundtracks can be used very effectively to generate a sense of character. Soundtracks can establish whether a character is evil or good, a victim or a hero. If a character regularly has a piece of music

attached to them – one which is repeated to indicate their presence – then this piece of music is called a character theme. Character themes can indicate the status of the character within the scene or the film as a whole; they can also be used to indicate the impact of a character on other characters within the scene or the film. If, for example, the hero of a film is not on the screen, but their character theme is being played, then it may be signalling that another character is thinking about the hero (perhaps in a romantic way), or that the character needs the hero's help. Aural motifs (pieces of repeated sound, not music) can also be used to signal the presence, either physically or emotionally, of a character. The heavy, rasping breathing of Darth Vader, in the 'earlier' *Star Wars* films, is ominous and threatening, and the viewer knows when they hear this sound that something untoward is probably about to happen.

Sound does not have to be repeatedly attached to a character, however, in order to relay information about them. A character's nervous state of mind, for example, could be expressed through a scene in which the character is seen nervously washing up, flinching at the diegetic sound of crashing pots and pans. A sudden shift in the non-diegetic soundtrack of a film into a sequence of long-held, low chords might indicate a situation of peril in which a character suddenly finds themselves. Both diegetic and non-diegetic sound can function to relay information about character. This can be done by using these two types of sound subtly or dramatically; and separately or together.

Sound and genre

Sound elements provide a key indicator to audiences of the genre of film they are watching. Both diegetic and non-diegetic sound can be used to establish the genre of a particular film. A significant amount of diegetic gunshots, explosions, screeching tyres and shattering glass sounds, for example, would be more consistent with an action film than a romantic comedy. Diegetic sounds of screams, knife slashes, howling winds and screeching doors would indicate the horror genre. In terms of non-diegetic sound, soundtracks can also help define the genre of a film. In some cases a composer even becomes synonymous with a particular genre. Ennio Morricone's haunting soundtracks immediately suggest Sergio Leone's 'spaghetti' Westerns. After *The Omen* (Donner, 1976), the first film in the *Omen* series, Gregorian chants seemed always to be associated with horror films, especially those concerning demonic possession.

EXERCISE 10

With a partner, choose two different genres of film. Make a list of the diegetic sounds you would associate with the genres and make notes on the type of non-diegetic soundtrack you expect to accompany the events on screen. Discuss your findings with the rest of your class.

Sound and setting

Both diegetic and non-diegetic sound can help to create information concerning the different settings that are evident within a film. Whether a particular setting is safe or not, whether it exists in contemporary or past time, or even in which country the setting exists, are all pieces of information that can be generated through the sound elements within a film. The isolation of a particular setting and its potential hazardousness, can both be evoked through sound. The diegetic sound of wind in leaves, for example, coupled with a soundtrack of haunting strings, could effectively generate a sense of the potential danger of a place. If the diegetic sound within a particular scene were of slaves being shouted at to make them row faster, of whips confirming the orders and of the swords of soldiers clanking against their armour, then it might be reasonably safe to identify the period as ancient Roman. The diegetic sounds of trumpet horns, chariot wheels, horses and the roars of the crowd in the coliseum within Ridley Scott's film *Gladiator* (2000), for example, confirm the Roman visuals we are offered. Soundtracks are extremely powerful tools in the evocation, description and confirmation of setting. Non-diegetic soundtracks can be used to evoke deserts, seas, fields, countries and cities. The magical forest within Ridley Scott's 1985 film *Legend* is introduced through a delicate series of light notes and bell sounds. At least at the beginning of the film, this is a forest of myth innocence.

Sound and narrative

Sound can generate narrative meaning in a number of key ways. Voice-overs are examples of non-diegetic sound, as they are only heard by the viewer and not by the other characters. Voice-overs allow one character from the story to narrate events. The character may be living, or, as in Billy Wilder's classic film noir *Double Indemnity* (1944), dead. Voice-overs are subjective in that they are the thoughts of one particular character. They may present an accurate picture of events, but they can equally present a biased version. The 'truth' of the story told within a voice-over has to be discerned by the viewer. Another sound device which allows for narrative information to be relayed to the viewer is the sound-bridge. A sound-bridge occurs when either a diegetic or a non-diegetic element of sound is carried from one scene, over an edit, into the next scene. If the character theme of a particular character is carried from a scene in which they appear into a completely different scene in

EXERCISE 11

Make notes on how the sound elements within a film sequence of your choice work to generate information concerning genre, character, setting and narrative. When your notes are complete, use the structure and content of the case study on sound that follows to write up your notes into your own case study on the use of sound in a film sequence.

which they do not, then this might indicate the influence of that character on other character's lives. Sound bridges are a very effective and subtle way for the film maker to suggest connections between two scenes.

Case Study 5: Sound analysis

The use of sound elements within a seven-minute sequence from Neil Marshall's *Dog Soldiers* (2002)

Source: British Film Institute

This case study will focus on the sequence in which the soldiers are first attacked by the werewolves.

Sound is used in this sequence to convey information concerning genre, character, narrative position and setting. *Dog Soldiers* is an example of the horror genre. It utilises elements of gothic horror e.g. the werewolves, but places the action in a very contemporary setting. This sequence begins with the central group of soldiers discovering the remains of another platoon and the barely alive leader of the dead men. The sequence moves the central characters fully into their nightmare and sees their first (very unsuccessful) encounter with the werewolves. As such this sequence needs to generate the tension that will not be fully released until the end of the film. The first important element of sound in this sequence is diegetic. The wounded captain they find explains, after watching the soldiers arm themselves: 'It won't make any difference. They won't die'; thus evoking one of the core fears within any horror film, that the threat is unstoppable and indestructible. The non-diegetic sound in the first part of this sequence is low, slow and brooding. It alerts the viewer to the potential attack to come, providing an ominous mood. The heightened diegetic sound of the soldiers loading their rifles and checking their ammunition functions to provide two meanings for the viewer. First, we understand that these are trained military men and are aware of how to prepare for standard battle, but seem (at this stage in the narrative) to be preparing for an altogether more powerful assailant. Despite their military knowledge, they appear vulnerable. Second, the diegetic sound of rifle chambers being loaded and checked reminds the viewer of the tension mounting and the fears of the soldiers.

The non-diegetic soundtrack then moves to the foreground and the viewer hears a drumbeat beginning as the soldiers begin to make tracks towards what they hope to be safety. The drumbeat echoes a heartbeat and signifies the soldiers' (and the viewer's) fear, as well as their military identity. What follows is a fusion of non-diegetic drumbeats and elongated, tension-generating strings, with the diegetic sound of feet crunching through the forest. Dialogue is often sparse in horror scenarios. It is the sound of fleeing feet and the soundtrack mirroring the fears of the protagonists that creates momentum and tension. When the soldiers stop, the non-diegetic soundtrack recedes in order for the viewer to hear the instructions given to the soldiers. The team leader addresses his troupe using nicknames and the viewer is shown the close relationship between the group of men. The viewer's understanding of horror/slasher films is evoked at this point. We can predict that the group of men will gradually diminish as they are picked off by the film's monsters. The fact that the group is close illustrates the impact that the killings the viewer predicts will have on the men. This short section also functions to provide information concerning the ranks within the group.

The non-diegetic soundtrack then crashes to a halt as the men are seen rushing towards and then stopping at the positions they have been given. The viewer's understanding of the horror genre helps them to read this silence. Even within a scene with lots of action, there are patterns of tension and seeming release, and the audience is well aware that the silence of this section will soon be broken by the appearance of the werewolves. The silence is initially broken by the diegetic sound of short, sharp breathing. The soldiers fear mirrors that of the viewer's and the subsequent diegetic sound of a werewolf howl and a frantically primed rifle adds to the tension. At this point in the sequence a shape, obviously one of the creatures, passes in front of the camera and the soundtrack recommences suddenly. The aural elements of a horror film are as powerful as the visual elements in the generation of fear and tension. One of the soldiers then attempts to fire his weapon, but finds it does not work. The narrative has now singled out the first of the victims and we focus on this soldier's desperate attempts to get his weapon to work. The diegetic sound of frantically checked ammunition indicates the desperation of this soldier and signals his future death. When sound elements within a horror film shrink to focus on the sounds generated by one individual character, the audience is prepared for that character's demise.

The soldier then begins to run and the diegetic sound the audience hears is that of him crashing through bushes. The non-diegetic sound also restarts and offers an echo of the frantic escape the soldier is attempting to make. It is obvious at this stage, from the sound elements we hear, that he is not only alone, but that he is running away from his group into diminishing space. As with any example of the slasher film (and in many ways *Dog Soldiers* utilises the standard conventions of this sub-genre), characters who are about to be attacked have a terrible tendency to run into smaller and smaller spaces. This soldier has run from open space into an area of thick trees and bushes, from which we know he is unlikely to escape. The sequence draws to its conclusion with a sudden end to the non-diegetic soundtrack as the soldier runs straight into a branch and impales himself. The audience are then only offered diegetic sound: that of the gurgling of blood coming from the soldier's mouth. We hear blood dripping onto the branch and understand that this is the end of the soldier's attempted escape. The final sound of this sequence is the diegetic roar of the werewolf, as it rips the soldier and the branch he is impaled upon away from the tree. Sound in this sequence has been used to create a micro version of the film as a whole. The sequence shows the fears of the soldiers, their relationships with one another and the fate that will befall the majority of the group.

Cinematography

Cinematography is a term used to describe all aspects of camerawork: shot types, camera positioning, camera movement and framing. The cinematography choices made within a film are a key means by which the film maker can convey meaning. Your discussions of cinematography will not only need to identify the element of camerawork being used, but discuss *how* it is being used and what the potential impact is on the viewer. The first stage of your study of cinematography should be to familiarise yourself with the potential shot types which could be used within a film and what information these shot types have the ability to convey. Shots are one of the basic 'building blocks' of a film. Many directors storyboard their films meticulously and plan each shot they want to use. In effect, a film is a sequence of carefully constructed shots, all contributing to the film's impact on the viewer.

Shot types

You will need to become familiar with the key shot types in the following list.

Extreme long shot (ELS). This type of shot is often used to introduce a setting or to indicate the overwhelming nature of that setting for the characters involved in the shot. An extreme long shot might show only environment, or tiny figures swamped by a particular place.

Long shot (LS). These shots are often used to show the relationship between a character, or group of characters, to a particular setting. The whole body of the character will be visible, as will much of the setting in which they stand. A long shot might be used in order to show the situation of a sole character within a hazardous setting or, alternatively, to indicate a character's escape into freedom.

Medium shot (MS). A medium shot is generally used to present characters talking to one another. The character(s) are shown from the knees up and the viewer is able to see the body

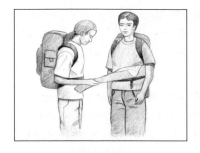

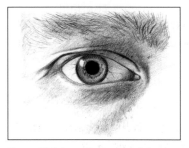

From ELS (previous page) to ECU.

language of the characters who are talking. Thus, the audience will be able to discern whether or not the conversing is amicable.

Close-up (CU). Close-ups frame the entire head, hand or foot of a character, or a part of an object. They can be used to draw the viewer's attention to a significant facial expression or to an object that might have significance within the narrative.

Extreme close-up (ECU). Extreme close-ups show only a section of a face or an object, or can be used to focus on a tiny object. ECUs are often used in order to focus the viewer's attention on a significant part of the face, a tearful or terrified eye, for example. ECUs take the viewer into extremely close proximity with a character. The discomfort the viewer might feel when positioned this close can be used to dramatic effect by film makers.

Establishing shot. This is the opening shot of a film or film sequence. An extreme long shot or long shot may be used to introduce the viewer to the main setting of a film.

Master shot. When a film maker is shooting a sequence, footage has to be taken that includes all of the action in that particular sequence. At the editing stage, any close-ups on character, or medium close-ups of conversations can be inserted into the master shot. Master shots provide a backdrop for any close-up or medium shot that might be cut to within a scene.

Cut-away shot. Within a sequence of action, the film maker might cut outside of the events within the scene being shown to show a character or object not in the scene. This is a cut-away shot. These are used to indicate connections between the events taking place in one scene, with characters or objects who exist in another place or at another time.

Cut-in shot. If the viewer's attention needs to be drawn towards a smaller element within a scene then a cut-in might be used. For example, if characters within a scene are discussing a crime and there is evidence for that crime within the setting that has not yet been discovered by the characters, then the film maker might cut-in to that evidence in order to provide the viewer with information not yet known by the characters.

Camera positioning

Another important element of cinematography that you will need to consider is camera positioning. The position of the camera when a shot is filmed has a significant effect on the meanings that are created for the viewer. The key types of camera positioning are listed below, with descriptions of the types of meaning that might be generated.

Eye-level shots. In order to create a sense of reality within a film, the film maker will often use a camera position that keeps the level of the camera roughly at eye height. This type of camera positioning creates a degree of normality for the viewer, as it does not suggest an angle of vision that is odd or unexpected.

Low-angle shots. Traditionally, low-angle shots are used to create an impression that what the viewer (or the character whose viewpoint the audience is adopting) is seeing is much bigger than they are. Low-angle shots can make what is being shown seem awe-inspiring, threatening or overwhelming.

High-angle shots generate the sense of something that is being looked down on. They might be used to indicate the smallness and vulnerability of the object (or person) that is being looked down on.

Point-of-view shots present action as if from the viewpoint of a particular character. This can encourage the audience to identify with a character or empathise with their situation.

Camera movement

As well as the type of shot that is used within a scene and the positioning of the camera, camera movement is also an important aspect of cinematography for you to discuss in your micro analysis. There are three key features of camera movement with which you should familiarise yourselves: panning, tilting and tracking.

1. Panning.

   Within a panning shot or 'pan', the base of the camera remains still, but the camera itself moves either right to left, or left to right. The movement is horizontal and might be anything up to 360 degrees in diameter. Pans can be used to introduce a film's audience to a particular setting, with the camera slowly revealing elements of a room, for example. A pan might also be from the point of view of a character, in which case the viewer is being invited to observe a scene and consider different elements of that scene at a rate that the character dictates.

2. Tilting.

   When tilting, the camera base again remains static, but this time the movement of the head of the camera is vertical, rather than horizontal. Two classic types of tilt shot would move either up or down a character, or up or down a building. The first type of tilt can indicate one character's sexual attraction to another. The second might indicate a 'sizing up' of a building to be climbed.

3. Tracking.

   A tracking shot occurs when the whole camera moves in, out, or sideways to follow the action. A tracking shot can be created by fixing a camera to a set of wheels, or 'dolly', which is then moved. Tracking shots enable film makers to follow moving action or characters through scenes.

Framing

Aside from shot type, camera positioning and camera movement, the other significant element of cinematography for you to consider is framing. If you pause a film, what you will see is a frame. The director and/or cinematographer of a film will make decisions regarding where the elements of a particular shot are positioned. The decision might be made that one character is to appear dominant, and thus they might be positioned in the middle of the shot, standing higher than the other characters. In order to convey the idea that events within the narrative are overwhelming a particular character, that character might be shown squashed in the frame by other characters, objects or buildings. Frames can be empty or full. Characters can be in the foreground or the background. They might be to the left or right-hand side of the frame. All of these possibilities of framing have the potential to generate meaning.

EXERCISE 12

With a partner, choose a short sequence from a film. Note down all of the different types of camera shot, position and movement that you find in this sequence. How does the cinematography you have identified help the viewer of the scene to understand the characters and events?

Now compare the notes you have made with the case study that follows. You should note in particular the way in which meanings generated by cinematography elements are discussed.

Case Study 6: Cinematography analysis

The use of cinematography within a seven-minute sequence from Todd Haynes' *Far From Heaven* (2003)

This case study will focus on the annual party that Kathleen and Frank Whittaker have thrown for the latter's work colleagues. This party has been alluded to in the narrative up to this point and would traditionally have functioned to present the Whittakers as a perfect example of a 1950s, middle-class, successful family. *Far From Heaven* is in many ways an homage to 1950s melodrama, in particular to the films of Douglas Sirk. Within Sirk's films, the surface elements of *mise-en-scène* and cinematography function to create an almost hyper-real context through which 1950s American society could be critiqued. The surface of *Far From Heaven* is also pristine, but what lies beneath is prejudice, lies and guilt. The party sequence is instrumental in deconstructing the myth that was perfect family life in the 1950s. The viewer is aware at this point in the film that Frank

Whittaker has homosexual desires that threaten to break apart his family. The climate of the time was generally intolerant to homosexuality and Frank's desires have to be kept secret. This puts incredible strain on his marriage. Kathy is presented as the perfect 1950s wife, loving and tolerant of anything her husband does, but this sequence is where we begin to understand the implausibility of the couple's situation. Kathleen has also befriended Raymond Deagon, the couple's educated, sensitive and articulate black gardener, and this is a friendship that is not tolerated by the middle-class, white inhabitants of Hertford, Connecticut. The cinematography in this sequence perfectly illustrates the prejudices and tensions that lie just under the picture-perfect surface.

The sequence opens with a crane shot of the street in which Kathleen and Frank live and the exterior of their house. This long shot signals their social position and the external perfection of their lives. The crane shot then moves to take the viewer inside the Whittaker's house and settles into a long shot of Kathleen Whittaker acting as the perfect hostess. The viewer is still held away from the party by this long shot and there is an observational tone to the cinematography employed here. It is as if we are being asked to pause and observe the seeming perfection of the scene, before moving to the truth. The camera crane then moves again to rest on a guest expressing her fears concerning racial integration. We are guided by the camera in this sequence to observe the attitudes of the guests. The camera is at a higher angle than this guest and Kathy, who is listening. This does not indicate some wholly passive position on her part, but the dominance of these kinds of problematic attitudes in her world.

The sequence then cuts to a close-up of the two guests who were discussing racial integration, now joking about the subject. Kathleen is positioned central frame. She is higher than her guests and shot using a mid-shot. The audience knows that her attitude to black rights is much more encompassing, and this is indicated by her framing at this point. The sequence cuts next to a mid-shot of a black waiter at the party and two more black characters serving drinks. This cut indicates the divisions within 1950s America and the fact that the black characters exist within a completely different frame to the white characters offers a stark indication of these divisions.

The next shot we see is of Kathy, positioned lower in the frame, being talked at by a male guest who is patronising her about her kindness to Raymond, her black gardener. Kathy's lower positioning within the frame makes it clear that she is being talked down to. Both her gender and her attitudes have made her the object of condescension. Kathy is then seen questioning where this male guest got his information. She is charming as ever, yet is blocked in the frame by her guests, signalling her entrapment by the other attitudes of the time. The camera then tracks with Kathy to another part of the party. She is clearly positioned as the central consciousness of the party, and indeed the film, and we follow her as she interacts with the other guests. She acts as a mirror held up to the attitudes of these guests.

The camera then tracks gently and stops in long shot, revealing Kathy central frame, with guests either side of her and Frank to the far left. Frank's framing seems to position him as marginal, yet the viewer is fully aware that it is his actions which have (and will) cause the main tensions of the film. The next camera set up is a medium/long shot of Frank seated on the sofa. He is blocked either side in the frame by two characters who are further into the foreground than him. Frank is trapped by this framing, as he is trapped by his secret, but he is still a powerful influence on the scene. Kathy may seem more free, and indeed the cinematography follows her elegant movements through the party, but it is Frank who can cause damage in this scene. When another guest flirts with Kathleen, he says: 'You should see her without her face on', thus indicating his inability to register his wife's attractiveness and his potential cruelty to her. The next cut reveals a mid-shot of Eleanor, Kathy's best friend, turning and looking concerned for Kathy after her husband's cruel joke. At this point in the narrative, the cinematography connected with Eleanor indicates her loyalty to Kathleen and care for her friend. This loyalty is, of course, revealed to be changeable in the latter stages of the film. The sequence cuts back to the same medium/long shot of Frank blocked by two of his guests and then cuts to a long shot of Kathy charmingly dismissing his slight. More than ever, it is evident that it is Kathy who attempts to keep their seemingly perfect world together and Frank who does not.

Kathy, still in medium/long shot, then moves over to her husband's side of the frame. His power to pull her into his world and his needs is evidenced by this movement. She is then seen in mid-shot, framed with Frank, attempting to persuade him that he does not need another drink. Kathy is not seen whole bodied at this point – only her torso is visible. Spatially, Frank might not seem to occupy as much of the party as Kathy, but he has the power to influence what goes on around him. He is constantly seated in this sequence and this lack of movement seems to reflect his intractability within the narrative as a whole. The sequence then cuts to a long shot of guests toasting Kathy, and then to Frank, who pulls her down into his frame. Throughout the film Kathy attempts to compromise with her husband but he never reciprocates. This is indicated by the focus shift in this sequence. Kathy moves around the party (and their world) with seeming ease, attempting to create the perfect image for their family. Frank, conversely, remains seated; forcing his wife to enter his frame and his world of deceit. The sequence ends with the toast: 'To Frank and Kathy. Truly Mr and Mrs Magnatec', but the reality of this perfect image has been fractured by what has been indicated by the cinematography within this sequence.

Mise-en-scène

Mise-en-scène is a French term, which literally translates as: 'put into scene'. If you look at a paused image from a film, or still images from posters, the elements of setting, decor, lighting, body language/movement, props, costume and make-up you would see are all studied under the heading *mise-en-scène*. As with all of the micro elements, a multitude of different meanings can be generated through choices made concerning *mise-en-scène*. Information regarding genre, character, mood, time, atmosphere and narrative point can all be relayed through elements of *mise-en-scène*.

Setting

A setting provides not only a geographical backdrop to a film, but also an emotional or psychological one. The place in which a film, or a scene from that film, is set can be indicative of the historical time of the film, the state of mind of the film's protagonists and the point in the film's narrative that has been reached. Settings provide atmosphere and even tone to a scene. Woody Allen's use of Manhattan for many of his films (*Annie Hall, Mighty Aphrodite, Manhattan*) provides not only a recognisable urban context for the narratives he portrays, but also a fitting, frenetic cityscape which mirrors the neuroses that many of his characters exhibit. Whether a film is set in an urban or rural context is also significant to the meanings generated within a film. The urban deprivation of Lynne Ramsay's 1999 film *Ratcatcher* presents a Glasgow estate that is so rubbish strewn and inhospitable that the central child protagonist of the film has to create his own fantasy of a new housing estate with golden fields in order to escape his day-to-day existence. Settings can also help to describe the psychological state of a character. Rain-saturated, squalid or oppressively busy settings, for example, are often indicative of a character's panic, confusion or desperation. It is significant that within Hitchcock's *Psycho* (1960), Marion Crane drives away from her crime and on to the Bates Motel along an isolated road during a rainstorm. Her guilt and desperation are evoked, as is the horror she is about to encounter.

Decor

How a room is decorated, and the objects that are used to furnish that room, provides another way by which meaning can be evoked. The decor within a room can relay information regarding character, genre and atmosphere to the viewer. Patrick Bateman's apartment in the film *American Psycho* (Harron, 2000) is clinically pristine and expensively furnished with ultra contemporary designs. The absolute coldness of his flat, and his obsession with conspicuous consumption, contribute to the viewer's reading of this character as self-absorbed and potentially psychotic. Decor can also provide key information for the viewer to use in their identification of the genre of a film. A room in which the walls are covered with torn-out sections of newspapers tends to indicate that the film is a thriller or a horror film. A room in which the furniture and other objects are futuristic indicate the science fiction genre. Decor can also contribute to the atmosphere of a scene. Darkly painted walls and an absence of furniture in a room evoke threat and an ominous atmosphere, for example. John Doe's apartment in David Fincher's 1995 film *Se7en* provides an example of decor used to convey information concerning character, genre and atmosphere. His apartment is painted black and red; on the walls are cabinets containing 'souvenirs' from previous killings and the shelves are full of obsessively compiled journals and cuttings of crime articles from newspapers. The film's thriller/horror credentials are obvious, as is the serial killer psychopathology of John Doe. The atmosphere of threat and horror that the decor in this apartment generates is also evident.

Lighting

The lighting of a scene is an important factor in the generation of mood and atmosphere. Characters, objects and settings can all be lit for effect. Different types of lighting can make a character's features exaggerated, throw ominous shadows into the corners of a room, or create a setting of disturbingly bright colours. In order to light a piece of action, three main types of light are used, as illustrated below.

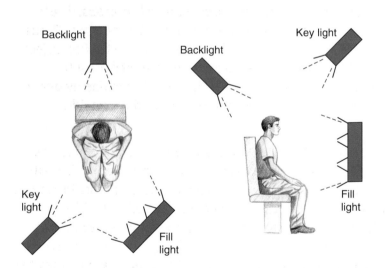

The choices that have to be made for the lighting of a scene are not merely concerned with the amount of light to be used. The positioning of the lights within a scene is also crucial to the scene's effectiveness. As with camerawork, the angle used is important and very different effects can be created by shifts in the positioning and angle of light. If a character or an object is underlit, then the light source is from below. This can have a distorting effect on the object or character being lit, making the object or character seem dangerous or threatening. Top lighting has the opposite effect. A light source which is above an actor, for example, will highlight that actors features in a flattering way. Top lighting can be used to exaggerate the beauty or glamour of an individual. If a character is backlit, then the light source comes from behind. Silhouettes can be created, thus adding mystery and suspense to a scene. When you analyse the use of lighting in your seven-minute sequence, begin by trying to identify the types of light used and the positioning of those lights. Then consider the effects that the lights are generating. You could consider how atmosphere and tone are created through lighting, how character information is relayed, how lighting helps to indicate which section of the narrative your sequence is in, and how choices of lighting might help to indicate genre.

Body language/movement and blocking

Body language can be an indicator of how a character feels at a given point within the narrative and can indicate one character's response to another. A reading of a character's body language as furtive, relaxed or panic stricken can of course help the film audience to understand the relationship between a character and the events that surround that character. Certain body language or body movement can become synonymous with particular actors and can even become an actor's signature. The gymnastic abilities of Jean-Claude van Damme, shown in films such as *Time Cop* (Hyams, 1994) became an expected element within his films. John Wayne's walk became so famous that it spawned many impersonations.

Blocking occurs when one character is shot with an object or other character partly obscuring the audience's view of the character on whom the audience is trying to focus. If a character is partially obscured from view, many potential meanings can be generated. The film maker might be attempting to present a character as trapped, vulnerable, confused or dangerous.

Props

The objects within a scene that contribute to narrative information are called props. These objects help to relay information to the viewer and can be used in a number of ways. Props can indicate genre, and an audience for a particular genre of film would expect these objects to be evident. Bows, arrows, guns, sheriff's badges and stetsons would immediately be recognised as consistent with the Western genre. Knives and masks would provide evidence that the film were an example of the slasher genre. Props can also be used to provide information about character.

Leonard Shelby's constant need for pens in Christopher Nolan's *Memento* (2000) help the viewer to understand his obsessive need to write information down. He only remembers the previous 15 minutes, so without a pen he cannot 'fix' his thoughts or observations. Props can provide the enigma or secret within a film's narrative or the goal of the narrative. The enigmatic prop within *Citizen Kane* (Welles, 1941) turns out to be a children's sledge, but the viewer is left guessing for the majority of the film why Kane's dying word was 'Rosebud'. The lost Ark within Spielberg's 1981 film *Raiders of the Lost Ark* is the prop that provides the goal, but also the conflict within the narrative.

Costume and make-up

The costume and make-up that are chosen for a film are an important factor within the creation of meaning for the film's audience. They can evoke historical time, relate information about character or help to create the fantasy elements within fantasy films. Costume drama is a genre in its own right and the costumes have to be historically accurate in order to sustain the audience's willingness to believe that the film is representing a previous time. Ang Lee's *Sense and Sensibility* (1995), for example, had to evoke Jane Austen's England and did so through a variety of means, including costume.

Make-up can also help to recreate historical time. The 1970s of Paul Thomas Anderson's 1997 film *Boogie Nights* was evoked through costume and an authentic recreation of the make-up of the period. Science fiction and fantasy films often use costume and make-up in order to signal a futuristic or 'other worldly' context to the viewer. *The Fifth Element* (Besson, 1997) engaged the services of the designer Jean-Paul Gaultier in order to create the futuristic outfits worn by the characters.

Costume changes can also be used to indicate changes in character situations, or in a character's state of mind. The 'rags to ballgown' narrative movement of the Cinderella story is at the root of many contemporary films, often signalling a change in status and attitude of the character involved. As with the Cinderella myth, however, this costume change is primarily for the female character and invariably means that she is then noticed by the male character. Sandra Bullock's character in *Miss Congeniality* (Petrie, 2000), for example, swaps her understated casual look for the glamour of a beauty pageant contestant in order to go undercover and investigate a crime. Her transformation also allows her to become the object of male desire within the narrative.

EXERCISE 13

Look at the two stills below. For each, try to identify which aspects of *mise-en-scène* are evident and what kinds of meanings are being generated by the *mise-en-scène* used.

Source: British Film Institute

Case Study 7: *Mise-en-scène* analysis

The use of *mise-en-scène* within a seven-minute sequence from Jane Campion's *In the Cut* (2003)

This case study will look at the opening credit sequence of Jane Campion's film and consider the key elements of *mise-en-scène*.

Setting and decor

The opening shot of the film is of the New York skyline. It is sunrise and the red glow of the sun can be seen behind the skyline. The sun in this shot might be warm and glowing, but the city is grey and uninviting. The *mise-en-scène* of this establishing shot seems to suggest the contradictions to come. The city has an ominous colouring and feels lifeless. The opening sequence then moves through a series of more focused establishing shots, all of which signify this as an environment that is at best uninviting and at worst, claustrophobic, tawdry and dangerous. The audience sees piles of rubbish and graffiti. This is an inhospitable urban environment. Two of the opening shots are filmed through fences or bars, and we are invited to read this setting as one in which the characters feel trapped. These images of fences and bars predict both the psychological entrapment of the main character of Frannie (Meg Ryan) and the narrative entrapment of the characters within the brutal events which occur in the film.

In contrast to the grey palette of the city, the garden shown in the second half of the opening credit sequence is almost hyper-real. This is a Garden of Eden, in which flowers and shrubs abound. The garden is a place of fertility, beauty and life. The contrast of this setting to that of the city is stark and indicates the destruction of such beauty to come. There is a fantasy quality to this garden, that can perhaps be read as symbolic of the dreams of the main characters that are destroyed by the events within the film.

The third and final setting used in the opening credit sequence is that of Frannie's apartment. She is seen sleeping peacefully in bed as the camera pans around her bedroom. There are wind-chimes and artificial butterflies hanging from the ceiling. The colours are muted but stylish and the apartment feels warm, safe and comfortable. This is a safe environment at this stage in the film, indicated by Frannie's peaceful sleep and the gentle noises of the wind-chime. As with the garden, the viewer fears that the apartment is a safe space that will be invaded by whatever horrors the grey and uninviting city holds.

Props

If the rubbish and fences of the first part of the credit sequence indicate the tawdry and stultifying nature of the city, then the flowers and petals within the garden indicate the opposite. The character we see in the garden is Frannie's sister. She is holding a cup of coffee and surveying the morning. As petals begin to fall from the trees and bushes, she watches them. The snowstorm of petals is beautiful and indicates the idyllic quality of the fertile garden environment. There is an unreal quality to the shots of the petals raining down on the garden and we are invited to understand not only how peaceful the characters feel at this point in the film, but also that this dream-like environment cannot last.

Lighting

The first part of the opening credit sequence uses naturalistic lighting for ominous effect. The contrast between the sun and the city in the establishing shot is extreme and, as has already been highlighted, indicates an urban environment which is often sombre and inhospitable. The light in the garden is heightened and gives a surreal, fairy-tale quality to the setting. Everything is bathed in light and, by extension, life. Frannie's apartment is not as light as the garden outside, but she can see the sun through her window. Access to light diminishes in this film as the events become more frightening. The dark events of the narrative are echoed by the diminishing light of the settings in which the characters find themselves.

Body language

Body language is a key indicator of character state of mind and in the opening sequence we are given a clear picture of how both Frannie and her sister are feeling at the beginning of the narrative. Frannie's sister walks slowly and in a leisurely way through the garden. We see shots of her feet on the cobbled path and understand her state of relaxation and peace. She is seen turning around slowly to view the garden and the shower of petals, and reaching up, smiling, to touch the shower, and we feel more than ever that this is a character who enjoys being alive. Of course, within the thriller genre, this also means that this character will probably become one of the victims of the narrative. As has already been stated, Frannie is asleep when we first see her. She then wakes, turns over, moves position, sighs peacefully and goes back to sleep. These are two characters who might have their own personal concerns, but seem essentially happy. The events to come will, of course, destroy their sense of peace.

Costume and make-up

Both women in this sequence are to some degree partially clothed and both are free of obvious make-up. Frannie is in her night clothes and her sister has walked into the garden in her skirt and camisole. They are not being sexualised by this lack of clothing, however, but made to appear free and relaxed. They are not presented as women who obsess about their appearance but as women who are probably happy with who they are. Transferred to a later part in the thriller narrative, a lack of clothing might indicate vulnerability, but here we are presented with characters who have not yet become vulnerable.

Editing

The role of the editor of a film is to select and arrange shots in a way that conveys specific meanings to the film audience. Editing is as important as any other of the micro elements in the creation of meaning and the importance of the editor should never be underestimated. The editor will often work with the director to select pieces of footage to be used, but this is not the only important type of decision that needs to be made at the editing stage. The type of edit between shots (known as transition), is of equal significance. There are four main types of transition that can be used by the editor and each can play a part in the creation of meaning.

1. Cuts.

    These are the most common and 'invisible' form of transition. If one shot moves instantaneously to the next, without the audience being conscious of the transition, then a cut will have been used. Cuts help the film to retain its reality, as they do not break the viewer's suspension of disbelief.

2. Dissolves.

    This type of transition is achieved by fading one shot off the screen while another shot is fading in. The audience will be able to see both shots on the screen at the mid-point of the dissolve. If the film maker wants to show the connection between two characters, objects or places, then a dissolve might be used to indicate the connection.

3. Fades.

    A fade occurs when there is the gradual darkening or lightening of an image until it becomes black or white. One shot will fade either out or in until the audience is left looking at a white or black screen. Fades can be used to signal the end of a particular section of time within the narrative, or to suggest the importance of the image which has just 'faded'.

4. Wipes.

    If one image is pushed off the screen by another, then a wipe has been used. Images can be pushed right or left, although it is more common for the image to be pushed off the right-hand side of the screen, as this movement is more consistent with the sense of time moving forward. Wipes are often used to signal a movement in a film between different locations that are experiencing the same time.

Continuity and montage editing

There are two types of editing with which you will need to familiarise yourselves. First, continuity editing. This is the most common form of editing type, as it retains a sense of realistic chronology and generates a feeling that time is moving forward. Continuity editing takes the film from one shot or scene to the next, moving forward in time. The film's narrative thus seems to be progressing in an expected and realistic way. Films may use flash forwards and flashbacks within their structure, but still be described as continuity edited, because the overall sense of forward movement is still retained. Montage editing is the second type of editing that you will need to be able to recognise. A montage-edited sequence will contain many very different images, quickly edited together. The images do not provide a sense of the narrative moving forward, but the sequence can still be full of meaning. The rapidity of cuts within a montage sequence creates impact and the viewer is forced to consider the connections between the images shown. There may be no obvious connection, but if, for example, the montage sequence is being used to represent the thoughts of a particular character, then the state of mind of that character would be clearly indicated. Montage sequences are often used to reflect chaos, tension or disturbance. The images edited together might have an overall thematic or visual connection, in which case the film maker might be attempting to make a wider point. However, montaged images can be deliberately disparate and unconnected, allowing a different kind of meaning to be evoked.

EXERCISE 14

With a partner, choose a short sequence from a film. Note down the style of editing used in your sequence and the transition types used. What are the meanings being created by the editing in your chosen scene?

Case Study 8: Editing analysis

The use of editing within a seven-minute sequence from Sam Mendes' *American Beauty* (1999)

Source: British Film Institute

This case study will look at the opening seven minutes of the film.

The purpose of any opening sequence is to draw the viewer into the narrative by introducing characters and plot elements. The opening sequence to *American Beauty* introduces the viewer to the world of Lester Burnham, the central character within the film, and his family. It also establishes for us the crushing tedium of Lester's daily routine, his dissatisfaction with his life and the unhappiness which is beneath the seeming perfection of his world.

This sequence uses continuity editing in order to establish a sense of real time moving forward. This is not a film which utilises montage sequences in order to make its points, rather one that provides a story of a year in Lester's life. As such, the viewer needs to experience time progressing. The opening crane shot of the film shows Lester's street and the series of edits that make up the rest of this sequence introduce us to the mundane routine of his life as well as the different life experiences of other members of his family. From the establishing shot we cut to Lester in bed. He is asleep, but is still represented as the focal point of the following story. The fact that the non-diegetic sound is his voice-over confirms this for the viewer. The scene then cuts to a closer, mid-shot of Lester lying in bed. The implication is already that what will follow will be a closer and closer inspection of Lester's and his family's lives.

Cuts are the only type of edit used in this sequence. They act as invisible, non-obtrusive edits, which do not distract the viewer's attention away from either the characters seen or the information heard. It is not the mechanics of the film-making process that are being shown here, but the characters who will occupy the film; it is essential that the viewer understands Lester's psychological predicament without being distracted by the edits. Having edited to a low-level shot of Lester putting on his slippers, the viewer is aware that what is likely to follow is a 'portrait' of one of Lester's typical days. The next cut shows us the 'high point of my day', as we see Lester masturbating in the shower. The film's tag line is: 'Look Closer' and the series of cuts the audience has encountered so far are indeed taking us into intimate proximity with Lester.

The viewer is then taken outside Lester's house for the first time. The cut is to a rose, of a variety called 'American Beauty'. As we progress through the film, it becomes obvious how significant this first shot was. Red petals become a motif within Lester's fantasies. Red flowers feature in many scenes, with many connotations. In this sequence, the image of the rose is used to introduce Carolyn Burnham, Lester's wife. She is seen cutting the rose in order to use it in a flower arrangement. The rose is perfect, as is the house in which Lester lives. Carolyn is perfectly dressed and seems to exude control over her environment. The next edit explains to the viewer what Lester's response is to this image of his wife in the garden. The cut takes us into a point-of-view shot through the window out into the garden. Lester's voice-over indicates his exhaustion 'with just watching her' and the viewer at once understands the distance between the couple and Lester's apathy concerning his wife's attempts to keep their imperfect world seemingly perfect.

The next cut is to a shot through a white picket fence. The imagery of confinement that is repeatedly used to indicate Lester's mental state is begun here. The fence also functions as yet another image of the perfect, suburban, middle-class American Dream-like world, which will be deconstructed throughout the film. Lester then narrates the viewer over the next series of cuts. We cut to 'next-door neighbour Jim', then to 'and that's his lover, Jim'. Lester's tone is not derogatory of the gay relationship, but more desultory at the seeming perfection of his neighbours' relationship: even they seem to have a perfectly ordered world, to the extent that they even share the same name. The next cut turns the camera around and shows Lester inside his house looking through the window. He is framed through the window, as if behind bars, unable to experience the scene he is seeing as anything other than further evidence of the prison-like world which he inhabits. The next edit offers further indication that he feels excluded from the lives of his wife and neighbours, and is trapped in his own disillusioned world. The cut takes the viewer into a position behind Lester. We can see what he is watching through the window. He is blocked on one side of the frame by a curtain, from the front by the window, and from the back by the audience's position – almost as if we have involuntarily contributed to his entrapment.

The sequence then cuts to Janie, Lester and Carolyn's daughter. This opening sequence is gradually revealing important characters and their emotional and psychological realities to us. Janie is seen at the computer, which seems a perfectly ordinary pursuit for a teenage girl. It is only when the sequence cuts to an image of what is on the computer screen, that we understand that it is not just Lester Burnham who is dissatisfied with his lot. Janie is studying her accounts as well as an internet site featuring breast augmentation. As is soon evident in this narrative, none of the Burnhams are happy with themselves or their lives as they are, and all are desperate for change. The next two cuts take us further into the mindset of Janie. We see her standing in front of her mirror, examining her appearance with evident displeasure. Looking beneath the surface is not something which the characters in this film seem able to do at this point in the narrative.

The next series of edits bring Lester, Carolyn and Janie (the three main protagonists) together. The sequence edits to Carolyn, waiting to take her husband to work and daughter to school. Everything about her body language and dialogue at this point in the sequence indicate her annoyance with the other members of the family and the cuts within this sequence clearly demonstrate the distance from and annoyance with each other that all three family members feel. The film cuts away from Carolyn to Janie, who is being criticised by her mother for her appearance. The cut back to Carolyn waiting impatiently then moves via a cut to Lester, who walks down the path, then drops the content of his briefcase all over the floor. The editing here does not allow us to linger on each of the characters, but acts to establish the awful tension felt within the family. Although the family is brought into the same section of this scene via the edits and they are obviously speaking to each other, they have still not occupied the same frame. Although the editing up to this point in the film has been organised to show us a comfortable middle-class family, it has also been subtly used to show the significant cracks in this family unit.

How to write the micro essay

Once you have completed all of your study and research into the micro elements, you will be at the stage when you can complete your micro essay. This should be between 1000 and 1500 words and should focus on a seven-minute sequence from a film. Below is an essay plan that you could use to organise and guide your essay writing.

Introduction to essay

Your introduction should show your reader that you understand the importance of micro elements in the creation of meaning and audience response. You should summarise the main types of meaning that can be generated by the micro elements you have chosen to study. Your introduction should end by identifying the film sequence that you are going to use in your analysis. Remember to give the director and date of the film.

Middle paragraphs

The main paragraphs within your essay should show a systematic and thorough evaluation of the impact of your chosen micro elements on your film's audience. You could evaluate one micro element in the first few paragraphs and then move on to the next micro element. However, your essay will appear more fluid and fluent if you work systematically through your sequence, identifying and discussing micro elements as they 'appear'. Micro features are used interdependently by film makers and you will need to discuss how your chosen elements work together, as well as separately, to create meaning and response. Don't forget to back up each of the points you make with a clear example from your film.

Essay conclusion

Your conclusion should summarise the meanings and responses you think your chosen micro elements have generated. You should also comment on whether or not you think the micro elements you have analysed have produced meaning and response effectively in your chosen sequence.

Before you begin planning your micro essay, read the example essays that follow and consider how the analysis within them has been organised.

Exemplar micro essay 1: Analysis of *mise-en-scène* and cinematography within a seven-minute sequence from Stephen Daldry's *The Hours* (2003)

The choices made concerning *mise-en-scène* and cinematography within a film are an essential element within the generation of meaning for the film's audience. A sense of historical time, mood, the characters' state of mind and even place within the film's narrative can all be indicated through cinematography and *mise-en-scène*. This essay will analyse how these micro elements generate meaning and create response in a seven-minute sequence from Stephen Daldry's 2003 film *The Hours*. The focus sequence depicts the character Laura Brown's near suicide.

The Hours is an adaptation of the novel of the same name, which itself uses Virginia Woolf's modernist novel *Mrs Dalloway* to inform its narrative. Daldry's film focuses on the lives of three women: Virginia Woolf, Laura Brown and Clarissa Vaughn. Woolf is the writer of the novel, Laura Brown the reader and Clarissa Vaughn plays a late-twentieth-century version of the character of Mrs Dalloway from Woolf's novel. There are three distinct times represented within the film: the 1920s, 1950s and 1990s and the sequence on which this essay will focus depicts the first two.

The character of Laura Brown exists in America in the time immediately following the Second World War. The hardship of the war years has been replaced by a new affluence and sense of security for many Americans and Laura's life, at least on the surface, is free from want. Her family live in a comfortable house, in a comfortable suburban neighbourhood. She has a devoted husband and one child, and is pregnant with her second. Her days are spent looking after her son, but apart from this she seems to have few responsibilities. Underneath this happy surface, however, is Laura's crushing sense of dissatisfaction with her life, and it is her reading of Woolf's novel that seems to confirm for her the pointlessness of the life she has.

The sequence begins with Laura taking her child to the babysitter. As she drives, the viewer is presented with images of the clean, ordered and comfortable neighbourhood in which she lives. There is, however, a silence between mother and son, which indicates both their anxieties. As Laura gets out of her car at the sitter's house, she is seen in long shot. Her pregnancy is clear, as is her difficulty of movement because of it. The audience is made increasingly aware that the pregnancy is part of the entrapment that Laura feels. The next shot is a close-up of Richard, Laura's son, who remains still in the car, rather than getting out. His sense of panic at his mother's departure is introduced, and then confirmed when he says, 'Mommy, I don't want to do this.' The close-up shots of Laura and Richard's strained faces add to the sense of tension within the relationship and the scene.

The surface elements of the film at this point contradict the emotional reality of the scene. Both Laura and Richard are dressed neatly, in clothes that confirm the decade as the 1950s. The settings in which we see them are uncluttered and clean, and yet both characters are experiencing life-changing events. The mid-shot of Laura, walking away from leaving her son, allows the viewer to see the control and order of her clothes, but also the emotional turmoil of her facial expression and body language. Symbolically, she has turned her back on her family, yet this is not done out of callousness but desperation, as her tears confirm. The camera tracks back in front of the distraught Laura, establishing her distress at her planned abandonment and the fact that she is the viewer's focus within the scene. As she reaches the car, we see Laura in mid-shot waving to her son. She has held back her tears before turning to wave to him, thus indicating the continued pent-up emotion of her life. Richard's face, also shot in mid-shot, is serious. The next series of cuts in this sequence present a series of mid-shots and close-ups of Laura and her son. She is now the central focus within her frame and is shown, not looking back, determined to carry out her plan. His mother's determination is contrasted with the increasingly close-up shots of Richard, becoming more and more hysterical as his mother's car pulls away. The next shot of Richard within this sequence is a long shot of him standing in the road, looking at the back of his mother's car as it departs. He is small, vulnerable and alone within this frame, and as the viewer realises later in the film, this theme, abandonment, is one of the key causes for the adult Richard's tendency towards self-destruction.

The next series of shots within this sequence show Laura driving and Richard in the living room of his baby-sitter. The *mise-en-scène* of the sitter's house indicates the 1950s setting of Laura's narrative. The huge-flowered wallpaper of the room combines with the Meccano set Richard is playing with to root the sequence in this period. Richard is seen building a house with his Meccano. The parallel shots are of Laura driving increasingly quickly towards her destination. As a long shot shows her swerving off the freeway, we see a medium shot of Richard destroying the house he has built; symbolically indicating the destructive impact that his mother's actions are having on his sense of safety and security.

The sequence then moves to Laura's destination. She has arrived at a hotel, the *mise-en-scène* of which is grand, yet anonymous. Laura is then shot in central frame, over the shoulder of a porter. As the porter moves out of shot, Laura is left, alone, in a large, stylish, but lifeless room. The colours within the room are muted creams and beiges. There is little natural light and the impression is of a room with shadows. The psychological situation of Laura is extremely apparent. An overhead shot is then used to show Laura lying on the bed. She looks swamped by the room. So far in the sequence, the viewer has feared that Laura will do something desperate, but has no evidence related to *mise-en-scène*. The next shot, possibly a point of view shot from Laura, shows her taking out a book and bottles of pills from her bag. The viewer's fears are confirmed by the sight of these props and the next shot, a cut away to the birthday cake she has made for her husband and placed on the kitchen table, suggests the life she has chosen to leave.

The camera then pans around Laura lying on the bed, reading Mrs Dalloway. The viewer hears the voice of Virginia Woolf reading a line from the book – 'Did it matter that she would cease to exist?' As we hear this line, Laura pulls up her shirt to reveal her pregnant stomach, indicating to the viewer one of the sacrifices she will have to make in order to escape her unhappiness. The next cut is to Virginia Woolf and the camera continues to pan, but in the opposite direction. This cinematography links the two characters' states of mind and quandaries. The *mise-en-scène* of Woolf's clothes and room locate the time as the 1920s. Her stillness mirrors that of Laura Brown. The viewer then hears the thoughts of Woolf, as she states: 'It is possible to die' and the next shot shows the impact that this line has on Laura Brown. Laura's face and body are partially in shadow. She is inert on the bed, seeming to give herself up to the prospect of death. As the scene cuts back to Woolf, the viewer hears her sister Vanessa Bell's attempts to break her out of her reverie. It is not Bell's question which brings Woolf back, however, but the entry of her daughter, Angelica, into her aunt's frame. A two-shot of Woolf with Angelica on her lap follows and although the child has perhaps introduced something positive into Woolf's thoughts, her aunt's expression is still quite disengaged. Neither Virginia Woolf nor Laura Brown can quite step outside of their own troubled thoughts, even when presented with a child.

Angelica asks her aunt 'What were you thinking about?', but the answer to this question is postponed as the scene cuts back to a point-of-view shot from Laura, as she looks at the bottles of pills on the bedside table. The viewer may, at this point, have been positioned as if they were Laura, yet the scene still generates a sense of powerlessness to stop events. There are very few point-of-view shots from Laura's perspective, and it is as if the viewer were not being asked to enter into her mindset, but to observe solely the emotional turmoil it causes. An overhead shot then places Laura centrally in the frame on the hotel bed. She is lying on a white bed cover and is shrouded in shadow. The connotations of death are clear at this point for the viewer. The sequence then enters a kind of dreamscape. Laura's psychological state is mirrored by the presence of river water filling the hotel room. This *mise-en-scène* element clearly links Laura Brown and Virginia Woolf. Laura is engulfed by her unhappiness and metaphorically feels as if she is drowning. Virginia Woolf, as we have seen in the opening sequence to this film, did drown herself in a river in 1941. The water is shown covering Laura Brown and the audience fears that she has taken the pills and died in her sleep. However, the cut to Virginia Woolf, and the close-up of her suddenly seeming to wake from her reverie, stops the viewer from having this fear confirmed. Woolf smiles and says to Angelica, 'I was going to kill my heroine, but I've changed my mind' and the connections built between Woolf and Laura, through the previous cinematography within this sequence, give the viewer hope for Laura. The cut-back to Laura in mid-shot shows her waking suddenly and gasping for air, stating: 'I can't'. The camera then tracks slowly back from Laura as she begins to cry, hold her pregnant stomach and rock. The camera and the viewer may be able to leave Laura at this point, as she has not committed suicide, but her body language indicates that her unhappiness is still very real.

The cinematography and *mise-en-scène* used in this sequence have contributed to the viewer's increased understanding of the character of Laura Brown. These micro elements have shown the dissatisfaction that can lie beneath the American Dream of the post-war years. The differences in *mise-en-scène* between Laura Brown and Virginia Woolf's scenes have distanced them in terms of chronological years, but the cinematography has clearly shown the connection between the two characters.

Assessment comments

This essay shows an extremely clear understanding of the meanings that can be generated by micro elements and their potential impact on the film spectator. The essay moves systematically through the sequence, discussing the micro elements individually and also how they work together to create meaning. The candidate shows an excellent level of film form knowledge and explores in detail the different reactions of the viewer at different points within the sequence. There is a real sense of individual voice in this essay, with the candidate exploring the different possible functions of cinematography and *mise-en-scène* with confidence and originality. This essay would achieve a high grade 'A'.

Exemplar micro essay 2: An analysis of sound and editing within a seven-minute sequence from The Coen Brothers' 1996 film *Fargo*

The micro elements of a film are an essential element within the generation of meaning. The sound used within a film can convey information concerning character state of mind, genre, atmosphere and the narrative position of a particular sequence. Editing can be used to indicate the relationship between characters within a scene, and the tone and atmosphere of a sequence. Each of these micro elements helps to contribute to the impact that a scene has on its audience. This essay will focus on how sound and editing are used to generate meaning and response within the sequence from *Fargo* in which Margie finds Gaer at the hideout.

The sequence begins with Margie, in long shot, shown getting out of her car. The sound is purely diegetic at this point. The audience can hear the crunching of her feet on the snow, as well as the distant sound of the wood chipper. The diegetic sound of Margie's steps in the snow indicates not only the environment she is in, but also her isolation. The snow, ice and fog of *Fargo* have already been experienced by the film's viewer and we are aware of how this *mise-en-scène* makes movement and vision difficult. The sound of Margie's steps confirms that she will have to confront Gaer alone, and in a snowbound environment that is likely to make her situation even more vulnerable and hazardous. It is only retrospectively that Margie and the film viewer realise that the noise she initially hears is a wood chipper. At this point in the sequence, the noise is unidentifiable. This has the effect of making the high pitched, mechanical sound even more ominous and threatening for both Margie and the viewer.

The sequence then cuts from the long-distance shot of Margie, to a medium/long shot of her, walking in the direction of the sound. The sound used here is still diegetic and seems to demand our complete focus. Margie's movement is towards the sound and the edit has taken us into another stage of her movement towards her final confrontation with Gaer. What follows is a panning shot that sees Margie walk away from the camera, towards the sound of the wood chipper. There are few edits at this point and the viewer is forced to watch Margie moving slowly away from the camera. The lack of edits here reinforces the idea that Margie is the central focus in this sequence and that she is the audience's hope for narrative resolution. The lack of edits also works to hold our concentration and to increase the level of tension within the scene.

The next cut takes the audience into a head-on close-up of Margie. We see her confused expression and thus have our own anxieties mirrored. The diegetic sound of the wood chipper is becoming increasingly louder, as if signalling the narrative movement towards the film's climax. This sequence, as well as the entire film, is continuity edited. Montage elements would distract from the increased tension of the sequence and halt the film audience's movement towards the unveiling of Gaer and the wood chipper. The use of cuts in this sequence, rather than any other form of edit, provide the kind of 'invisible' movement from one element of the scene to another, which works to sustain tension and retain audience engagement.

As the sound of the wood chipper becomes even louder, the edits have taken the viewer from one shot of Margie alone, to another. The cuts in this sequence continually confirm that Margie's confrontation with Gaer will be one without help. The next cut in the sequence moves the audience in front of Margie, into a close-up, so that we can see her expression when she finally discovers the source of the diegetic sound. The audience's expectations are met, and their fears confirmed, when the next cut takes them into a point of view shot, showing Gaer standing next to a wood chipper, with blood spitting out of it onto the snow. The edits have drawn the viewer towards the unveiling of this horrible sight. The sequence then cuts to Margie, having taken out her gun, heading towards Gaer. The diegetic sound of the wood chipper is now so loud that it masks her approach. This allows her initial approach to be unnoticed, but also adds to the feeling of anxiety for the viewer. The diegetic sound of the wood chipper is loud and terrible, it seems to indicate its own threat to Margie.

As Margie approaches Gaer, the non-diegetic soundtrack begins. The soundtrack is instrumental and uses long chords in order to increase the tension within the sequence. The dual effect of the loud, mechanical sound of the wood chipper and the long ominous chords of the non-diegetic soundtrack is intense and unsettling. Margie and the viewer have moved close enough to Gaer now to be in danger. The next cut does nothing to diminish the viewer's sense of panic and dread. We now see Gaer, standing over the wood chipper, attempting to force a leg into the grinding mechanism.

The audience knows from a previous sequence that Gaer has killed his partner in crime and we now assume that this leg is his. The non-diegetic soundtrack begins to rise to a pitch at this point, as if to mirror the horror that both the audience and Margie experience at seeing what Gaer is doing. As Gaer attempts to force the leg into the wood chipper, the diegetic sound of the wood chipper rises in pitch. Almost scream-like, it also echoes the horror of Gaer's actions.

The next cut is to Margie who shouts 'Police' at Gaer, in order to get him to stop. Margie's law enforcement credentials have never been in question in this film and the audience has been in little doubt that she will eventually catch the criminals. However, as the diegetic and non-diegetic sound overwhelm what Margie says, tension is increased and the viewer is even more fearful for her safety. This discordant wall of sound which surrounds Margie works to isolate her further from potential help and safety. She shouts 'Police' for a second time and the sequence cuts back to Gaer, still oblivious to her presence. The cuts have taken the viewer uncomfortably close to Gaer and to the terrible thing which he is doing. This proximity generates tension and the viewer becomes desperate for the tension to break, in order that they can pull out from shots of the blood and the wood chipper. The sequence then cuts back to Margie whose cry of 'Police' is heard this time. She also points to her badge, signalling her position. The diegetic and non-diegetic sound are still loud and relentless, as the next cut shows Gaer looking up from the wood chipper, turning and running from Margie.

The next cut pulls the audience out from their close proximity to Gaer and we watch in long shot as he tries to flee across the frozen lake. The sequence cuts to Margie pointing her gun at the fleeing Gaer. Just before she shoots, the diegetic sound of the wood chipper ceases. The wood chipper has now been replaced as the focus of the sequence by Gaer's attempted escape: the presence of its sound in the story is no longer needed. The audience hears the gun shot, as well as the mounting tension within the soundtrack. The non-diegetic sound is still rising because Gaer has not yet been captured and it is not until the sequence cuts to the results of Margie's second shot that the non-diegetic sound calms. Gaer is shown, wounded, lying in the middle of the snow-covered lake. The non-diegetic sound has become less urgent and discordant, and settles now into a series of lighter, rising chords which imply a resolution to events. As the next cut takes the viewer out to an extreme long-shot of Margie approaching Gaer on the lake, this new, less frantic section of the soundtrack continues.

This scene finishes at this point, but the non-diegetic sound does not. The next cut takes us into a new scene and a point-of-view shot from Margie, through her patrol car window. The non-diegetic sound from the previous scene has bridged over into this scene, as if to indicate the fact that the viewer's anxieties are not quite over. It is only when this scene cuts to a shot of Gaer behind the grill, in the back of Margie's police car, that the non-diegetic sound resolves and stops. The viewer can see that Margie has ended the chaos of the narrative and has caught one of the major agents of disruption within the film. Therefore, the non-diegetic sound that 'narrated' the climactic scene can come to an end.

In this sequence, sound and editing are inextricably linked. They function to give the viewer information concerning the climactic nature of this sequence within the narrative as a whole, to express the fears and feelings of the film's protagonist, Margie, and to draw the viewer into the tensions and anticipation associated with this kind of film sequence. Sound and editing elements are absolutely essential in the creation of an engaging and effective film sequence.

Assessment comments

This essay shows clear understanding of the ways in which the chosen micro elements function independently and together, in order to generate meaning and response. The essay offers a thorough and accurate evaluation of the different types of meaning created by film sound and editing. A very good level of film form knowledge is evident here and textual examples are used clearly to substantiate points made. There is clear indication in this essay of an independent voice, with the candidate speculating on potential meanings and responses, as well as utilizing their knowledge of macro elements in order to discuss micro elements within this sequence.

Practical Application of Learning (PAL)

Having completed your micro and macro essay, your last FS1 task is to come up with an original idea for a film and then to create a storyboard or a screenplay for a sequence from that film. The skills and knowledge you gained during the micro and macro tasks will be invaluable in this practical work and you should think very carefully about how choices related to macro and micro elements work to create meaning and affect the film audience. This task provides you with the opportunity to create the film you have always felt was absent from your cinema-going experience: the greatest film never made!

In the practical work, you should produce:

- EITHER, a storyboard of 15 to 25 different shots
- OR, a screenplay of between 500 and 800 words
- AND written work of between 800 and 900 words.

The written work is broken down into:

- a synopsis of your imaginary film (200 words)
- an account of the cinematic ideas you are going to use in your practical work (200 words)
- an evaluation of your finished practical work (400 to 500 words).

How to begin your PAL work

The first step in the production of any practical work is a brainstorming of possible ideas. You have had plenty of experience of watching both mainstream and independent films by this point in the course and you should consider in your brainstorming of ideas elements within these films that you found particularly effective. Consider cinematography you have found particularly powerful, sound elements you considered evocative, editing techniques that created drama and meaning, and *mise-en-scène* choices that you thought gave the film impact. You could also think about how generic conventions have been used to affect the viewer and how narrative strategies engage the film audience's interest. Once you have brainstormed your ideas and settled on one in particular, try to flesh out the different ideas you have into a whole film idea. You could use the following questions to prompt you:

1. What are the main events that happen in your film?

2. Who are the main characters? What do they look like? What are the relationships between the characters? What are their roles within the narrative?

3. Does your film have a recognisable genre? Which conventions of that genre will be evident?

4. Who will be the audience for your film?

5. Where will it be shown? Are you going to produce a mainstream or an independent film?

Once you have all of the background information for your imaginary film, you can move on to writing your synopsis.

The synopsis

The main function of a film synopsis is to provide the reader with information concerning the key events within a film. A synopsis should be engaging as well as informative, and make the reader want to go out and watch the film described. A synopsis indicates the genre of a film, as well as the time in which it is set, the main locations, main characters and significant events. You have only 200 words in which to describe your film, so subplots and subsidiary characters do not need to be included.

Here are two examples of film synopses.

1. Synopsis 1.
   It is the present day in small-town middle America. Louise works as a waitress in a cafe and Thelma is unhappily married to a man who takes very little notice of her. The two women are planning a weekend away to escape from the tedium of their lives. On route to a mountain cabin, they stop at a bar and Thelma is nearly raped. Louise saves her, but shoots Thelma's attacker dead. The two women then flee the scene. They agree to escape to Mexico. Louise's boyfriend brings her savings to her, but these are stolen by a young man who has spent the night with Louise. The women are now desperate and Thelma resorts to holding up a store in order to get them some money. The women are pursued

by the police and cornered near the Grand Canyon. They decide to choose death, rather than imprisonment, and drive over the edge of the canyon.

2. Synopsis 2.

It is the present day in North London. Shaun, who is 29 and a junior manager in an electrical goods shop, lives with Pete. Shaun's girlfriend is Liz, who is becoming increasingly unhappy with the routine of their relationship. The characters are so absorbed in their own minor worries that they do not notice a recent outbreak of flesh-eating zombie activity. Liz dumps Shaun after yet another let-down. Pete then returns to the house one day having been bitten by a zombie and Shaun finds two zombies in his garden. Shaun is concerned about Liz and sets off to rescue her from the zombie threat. He finds her and saves her from the zombies. Shaun and Liz are reunited and live happily ever after together.

EXERCISE 15

Read the two synopses above. First, see if you can identify the film that is being described. Then note down the key information that is being given. Finally, choose a film you have seen recently and try to create an effective synopsis for that film.

When you have practised synopsis writing, you should be ready to create your own synopsis for your imaginary film.

Cinematic ideas

Your cinematic ideas should be written before you begin the practical work, as they provide an indication of the stylistic choices you are going to use. This piece of writing should include details of the technical devices (such as camerawork, *mise-en-scène*, editing and sound) you are going to use within your screenplay or storyboard, and the effect that these technical devices will have on the film's potential audience.

Within your cinematic ideas, you should refer to actual films and to the cinematic ideas within them that have influenced your decisions concerning your own film. You have 200 words in which to outline your cinematic choices.

The storyboard

A good storyboard will provide a template of ideas which the film-maker can use to help plan and execute the shooting of scenes. Storyboards need to contain information concerning *mise-en-scène*, sound, editing and cinematography. Through these elements, narrative and genre information can be relayed. Storyboards need to be easy to read, in the sense that they should move clearly from shot to shot, allowing the 'reader' to visualise and make sense of the action as they 'read' the storyboard.

You do not have to be an amazing artist to create a storyboard, but you do need to have a clear sense of how each of the shots you draw offers information. Each shot will need to be clearly drawn, with enough information included to allow a potential film-maker to shoot whatever you have indicated in the shot.

Look at the industry example of a storyboard below. It includes all of the necessary information to eventually shoot the scene.

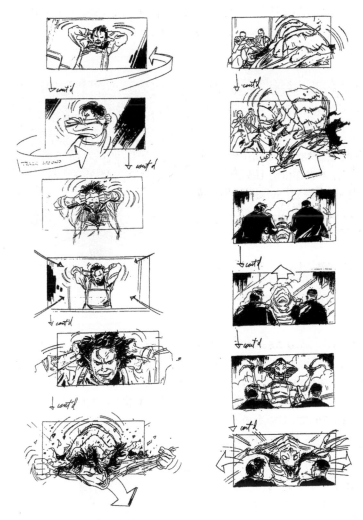

Sony Pictures Entertainment

Your storyboard does not have to be as well drawn, but it does need to include the same information. Below is a list of micro and macro elements that are used to relay meaning in the industry storyboard. You should consider them when creating your own storyboard.

1. Camera angle
2. Camera distance
3. Camera movement
4. Character movement
5. Sound
6. Edit type
7. Genre elements
8. Narrative information.

Now look at the series of illustrations. Each one shows how you can relate micro and macro information visually.

1. **Camera angle.**
   The angle of the camera is evident from what can be seen in the drawing. It appears as if the camera is looking up at the top of the mountain, thus indicating the size of what is being shot and potentially the anxious state of mind of the character who is about to climb the mountain.

2. **Camera distance.**
   The camera distance being indicated in this illustration is an extreme close-up. The camera is placed in extremely close proximity to the character's eye and it is obvious to the viewer that the character is terrified.

3. **Camera movement.**
   The arrows in this illustration indicate a panning of the camera, or 180 degrees right to left. The camera is at eye-level and this camera angle contributes to the feeling that the panning approximates a character's gaze around a room.

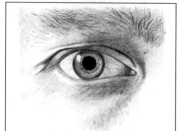

4. **Character movement.**
   The arrows in this illustration indicate that the character has turned from having his back to the camera, to facing it. Again the camera is at eye-level, so the movement of the character seems to suggest that he has turned to face another character who has been following him.

5. Sound.
The information under this illustration states that the sound is diegetic. The sound of wind in the trees is shown. As it is shown to be night-time and the trees are shot from a low angle, the sound used seems to contribute to the feeling that this is an unsettling and ominous scene.

Sound of wind in the trees

6. Edit type.
The edited type indicated between these two shots is a wipe. The shots show two different characters, both sitting on their beds, both with their heads in their hands. The use of the wipe indicates that the moods of these two characters are linked, that they might have been contributing factors in each other's upset states of mind.

Tom, head in hands

Wipe to

7. Genre elements.
This illustration includes genre-specific props and costumes. The technology in the room is obviously futuristic and the outfits worn by the characters also indicates the science fiction genre of the film.

Gina's room, head in her hands

8. Narrative information.
There is no action evident in this shot, but a black background with the words *Five Years Earlier* written over the top. The shot relays information concerning narrative movement and will obviously be followed by a flashback sequence within the narrative.

You should use the 'checklist' of eight elements outlined above, the comments on how these elements can create meaning, and the illustrations in this section to begin creating your own storyboard.

The screenplay

A screenplay includes all of the information necessary for a film to be made. It includes detail concerning characters, dialogue, action, locations, props and camera angles. Your screenplay should give all of the information needed for a potential film maker to be able to commence shooting. Dialogue is not the only element within a screenplay and you should make sure that you include all of the other types of information necessary for your 'reader' to visualise the film sequence.

Five years earlier

As with the storyboard task, you should use all of the knowledge you have gained during the micro and macro tasks to create an effective screenplay. Consider the questions below before you commence writing.

1. What is the genre of your screenplay? Which generic conventions of that genre are you going to use in your practical work?

2. Where does the sequence come in the overall narrative of your film? How is it evident that the sequence is from the exposition, development, complication, climax or resolution segment of the narrative?

3. Who are the characters appearing in this scene? What do they look like? How do they feel? How do they interact with one another?

4. Where is the scene set? How does the location and setting of the scene help to convey information to the film's potential audience? How is the scene lit? What meanings does the lighting help generate?

5. Are there any props evident in your scene? Are they significant to the film audience's understanding of character, genre, themes or narrative?

6. What sound is evident in the sequence? Is there non-diegetic sound? If so, what type? Is there dialogue? How is the dialogue delivered? What kinds of information is being conveyed by what is said? Is there other diegetic sound? How does this help convey meaning?

7. What kinds of camera angle, movement and distance are used? What information does the cinematography you have chosen help generate?

8. What edit types will be used? Are these consistent with the mood, atmosphere and narrative information created within the sequence?

When you have the answers to all of the questions above, you will be nearly ready to begin writing your screenplay. The last important issue to consider is how a screenplay is structured.

EXERCISE 16

Look at the extract from an industry example of a screenplay below. Take particular note of the layout of the screenplay. Your own work should use the same structure and also use the same kinds of abbreviations. When you have studied the structure, use the eight questions above to consider how the screenplay generates meaning for its audience.

Extract from the screenplay for *Fight Club* (Fincher, 1999). Opening sequence:

SCREEN BLACK

JACK (V.O.): People were always asking me, did I know Tyler Durden.

FADE IN.
INT. SOCIAL ROOM – TOP FLOOR OF HIGH RISE

Tyler has one arm round Jack's shoulder; the other holds a handgun with the barrel lodged in Jack's mouth. Tyler is sitting in Jack's lap. They are both sweating and dishevelled, both around 30; Tyler is blond, handsome, and Jack, brunette, is appealing in a dry sort of way. P.O.V. Close-up as Jack looks at his watch.

TYLER: One minute. *(Looking out of the window).* This is the beginning. We're at ground zero. Maybe you should say a few words to mark the occasion.

JACK: . . . i . . . ann . . . iinn . . . ff . . . nnyin

JACK (V.O.): With a gun barrel between your teeth, you only speak in vowels.

Jack is seen in close-up. He tongues the gun barrel to the side of his mouth.

JACK (*still distorted*): I can't think of anything.

JACK (V.O.): With my tongue, I can hear the rifling in the barrel. For a second I forgot about Tyler's whole controlled demolition thing and I wondered how clean this gun is.

Tyler checks his watch.

TYLER: It's getting exciting now.

JACK (V.O.): That old saying, how you only hurt the one you love, well, it works both ways.

Jack turns. In a P.O.V. shot he looks down 31 storeys.

JACK (V.O): We have front row seats for the Theatre of Mass Destruction. The Demolitions Committee for Commission Mayhem wrapped the foundation columns of ten buildings with blasting gelatin. In two minutes, primary charges will blow base charges, and those buildings will be reduced to smouldering rubble. I know this because Tyler knows this.

Now you are ready to begin writing your own original screenplay.

Your evaluation

This is the only piece of writing that should be completed after your practical work. In your evaluation you should assess the effectiveness of your storyboard or screenplay. You will need to comment on whether or not you were able to translate your cinematic ideas into the practical work effectively. Did your storyboard or screenplay have the audience impact you hoped for? In order to get feedback on your work, you should show it to other members of your film studies class and ask them whether it made sense and whether it would make an effective film.

Exemplar PAL 1: Storyboard and writing

Synopsis: *Meant to be*

In a time of pre-war tyranny, Alexander and Lucia, two childhood sweethearts, are fatefully separated by the death of Alexander's father. Tears are shed, but unknown debts are to be paid, changing Alexander's life of luxury to one of poverty. As Lucia grows up the proud daughter of Lord and Lady Cunningham, war begins and Alexander is conscripted to fight in the Battle of Waterloo. Alexander returns from war a hero and brings with him his friend, Colonel Westwood. A party is held at the Colonel's house in honour of the pair's safe arrival home. Unbeknownst to Alexander, Lucia has become engaged to the Colonel's son, Nicholas. When the two childhood sweethearts meet at the party, their feelings for each other immediately return. They begin an affair, but this is discovered by Nicholas, who becomes enraged and attempts to force himself on Lucia. The couple flee, but leave the Colonel desiring revenge for his son's abandonment and subsequent suicide. The story then leaps forward two years, with the happy and unsuspecting lovers living in Devon. The Colonel's men have tracked the pair down, and capture and drown them.

Cinematic ideas

The sequence begins with the arrival of Alexander at the party and ends with the two childhood sweethearts recognising each other. As the sequence opens, an overhead shot will be used to show Alexander in the party. He is swamped by the crowds. The *mise-en-scène* used will evoke the aristocratic circle of the Colonel and his friends. The camera will be at a low angle when the audience sees the Colonel, thus indicating his status. Alexander is then seen looking around the room. A panning point-of-view shot is used to show his viewpoint, but the panning stops abruptly when he sees a stunning young woman. The party seems to have shrunk at this point to just Alexander, the young woman and the man whose arm she is holding. The viewer is kept within the point of view of Alexander, as the camera pans down Lucia's body and settles on her hand. The subsequent close-up reveals that she is wearing a huge engagement ring. The next shot will show the introduction between the pair. As

Alexander looks up from kissing Lucia's hand, the expressions of both protagonists show that they have recognised one another. The main cinematic and narrative influence for this scene is *Onegin* (Ralph Fiennes, 1999). In this film, Onegin and Tatyana have not seen each other for some years, but are reunited at a ball. Although *Meant to be* is set within a different time frame, the cinematography within the sequence from *Onegin*, which uses point-of-view panning to show Onegin's gaze around the ball, his sudden sight of Tatyana and their recognition, was an influence on the scene from *Meant to be*. My storyboard was also influenced by other great romantic dramas, such as *Titanic* (James Cameron, 1997) and *Romeo and Juliet* (Franco Zeffirelli, 1968).

Storyboard

DAISY. GLOVER-MAIN

STORY BOARD - CINEMATIC IDEAS

1.

Camera looking down on Alexander as he enters the Party.

2.

Wide shot, looking left & right at the party as from Alexander's eyes.

3.

Camera cuts back at eye level to Alexander as he notices the Colonel.

4.

Zooms in to Colonel talking to friends from accross the room.

5.

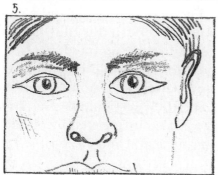

Close up of Alexander's face as he prepares to head over to the colonel.

6.

Camera drops to floor level and moves with Alexander as he moves 8 side steps in the congestion of the party.

7.

Camera stops, still at floor level, as we meet the Colonel's feet with Alexanders.

8.

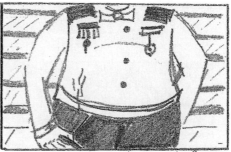

Camera angle stays at floor level, but the angle more up the colonel's body which helps represent his authority as the host of the party.

9.

Cuts and zooms in to closeup of the handsake between Alexander and the Colonel, before introducing Alexander to the other members of the group.

10.

Alexander turns from the group with camera angle at eye level, to look around the party.

11.

Zoom in to beautiful girl he spotted across the room.

12.

Wide shot as Colonel distracts Alexander back into the group, talking of thier past in war.

13.

Alexander turns again to see if he can spot the girl in a wide frame, including the other members of the group.

14.

Close up, at eye level, of Alexander's facial expression of confusion & then delight as he recognises the girl as his childhood sweetheart.

15.

As he turned back close up of two new members arm in arm, within the group. Lucia!

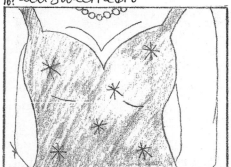

16.

The camera pans down her body and stops at her left hand.

17.

Camera zooms in to her hand, as Alexander noticed Lucia's engagement ring on her finger.

18.

Wide shot as the Colonel introduces his son and his son's fiancée, Lucia. and Alexander shakes his hand.

19.

Close up of Alexander kissing Lucia's right hand, without loosing eye contact with her, in aknowledge-ment to their introduction.

20.

Zooms in to Lucia center framed face, looking at Alexander in disbelief, with a shy smile as she recognises him. Her TRUE love.

Evaluation

Meant to Be would fall into the genre of romantic drama/tragedy. As such, it contains some of the main conventions of that genre. The narrative of love and loss that is typical of this genre of film is evident in *Meant to Be*, as is the hurdle the lovers have to face. The sequence I storyboarded indicates the hurdle for the lovers: Lucia's engagement to another character. The tension in this sequence is generated through the cinematography used. Through the decreasing distance of the camera, the audience feels the suspense and anticipation of the meeting between Alexander and Lucia, as Alexander moves from looking across the room to seeing Lucia in close-up.

The feedback I received from classmates was that the anticipation and surprise within this scene was clearly imagined within the storyboard frames. The representation of subsidiary characters was also mentioned and the feedback suggested that it was clear that the Colonel was a powerful man and could potentially provide the threat to the lovers within the narrative. It was felt by my classmates that the storyboard presented time and place well, with comments made concerning the aristocratic costume and *mise-en-scène*.

The cinematic influences on my screenplay were also noted and the conventions of romantic tragedy apparent in the *Romeo and Juliet* story were often mentioned. I enjoyed the process of creating the storyboard for *Meant to Be* and especially the challenge of evoking a doomed and conflicted relationship. I was particularly pleased with the feedback I received regarding how a sense of memory, loss and emotional engagement were generated through the movement of Alexander towards Lucia. I wanted this movement to be one of remembrance and resurgence of feeling and the feedback I gained confirmed this meaning was being created. The title of the film was also commented on and it was felt that this implied a fated union, one which would ultimately end in tragedy.

Assessment comments

The synopsis for *Meant to Be* is well organised and clearly expressed. It immediately evokes the generic credentials of the film and these are sustained throughout the elements of the practical work. The cinematic ideas section shows a real sense of engagement with how stylistic features can be used to generate meaning and audience response. It also acknowledges the film's debt to real romantic tragedies. The storyboard is very well drawn and proceeds through this pivotal moment in the film's narrative with confidence. The sequence makes cinematic sense and works extremely well to sustain the viewer's interest in the relationship between the two protagonists. The evaluation is honest and reflective, using classmates responses to consider the effectiveness of the ideas and meanings within the storyboard. Grade 'A'.

Exemplar PAL 2: Screenplay and writing

Synopsis: *The Synergy*

The film centres on a businessman, Pip Warwick, who lives and works in London. Pip's father, a severe man whose only motivation in life was the acquisition of money and status, repressed him and his free-spirited mother. Knowing nothing else, Pip grows up to emulate his father.

Pip's devotion to his career is tested when he discovers hidden corruption within the company for whom he works. This affects Pip deeply and he becomes disillusioned about his life up to this point. Throughout the film, the audience gain information about Pip's troubled childhood through flashbacks. As Pip's breakdown deepens, he begins to hear his late father's and mother's voices in his head, delivering conflicting messages of peace and violence. Under the influence of these voices, he becomes involved with an anticorporate anarchist group: Jones1. Pip is dragged deeper into more and more radical and anticorporate actions. However, in a chance meeting in a psychiatric wing of a hospital he meets Manos, a member of the Synergy Project, a peaceful protest community. Through the help and guidance of Manos, Pip overcomes the visions of his father and makes peace with his dead mother. At the climax of the film, Pip finds the strength to leave Jones1 and bring about justice.

Cinematic ideas

This scene is one in which the audience is given information concerning Pip Warwick's childhood through flashbacks. The scene opens with a black screen. Gradually, in the centre of the screen a pale spot appears and grows bigger, as if the camera were speeding towards it. As the spot comes into focus, it is revealed as an ashtray. The ashtray is shot from below and through it the audience can see the 1970s decorations of the room. Two figures, a man and a woman, can be seen through the ashtray, pacing around the room. The couple are in the middle of an argument, their voices slightly muffled. The shots change to eye-level close-ups and medium shots of the couple. As the argument reaches its peak, the audience sees the male character strike the female character. At the end of the scene the shot cuts back to under the ashtray. The audience sees the man walk to the table and stub his cigarette out.

The cinematic influences for this scene (and the film) include *Being John Malkovich* (Spike Jonze, 1999), *Fight Club* (David Fincher, 1999) and *Memento* (Christopher Nolan, 2000). The disorientating cinematography evident in these films, which is used to imply disturbance in the scene, is something which I also incorporated to show the memories of the character of Pip. The emphasis on memory, the distortions within remembered events and the impact of the past on the present state of mind of a character, are also elements within my screenplay, which were influenced by the latter two films.

Screenplay

BLACK SCREEN.
In the centre of the frame a pale dot appears. The camera appears to be speeding towards the dot and it becomes increasingly clear that the pale dot is in fact a glass ashtray. The ashtray is shot from below and the viewer can see through the opaque object, though not clearly. After five seconds the shot is fully revealed and through the glass base, two distorted figures - a man smoking a cigarette and a woman with long dark hair - can be seen moving in and out of shot.

INT. A COUNCIL HOUSE. DAY
The decor and clothing suggests that the setting is the 1970s. A slither of bold orange and brown wallpaper can be seen and in the centre of the shot there is a paper dome light shade hanging from the heavily textured ceiling. Faintly in the background, the diegetic sound of a radio can

be heard. The track is 'Pale Moon Rising' by Creedence Clearwater Revival. The room is flooded with the dull natural light of a rainy day. The couple are in the middle of an argument.

MAN (*muffled through the glass*): That boy will never amount to a ****ing thing and you wanna know why? Because of you!

WOMAN (*fighting back tears, in little more than a whisper*): I've only ever wanted the best for Pip. For him to discover the world on his . . .

MAN (*interrupting abruptly*): Oh, shut up with that new wave shit! I'm the one who wants the best for him. I'm the one who wants to see him a success ! You'd rather see him on the streets, like some kind of tramp!

Cut to a long shot of the room. An eye-level shot is used from the corner of the room, furthest from the interior door, next to the window. A brown sofa can be seen to the right of the frame and in between the arguing couple is the coffee table holding the glass ashtray, along with a collection of newspapers. The camera tracks into the room and rests on a close-up shot of the woman's face, as she begins to cry quietly.

MAN (*raising his voice slightly in anger*): What are you crying for? It's the truth. I've told you about all of this hippy shit before, wanting the boy to go abroad . . .

Cut to an extreme close-up of the man's face. Only the eye area is visible. His cheeks are red with anger. His eyes are a cold glistening blue and he is spitting his words in a low, menacing, tone. The camera tracks out slowly to a medium shot, as he begins to move slowly around the coffee table towards the woman. The camera tracks along with him.

MAN (*continuing as he moves*): . . . letting him out all times of the night and day.

Cut to a medium shot of the woman. She is clasping her hands together at her chest. Everything about her suggests timid submission.

WOMAN: But . . . I . . . just think you should let him make his own mind up about his career and . . .

The woman stops mid-sentence. The camera tracks back revealing the man standing less than two feet from the woman. It is clear that she is afraid. Next to her powerful husband, the woman seems little more than a mouse.

MAN: Don't you remember what happened the last time you interrupted me?

WOMAN: Sorry, I . . . I'm . . . sorry.

The woman begins to cry more profusely. Cut to a close-up of the man's face. He is sweating and clearly becoming more anxious.

MAN (*with urgency in his voice*): Shut up! Stop it! Do you want the whole street to hear you!?

Cut to a medium shot of the couple. The woman does not stop. Her crying becomes more desperate and uncontrollable.

MAN (*through gritted teeth*): Shut up, you stupid bitch! They'll call the police if they hear your wailing!

There is evidence on her face that the woman knows what will happen if she does not stop crying. Her fear, however, makes her cry more. The man raises his fist and a defeated look comes over the woman's face. He brings down his fist and a dull thud can be heard as it connects with her cheekbone. She falls to the floor in silence, out of shot. He takes a step back and a drag of his cigarette. All that can be heard is the radio still playing in the background and the occasional broken exhalation from the woman at his feet.

Cut back to the shot from under the ashtray at the beginning of the sequence. The man's blurred shape can be seen to the right of the frame.

MAN (*quietly, yet coldly*): Go and get some make-up on before the man comes down for dinner.

The man stubs his cigarette out in the ashtray and as the ash covers the glass, the screen fades to black with the sound of the cigarette being extinguished. This forms a sound bridge to the next scene. The sound of a kettle hissing mixes with the dying hiss of the cigarette.

Fade from black to a shot of a kitchen. It is the present day and Pip is making a cup of tea in a modern, white and stainless steel kitchen.

Evaluation

The sequence is a flashback in which the main protagonist's past is revealed. *The Synergy* screenplay includes many of the generic conventions of a thriller. The shots from under the ashtray muffle the dialogue and obscure the images of the characters in the scene. This character enigma is a generic convention of the thriller and works to hold the viewer's attention. However, this shot may prove uncomfortable for the viewer to watch and this might be a weakness of the screenplay. The era-defining elements within the scene, such as the decor and costume, help root the sequence in the 1970s and in Pip's past. The diegetic sound within the sequence, for example, the Creedence Clearwater Revival track, also helps to create chronological authenticity.

When the screenplay received audience feedback, it was agreed that the meanings I wanted to relate were those that were understood. Those classmates who read the screenplay all said that they felt the disturbance within Pip's past and that the difficulty he would subsequently have with getting out from the influence of his father was all made very clear. There were a few 'readers' who said that they felt that the shot changes were rather confusing. This may indeed be another potential weakness of the screenplay, but I would hope that when on a cinema screen the shot changes would be engaging, rather than confusing. My aim was to evoke the selectivity of memory through the shots chosen. Overall, the feedback I received suggested that the screenplay was effective. The authentic recreation of the 1970s was mentioned as a positive point within the screenplay and the emotional reality of the scene also seemed to affect 'readers'.

Assessment comments

The synopsis for *The Synergy* is clear and evocative. The main events and significant protagonists within the imaginary film are clearly outlined. The cinematic ideas section is detailed and shows a confident application of past micro and macro learning. The cinematic influences indicated are explained effectively. There is a clear sense of the candidate considering how stylistic choices inform potential generation of meaning. A comment on the potential target audience for this film would have been a useful addition. The screenplay itself is extremely original. It has a real sense of form and movement, evoking a remembered incident through an engaging use of stylistic elements. The candidate's self-evaluation is reflective and considerate of the feedback received. Overall, an excellent screenplay that follows shape and content requirements accurately and presents an extremely engaging sequence from a film. Grade 'A'.

Chapter 2

Producers and Audiences: Hollywood and British Cinema (FS2)

Overview of the FS2 Unit

The second unit in your AS Film Studies course requires you to focus on the film industry and film consumption. You will need to show a good understanding of the business of film and the issues involved in how audiences respond to film. Your focus will be on the industries of British and Hollywood cinema. The work you have done for the FS1 macro analysis essay, which concentrated on mainstream Hollywood cinema, will be useful for this unit, but you should remember that the FS2 focus is on the film industry and audience rather than on textual analysis.

The FS2 exam is worth 30 per cent of your AS grade and 15 per cent of your whole A level. The exam lasts one and a half hours, in which time you will have to answer two questions. The questions are each marked out of 25, so your total mark will be out of 50. Because each question is worth an equal number of marks, you should make sure that you spend an equal amount of time on each. The exam paper usually suggests that you allow 10 minutes to read the exam paper thoroughly and 40 minutes to answer each of the questions.

There are eight key areas that you should cover in your preparation for this exam. It is worth organising your notes into these key areas. You should remember, however, that the questions in the exam will ask you to draw from your knowledge of several of the key areas at the same time. As you read through your notes, remember to mentally cross-reference and find connections between the areas. The key areas are listed below and this chapter is organised using the same headings.

- The Hollywood film industry, then and now
- Film finance and film production
- Film distribution
- Film exhibition
- The British film industry, then and now
- Film consumption: the cinema audience
- The star system
- Film and new technologies.

Skills required for Unit FS2

There are two important skills associated with the Producers and Audiences exam:

1. The ability to articulate your understanding of how cinema functions as a business and how this business interacts with its audience.

   For this first skill, you will need to show your knowledge of the mechanics and functioning of the film industry. You will need to evaluate how film financing, production, distribution and exhibition are structured within the British and Hollywood systems. It is important to identify similarities as well as differences between the film industries of both Britain and Hollywood. In order to substantiate the points you make, you will need to use concrete, specific examples. Discussion of the film industry's interaction with its audience is also an important area within this skill. You should comment on how audience expectations affect the films that are produced; how different consumption modes and contexts affect the viewing experience; and how audience feedback on films affects a film's performance.

2. The ability to articulate a critical understanding of your own experience as a consumer, fan and critic of cinema.

   To demonstrate the second essential skill in the FS2 unit, you will need to reflect on your own experience of film from a variety of different standpoints. Consider your own expectations of both Hollywood mainstream products and independent films. You should also reflect on how publicity and advertising affect your choices of film viewing. The place where you watch films, on what format, and with whom should also become part of your discussions.

The Hollywood film industry, then and now

The profile and structure of the Hollywood film industry has changed much over the years. Legislation and economic factors have meant that Hollywood 'then' and Hollywood 'now' are significantly different from each other. You will need to consider three key areas within your discussions of this topic:

- the changes that have occurred in the Hollywood film industry
- the difference between the film industries in Hollywood and in Britain
- the types of film product that the contemporary Hollywood film industry produces.

The Hollywood studio system

The Hollywood studio system had its 'Golden Age' between 1930 and 1948. This period in film production was on a 'production line model', which caused critics to argue that the films produced lacked imagination and were created to a formula. Five companies dominated the film industry during this period: Paramount, Loew's (the parent company of MGM), Fox Film, Warner Bros. and RKO. Three other, smaller companies existed in Hollywood (Columbia,

Universal and United Artists) but they did not own exhibition outlets (cinemas) and were therefore reliant on the 'big five' to be sure of wide cinematic release. These five film companies were vertically integrated – they owned the means of production, distribution and film exhibition, which allowed them to dominate American cinema screens and the global film market until 1948.

In the years after the Second World War, however, the social climate in America began to change. Many families moved to the suburbs in order to escape the cities and the once guaranteed urban cinema audience could no longer be relied upon. Box-office takings began to drop and many of the big movie palaces were forced to close. The year 1948 marked the end of the supremacy of the big five. The Paramount Decree, a Supreme Court ruling that forced the five major companies to sell their cinemas, was passed and they lost their monopoly. An outline of the companies that made up the big five of the Hollywood Golden Age follows. Some of them survived the Paramount Decree, but as you will see, some did not.

Paramount

Paramount Studios came into existence in 1916. Although one of the major five studios during the so-called 'Golden Age' of Hollywood, the focus of Paramount was slightly different to the other big studios. Production was not rigidly controlled by a mogul figure and directors had far more control over their work. Paramount became known as more of a 'director's studio' and in this sense auteurism was more prevalent. Cecil B. DeMille was one of the directors at the forefront of the fledgeling Paramount's success and *The Ten Commandments* (1923) proved to be not only a critical but also a commercial success for the studio.

Paramount had a huge 'stable' of stars, both American and European, and this meant that the appeal of its films was wide-ranging. It also became the first studio to establish a global system of distribution for its films and these two factors, combined, meant that Paramount's big studio status was quickly established. The beginning of the 1930s saw massive profits for the studio and with directors such as Billy Wilder and Josef von Sternberg creating individual and popular films, the position of the studio seemed solid.

Paramount's stars included Marlene Dietrich, who made *Morocco* (1930) and *Blonde Venus* (1932) for the studio, and the Marx Brothers, whose 1933 film *Duck Soup* was also very successful. Paramount also signed Bob Hope, Bing Crosby, Veronica Lake, William Holden and Barbara Stanwyck, swelling its already impressive star pool. Quite amazingly, however, given the studio's stars and directors, by 1933 Paramount had declared itself bankrupt and only emerged from financial problems in the late 1930s.

During the period of the Second World War, Paramount once again reached its previous successful heights. A combination of the stars Paramount had available for audiences and its massive chain of theatres for cinema exhibition, as well as the fact that the films being produced satisfied audiences' wartime tastes, meant that it was once again succeeding financially. The Bing Crosby, Bob Hope and Dorothy Lamour vehicle, *Road to Zanzibar* (1941) and Billy Wilder's classic film noir, *Double Indemnity* (1944), were both made during this period and together provided the studio with box-office profits and critical acclaim. The 1948 Paramount Decree brought an end to this period of dominance, however. As the first studio to be forced to break apart its exhibition and production divisions and deconstruct its vertically integrated process, Paramount never reached the same kind of dominance again.

Metro Goldwyn Mayer (MGM)

Unlike Paramount, MGM was very much controlled by its executives rather than its directors. This high level of studio control was criticised by some and accusations of blandness were levelled at MGM products during this period. The studio came into existence in the early 1920s through a merger 'directed' by Marcus Loew's company, Loew Inc. The distribution company Metro Pictures and Goldwyn Pictures (which had impressive studio and production facilities) were the first two companies to merge. Louis B. Mayer Productions became part of the merger when it became clear that Mayer and Irving Thalberg, who were in charge of production at the Metro-Goldwyn company, were guiding forces in the larger studio.

MGM had an impressive array of stars to choose from. Lon Chaney, Lillian Gish, Joan Crawford, Greta Garbo, Mickey Rooney and Judy Garland all became major stars for the studio and secured many box-office successes. By the end of the 1920s, MGM had become a major player in the film-making business. It was one of the few studios that did not seem to be too harshly affected by the Wall Street Crash of 1929 and increased its profits year upon year. Irving Thalberg was a driving force within film production and oversaw the films made by Paramount during this period. Thalberg's dominance was cut short, however, by his early death, at the age of 37, in 1936. David O. Selznick took over production, but left in order to begin his own studio. In response to these two events, Mayer then took charge of the production operation at MGM.

The 1940s saw a lessening of success for MGM. Like the other big five studios, MGM attempted to function much as before following the 1948 Paramount Decree, but this was eventually impossible. MGM's legacy for audiences was a collection of films such as *Grand Hotel* (1932), *Mutiny on the Bounty* (1935), *The Wizard of Oz* (1939) and *Mrs Miniver* (1942).

Warner Bros.

The Warner Bros. studio produced the very first film with sound, *The Jazz Singer* (1927). The 1929 financial crisis of the Wall Street Crash did affect the studio, but only minimally because of the more independent financial structure of the company. The response of the Warner Bros. studio to the events of 1929 was extremely significant, however. Warner Bros. began an almost 'production line' ethos of film making, which created an astonishing output of around 60 films per year.

Unlike Paramount, therefore, Warner Bros. was not director-focused. Its film products were mainly genre-driven and targeted at the broadest possible audience. Darryl F. Zanuck was the production executive/mogul who oversaw production in the Warner Bros. film 'factory'. The gangster and musical genres were most heavily utilised by Warner Bros. at this time and films created within these genres proved very successful at the box-office. *Little Caesar* (1930), *The Public Enemy* (1931), *The Roaring Twenties* (1939) and *To Have and Have Not* (1944) were all genre-driven pieces that proved extremely popular with cinema audiences. James Cagney and Humphrey Bogart were Warner Bros. stars whose names would become synonymous with the gangster genre. By the late 1940s, however, Warner Bros. was a very different place to the film-producing machine of the 1930s. Zanuck had left to set up his own production company and the Paramount Decree had taken its toll.

Twentieth Century Fox

Founded in 1914 by William Fox, the Fox Film Corporation really began to take off when it purchased sound processing technology and a chain of exhibition outlets in 1925. 1930 saw the departure of Fox from the board of the company, which was suffering losses due to his penchant for producing extremely expensive films. 1935 was a highly significant year for Fox Film, however, as this was the year in which it merged with Twentieth Century Pictures to become Twentieth Century Fox. Darryl Zanuck, formerly production head at Warner Bros., was in charge of Twentieth Century Pictures, which meant that Fox Film had not only gained a partner company, but an established and very powerful film 'mogul' as well.

Twentieth Century Fox did not have the huge stable of stars of Paramount and was not as star-driven, but it did have a child star, Shirley Temple, and a Western star, Roy Rogers, both of whom had massive box-office appeal. Twentieth Century Fox also had a level of critical success which eluded some of the other big five studios. The 1940 film adaptation of John Steinbeck's novel *The Grapes of Wrath* won two Oscars and gave the studio a useful critical reputation. Alongside the successes of Shirley Temple films, such as *The Littlest Rebel* (1936), and the continued success of the Roy Rogers' Westerns, the critical reputation of films from Twentieth Century Fox secured the studio's position. As with all of the other big five, however, the shape of the studio was to change significantly after the 1948 Paramount Decree.

RKO

RKO was created in the 1920s through the merger of the Radio Corporation of America, the cinema chain Keith-Albee-Orpheum and the film production company FBO. In 1931, the head of the studio, David O. Selznick, began a unit production system, which meant that independent producers were drafted in, in order to produce a set amount of films. However, by 1932, Selznick and RKO had parted company due to financial losses. 1933 was an important year for RKO because it was in this year that perhaps their most famous film was produced: *King Kong* was a major box-office success for the studio and a ground-breaking piece of animation, which helped to seal the studio's reputation.

The Gay Divorcee (1934) and Top Hat (1935) also proved to be very financially successful for RKO and brought together Fred Astaire and Ginger Rogers, in what was to become a hugely popular pairing. Unlike the other major studios, the pivotal year for RKO was not 1948. The Paramount Decree did have an impact on the company, but it was Orson Welles' 1941 film, Citizen Kane, that really sealed the future of RKO. Kane is a thinly veiled account of the life of the publishing tycoon, William Randolph Hearst. When Hearst discovered Welles' film he instructed his publications not to carry advertising for the film. He also initiated a press campaign against it and caused so many problems around the film's release that it was taken out of circulation, not to emerge again until the 1950s. Following the problems with Citizen Kane and the 1948 Paramount Decree, RKO was in severe financial difficulty. Howard Hughes eventually bought a controlling share in the company, but RKO never again attained its previous status.

Hollywood today

In today's Hollywood, the vertical integration of the Golden Age is no longer in existence. Studios do not work on a production line model and do not control the means of production, distribution and exhibition. Film studios might bring finance and studio facilities to a deal, but films are not exclusively generated 'in-house'. An independent producer might bring a package to a studio, which consists of a treatment for a film (longer than a synopsis, but not yet a full script); details of actors/actresses attached to the project; and details of the proposed director and locations. The studio will then consider whether to finance and 'house' the project. Today's Hollywood is home to many studios, the biggest of which are MGM, Warner Bros., Sony Pictures Studios, Paramount, Universal, Twentieth Century Fox and Dreamworks. As you can see, four out of the big five studios of the Golden Age still exist, but their remit and control has changed somewhat.

The types of products that come out of the Hollywood film industry today have also changed. Many films are still star vehicles, but these stars are not attached to any one studio and can therefore switch studios for different films. It is also significant that many of today's stars have their own production companies, which not only produce some of their films, but operate in a production capacity for other stars, actors and directors, too. One of the most significant types of product on offer today from the Hollywood film industry is the 'blockbuster'. The fact that blockbusters share a set of characteristics almost renders them a genre in their own right. These types of films provide much of the scheduling at cinema outlets and are an essential area for your consideration.

The function of blockbusters is predominantly economic. The success of a blockbuster can bankroll many of the smaller film projects that a studio or a production house wishes to develop. Producers will consider the release date of their blockbuster very carefully in order to attempt to secure maximum return. The failure of a blockbuster can signal economic disaster for investors.

The four main characteristics that blockbusters share are designed to attract the broadest possible audience.

1. Blockbusters have very simple storylines that are easy to understand and have universal appeal.
   These films are created to be accessible to global audiences and therefore omit the kind of culturally-specific detail that would alienate a particular nation's potential viewing audience. Blockbusters are constructed around tales of 'good versus evil' (*The Lord of the Rings* trilogy, the *Star Wars* films, *Spiderman*). They present stories where global destruction is averted (*Armageddon*, *Men in Black*, *Independence Day*). They engage audiences with stories that relate to universal hopes and fears.

2. Blockbusters are populated by characters who are easy to understand.
   They do not tend to have characters whose complex psychological states might not be understood by young viewers and they do not tend to present characters whose attitudes and ideological stances might alienate different cultures. Blockbusters include characters whose motivation is to 'save the world' or to save the person they love (*Terminator II*, the *Die Hard* films, *Titanic*, *The Lord of the Rings* trilogy). Having said this, it can be argued that many blockbusters do adopt an ideological position that is centred on America, but this is rarely articulated as being against another culture, as that could damage the film's global appeal.

3. Blockbusters are marketed on their 'look'.
   They tend to include exciting special effects, such as pyrotechnical displays and computer-generated imagery. They look expensive and do not use experimental or unexpected film stock. Blockbusters are spectaculars. They excite audiences through visual display and do not rely on dialogue to engage the viewer. The huge action set pieces of *Pearl Harbour*, *Mission Impossible* and *Titanic*, for example, are fundamental to their appeal.

4. Blockbusters become a brand.
   The enormous initial financial outlay a blockbuster requires will not be recouped through the box-office alone. DVD and video sales are an essential part of the securing of financial return and the universal appeal of the film is an extremely important factor within continued video and DVD sales. The selling of television rights is also important to the continuing return on a blockbuster. It is merchandising, however, that can often bring the greatest reward and the universal nature of the blockbuster is ideally suited to the global sales of toys, games, clothes and myriad other types of merchandise.

EXERCISE 1

Choose a film that you consider to be a blockbuster. Use the four key characteristics of the blockbuster, outlined above, to research information for your own blockbuster case study. When you have completed this research, bring your notes into your film studies class and present what you have gathered to the rest of your group.

Case Study 1: *Titanic* (Cameron, 1997)
Is it a blockbuster?

The budget for James Cameron's *Titanic* was $200 million. An extraordinary amount of money, equalled only by *Spiderman 2* in 2004. Distributed by Twentieth Century Fox, Cameron's film eventually made a profit, but it was feared during production that it would become another *Waterworld* (Kevin Costner's box-office flop). *Titanic* was released on 19th December 1997 and very quickly became a huge, global success.

Titanic has very clear blockbuster credentials. It has one of the simplest of all storylines – that of love and loss. The characters of Rose and Jack are from different classes, they stay on different decks within the ship. Their costumes advertise their class differences. The difference between the characters and the hurdles their love has to cross are clear. Rose is about to marry a man she does not love and Jack has to overcome the rigid class divide of the time. The universality of their character construction and story is clear and eminently translatable to other nations and cultures.

In terms of the look of the film, its high production values and special effects clearly define it as a blockbuster. Cameron and his team used cutting-edge CGI effects to create the shots of the ship and of many of the extras who are seen on it. The film was marketed as a spectacular love story and the backdrop of the special effects only served to give the film increased appeal. The narrative of the film moves inexorably towards the tragedy, which many members of the audience would already be expecting, and it is this combination of love story and disaster movie that helps to make the film's appeal so broad.

As a mainstream film with a broad potential audience, the film's TV rights were a guaranteed seller. DVD and video sales also enjoyed the broadest possible potential market. In terms of the 'branding' of the film, calendars, 'the making of' books and numerous other pieces of merchandising appeared after its release. The success of the Celine Dion track, which echoes the love story within the film, also served to keep the film in the consciousness of its consumers.

Film finance and film production

The first stage of any film's production is the attempt to secure financial backing. Securing the finance for a film is often a complex and lengthy task. In many ways, the attempt to secure financial backing is an exercise in confidence building. The production company must generate confidence in the potential revenue of their planned film in order to create an environment in which investors feel they *must* invest, rather than have to be persuaded to back the film.

Film is one of the biggest potential exports a country can have and the returns can be enormous. Of course, the losses can also be staggeringly high if the film does not make enough of a return. In such a potentially insecure financial climate, it is no wonder that investors tend to be drawn by those film projects that seem to promise the best financial return. The potential backing for a blockbuster, although it might be of a much greater amount, is often more forthcoming than for a film that has a lower budget, but less potential in the global market. Statistically, within the Hollywood film market, for example, only one in ten films released will make a significant financial return for investors. It is these films that generate enough revenue to cover the losses made by the majority of film releases.

The package

To generate the kind of confidence that will secure investors, the producer of a film must put together an attractive proposal. This proposal is called a 'package' and consists of a number of essential elements. Obviously, the core of the package is the idea for the new film. This may have been generated by a writer, a director, the producer, or even a star. The idea might originate from an existing book, play or from a previous film. The idea, however, is not enough to take to potential backers and it is the job of the producer to create a comprehensive and enticing package of information, to present to investors. Typically, a package will consist of the following elements.

1. A script 'treatment'.
   This is far more involved than a synopsis and can run to over ten pages of information concerning storylines, characters and locations.

2. The generic profile of the film.
   In order to help investors 'place' the film idea within the film marketplace, the package will include details of the genre of the film. It might also describe how genre elements will be developed, in order to offer potential audiences a different experience of that genre. Of course, if the film being presented to investors does not have a clear generic profile, then key stylistic or thematic features might be outlined.

3. The proposed budget of the film.
   Obviously, investors need to know what their potential outlay might be and the package will contain a breakdown of the film's proposed budget.

4. Visual representation of key scenes.
   In order to help potential investors visualise the proposed film, the package may well contain storyboard frames for key narrative moments.

5. Key personnel.
   If the proposed film already has a director or actors attached, and these individuals have already had box-office success, then the inclusion of their names will act as an encouragement to potential investors. The package could also include the potential actors and director, but this would seem more speculative to those who might invest.
   Key personnel, such as editors and cinematographers, might also be mentioned in the package, especially if they have a reputation that would attract investment.

6. Potential spin-offs, merchandising and tie-ins.
   As has already been stated within this chapter, the exhibition of a film is often only the beginning of its money-making journey. Sales of television rights, merchandising opportunities and other post-exhibition opportunities will also be outlined in the package. Investors need to know the potential overall return they could make on their investment.

Investment

Potential investors and backers for a film may be many and varied. In today's climate it is common for a film to have numerous sources of backing. Whether a producer secures backing from individual investors or city corporations, or manages to obtain subsidies such as government money or lottery funding, the 'green light' cannot be given to a film project unless all necessary financial backing is secured. Producers might even pre-sell the film to a distribution company in order to generate the finances for production. Once the producer has the money behind their project, the next stage of the production process is to get the script for the film developed and the project underway.

Costs

There are two types of costs that are incurred during the film-making process. First, there are 'above-the-line' costs. These are the most predictable types of cost for the producer of a film to consider. The list includes the salaries and fees for the film's stars, director and personnel. These costs would have been calculated before the film went into production. They are fixed costs – they do not change during production. 'Below-the-line' costs are not so easy to predict. They include costs for locations, film stock and costumes. These types of costs can easily escalate during the production of a film. If extra days of shooting are needed, the script needs to be rewritten or extra equipment has to be hired, then the below-the-line costs can go through the roof.

Production

Once the above-the-line costs have been determined, the first draft of the script has been completed and the budgeting of the film has been organised, the film is ready to leave the pre-production stage and enter production. The production stage is primarily that of filming. This is the most potentially hazardous and expensive part of the whole process and it is the job of the producer at this stage to attempt to keep actors, directors and personnel within budget. The shooting schedule of the film should, in theory, act as a means of organizing time and personnel. Variables such as weather, illness and artistic differences between key personnel, can, however, extend a shooting schedule and inflate the film's below-the-line costs.

Post-production

Once all of the filming has been completed, the next stage is post-production. This is the stage in which the film is edited. The producer, as well as the director and the editor of the film, will often have an input into the editing process. It is not just a question of editing images at this stage – the sound editing of the film is of equal importance. Editors have more, or less, influence over a film depending on who they are and what kind of relationship they have with the director and producer. The standard process, however, is for the editor to construct a 'rough cut' in which the scenes of the film are loosely assembled around the ideas within the script. The 'finished edit' is achieved when the final decisions have been made. The person who makes the finished edit decisions varies. Directors often have to fight for 'final cut' and the number of DVD and video versions of films that promise 'the director's cut' only serves to show that often it is the producer, the studio or the investors who have influence over the final look of a film. Once the finished edit has been achieved, any special effects needed have been included and the soundtrack for the film has been added, the film is ready for distribution.

EXERCISE 2

With a partner, look at the list of the biggest film budgets, below:

Titanic	$ 200,000,000
Spiderman 2	$ 200,000,000
Waterworld	$ 175,000,000
The Wild, Wild West	$ 175,000,000
Van Helsing	$ 170,000,000
Terminator 3	$ 170,000,000
Troy	$ 150,000,000
Tarzan	$ 145,000,000
Die Another Day	$ 142,000,000
Armageddon	$ 140,000,000

What factors do you think helped secure such huge amounts of investment in these films?

Case Study 2: Low-budget film box-office returns

For the film investor, it is not the initial budget of a film that is of most importance, it is the return on the money a film makes. Investment in a low-budget film can bring an enormous percentage return, for example. Below are some examples of (often very) low-budget films that went on to make $1 million at the US box-office. In other words, these are some of the best film investments there have ever been.

Date	Film	Budget
1993	*El Mariachi*	$ 7,000
1991	*Slackers*	$ 23,000
1995	*The Brothers McMullen*	$ 25,000
1994	*Clerks*	$ 27,000

Date	Film	Budget
1999	*The Blair Witch Project*	$ 35,000
2004	*Super Size Me*	$ 65,000
1998	*Pi*	$ 68,000
1977	*Eraserhead*	$ 100,000
1915	*The Birth of a Nation*	$ 110,000
1996	*Swingers*	$ 200,000

Film distribution

Film distribution is the process of launching a film into the marketplace and then attempting to sustain the public's interest in that film. In order for a film to be financially successful it has to be publicised, marketed and positioned effectively. Cinema is an extremely competitive business and distributors have to employ a whole range of strategies in order to make their film succeed. This section aims to take you through all of the important stages of distribution and to discuss each of these stages.

The first stage of the journey for any distributor is the acquisition of rights to a particular film. There are three possible stages at which a distributor will become involved with a film. First, the distributor might invest in a film's production – in this situation the distributor might have some say within the film-making process. Second, the distributor might buy the rights to a film after it has already been made. Third, if the distributor is part of the larger organisation that has made the film, then it will automatically distribute films made by the parent company. World-wide distribution is dominated by US-based companies, such as Paramount, Warner, Disney, Twentieth Century Fox, Universal and Columbia, and each will fight vigorously for part of the annual $60 billion generated within the global film entertainment business.

Positioning
One of the most important decisions a distributor will make is concerned with the positioning of the film they are distributing. Each distributor must decide on how and when to release their film. This decision is crucial. If the film is released at a slow time of year, or when there is such intense competition that the distributor's film becomes overwhelmed by another, then this can spell financial disaster. Films rarely break even through cinema release alone, but the success of a film's cinema release is crucial to the

kind of positive word of mouth that will help secure video and DVD sales, and the selling of film rights to TV companies.

One of the first factors a film distributor has to determine in order to get the film's positioning right is the target audience for the film. The most frequent cinema-going age group is 15–24, which means that this age group is the most lucrative for the distributor. The distributor's job is to try to target the film's audience correctly, while also attracting the widest possible audience. A publicity and advertising campaign that narrows the film's potential audience, or misidentifies it, will severely jeopardise the film's chances of making money at the box-office. One strategy available to a distributor in order to help identify a film's potential audience is the test screening. This occurs before the film's release. An audience made up of the target market that the distributor has identified for a particular film is assembled and shown the film. Each member of the audience then completes a questionnaire, commenting on the extent to which the film is the kind that they would pay to see. This can help the distributor identify the core audience for a film more accurately.

Circulation and release

Another major concern for the distributor is how many copies of a film to circulate to cinemas. The average 35 mm print costs around £1000 and it is essential that the appropriate number of prints are circulated. The distributor must decide whether their film requires a 'saturation release' (700–1000 prints, available at all mainstream cinema outlets) or an 'art-house release' (around 20 prints, circulated to art cinemas). A big-budget blockbuster would gain saturation release, as the distributor would assume a wide audience for the film and a foreign film would gain art-house release, because its potential audience would be much narrower.

As we have already acknowledged, the competition for space and profit within the film marketplace is intense and there are many questions which a distributor must answer as well as that of how many prints are needed of the film. The timing of a film's release is crucial to its possible success and the distributor has to consider this carefully in their pre-release decisions. School holidays are a prime time within the year for the release of blockbusters, whose primary audience are people who are of school age. If the film is one which might win awards (Academy Awards and BAFTAs, for example), then it will be released during the traditional season of awards competition: January to March. The distributor must also consider the competition which will exist for any film they release. Too many blockbusters released at the same time can limit the potential box-office success for each and there may not be screens available to exhibit a particular film if they are already full up with other big budget releases.

Marketing

The marketing campaign for a film can often cost as much as the making of the film and because of this distributors have to plan the marketing of their film extremely carefully. The primary objective of any marketing campaign is to create the feeling that this is a 'must see' film. Word-of-mouth is the most powerful marketing aid for a film. The distributor must create a marketing campaign that presents their film as unmissable. The key elements within any marketing campaign are listed below, with comment on how they can be used to generate interest in a film.

Posters

Source: British Film Institute

If a film is designated a potential blockbuster, then it might have a 'teaser' poster campaign as well as the main poster campaign. Teaser posters use a few of the key elements of a film to generate interest. There might be a series of teaser posters, each revealing one more important element of the film, before the potential audience is offered the full poster. This is an expensive, yet often effective, way of generating pre-release interest. Film posters contain standard elements that are used to sell the idea of the film to the potential viewer. Generic elements, such as an ominous *mise-en-scène* for a thriller, or images of the main characters (showing their differences from one another) in a romantic comedy, are used to capture the interest of audiences who have preferences for certain genres. Often the main image on a poster echoes a key moment within the film, thus illustrating to the potential viewer the tension, horror, comedy or romance that can be expected. A well-known director or star will have their name figure prominently on the poster in order to capture the attention of those members of the potential audience who have positive associations with these names. The USP (Unique Selling Point) of a poster is the element that appears different or special to the viewer. Regardless of whether members of the audience are fans of a particular director, star or genre, they need to be presented with a film that seems to be different from others they have seen before. The USP presented on a film poster seems to promise this difference.

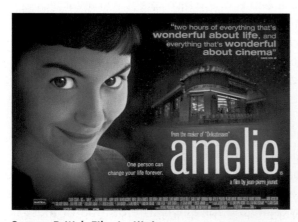

Source: British Film Institute

EXERCISE 3

Look at the two posters for *Amelie* and *Spiderman* and answer the questions below, making a set of notes for each poster. Then consider what the similarities and differences are between the two posters.

1. What generic elements can you identify on each of the posters? Include comments on props, actors, settings, iconography and use of colour.

2. How are stars or 'star' directors being used on the posters? What other films do you associate these individuals with and why might this be important within the marketing campaigns for the films?

3. How are the posters composed? What kinds of camera angles are being used in the posters? How does this affect the potential viewer?

4. Who do you consider to be the target audience for each of these films? What information is contained on the poster that helps you decide who is the target consumer?

5. What text is used on the posters? What is the tag line? Are there any quotes from reviewers? How do these elements affect the potential viewer?

6. What institutional information is included on the posters? What companies are involved in production? Is there any information on exhibition outlet? How do these elements affect the potential consumer of the film?

7. What do you consider to be the USP of each of the posters?

Trailers

As with posters, films that have a higher publicity and advertising budget might have teaser trailers that are screened before the main trailer. Trailers have to be given certification by the BBFC (British Board of Film Classification), just as films do, and it is possible for the trailer of a film to be given a different certification than the film itself. If a trailer for a film with a 15 certificate is screened prior to a PG film, then the trailer has to mirror this PG audience and be a PG itself. Distributors will wish to promote their film to the members of the audience of the PG film who are 15 and over, but cannot include elements within their trailer which are prohibited under the BBFC guidelines for a PG film. Trailers need to present a number of key elements to a potential audience. The genre of the film has to be apparent and this may be presented through key scenes, dialogue, iconography or sound elements. The key elements of the narrative also have to be included, but obviously not to an extent that would ruin the surprises within the narrative. If the film is star driven, then the potential viewer will expect to see sequences in which the star is acting. As with posters, any film must also attempt to distinguish itself from the other films being publicised, and will include a USP. This might come in the form of images of an actor playing a different role from that which the audience expects, or in a location that differs from that which is conventional within a particular genre; or it might be located within the presentation of a story which (apparently) has not been told before.

Media advertising

In order to reach the widest possible potential audience for a film, the distributor will employ a variety of different mediums and media texts to advertise. Scaled-down versions of posters appear in magazines and newspapers, and scaled-up versions might appear on the sides of buses or on giant hoardings next to the road. Trailers for upcoming films can be placed between TV or radio programmes. However, the cost of advertising on TV might be prohibitive, especially if the film the distributor is promoting is low budget.

The stars or director of a film often appear on television or radio shows to be interviewed about, and promote, their latest film. This kind of publicity can, of course, be double-edged. A bad interview can generate as much publicity as a good one, but will not necessarily promote the film in a way which the distributor hoped!

The internet

The internet can be an amazing tool for film distributors to promote certain films. Films may generate a 'buzz' even before pre-release promotion begins, and if a film becomes the subject of excited, positive debate in an internet chatroom, the subsequent good word of mouth can be invaluable to the distributor. Conversely, of course, negative 'buzz' can act to scupper a film's potential box-office success. Individual films may have their own website, which might include clips, message boards, poster images, interviews and a film synopsis and these official websites can positively contribute to public awareness concerning a particular film. Film production companies also often have their own sites with details of upcoming films. The internet can act as a massive marketing tool for distributors, yet it can also impede the publicity of a film severely. *The Blair Witch Project* 'teaser' site, which provoked huge debate around whether the film was based on a real incident or not, gave this low-budget film huge amounts of pre-release positive publicity. However, sites such as Harry Knowles' aint-it-cool-news.com, can severely damage the word-of-mouth about a particular film. Knowles' site is famous for its titbits of 'insider' information concerning on-set arguments and other production difficulties. Pre-release, bad opinion about the quality of a film, especially if it seems to come from someone working on the film itself, can be extremely detrimental to the film's word-of-mouth.

Promotions

Big-budget films, especially, often have tie-in promotional campaigns. These might come in the form of free plastic toys with fast food, displays for films in high street shops or children's meals themed with a particular film in restaurants. One aspect of the distributor's job is to arrange such tie-ins with appropriate outlets. Children's films can be promoted very effectively through the promoter's partnership with a chain of fast-food restaurants, but obviously the promotion of a French art-house film cannot utilise the same promotional possibilities.

Merchandising

Alongside TV deals, video and DVD sales, the merchandise connected with a film is where the actual profits will be made. The distributor will oversee the sale of licenses to approved companies, which will allow that company to use film images and logos in the marketing of other products. *Star Wars* was perhaps the first film to really profit through merchandising. Today, the potential marketing revenue of a film is so high that the stars of a film might take a percentage of the merchandising profits as part of their fee. Toy shops are often full of games, dolls and outfits that are associated with a particular film.

Premieres

Film premieres are a carefully organised distribution tool. They generate column inches in newspapers, TV interviews with the stars and any number of magazine articles on the film and the stars who attend the premiere. A premiere is the official launch of a film and the distributor has to make sure that the correct kind of press attention is attracted. A 'no-show' by the film's star, or a campaign against the film by a pressure group at the premiere, are events that could create very problematic, negative publicity.

Press junkets

As illustrated in the film *Notting Hill*, in the scene in which Julia Roberts' character (and the other stars of her latest sci-fi film) give endless short interviews to members of the press, a junket is an organised and official element within a film's publicity campaign. Journalists from different publications are given a very short time in which to interview the stars of a film about the film's content. Junkets are used in order to try and attract favourable publicity from film reviewers and are often lavish occasions in which the press are invited to luxury hotels and are plied with complimentary food and drink in order to persuade them to review the film positively.

Preview screenings

Preview screenings are different from press screenings in that the audience is shown the finished version of the film (after a test screening, particularly adverse audience comment might encourage the producers of a film to cut or alter different scenes). Free tickets for preview screenings might be given away or won in competitions in order to attract audiences for a particular film and persuade them to generate positive word-of-mouth. Distributors are careful to attract audiences for the preview screenings from groups that they have already identified as the target audience for the film. It would be pointless to offer preview screenings to the wrong audience, as the subsequent word-of-mouth might be negative.

Festivals

Film festivals have a dual function. They are competitions, in which a film might gain massive positive publicity if it is critically acclaimed and given an award. They are also a kind of film marketplace, in which distributors might compete with one another in order to secure the distribution of a film that has just been produced. The world's press is invited to festival events in order for the films shown to be reviewed and the film's stars and director to be interviewed. Festivals can act as a major publicity tool for the distributors of a particular film. There are many film festivals around the world but some with the highest profile are the Cannes, Sundance, Berlin, Toronto and Venice film festivals.

Case Study 3: *Amores Perros* (Gonzalez Inarritu, 2001)

Amores Perros was released in the UK in May 2001, with an 18 certificate. The UK distribution of the film was handled by Optimum Releasing, a company whose other releases have included *Elephant, Spirited Away* and *This is Spinal Tap*. Optimum is a distribution company that deals primarily with art-house and independent films. *Amores Perros* is an art-house, foreign language film. *Amores Perros* went on to win a BAFTA for Best International Language film and also became one of the highest grossing foreign language films to date at the UK box-office.

In terms of the film's journey to UK screens, things did not run smoothly. The film had been critically acclaimed at the Cannes Film festival in 2000, but it also contained controversial scenes of dog fighting, which potential distributors knew would cause problems with the RSPCA, and therefore the BBFC. There were calls for the film to be banned even before it hit UK screens. The film was screened to a number of potential distributors, but they had many concerns about taking on such a film. The main sticking points for distributors seemed to be the controversial content (dog fighting) of the film, the high cost being asked for UK theatrical distribution rights, and the fact that at nearly three hours long, the film would not be able to have many screenings per day, thus limiting potential box-office return.

It was not until many other distributors had turned down the project that Optimum Releasing took it on. Optimum's strategy for the release of *Amores Perros* was ingenious. They opened the film on the same weekend as *Star Wars: Episode 1. The Phantom Menace* was released and sold it as an alternative to those audiences who did not want to see Lucas' big-budget epic. The strategy was successful and audiences flocked to see the film. Even the public debate over the dog fighting scenes within the film only served to bring more publicity. Ten prints were distributed to cinemas within key cities around the country: London, Edinburgh, Glasgow and Newcastle. Optimum targeted publications such as *The Guardian*, *The Times*, *Total Film* and *GQ* for press reviews and publicity interviews. After a very difficult journey to UK screens, *Amores Perros* eventually proved its critics, and those distributors who considered the film 'too hot to handle', wrong.

EXERCISE 4

Using the information in this section and the case study above as a guideline, produce your own case study of the distribution of a particular film.

Film exhibition

The topic of film exhibition concerns the showing of films, primarily within cinemas. Exhibition could, of course, include the showing of films within festivals, but your most important concern within this topic should be the different types of cinemas, the films they show and how the cinema creates viewer interest in what they are exhibiting. The main distinction within this topic is between multiplex and independent cinemas.

The rise of the multiplex

Many countries, including Britain, did not have multiplex cinemas until the 1980s. Most cinemas up to this point were either independent or part of a nation-specific chain. Investment in exhibition outlets in Britain from the major American studios came about because of a concern from these big producers that there were not enough cinemas in which audiences could see their film products. In the 1980s, major US studios, such as Universal and Warner Bros., invested in the construction of multi-screen complexes that could exhibit films. Of course, these complexes could not solely show films from these studios. This would have constituted the kind of monopoly that was outlawed in 1948 with the Paramount Decree, but the new multiplexes could exhibit a substantial number of films produced by these studios.

Essentially, a multiplex is a large, purpose-built building, with ten or so cinema screens. The multiplex is often situated on the outskirts of a town or city. It is positioned outside urban centres for a number of reasons. First, it is often impossible to construct such a big, new building within a pre-existing urban sprawl. Second, the multiplex visitor is far more likely to spend money in the restaurants, bowling alleys and bars housed within the multiplex complex if going elsewhere would mean getting back in the car. Companies such as UCI, Virgin Cinemas and Odeon Cinemas present potential film-goers with a range of activities, alongside the viewing of a film. An individual or a family can potentially go ice skating, have a meal and then see a film, all of which are activities that generate income for the multiplex owner. The number of screens within a multiplex cinema also means that a variety of films can be shown at any one time. The main product for exhibition tends to be mainstream, but more independent films can also be screened, thus ensuring the widest possible audience and the biggest possible financial return. The scale of investment in multiplexes also means that the cinema technology used is the most recent. Surround sound and the latest in projection technologies also attract viewers because of the film experience they provide.

Independent and art-house cinemas

Independent and art-house cinemas are owned by individuals or smaller companies and of course, tend to exhibit different films to multiplexes. These cinemas do exhibit some mainstream film products, but they also show foreign language films, independently produced films and even experimental films. The experience of going to an art-house or independent cinema is also different from going to a multiplex. These cinemas are often housed in renovated buildings – they might have a cafe, but certainly not a choice of chain restaurants. The kinds of audiences who frequent art-house or independent cinemas are often those people who want a cinema experience that is very different from going to a multiplex. They are often looking for a type of cinema that does more than just entertain. The person who buys a ticket for a retrospective of a particular director's work, for example, is probably not the same kind of viewer who drops into a film that starts at the right time after a shopping trip. It would be a mistake, however, to formulate a class- or education-based profile of the multiplex and the art-house cinema-goer. These factors might have some bearing, but an individual might oscillate between the art-house and the multiplex experience.

The exhibitor

The role of the exhibitor is a crucial one in the continued publicity and marketing of a film. Exhibitors do not buy films from distributors, they rent them for a period of time. Exhibitors will research the cinema-going climate and decide on films to show that they think will be profitable and fit the profile of the cinema. It is also the role of the film exhibitor to give space to distributors who are advertising forthcoming film releases. All cinema foyers house posters and other promotional items that will potentially excite and engage the potential viewer. Exhibitors do not just show audiences the film they have paid to see. Trailers are played before the main attraction and these trailers are carefully positioned beside films that share the same profile of audience. Cinemas will also help to market a film they are showing through promotions and even competitions. They will also take out advertisements for the films they are showing in local newspapers and their own brochures and flyers. Essentially, the distribution and exhibition of a film are extremely closely linked. They are also mutually advantageous, providing a constant promotion of the films being exhibited and films that are to be exhibited to potential audiences.

Case Study 4: The Arts Picturehouse and Cineworld cinemas in Cambridge

Below are the programmes for one week's screenings in October 2004 in these two cinemas.

The Arts Picturehouse	
Hero (12A)	4.15 pm, 6.15 pm and 8.45 pm
The Motorcycle Diaries (15)	1.45 pm and 9.45 pm
Old Boy (18)	12.45 pm, 3.15 pm, 6.45 pm and 9.45 pm
Ae Fond Kiss (18)	2.30 pm and 7.30 pm
Late Night:	
La Haine (18)	10.40 pm
Hellboy (12A)	10.50 pm
Kids Club:	
The Three Musketeers (PG)	Sat 11.00 am

Cineworld	
Shark Tale (U)	11.00 am, 12.00 pm, 3.20 pm, 4.20 pm, 5.30 pm, 6.30 pm and 8.40 pm
Bride and Prejudice (12A)	11.30 am, 2.30 pm, 4.30 pm, 6.30 pm and 8.40 pm
Wimbledon (12A)	11.40 am, 1.20 pm, 3.30 pm, 5.45 pm and 8.45 pm
Saw (18)	7.40 pm and 10.00 pm
Layercake (15)	4.50 pm, 7.30 pm and 9.30 pm
White Chicks (12A)	2.40 pm, 5.20 pm and 9.30 pm
Resident Evil 2 (15)	4.40 pm, 7.00 pm and 9.30 pm
Dodgeball (12A)	11.30 am
Advanced screenings:	
Alien v Predator (15)	Thurs 21st October 5.15 pm and 9.45 pm

Differences and similarities between the two exhibitors:

1. Numbers of screens.
    The Picturehouse cinema is an independent cinema and has three screens.
    The Cineworld cinema, a multiplex, has ten.

2. The geographical location of the cinema.
    The Picturehouse is positioned in a converted building in the centre of Cambridge,
    whereas Cineworld is a very recent building that occupies a space about two miles
    outside the city centre.

3. The entertainment on offer, aside from film viewing.
    The Picturehouse has a cafe, which offers drinks and snacks. It also has film quiz
    nights and hosts Film Studies evenings and weekends. The Cineworld complex
    houses a bowling alley, a restaurant and a gym.

4. The types of films being exhibited at each cinema.
    The films available to audiences at the Picturehouse are mainly independent ones.
    Old Boy is a Korean film, *La Haine* is French and *The Motorcycle Diaries* is a Spanish
    language feature. *Ae Fond Kiss* is the latest film from Ken Loach, a director who
    often works with lower budgets and always in an independent film context. These
    films are not mainstream and do not offer the viewing pleasures usually associated
    with mainstream films (high production values, stars, big action sequences, special
    effects etc). The Cineworld screens offer many mainstream films and cater for a
    much broader audience. Although *Bride and Prejudice* is directed by Gurinda
    Chadha, a female, Asian, British director, and *Layercake* is the first directorial
    offering from British producer Matthew Vaughan, the majority of the other films
    on offer are Hollywood products. *Wimbledon* and *Dodgeball*, for example, are very
    clearly targeted at a mainstream audience and include stars who have a strong
    mainstream appeal.

5. The audience profiles of those who frequent both types of cinema.
    Attempting to identify audience profiles by any criteria other than age and
    experience requirements is not only difficult, but fraught with potential stereotyping.
    The certification of films on offer at both cinemas is equally varied, but the types of
    films shown are significantly different. If audiences for the kinds of films shown at
    a multiplex prioritise entertainment in their viewing expectations, then independent
    and art-house cinema audiences might be said to require more intellectual
    stimulation and challenge. An analysis of both the cinema programmes in this case
    study might highlight the differing content of the films shown. The majority of the
    Cineworld films could be said to elicit a physical response in their audiences. They
    generate laughter, tears or fear, but do not tend to challenge assumptions, ideas or
    beliefs. The films being exhibited at the Picturehouse cinema could be said to offer

a more enlightening experience. They offer stories from different cultures, comments on social ideology and deconstructions of relationships.

EXERCISE 5

Using the case study above as a guide, investigate what is being shown at a multiplex and at an independent cinema in your region. You should make sure that your research includes information about the following.

1. Numbers of screens.
2. The geographical location of the cinema.
3. The entertainment on offer, aside from film viewing.
4. The types of films being exhibited at each cinema.
5. The audience profiles of those who frequent both types of cinema.

The British film industry, then and now

As well as considering the similarities and differences between the British film industry during the 1940s and the British film industry today, there are two other important issues to consider when preparing for this topic. First, as has already been indicated in the section on Hollywood in this chapter, you will need to consider those factors and features that are the same or different between the British and Hollywood industries. The second question to consider concerns a definition: what is a British film? Whether you ultimately identify the main consistent factor in your definition to be financial, thematic, or to concern narrative, you should attempt to formulate an answer to this question.

The 'Golden Age' of British cinema

The 1940s in British cinema is often considered to have been a Golden Age in British film production. The commencement of the Second World War in 1939 had dealt a significant blow to the British film industry: cinemas were closed, because of the threat of bombing. Of course, within a period of wartime, where national morale was low and individuals craved an escape from the deprivations brought on by the war, film was a potential means of escape and the closing of the cinemas did little to improve the spirits of the British public. The British government quickly realised this, but also realised the importance of film within propaganda campaigns. The role of film in the drawing together of the national community, and the demonizing of the threat to that community's safety, became evident in many of the films which were released during the early 1940s. What was also significant at this time was the particular representation of Britishness that was found in many films released. Not all film products were propagandist in tone and many presented the shifting nature of class and society in Britain at this time.

Two major British studios during this period that you need to consider were Ealing and Gainsborough Studios. Ealing Studios created films from 1938 to 1959. The studio became synonymous with a particular type of film, to such a degree that it is possible to detect a studio 'signature' in many of the films produced. Ealing comedies reflected a changing social world in Britain. The Second World War had produced a Britain that challenged class and social hierarchies, questioned gender roles and longed for a period without economic repression. The films that came out of Ealing Studios at this time were often comedies that presented authority and outmoded social codes as humorous. Those films of the late 1940s and early 1950s were especially satirizing of these social structures and issues. *Passport to Pimlico* (1949), *Kind Hearts and Coronets* (1949), *The Lavender Hill Mob* (1951) and *The Ladykillers* (1955) all enjoyed great box-office success.

Gainsborough Studios produced a very different kind of film product. If Ealing's films reflected a contemporary Britain and the concerns of British people at that time, Gainsborough films were far more escapist. These films were not without some political content, however, but this was presented in a much glossier and more dramatic way. Gainsborough's 1945 film *The Wicked Lady*, for example, has a central female highwayman, played by Margaret Lockwood. She is independent and will not be confined to the roles that have been prescribed for her by society. The women who took over the manufacturing and farming jobs made vacant by soldiers going to war would probably have been very sympathetic to a character who did not see why she had to stay at home and give up her independence.

Whether your case study films for this period in British cinema history include those already mentioned, or examples such as *The Lady Vanishes* (Hitchcock, 1938), *In Which We Serve* (Coward/Lean 1942) or *Brief Encounter* (Lean, 1945), you should consider the way in which gender and class roles are represented and whether these representations seem to be a reaction to what had existed before. Consider also the function of cinema during this period. Is the film that you have chosen as a case study propagandist, challenging or escapist? You should also bear in mind the role of the big studios and producers in the production of films, and consider whether any form of studio 'house style' is evident. The last important area of consideration is that of what understanding you have gained about Britain and British people during this period from the films you have watched. Do individuals seem to be fighting some type of repression? Are they anti-authority? Do they dream of community, or do they already have it? You should think about whether the particular representation of Britishness you find within the films of this period seems to confirm or challenge traditional viewpoints.

Contemporary British cinema – the 1980s and beyond

There was certainly a decline in cinema-going during the period when video was first introduced to consumers (during the late 1970s) and the British film industry was not exempt from the impact of this on the box-office. As we have seen in a previous section of this chapter, however, the introduction of the multiplex to Britain did help to bring audiences back into the cinema. The multiplexes of the 1980s were not just full of Hollywood blockbusters, however, and there were many British success stories during this period. *Chariots of Fire* (Hudson, 1981) and *A Room with a View* (Ivory, 1985) both did extremely well at the box-office and in the case of *Chariots of Fire*, at the Oscars, too. It has to be acknowledged, however, that films such as these presented a very specific type of Britishness to the consumer. Both are set within a previous historical context and both present an England of well-mannered, middle-class individuals. The reality of Britain in the 1980s, during the period of Margaret Thatcher's Conservative government, was not reflected in films such as these. The articulation of the gap between those who 'had' and those who 'had not' and the presentation of issues of race, gender and sexuality in contemporary 1980s Britain was left to films such as *My Beautiful Laundrette* (Frears, 1985) and *Sammy and Rosie get Laid* (Frears, 1987).

British film finance

In the contemporary British film industry, film finance continues to be one of the main topics of debate. Lottery funding of film has caused much argument and discussion and still remains a 'hot topic'. The original premise behind lottery funding was to invest in the framework of film making, rather than directly in the film itself. The idea was to establish studios, which would then invest in scripts and provide the means of production to new and established directors. Lottery money would not cover all of the expenses needed to make a film, but would provide a foundation from which film makers could then attempt to garner other financial support. The criticism of lottery funding revolves around the issues of quality and box-office return. Rather than allocate funds to particular films, lottery money was distributed widely, to many small projects. Money for script development was given to projects that either did not make it to the big screen, or when they got into cinemas the films were criticised for their poor quality and made little return at the box-office. The sheer volume of projects that received partial funding meant that few eventually succeeded. There are notable exceptions, however, including Lynne Ramsay's 1999 film *Ratcatcher*, which received much critical acclaim.

The Film Council was set up by Tony Blair's Labour government, with the aim of providing funding for film. The Film Council is now the body that allocates lottery money and manages investment into British films. Set up in response to the criticism over lottery money allocation, the idea behind the Film Council was to provide an organised and more focused means of getting British film projects off the ground. Film Council money comes from three sources:

- the Development Fund: £5m per year given to script development
- The New Cinema Fund: £5m per year given to projects that are deemed to be of a more original and independent type of cinema
- The Premier Fund: £10m per year given to film projects that potentially have a more global appeal.

TV companies can also be a source of finance for film production and you should also consider in your discussions the roles that the BBC and Channel Four Films have had.

What is a British film?

In terms of the kinds of films that have been produced in the contemporary British film market, there are significant groupings of films which you will need to discuss in your exam answers. The role of the 'heritage film', for example, in the representation of Britain and 'Britishness', is an extremely interesting topic. A discussion of films such as *Four Weddings and a Funeral, Notting Hill* and *Shakespeare in Love*, for example, should consider the ways in which Britain and Britishness are being represented to our own and foreign audiences. The literary heritage of many films such as these and the class system they describe promotes a particular view of Britain.

In contrast, you should also consider those films that present scenarios that are specific to a region and thus acknowledge Britain as a nation that exists outside of London! *Trainspotting* and *Ratcatcher* (both set in Scotland) and *Twin Town* (set in Wales), establish a picture of a Britain that includes many different, specific regional identities. The multi-ethnic nature of Britain today is also reflected in many contemporary films and it would be very interesting to compare the box-office success of films such as *Bhaji on the Beach* and *Bend it Like Beckham*, with films such as *Four Weddings and a Funeral*, in which it is 'white' Britain that is in focus. Your discussions concerning the profile of British film products today could also consider genre. What impact have new gangster films such as *Lock, Stock and Two Smoking Barrels* and *Layercake* had on audience expectations of British cinema?

Having completed all of your research and preparation into the areas outlined above, you should end by making sure that you have answered the question posed at the beginning of this section: what is a British film? Your answer should come out of a consideration of a number of factors. These factors are included in the questions below.

Does the film you are studying have:

- a predominantly British cast and crew?
- British funding?
- discussions of issues which are pertinent to British audiences in particular?
- a British target audience?
- representations of Britain and the British way of life?

EXERCISE 6

Choose two examples of films you consider to be British. Then, use the questions above and your own research to determine whether or not these films really are British.

Case Study 5: Lottery 'failures'.

As we have seen from this section, initial National Lottery film investments were highly criticised. Many critics, and also interested members of the viewing public, felt that the films produced were of poor quality. Perhaps the most telling detail is financial. Below are a series of films that received lottery finance, but made a very poor return on this investment.

- *Hideous Kinky* (1998). A film starring up-and-coming British actress Kate Winslet. Lottery grant: £1,295,000. UK box-office takings: £687,088.

- *Love's Labour's Lost* (2000). Directed by Kenneth Branagh, this Shakespeare adaptation was given a £1,056,909 lottery grant. It took £324,656 at the UK box-office.

- *There's Only One Jimmy Grimble* (2000). Starring Robert Carlyle and following the success of *Trainspotting*, this film was obviously seen as a good candidate for a lottery grant. Lottery grant: £1,710,000. UK box-office takings: £293,000.

- *Amy Foster* (1998). Another film whose stars (Rachel Weisz and Sir Ian McKellen) seemed to guarantee some success. Lottery grant: £2,000,000. UK box-office takings: £48,711.

- *Downtime* (1998). Starring Paul McGann, this film was given a lottery grant of £768,898. It took £28,135 at the UK box-office.

Film consumption: the cinema audience

This topic is inextricably linked to the other topics you will study for the FS2 exam: study of film consumption and the cinema audience should, of course, be brought into discussions of the other topics. There would not be a film industry without an audience who provide revenue for film companies by spending their 'leisure pound'. It is also worth remembering that you are a film consumer and therefore part of a film audience. Your own expectations and experiences of film-going are very important to your answers. Your personal as well as your objective comments are an essential part of your exam answers.

The notes that you make concerning film consumption and the cinema audience in preparation for the 'Producers and Audiences' unit should address three main questions:

1. Is it possible to identify specific types of viewer for different films and their reasons for going to see particular films?

2. How do audiences consume film and has this consumption changed over the years?

3. What are the different contexts for film consumption and how do these affect the experience of watching a film?

Audience profile

Is it possible to identify specific types of viewer for different films and their reasons for going to see particular films?

The certification of a film identifies one feature of the viewer for that film. Obviously, many of the members of a film audience for a particular certificate for a film might be considerably older than the prescribed certification, but they should not be younger. Aside from age, gender certainly plays a part in the profile of audiences for particular films. It is not as simple as saying that female audiences like romantic comedies and male audiences prefer action films, as there are of course male and female viewers who enjoy both, or neither. However, generic preference does have a gender-related profile. Perhaps because many romantic comedies and 'chick flicks' are marketed directly at a female audience, many male viewers (especially younger ones) tend to say that they do not go to see these films. Similarly, the balance of action over dialogue and centralised male characters over female ones in action films does tend to draw more male than female viewers. This distinction, however, has most relevance within the audiences for blockbusters and other generically specific films. It is not so relevant when describing audiences for films that fall outside this type of film product.

The question of genre and audience profile can also be extended into a discussion of the importance of genre recognition within the viewer's choice of film. As you have already seen through your study of genre for the macro essay in FS1, film audiences have certain expectations of genre and generic conventions. If a film provides expected generic elements and presents them with an interesting twist, then audiences experience both a pleasure in having their expectations met and an added engagement with the film because it offers something new. As well as the age and gender elements within a film viewer's profile, therefore, there might also be a particular enjoyment and expectation of genre.

If we make a distinction between mainstream film products and those that are more independent, then a different type of audience profile comment can be made. The typical demographic for mainstream films is people aged between 14 and 24. This age group attends more cinema than any other, and therefore spends more money at the box-office. Many of the films on offer within multiplex cinemas, therefore, cater for this age group. This does not necessarily mean that the only type of film enjoyed by, or on offer to, people aged between 14 and 24 is the blockbuster, but what it does mean is that experiences and issues related to this group will form the basis of the majority of films shown. The last thing a multiplex would want to do is exclude its most lucrative market. The independent film viewer cannot be so easily described. They may be younger or older, but what these viewers share is an expectation for a type of cinema that offers different kinds of pleasures to a mainstream film. These viewers might want films that are less generically formulaic, do not follow standard patterns of narrative, and include discussion of issues that would not be of focus within a mainstream film.

EXERCISE 7

Using the questions below, interview four or five people of different ages, genders and backgrounds. What points can you make about different types of film viewers from the answers you receive?

1. How many times a month do you go to the cinema?

2. Do you watch films in a multiplex cinema, an independent cinema, or both?

3. Do you make your decisions about which film to see based on genre, stars, the film's director, or any other consistent factor?

4. Would you say that you go to the cinema to be entertained, educated, inspired, or any other motivating reason?

5. Have your viewing tastes changed over the last few years? If so, why?

Audience consumption of film

How do audiences consume film and has this consumption changed over the years?

There are two different types of answer to the question of 'how' audiences view films. The first concerns the technologies via which films and film information is consumed and the second concerns the relationship between the viewer's attitudes and those presented within the film.

Consumption formats

In terms of technology and formats, there is a difference between the viewer's experience of a film on the big screen, on video or on DVD. You could consider the difference in experience between sitting in the dark in a cinema, surrounded by other viewers, listening to a surround sound system and watching a cutting edge projection of the film, and watching a DVD or video recording, alone, at home. Of course, with the advent of home cinema systems, surround sound is possible in your living room and DVD images do offer a very clear visual experience, but the collective viewing experience of sitting amongst 200 or so other people cannot be recreated in your living room. You will need to ask yourself whether you think viewers watch different types of films at home and whether they have a different response to the films that they view there. The issue of the changing nature of film consumption in relation to developing viewing technologies could be researched through discussion with older members of your family. What kinds of technological changes have occurred within your grandparents' and parents' lifetimes, or even your own? Do you think the advent of digital technologies (cameras, editing equipment, projectors) has radically changed the viewing experience?

The relationship between viewer and film

The other side of the 'how' question concerns the dynamic between the viewer and the film text. You do not need to enter into any complex discussion of consumption theories here, but it would be very useful to try to formulate your own opinions regarding how viewers consume films. Whether you think film viewers merely absorb what they see unquestioningly, or whether they question and challenge what the film text offers, should at least be discussed in your notes and your exam essays. You need to acknowledge to your examiner that you understand that each audience member comes to the film-viewing experience with an individual collection of expectations, attitudes and cultural assumptions, and that this has an impact on the way they respond to the film. Whether an audience member accepts or challenges the messages and values within a film depends on many factors, including their own attitudes, experiences and requirements from the film-going experience. Even the most challenging of film viewers might just sit back and absorb, if they are tired and just want to be entertained!

Contexts for film consumption

What are the different contexts for film consumption and how do these affect the experience of watching a film?

In considering how audiences view films, you have already touched on the issue of cinema versus home consumption in terms of how these contexts might affect the viewing experience. Your evaluation of 'where' a film is consumed might extend your notes into comment on the impact of the multiplex cinema and the (not merely film viewing) experiences it offers. You should consider why so many people visit multiplexes. Is it because they offer convenience, choice, a whole evening's entertainment? Is it because the technologies they have at their disposal for film screenings are of such high quality? You should also consider the similarities and differences between the multiplex and the independent cinema experience. Your discussions should then extend to analysis of the different experiences of watching a film alone, as part of a small group or as part of a cinema audience. Is there a sense of collective response within a cinema auditorium? Does having others around you laughing or crying encourage you to do the same, regardless of your initial response to a particular scene or character? Does watching a film with your peer group liberate or prescribe the responses you have to a film? Are you more likely to watch films that are controversial, shocking and outside your certification band at home?

You will need to consider the three questions outlined above carefully in your preparation for this exam. Also remember that this particular topic does not stand alone and should be part of all of your discussions. A comparison of the British and Hollywood film industries, for example, would need to identify similarities and differences in audience profile. Any discussion of the 'star system' would require a detailed evaluation of the relationship between star profile and audience expectations and aspirations. Any analysis of the impact of new technologies on the film industry would be lacking if it did not include details about how these technologies affect those viewers who use them.

The star system

Your discussions of the star system will need to cover four essential areas. First, you will need to show your examiner that you understand what a 'star' is and how this person differs from ordinary actors. Second, you will need to describe clearly in your exam responses the way in which the film industry uses stars within the marketing and promotion of a film. Third, you should make sure that your notes include information about the way in which the film viewer relates to the star. Your comments about the difference between stars in contemporary cinema and stars from past eras of film will provide the last important area of discussion.

What is a 'star'?

In terms of the factors that combine to produce a star, you will need to consider a series of questions that help to identify the characteristics of an individual who has been elevated above the level of a 'mere' actor. Below are questions you should use when evaluating an individual's potential star status.

1. Does the individual you have chosen have global appeal and would the producers of a film be able to ensure they are universally recognisable?

2. Does the presence of this individual's name on posters and in other marketing material give investors potential financial security? In other words, can this actor 'open' a film?

3. What level of fee does this individual receive for a film? Does their potential box-office 'pull' mean that they can command high fees on a regular basis?

4. Does the actor you have chosen generate press interest? Do they have a level of media interest (in their life and career) that not only helps promote a film, but also ensures that they remain in the public consciousness?

5. Has this individual become closely associated with particular types of role or genre of film? For universal appeal to be sustained, stars tend to stick to particular types of role (usually the roles that have universal appeal and are easy to translate to other cultures).

6. Can the film viewer identify with the star and the characters they usually portray? This question is especially interesting, because it throws up a difference between stars 'then', and stars 'now'. There is still an aspirational quality to an audience's responses to stars today, but because of the increased amount of information we have about stars and their lives, they tend to appear less aloof than stars whose 'real' lives were masked by studio publicity.

The film star is, in many ways, as much of a product as the film itself. With the advent of new media technologies such as the internet, the potential contexts in which both a film and the film star can be promoted are now many more than in previous times. Stars have both official and unofficial websites, for example, which sustain their appeal. A star is an essential part of the marketing and promotion of a particular film, and producers will make sure the

EXERCISE 8

Use the questions above to analyse the position of your chosen star within the film industry.

star is at the forefront of any marketing strategy. Producers will create press packs for the media which include biographical and filmography information about a particular star. Stars will give both TV and print interviews, which help to promote a film. They will appear at premieres in order to help attract attention for the film in which they are starring. The star of a film has an essential role within both the pre- and post-production publicity of a film. As we have already seen within the production section of this chapter, the inclusion of a star's name in the package of a film can help secure backing. Post-release, the star will not only give press and TV interviews and attend premieres, they might also provide interviews for DVD releases and attract 'buzz' around a film via comments on their internet sites. Of course, not all of the publicity surrounding a star will be positive, but unless the accusation surrounds that individual's film performance, this unofficial publicity does not tend to damage the film's financial potential.

The star as promotional tool

For the film viewer, the star has a dual existence. They exist within films and also within the media. In the contemporary film world, a star's press cannot be as heavily controlled as it was in the days of the Hollywood Golden Age. Details of the life of the star outside of any films in which they appear are more freely available and today's viewer understands the difference between fantasy and reality much more clearly. The idea that a star and the characters they play are inextricable is not really possible in an age where we can pick up a magazine and see that person looking scruffy, walking their dog! There is still a tendency to attach the particular characteristics of a character to the individual who plays him or her, but the inextricability of star and character is less likely today. The idea of a star as a kind of blank canvas, onto which the film viewer can transpose their hopes, dreams and aspirations, remains part of the star/viewer dynamic, but this might be altered when we know something of the real individual beneath the star image. Viewers do still have expectations about the roles a star takes on, however, and it is often difficult to accept a star within an unexpected role. If the star has made their name in certain genres or roles, a series of expectations is established around them and audiences might not respond well if these expectations are not met.

As we have already seen within the section in this chapter on the Hollywood Golden Age, stars at that time were very much a product of a particular studio. Often tied into a contract for seven years, stars were created and 'groomed' by the studio that owned their contract. The acting stables during this period honed many actors and actresses who dreamed of becoming a big name. The studio would nurture individuals who they thought had potential star quality and bankability. Everything from what a star looked like to where they lived and who they were seen in public with was, to a large extent, controlled by the studio. The image of the star was constructed through both the roles they played and their public persona, and in these times of much less press intrusion, it was possible for the studio to create a sense that the star was remarkably similar to their on-screen persona. The star during this period would often become synonymous with a particular characteristic, such as integrity, vulnerability or honour, and this would become part of the viewer's expectation of that individual, both on and off screen. Given the fact that stars were tied to studios by contracts, a successful screen role often meant that the studio then cast that star in a succession of very similar parts. In today's film arena, where stars are not controlled by studios, typecasting can be (but is not always) avoided. Stars today have more choice and potential control than their predecessors. Today's stars might have their own production company, or take on the role of producer within one of their films. Hugh Grant's 'Simian Productions' and Jude Law's 'Natural Nylon Films' are both examples of star-run companies.

EXERCISE 9

Look at the two lists of stars below. The first list contains stars 'then' and the second list contains the names of stars 'now'.

Stars 'then'

- Humphrey Bogart
- Rita Hayworth
- Shirley Temple
- Orson Welles
- Jane Mansfield
- Cary Grant

Stars 'now'

- Julia Roberts
- Tom Cruise
- Meg Ryan
- Tom Hanks
- Nicole Kidman
- Hugh Grant

Using the internet, magazines and any other types of resource material, make notes under the following headings:

1. Filmography and most famous films.
2. Box-office successes.
3. Attachment to any studios or production companies.

4. Press and public persona.

5. Awards and nominations.

6. Key roles and character types.

7. Genres of film associated with the star.

8. Roles within film-making other than star e.g. director or producer.

9. Length of film career.

10. Differences between the stars in the two lists.

Case Study 6: Julia Roberts and Bette Davis

Julia Roberts

Julia Roberts was born in Georgia, USA in 1967. She has become one of the highest-paid actors in Hollywood and can command fees of $25,000,000 per film, rivalling the fees of male stars such as Tom Cruise and Harrison Ford. Although known for her acting, Julia Roberts has become involved in production and was credited as 'executive producer' for *Stepmom* (1998) and the TV series *Queens Supreme* (2003). As an actress, she has made around 35 films to date, often starring as the love

Source: British Film Institute

interest, as in *Ocean's Eleven* (2001), *Runaway Bride* (1999) and *Pretty Woman* (1990). Roberts has been careful to try to avoid typecasting and has also made films in which she performs a very different role: *My Best Friend's Wedding* (she doesn't get the man), *Erin Brockovich* (she battles to help a small community find justice). Although associated with a number of genres, including romantic comedy and drama, this actress can be most attached to big budget feature films. *Ocean's Eleven* and now *Ocean's Twelve*, *Conspiracy Theory* and *America's Sweethearts* are all films targeted at a very mainstream audience. In terms of awards, Julia Roberts had to wait until *Erin Brockovich* to win a Best Actress Oscar and a BAFTA for Best Performance by an Actress in a Leading Role.

Source: British Film Institute

Bette Davis

Bette Davis was born in Massachusetts, USA in 1908 and died in 1989. She acted as producer on one film – *A Stolen Life* (1946) – but is best known for her screen persona. In 1932, Bette Davis signed a seven-year contract with Warner Bros. Studios and because of her continued successes for that studio, was sometimes nicknamed 'the fifth Warner brother'. In total, she starred in 102 films and made her last film, *Wicked Stepmother*, in the year of her death. Throughout an extremely long career, Bette Davis played a number of different roles, from femme fatale to psychotic middle-aged woman. She won Oscars for her roles in *Dangerous* (1935) and *Jezebel* (1938) and it was in the 1930s and 1940s that Bette Davis was at her most prolific and successful. Bette Davis won eight other Oscar nominations, mostly during the 1930s and 1940s, but was less successful in the 1950s and 1960s when her films lost money. With perhaps one of the most striking film comebacks in history, it was the film *What Ever Happened to Baby Jane?* (1962) that returned Davis to film audience's attention. Her sadistic and psychotic portrayal in this film marked a stark difference to her glamorous earlier roles.

Film and new technologies

Advancements in film-related technologies have had a significant impact on all stages of the film-making process, from pre-production, through production, distribution and exhibition, to consumption. Your preparation for this particular topic should consider the impact of new technologies on both the film industry and the film consumer. You could begin by considering the following technologies:

- CGI (computer-generated imagery)
- the internet
- digital cameras and editing software
- DVD (digital versatile discs)
- big screen technologies
- video and computer games.

Computer-generated imagery (CGI)

Computer-generated imagery, or CGI, is becoming more and more commonplace within the film-making process, especially within particular genres, such as fantasy and science fiction. CGI elements can be used in a number of ways, ranging from the invisible to the highly visible. An increasing number of films are generated purely through a CGI process, including *Shark's Tale*, *Shrek* and *Finding Nemo*. These films are for a predominantly children's audience and it will be interesting to see whether or not wholly CGI film making will ever become more of a part of the consumption of adult audiences.

Film makers also use CGI when they have an element within a film that is too large in scale or too expensive to construct in reality. The makers of *Gladiator*, for example, created the cityscapes of Rome via CGI technology and many shots of the ship and its passengers in *Titanic* were created using CGI. Films such as *The Lord of the Rings* trilogy have used CGI in order to create fantasy elements. If an audience has no reference point in reality for certain kinds of images, a CGI component can be used as it will not be judged against the 'real thing'. Creatures such as Gollum do not exist and therefore can be CGI-generated with impunity. There has also been a move within the film industry to remaster films using CGI. Jabba the Hutt, for example, from the original *Star Wars* trilogy, was created in CGI for the re-release of the films and this creation was then added to the original footage. A cynical reading of this kind of CGI use, however, might highlight the revenue generated from a re-release, rather than any improvement to the original, as the guiding force behind remastering.

The importance of CGI for the film industry is twofold. CGI elements can make a film more spectacular and more of a draw to potential audiences. If one of the elements of appeal with a blockbuster is the promise of ever bigger and more spectacular sequences, then CGI is certainly one way to generate such appeal. Of course, if the producers of a film do not have to construct expensive sets, but can create the set on a computer, economy can also be a factor in the choice of whether or not to use CGI. For the mainstream/blockbuster film consumer, a CGI component has become part of the package of expectations he or she will bring to the viewing experience.

The internet

The global nature of the internet, and its presence in an increasing number of homes around the world, makes it a powerful marketing and promotion tool for the film industry. Individual films have increasingly sophisticated websites on which a film can be promoted, discussed and even seen (in clip form). These websites include information about the film's story, its cast, its production and associated merchandise. They include trailers and competitions to engage and entice potential viewers. They might even include message boards on which fans can discuss the film. The interest in a film expressed by the number of visitors that any one site receives can also act as a prediction mechanism for the film's producers, attempting to gauge how successful the film will be on release. Websites are not static like a poster – they can be updated – and can therefore evolve to suit the needs of potential viewers and reflect the latest events surrounding a film. It is less expensive for a website to be updated to include award nominations, for example, than it would be to produce new posters.

The internet is not just home to official websites concerning particular film releases, however, and many fansites will pop up either during a film's production or after its release. These sites might focus on the film's stars, story, director or a combination of these elements. The sites might contain positive criticism for a film or they might include negative criticism. The globally accessible nature of the internet does make for a relatively democratic discussion forum, but even negative criticism can be of use to the industry. Distributors might be able to amend marketing campaigns or 'spin' publicity in response to negative comment. Film producers and distributors have even been known to create what appear to be unofficial sites in order to attempt to generate positive word-of-mouth surrounding their latest film release.

It is not just distribution that can be affected by the use of the internet, however, as this new technology is being increasingly used as an exhibition forum. For the makers of low-budget films especially, a relatively inexpensive context in which their film can be shown to potentially millions of people is a very attractive option. If someone has shot a film with a digital camera, edited it at home with a software package, and then created a website, the production crew for a low-budget film could have as few as one member.

All of the above comments concern the potentially positive uses to which the internet can be put. There are some more problematic issues, however, of which you should be aware. First, there is the issue of piracy and illegal downloads. As with the problems faced by the music industry concerning illegal downloading of music files, the film industry could face a problem of illegal 'film sharing' if home technologies advance to a point where the time it takes to download a whole film and the quality of the download do not make the exercise pointless. Second, there are websites that deliberately publish 'spoiler' information about a film. This information might come in the form of revelations concerning the film's plot, or debilitating production difficulties. Not all publicity is good publicity, and the nature of the internet makes it impossible to track all information that appears on websites.

Digital cameras and editing software

As you may know from your own experience of amateur film-making, digital cameras and editing software have brought about significant changes in both the way films can be made and who can make them. The budding film maker can now buy a digital camera and editing software relatively cheaply and produce films that have very high audio and visual quality. The potential production values of a film made on digital equipment are extremely high, and with the internet now providing an accessible means of film exhibition, there is now far more opportunity for film makers with lower budgets not only to make a film, but to show it to potentially millions of viewers. You only have to look at the phenomenon that was the *Blair Witch Project* to understand the difference that digital can make. Made on digital equipment, with a budget that in industry terms was miniscule, this film introduced itself to audiences via an internet teaser site and then went on to extraordinary box-office success.

Digital film-making technologies are not just used by amateur or the makers of low-budget films, however. Many mainstream film makers have created films with digital technologies. The convenient size of digital cameras, as compared with film cameras, and the compact accessibility of a computer, as opposed to a full editing suite, proved attractive to the likes of director Mike Figgis, for example, when he made *Time Code*. Digital tape is cheaper than celluloid and digitised images are eminently more manipulatable than those created on film. In terms of distribution, a digital tape copy of a film can be replicated easily without the original quality being slowly corrupted. Of course, a film distributed on digital tape requires a digital projector, but even these are becoming far more common within cinemas today.

DVD (Digital versatile discs)

Your study of new film-related technologies should also consider the impact of the DVD on both the film industry and film consumers. Although DVDs have been around for some years, they have not completely superseded video and viewers are still likely to watch both DVD and video-taped copies of films at home. For the film industry, the DVD provides an interesting marketing tool. The huge storage capacity of a DVD means that it can hold much more information than a standard VHS tape. A DVD copy of a film will invariably house not only the film, but extras such as deleted scenes, audio commentaries and behind the scenes documentaries. These additions, of course, add to the attractiveness of buying a copy of a film on DVD, as opposed to video. DVD technology also promises much improved audio and visual quality, which again will attract consumers. Many viewers will buy films they already have on video on DVD, in order to experience the increased quality of this format. This, of course, can be a never-ending practice. Once the consumer has a DVD copy of their original video film, they might be tempted by the director's cut or the special edition, both of which promise something more, and all of which means increased revenue for the film industry.

For the DVD consumer, the experience is not just different because of the increased quality in sound and image or the extras available. The way in which a DVD is accessed and potentially viewed differs greatly from the video experience. DVDs have menus through which either the whole film or selected scenes can be accessed. The consumer can, therefore, move straight to a scene rather than have to fast forward or rewind. The ease with which a viewer can move through a film on DVD might even mean that on second or third viewing, scenes are jumped. The context of a film's production can also be experienced alongside a film and it would be interesting to debate whether or not the inclusion of behind the scenes information, as well as the film text, makes for a more informed film viewer. There is also potential for the viewer to be told what certain moments or scenes mean, using audio commentaries from the director or other key film personnel. Whether this reading is accepted or challenged will depend on the individual viewer, but the existence of this kind of interpretation does potentially create a dialogue between film maker and film consumer.

'Big screen' technologies

The most common form of 'big screen' experiences that exist in the early twenty-first century are either on IMAX screens or in theme parks. The effect of the experience in a cine 180-degree theme park attraction is predominantly physical. These attractions do not show feature films or any narrative form of presentation, but tend to offer an 'immersion' experience, such a riding a roller coaster or flying. For the IMAX viewer, the experience is different. IMAX is an integrated system of film production that uses cameras, film stock, screens and projection equipment especially designed to offer a thrilling experience. IMAX cinemas have a projector the size of a small car, screens the size of three double-decker buses and film stock double the size of the film industry standard of 35 mm.

Still in its early stages, IMAX does not tend to produce feature films, but relies on a programme of dynamic and dramatic experience-driven films, which places the viewer in a scenario they would not ordinarily find themselves in. Whether the experience is in space or under the water, what the IMAX viewer gets is immersion into another world. This immersion experience is generated through numerous devices. Viewers sit at a much closer proximity to the screen than in a standard cinema and their peripheral, as well as central vision, is bombarded with images. The enormous sound system within an IMAX theatre completes the impression that the viewer is within the experience, rather than merely observing it.

There have been question marks raised over the viewer's potential tolerance of this kind of experience and the full sensory immersion offered was thought to be unsuitable for feature film viewing. However, *The Lion King* and many other films now have IMAX prints, so the question of whether the decision to transfer feature films to the IMAX experience was purely financially driven, or whether an immersion viewing of a feature film will enhance the viewer's experience, could provide you with an interesting debate.

Video and computer games

With such a high level of interest in computer and video games among teenagers and adults today, it is hardly surprising that they have a significant connection to the film industry. The relationship between the gaming and the film industry is two-way, involving the transfer of games to film and vice versa. As with comic books, games that are transferred onto film have a pre-existing group of consumers, and the producers of the film hope they will also want to see the film version. Those individuals who were fans of the *Tomb Raider* and *Resident Evil* games, for example, were relied on to also make up part of the film audience. It is not just the film audience, however, who are exploited by film producers. The storylines, characters, even *mise-en-scène* of a game is also brought across to the film version. This retains visual and thematic continuity, but also provides the film industry with elements that are already created. The player of a game will not automatically become the viewer of a film version, however, and you will need to acknowledge the different experiences of game playing and film viewing. The interactivity of a game cannot be transferred to the film experience and gamers might not enjoy the more static experience of watching a film version. As a piece of merchandise connected with a particular film, the video or computer game is potentially highly lucrative. The *Harry Potter* game is extremely successful and has provided the film's producers with yet another means of income generation.

EXERCISE 10

With a partner, prepare a presentation on one film-related new technology. You could choose one that has been discussed here, or concentrate on something completely new. You should prepare notes, specific examples and film clips (if appropriate) that include details of how the new technology has affected both the film industry and film consumers.

Case Study 7: The role of *Industrial Light and Magic* in the creation of film-related new technologies

Below, in chronological order, are the film-related new technologies and effects that have been created by Industrial Light and Magic (ILM).

1982:	ILM create the first completely computer-generated sequence for the film *Star Trek II: The Wrath of Khan*.
1988:	ILM produce the first 'morphing' sequence in the film *Willow*. This technology was subsequently used to create the morphing effects in James Cameron's films *The Abyss* and *Terminator 2*.
1993:	ILM create the first example of computer-generated human skin texture in the film *Death Becomes Her*.
1994:	ILM create the dinosaurs for *Jurassic Park* and generate the first examples of living, breathing creatures through CGI.
1995:	ILM create the first example of a 'photo real cartoon' using CGI technology for the film *The Mask*.

1996:	ILM combine a human face (that of Sean Connery) with animation to create the face of the dragon in *Dragon Heart*.
1999:	George Lucas' *Stars Wars Episode I: The Phantom Menace* is created using digital terrains, CGI lead characters and digital extras.
2001:	ILM creates the attack scenes for *Pearl Harbour*.
2002:	*Star Wars: Episode II: Attack of the Clones* is created entirely on digital HD video and includes over 2200 digital effects.

Exemplar essay: Section A

Question: To what extent does the age of the target audience for a film have an impact on marketing strategies for that film?

The producers and distributors of a film are predominantly interested in the eventual financial return a film will make for them. A marketing campaign for a film is carefully organised and is comparable to a military campaign. Each aspect of the distribution process takes into account numerous factors, including the age, gender and cultural interests of the film's target audience. If a distribution campaign does not engage the appropriate target audience, then financial disaster can ensue.

A distributor uses numerous strategies to make an audience aware of a film that is about to be released. These strategies include trailers, poster campaigns, press advertising, tie-ins and merchandising. The age of the target viewer is an absolutely crucial factor in the creation of these different aspects of distribution. If the film being introduced to its potential audience is a mainstream blockbuster, for example, and has a certificate of PG, 12 or 15, the distribution behind it will have to echo the interests and expectations of that target audience. Blockbusters, for example, which have mainly under-18 certificates might have a series of teaser trailers, as well as a main trailer. Each of these trailers will reveal an increasing number of film elements, all of which have to engage this young audience. The teaser trailers for *Godzilla*, for example, implied the presence of the creature, rather than showing it. This caught the imagination of young audiences. By the time the main trailer was released, which showed the monster nearing a harbour and then looking straight into the camera, the full impact of the creature could be felt. This main trailer also included special effects shots and big action sequences, both of which would engage the interest of this blockbuster's young audience.

If a poster campaign is targeted at an adult or independent film audience, the elements used to introduce the film and engage the potential consumer will be less spectacular and less driven by special effects. The USP (Unique Selling Point) of an independent film, for example, is unlikely to be a CGI element. It might be the characterisation, the interaction between characters, the political backdrop or the historical context of the film that is used to encourage the adult or independent film viewer to see the film. The *American Beauty* posters, for example, which included images of the character of Angela, covered in rose petals, with the tag line 'look closer', implied a drama, and perhaps one which involved discussions of sexual desire, hardly something that would encourage the PG audience to watch the film.

The publications in which adverts, interviews and articles concerning a 'soon to be released' film are positioned by the distributor are also crucial to its potential box-office success. It could be argued that for very young audiences, any press advertising is pointless because they do not read newspapers. However, it will be the relatives of very young children who take them to the cinema and they *do* read press adverts. In terms of press positioning, there is a significant difference between the target readership for publications such as *Premiere* and *Empire*, and *Sight and Sound* magazine. The two first publications cater predominantly for the mainstream film audience. *Sight and Sound* tends to be for those viewers who want to extend their experience of film outside of the multiplex. *Premiere* and *Empire* have a younger target readership than *Sight and Sound*, and see film as an entertainment, rather than a topic for debate and criticism. Posters, articles and adverts for *A Shark's Tale*, *Spiderman 2* and *The Day After Tomorrow* would find themselves in the former publications. Those pieces and posters which advertise *Amores Perros*, *Talk to Her* and *The Motorcycle Diaries* would probably find themselves in the latter.

In terms of merchandising and tie-ins, distributors know that young children and teens are much more likely to buy fast food with free gifts and toys that are connected with a particular film. You would not find a plastic model of a character from *Lost in Translation* in your Happy Meal, for example, but you could potentially find one of the animated characters from *Toy Story*. Because of the huge initial investment needed by a blockbuster film, merchandising and tie-ins are an essential form of revenue. For films targeted at an older market, game and toy sales are unlikely to be lucrative.

Distributors, therefore, have to identify the age of their target audience very carefully. They have to understand the expectations, interests and film experiences of that age group clearly in order to target marketing campaigns effectively.

Assessment comments

A very clear response, which consistently answers the question set. There is a very good level of knowledge here concerning the role of the distributor and distribution strategies within the marketing of a film. The essay is clearly structured and presents appropriate examples for each of the points made. Grade A.

Exemplar essay: Section B

Question: To what extent do you think British films today are aimed at an international film market?

There is often a tension within a national film industry, between producing films that reflect the contemporary nature of that nation and producing films that make a lot of money through international sales. There have been many examples of recent British films that seem to have been produced with an international market in mind. This is not the whole story of the British film industry today, however, and there are many other examples of recent films that very consciously reflect Britain and British people today.

For a film to do well on the international market, it needs to do a number of things. First, it needs to have a storyline and characters that can be transferred to different national audiences. Second, it helps if the film presents its home nation in a way international viewers can easily understand. Lastly, the film might use actors who are already established within the global film market. In terms of British films released in recent years, international success stories have included *Four Weddings and a Funeral*, *The Full Monty* and *Shakespeare in Love*. The universality of the storylines in these films is the first factor to be considered. *Four Weddings* and *Shakespeare in Love* are love stories, while *The Full Monty* tells the tale of ordinary individuals breaking out of hardship. These are eminently relatable stories, with relevance regardless of the viewer's nationality. In terms of the representation of Britain and Britishness in these films, they include three particular types of representation that would have resonance for an international market. *Four Weddings* is set within a very middle-class England. The characters are well-spoken, live in nice areas and present the kind of 'floppy-fringed' England that, although unrepresentative of the majority of Britain today, does tap in to a particular view of England from a (mostly American) perspective.

The Full Monty, although set in Sheffield after the demise of the steel industry (and therefore contrasting with the setting of *Four Weddings*), still presents Britain in a way that mirrors certain global pre-conceptions about British life. A Britain populated by struggling, yet dignified working classes, echoes an expectation that class divisions are still very stark and the class system is still in existence. Heritage films and literary adaptations, such as *Shakespeare in Love*, are also, for many foreign viewers, synonymous with British cinema. *Much Ado About Nothing*, *Emma* and *Sense and Sensibility* all did well at the international box-office, confirming this idea that Britain's literary heritage is supremely marketable.

These films do not make up the entirety of British film products, however, and it would be wrong to say that the only products produced by the British film industry are those aimed at an international audience. Many contemporary films have sought to mirror the actual situation of Britain today and the issues faced by British people. The multi-cultural nature of Britain has been presented and discussed in films such as *Bend it Like Beckham* and *Babymother*. The regionality of Britain has also been reflected in films such as *Trainspotting* and *Twin Town*. The real impact of urban deprivation, glossed over in films like *The Full Monty*, is presented in all its lifelessness in films such as *Ratcatcher*. The issues associated with immigration are starkly presented in *The Last Resort*.

Although films such as *Four Weddings*, *Sliding Doors* and *Notting Hill* seem to be explicitly and consciously aimed at an audience wider than just Britain (the inclusion of American stars only serves to confirm this), not all films that gain international success seem to have consciously sought it. The success of *The Full Monty* in America, for example, was something of a surprise. Unfortunately, from an economic point of view, breaking the American and international markets is important to the British film industry. Huge international box-office receipts for one film can help finance other, perhaps less commercially orientated films.

Assessment comments

This answer shows an excellent level of knowledge of the British film industry and the films it produces. The candidate challenges the questions and deconstructs assumptions about British film with confidence. A wide range of film examples are used in this essay, all of which are appropriate to the essay question and the candidate's line of argument. An assured response. Grade 'A'.

Formal questions to consider

1. Below are the top ten box-office successes in the UK in 2003.

1. *Finding Nemo*
2. *The Lord of the Rings: The Return of the King*
3. *The Matrix: Reloaded*
4. *Love, Actually*
5. *Pirates of the Caribbean*
6. *The Lord of the Rings: The Two Towers*
7. *Bruce Almighty*
8. *X-Men 2*
9. *Calendar Girls*
10. *Johnny English*

Using the examples from this list and your own references, answer the following question: What do you consider to be the main difficulties with British film's challenge to Hollywood products?

2. Look at the two examples of posters below:

Source: British Film Institute

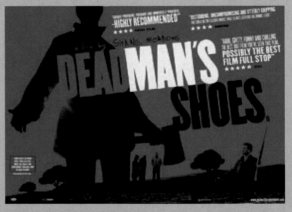

Distribution: Optimum Releasing. Production: Wrap Films

Making reference to the two posters in your answers, discuss what you think the differences are between the distribution of a mainstream and independent film.

3. With reference to specific examples of stars and films, discuss the role of the star within the marketing of a new film release.

4. What role do you think audience expectations play in the types of films released by Hollywood today?

5. What strategies are used by multiplex exhibition outlets to encourage new viewers to their complexes?

Chapter 3

Messages and Values: British and Irish Cinema (FS3)

Overview of the FS3 Unit

This unit in your AS Film Studies course requires you to focus on how messages and values are produced in British and Irish films. The micro and macro skills you learned during your FS1 studies will be very useful in this unit as a foundation to your discussions.

The key area you will need to consider for this unit is representation. Your studies for the exam require you to look at how representation is constructed and what messages and values are indicated by the representations you identify. Micro and macro textual elements help to construct representation – your essays will need to identify and evaluate the micro and macro elements that are used; the type of representation that is produced; and what this indicates to the film viewer about messages and values.

The FS3 exam is worth 30 per cent of your AS grade and 15 per cent of your whole A level. The exam lasts one and a half hours, in which time you will have to answer two questions. The distribution of marks for this paper is not equal across the two sections of the exam. Section A questions (Topic Study) carry 35 marks and Section B questions (Close Study) carry 25 marks. You should allocate your time in the exam in accordance with the mark distribution i.e. 50 minutes for Section A and 40 minutes for Section B. At the beginning of the exam, you will need to identify the questions that you are going to answer quickly. You will be prepared for one of the topic questions in Section A and for one of the single film questions in Section B.

Skills required for Unit FS3

The Film Studies syllabus outlines four main skills that you will need to show in your FS3 answers, as follows:

1. An ability to identify messages and values, both explicit and implicit, in films.
   This skill requires you first to be able to distinguish between explicit and implicit meaning. Translated further, this means the ability to identify what the film makes obvious about a particular issue and what the film implies about an issue. It might be as simple as distinguishing between what the characters say about race, religion, gender or nationality and what is implied about these areas through the film's use of micro elements.

2. An ability to critically evaluate representation within film texts.
   The ability to discuss representation is one of the key skills of Film Studies and you will be asked to evaluate what a film is saying about a particular social group or social issues many times during your Film Studies course. The simplest way to identify the process through which representation is established, what this implies about the film's attitudes and how these attitudes relate to dominant social ideas is to follow a three-point plan:

   • Use your knowledge of micro and macro elements to determine what the film seems to be saying about a particular individual or social group. The choices of cinematography, sound, editing and *mise-en-scène* surrounding a character, and the narrative importance of that character, will imply a certain response the viewer is encouraged to have to an individual or group.

   • Using the notes you have just made, comment on the attitude of the film towards particular groups of people and the issues related to them.

   • Consider whether you think this attitude of the film mirrors, or challenges, the dominant attitudes that existed in the world at the time the film was made.

3. An ability to contextualise films, both historically and socially.
   Your notes on representation will extend into this skill. You should research into the time in which the film you are studying was made and consider whether the political or social events of the time had any impact on the film you are studying.

4. An ability to reflect on your own personal response to a film's messages and values.
   Last, but by no means least important, is your own response to the attitudes you have identified in your film. What do you think about the way in which the film discusses certain issues or represents certain social groups? Does the film enlighten you about any social or historical event?

Approaching Section A: Topic study

Section A of your FS3 exam asks you to consider a group of films under a particular heading. There are six topics for the comparative section of this exam. Your teacher will have chosen one from the following:

• The 1940s – the war and its aftermath

• Swinging Britain 1963–1973

• Passions and repressions

• Social and political conflict

• Scottish cinema

• Comedy.

The focus of your study within Section A will be to consider how representation is constructed within the films you have chosen and whether the individual films within your topic have similar or conflicting messages and values. Your topic may be Scottish Cinema, for example, but the representation of Scotland, gender or age, for example, in the films you study might be very different. The headings of the topic sections in Section A will provide you with a historical, generic or regional means of connecting the films you evaluate, but these groupings do not imply that each of the films you might study for this topic are saying the same things.

Focus films in Section A

For each topic in Section A two focus films are prescribed. You will need to use at least one of the two films given for the topic you are studying within your essay discussions. Analysis of the focus films does not have to dominate your essay content, but it does have to be evident. Whether or not the title of your topic has a chronological boundary, it will be worthwhile considering the historical and social context of the films you discuss. As we have seen in Chapter 2, the context of a film's production may have significant bearing on the representations that are evident within the film, so this element should be an important part of your discussions.

Representation

As we have already seen, demonstrating an understanding of representation in your exam answers is extremely important. Representational analysis should begin with an analysis of micro features. For example, a consideration of the different camera angles used to present a character will tell you what kind of position they have within the film and how they are seen by other characters within the film's narrative. You should also identify the diegetic and non-diegetic sound elements that have been used in connection with this character, what kind of *mise-en-scène* elements are used to present them, and how a scene uses transitions to relate meaning about that character. All of these micro elements contribute towards your understanding of the way in which the film uses the characters and what it seems to be saying about them. You can then move on to a discussion of whether or not the film seems to be presenting a certain individual or group of characters in a stereotypical way; whether the film is challenging the viewer's perceptions about a particular group and their associated issues; and whether the representations in the film seem to confirm dominant social attitudes, or challenge them.

The attitudes and ideas that seem to be the most commonly held and influential within a society at any one time are called 'dominant social ideologies'. It is the relationship between these attitudes and the ones you have identified in your film text that will provide you with the core of your discussions. For example, if your film seems to be suggesting that Britain does not appear particularly accepting of ethnic minorities, you will need to discuss to what extent you think this suggestion from the film is confirmed in the social reality surrounding the film. An ideology is a set of shared beliefs. These beliefs might concern gender, sexuality, religion, nation, regionality or age. Your task will be to compare and contrast the ideologies apparent both within your film and within the society around it.

Using your own examples

Alongside your focus film and the other films that your teacher presents to you in class, you can also use your own choices of relevant film examples within your essays. One of your main goals in any exam is to differentiate your work from other candidates and an FS3 essay that includes a variety of film references, including your own, will help you distinguish your work from the rest.

The 1940s – the war and its aftermath

For this topic you are asked to consider issues of representation in films that were made during the Second World War and films made after the war up until the end of the 1940s. There are many possible representational areas that you might consider for this topic, including gender, nationality, class, power, authority and community. The two focus films for the topic are *Went the Day Well?* (Cavalcanti, 1942) and *Fires Were Started* (Jennings, 1943). You may use one or both of these films in your answers.

There are many different issues and debates that you could consider for this topic. In effect, you have an 11-year timeframe (1939 to 1950), from which to draw your examples and within this time a great deal happened in Britain. The films you study might speak directly of the experience of fighting in a war, or being at home suffering the effects of wartime deprivation. You might see examples of films that were made after 1945 that discuss the effects of the war on Britain. These post-war films might articulate the problems of reconstructing Britain after the ravages of the war. Not all films during this period were related to wartime events, or discussed the war at all, and you may look at examples of films that were made to help British viewers escape from their pressures into a world of comedy or romance.

Films made during the war

You should analyse films made during the war in terms of intent. Given the fact that most British cinemas were closed by the government at the beginning of the war for fear of bombing, and only opened after the government acknowledged the potential place of film within wartime propaganda, one area of analysis should concern the representation of Britain in relation to the 'aggressor': Germany. Do the films you might study during this period represent a demonised German threat? Do they imply that the whole blame for the war is Germany's? Or, do they attempt to build the morale of the British public by describing a better, post-war future for Britain? You should not think, however, that only films fuelled by propaganda existed on British screens during the war. Ealing Studios was highly productive during the early 1940s and produced a number of 'Ealing comedies', which presented a much more satirical view of Britain, British people and British institutions.

Films made after the war

The films that entered British cinemas after the end of the war were again very varied. Some of them presented 'reconstruction' directly, and considered not only the economic reconstruction that was necessary after the war, but the reconstruction of community and national morale.

Towards the end of the 1940s, the cinema arena was extremely diverse. *Passport to Pimlico* (Ealing, 1949), for example, represented the aftermath of the Second World War and its impact on a local community. The film explored the issues connected with a Britain still in rationing. A local community set up a 'ration-free' state in order to counter the depressing effects of post-war restrictions. Eventually, however, this new state was overwhelmed by precisely the kinds of bureaucracy and hierarchy that the inhabitants of Pimlico were trying to avoid. The film not only reflects the fact that even though the war was over, the effects of it were still being felt, but also the nature of independence. For the inhabitants of Pimlico, independence comes with a price. However, the satirical and humorous nature of the film made it less a tale of hardship and more a story of misadventure.

A very different film was released in the same year, by the same studio. *Kind Hearts and Coronets*, starring Alec Guinness in multiple roles, told the tale of a multiple murderer who 'picks off' the remaining members of his family in order to inherit his birthright. *Kind Hearts* was a huge success and was not a film that directly reflected issues connected with the war. The film did satirise the British class system, however, and reflected another important area of representation within this FS3 topic.

Whether your chosen films include representations of the wartime experience, the economic impact of the war, post-war reconstruction, the class system, the family or Britishness generally, you should make sure that you do two things. First, carefully describe and analyse the particular nature of representations in each of the films you have chosen. Then draw those particulars together into an overall analysis of the topic. Are there any themes or representational areas that seem to be consistent across all of your films?

EXERCISE 1

Look at the opening sequences of two of the films you are studying for this topic. Using your knowledge of micro elements, make notes on how the textual features of the films are working to establish their themes.

Case Study 1: *Went the Day Well?* (Cavalcanti, 1942)

Went the Day Well? is the tale of the invasion of a remote village by a group of undercover German troops masquerading as Royal Engineers. The film describes the mounting distrust that occurs in this village when the inhabitants become suspicious of the disguised soldiers. Cavalcanti's film uses the story of the village and undercover German troops to point to one of the psychological after-effects of war: pervading national suspicion. Cavalcanti constructs a very traditional image of the British village, full of community meeting places and community spirit. This is, of course, shattered when suspicions mount. Ultimately, it is the anger and distrust generated by the invaders in the minds of the villagers, rather than what the invaders actually do, that destroys the rural idyll. The villagers' anti-German feeling is both violent and all-consuming. The 'enemy' becomes de-humanised and the villagers are shown carrying out the kind of violent (even sadistic) attacks that they would previously never have dreamed of. This film functions as a discussion of the impact of war, war-mongering and propaganda on the individual psyche. It is almost as if the fear of barbarity and brutality comes to justify these characteristics within those who fear them.

Case Study 2: *Fires Were Started* (Jennings, 1943)

Source: BFI Stills, Posters and Designs

Humphrey Jennings was perhaps best known as a documentary film maker. By 1945, he had already created more than twenty documentaries, with wide ranging subject matter. During the war years, his work reflected the mood of ordinary British people and described not the grand themes of war, but the day-to-day hardships and difficulties. *Fires Were Started* follows a group of real firemen, as they struggle to put out the fires that covered Blitz-stricken London. The film used real fires, as well as real fire-fighters, to illustrate the struggles of these men, who, day after day, sought to keep London from the brink of total ruin. The fire-fighters are very clearly represented as valiant in their attempts to stop an ever present threat. The relentlessness of their task, and the psychological impact of the constant threat to the fire-fighters and the inhabitants of London, also reflects the reality rather than the glamour of a wartime situation.

Swinging Britain 1963–1973

As with the last topic (The 1940s – the war and its aftermath), Swinging Britain 1963–1973 has a prescribed timespan. The ten years you have available within this topic encompass both the period often referred to as the 'swinging sixties' and the few years that came directly after it. You could, therefore, consider the impact of the films released in the 1960s on film audiences and compare this with the films released at the beginning of the next decade. You might equally consider if there are any stylistic differences between the films of the 1960s and early 1970s, and compare the representations that are constructed in these films. The focus films for this topic are *A Hard Day's Night* (Lester, 1964) and *Darling* (Schlesinger, 1965).

The expansion of this topic into the early 1970s makes for a very interesting variety of themes, ideas, issues and representational areas that can be discussed. The changing nature of this period in history is also an important factor for consideration. The hardships of the war years were over and the Britain of the 1950s, in which gender and class roles were still very clearly defined, was being challenged. During this ten-year period, young Britons especially challenged the politics and lifestyle choices of their predecessors. The feminist movement had begun to articulate some of their concerns and young people were expressing their challenge to tradition and authority through their attitudes, clothes and music.

Representations of London

The notion of a 'swinging London' during this period will provide a central area for debate within this topic. Whether this title has been applied retrospectively, or whether it was the experience of those individuals who lived in the capital at the time, is something you will need to debate. What went on in Britain's capital, as compared with the events and attitudes of the rest of the country, will also provide a central topic of discussion. Was London representative? Within the films you will study for this period, there are certain other key areas of representational debate. Attitudes towards gender, the class system, the family and authority figures and institutions should be acknowledged and discussed in detail.

In terms of the representation of London, in comparison to the representation of other films during this period, your task will be to consider whether or not the capital is presented in contrast to the rest of the country. Films such as *A Hard Day's Night* do represent a London in which fashion and music are all consuming and the young playfully jostle with the 'old'. You might even bring in examples of TV dramas, such as *Cathy Come Home*, in order to draw contrasts between a glamourised notion of a city, such as that shown in *A Hard Day's Night* and the mundane, difficult reality of life in a city.

The sexual revolution?

The 'sexual revolution' of the 1960s, in which the pill made it possible for women to have sex without fear of pregnancy, is also an issue to consider. Is this represented as liberating for women in the films you have chosen to study, or are there problems related to such freedom?

Silvio Narizzano's 1966 film *Georgy Girl*, for example, in which a frumpy young woman's only means of escape from loneliness is to marry an older man, and her glamorous flatmate's enjoyment of the sexual revolution is curtailed by an unwanted pregnancy, is in fact a very bleak portrait of so-called sexually liberated London.

Contentious films

Nicolas Roeg's 1970 film *Performance* would also provide much useful debate under this topic. At once a thriller and a tale of sexual freedom, the film includes quite explicit images of violence and sexual encounter. The setting of this film is one in which gangland violence is a perennial threat and what might be initially liberating sexual encounters can prove ultimately destructive. The film caused much censorship debate and provided a very stark and often shocking contrast to the more sanitised films from this period. What must be acknowledged within a study of this topic is the variety of films made during this period and the variety of representations they contain. For example, it is surprising to note that the decade that included the 'pop film' energy of *A Hard Day's Night*, also included Kubrick's 1972 classic *A Clockwork Orange*!

Whether your focus for this section is on films that seem to reflect the euphoria of the social and sexual revolution, or whether your film examples seem to scrape away at this attractive surface, you will need to focus on the way in which the representations on offer in your film texts interact with the contemporary world around them of 1963–1973.

EXERCISE 2

With a partner, choose one focus area from the list below:

1. 'Swinging London'
2. The social revolution
3. The sexual revolution
4. Music and fashion.

For your chosen focus area, make notes together on what the films you have chosen to study seem to be saying about this area, and how these messages are relayed to the film viewer.

Case Study 3: *Darling* (Schlesinger, 1965)

As a proponent of the so-called 'British New Wave' of cinema, John Schlesinger created films that were designed to develop British cinema out of what had gone before. Schlesinger also had a documentary film and acting background, which influenced his film making. *Darling* was a critical success for both the director and its star, Julie Christie (she won the Best Actress Oscar for this film in 1965).

The film examined upper-class decadence and the loneliness that can be brought about by a jet-set lifestyle. The representation of the class system in this film is created through this focus on the upper-middle classes. It shows how too much money and too little time can corrupt and stultify people. Schlesinger's film was shot in a style reminiscent of the French New Wave films of Godard and Truffaut. It picks at the perfect surfaces of the characters it uses and points to decadence as the end result of over-indulgence.

Case Study 4: *A Hard Day's Night* (Lester, 1964)

Source: BFI Stills, Posters and Designs

Richard Lester's *A Hard Day's Night* was originally conceived as a promotional vehicle for the Beatles. The film discusses a number of issues that would have been current at the time the film was made. The film discusses issues of age and class, as well as the impact of pop music during this period. The Beatles are seen in this film in a number of scenarios in which the exuberance of youth is pitched against the dullness of age. However, there are also scenes within this film in which age does not seem to be an indicator of common sense. Whereas the four 'boys' are shot getting up to mischief, causing great anxiety to their management team and generally having a great time, it is Paul's 'grandfather' who is perhaps the most irresponsible character in the film. It is as if this film, aimed very specifically at a young, Beatles' 'fan' audience, does not want to represent young people as too out of control.

The main focus of the film is, of course, the band and their music, but alongside comments about age, there are also scenes within this film that represent the class divide. The Beatles are working-class boys who, through musical appeal, have

🎞 become wealthy. They represent a dream for those young fans wanting to break out of their normal lives and make it 'big'. The Beatles also represent a challenge to the kind of class snobbery that they encounter on a train. They have elevated themselves into an altogether different class: that of the 'star'.

London, in this film, as has already been mentioned in the main section of this topic, is safe, secure and exciting. The only threat the Beatles encounter is from over-zealous fans and there is no hint of the violence and corruption that can be seen in other films from this period. There is also no sign of the sexual revolution in this film. The Beatles might well have been exploring their sexual worlds, but the particular representation of this band as constructed in Lester's film does not include sex or sexuality.

Passions and repressions

The focus of this topic area is the representation of sexuality and desire in specific social contexts. Your task for this topic area will be to consider the different representations and discussions of passion and repression within the same social context or across different social groups. As with all of the Section A topics for the FS3 exam, you can bring in your own examples of films, but you will have to discuss your focus film, too. For this topic, your focus films are *Brief Encounter* (Lean, 1945) or *Beautiful Thing* (MacDonald, 1996).

There are three key areas for this topic that would provide much useful debate within your essays:

- sex and class
- sex and race
- heterosexuality and homosexuality.

The films you choose will probably be from differing historical periods. An analysis of the shifting attitudes towards sexuality and desire should make up part of your preparation for this topic. Consider also the interaction between the way sexuality and desire are represented in your films and the attitudes of the social world surrounding the film. Do these attitudes seem to be in agreement, or do they conflict?

Sex and class

This topic has no chronological boundaries, so as long as your film is an example of British or Irish cinema, you can use it within your discussions. If you are concentrating on the sub-topic of sex and class, for example, alongside *Brief Encounter* as your focus film, you could look at *The Remains of the Day* (Ivory, 1993), *Letter to Brezhnev* (Bernard, 1985) or *Saturday Night and Sunday Morning* (Reisz, 1960). *The Remains of the Day* tells the story of a repressed relationship between two servants who work in a stately home. The character of Stevens, played by Anthony Hopkins, cannot exist outside of his role as head butler. Miss Kenton, played by Emma Thompson, tries, unsuccessfully, to liberate him from his state of abject repression. The film represents the class system at this time in British history as so repressive that it even infects the emotional life of those stultified by it.

Letter to Brezhnev is set in the 1980s. One of the central female characters works in a factory, the other is unemployed. They have little, or no, money, and dream of some form of escape. The setting of this film is Liverpool and the story is of individuals who have not flourished under the Tory government of the time. The female characters in this film are working class, and the sailors they eventually meet can be presumed to be from that class, too. This is not a story about how love can be liberating. One of the characters has a sexual encounter and then returns to the chicken factory, fully aware that her life is not going to change because of one night with a Russian sailor. The other female character is more hopeful, even writing to the Russian president to ask about her sailor. The characters in this film are not sexually repressed, but they are socially and economically immobilised.

Saturday Night and Sunday Morning was a big box office success for the British New Wave. The film tells the story of a Nottingham factory worker who rails against his working-class family background and the economic repression he endures. He attempts to escape through sexual encounter, as well as acts of physical defiance, but is ultimately left with nothing. The passion in this film comes mainly in the form of anger and the repression is economic and social. The lead character's tendency to leave his sexual conquests does little to relieve the bleakness of this film. As a contrast to the heightened romanticism of *Brief Encounter*, a discussion of *Saturday Night and Sunday Morning* would provide very useful comment.

Sex and race

Comments on the relationship between sex and race could use the film *My Beautiful Laundrette* (Frears, 1985) to good effect. This film could also provide an interesting study of the representation of homosexual passions and repressions. Frears' film is set in London, in an Asian community. The central family in the film have opened a laundrette and it is to be run by the son of the family. The story centres around the relationship between this young Asian man and an ex-National Front thug, who befriends him and helps him open his dream laundrette. It is not just the gay relationship that has to be hidden by the main characters, but the inter-racial nature of this relationship too. The Asian characters in the film have economic power and the white characters are mainly those who hurl abuse. This film provides a very interesting study of a passionate sexual relationship between a white and an Asian man, within the context of 1980s Thatcherite Britain.

Whatever films you choose to study and whatever focus you decide to take for this topic, there are important central issues that you will need to consider. First, you will need to define the nature of the passion represented in your chosen films and consider what the pressures on this passion are. Then you should ensure that you consider the social context of the film and consider whether or not the film is articulating a view that was socially prevalent.

EXERCISE 3

Using your case study film and one of the other films you are studying for this topic, research into the reception of these films at the time they were made. You might use the internet, other archives or film journalism. You should evaluate the kinds of comments that were made about the film's content, messages and values. What was the attitude of critics at that time to the film's representations of passions and repressions?

Case Study 5: *Brief Encounter* (Lean, 1945)

David Lean's famous 1945 film *Brief Encounter* tells the story of the affair between two, upper-middle-class characters, who are both married. The events shown in the film are Laura's version, as is indicated by the fact that the voice-over is hers and thus the reliability of the version of events offered needs to be debated. The passion that the characters feel for each other is deemed unacceptable by both the characters and the film's narrative itself. The fact that both characters ultimately repress their feelings and return to the life that is more socially acceptable, only serves to confirm the film's viewpoint. Although the character of Laura, in particular, is seen to be repressed by the very strict gender roles within her marriage, she ultimately returns to it. Her representation does not challenge the social attitude towards women and their place in society that was dominant in the 1940s. The characters within Lean's film express the kind of restraint that would have been deemed the only true option within 1940s morality.

Case Study 6: *Beautiful Thing* (MacDonald, 1996)

Source: British Film Institute

Hettie MacDonald's film, about the difficulties of having a gay relationship, would make an excellent comparison with *My Beautiful Laundrette*. The character of Jamie falls in love with his next door neighbour Ste. Although these two characters live in a historical context that one would like to assume is more aware and less prejudiced, the relationship does not run smoothly. The film is set in Thamesmead, South London, a far cry from the rarified middle-class world of *Brief Encounter*. The film considers the issues faced by young gay individuals in a contemporary setting. The pressures on the relationship come from many different quarters, including Jamie's mum, whom he is terrified of telling. It is the social and familial impact of this relationship that is discussed in the film and it presents a 1990s context in which attitudes to gay relationships are not quite as open as many viewers would have hoped.

Social and political conflict

For this topic your area of focus will be films that represent social or political conflicts. Your films might deal with many types of conflict, including situations of ideological confrontation or social injustice. The focus films that have been prescribed for this section are *It Happened Here* (Brownlow/Mollo, 1966) or *Bloody Sunday* (Greengrass, 2002).

This topic might initially appear daunting because of the scale of possible areas of debate the title implies. However, there are certain key areas of discussion to bear in mind that will help you to focus your comments within your exam essays. You might look at the way a particular event or a period of social conflict has been represented in a number of films. The situation in Northern Ireland, for example, and key dates and events connected with this, has provided the impetus behind the making of a number of films. You might consider the way in which perceived threats to Britain have been discussed within films. You might also bring the topic of conflict into a more domestic arena and discuss films that represent the effects of social or political issues on particular families.

Representation of historical events in British and Irish history

In terms of particular key points in British and Irish history and the events of that time, the focus film *Bloody Sunday* will provide an important part of your debate. The film tells the real story of events that occurred in Londonderry on Sunday 30th January, 1972 and represents a particular version of the tragedy that happened. Jim Sheridan's 1993 film, *In The Name of the Father*, also deals with the Anglo-Irish conflict. This film is a fictionalised account of the events that followed the Guildford pub bombing in 1974. Sheridan's film tells the story of Gerry Conlan and his father Guiseppe's (wrongful) imprisonment for this crime and their fight to be released. The imprisonment of the 'Guildford Four' is very clearly represented as a miscarriage of justice in this film, with the Conlons and their friends depicted as scapegoats for a nation's anger and the police and judicial systems' need to be seen doing justice. The scenes in which Gerry is harassed and beaten by the police confirm the film's standpoint. The IRA may have been responsible for the Guildford murders, but both the police who beat Gerry and the courts who imprisoned the Guildford Four are also seen as reprehensible. Scenes such as those of Guiseppe Conlon's death in prison pull audiences' sympathies firmly towards Gerry and his friends.

The threat of invasion

The threat of 'invasion' is another key thematic area that you could explore within this topic. Whether the invasion is fictional, such as that of the Nazis invading Britain in *It Happened Here*, or is real, the central issue for you to discuss is that of the fear behind the threat. Pavel

Pavlikovsky's 2000 film, *The Last Resort*, for example, is a discussion of the plight of those individuals who come to Britain as immigrants. The issue of immigration is continually debated, but in Pavlikovsky's film the answer is fairly clear. Tanya and her son arrive in Britain, hoping to join her fiancé. However, her fiancé is not there to meet them and they are sent to 'Stonehaven' to await the processing of Tanya's request for political asylum. The *mise-en-scène* of this town is incredibly bleak and mother and son have to live in a soulless block of flats. In an attempt to earn money, so that they do not have to live on the food vouchers they are given, Tanya even resorts to internet porn acting. One only has to look at many newspaper articles concerning immigration to know that Pavlikovsky's sympathies towards immigrants are not shared by all of Britain.

Social and political conflict and the family

The impact that social and political conflict has on the family can be seen clearly in *My Son the Fanatic* (Prasad, 1997). This is the story of a family which is eventually torn apart by the differing religious and political convictions of a son and his family. The story revolves around a Pakistani taxi driver, who is accepted by those around him and has absorbed much of the culture of the British context in which he now lives. The conflict in this film is between this character and his son, who rejects Britain and British customs in favour of Islamic fundamentalism. The son becomes increasingly fervent; he invites an Islamic leader into his father's house and attacks white characters, whose behaviour he deems shameful. One of these characters is the prostitute, Bettina, with whom his father is having an affair. The criticism in this film is not just for the son, who destroys his family through his own fanaticism. It is also for the Islamic leader, who eventually attempts to remain in the culture he apparently despises. And it is also for the foreign businessman who uses the prostitutes who are eventually attacked and seems to have the least morals of any character within the film. Prasad's film is a study of what happens to individuals and families when social and political conflict occur.

In order to maintain a sense of organisation and realistic limits in your answers for this topic, try to group the films you have chosen to study under the three main areas of discussion outlined above. There will obviously be differences between these films, but this type of organisation will help you maintain a systematic approach to the topic of Social and political conflict.

EXERCISE 4

With a partner, discuss the closing sequences of your focus film and one other film you have chosen to study. What do these sequences seem to be suggesting about the conflicts that have been apparent in the narrative? Are these conflicts resolved at the end of the films? Why do you think the director chose to either resolve the conflict or leave it open?

Case Study 7: *It Happened Here* (Brownlow/Mollo, 1966)

Source: British Film Institute

It Happened Here is a film in which a real fear is articulated through a fantasy scenario. The film represents a situation of a Nazi invasion of Britain. The low-budget nature of the film and the style of cinematography do make it reminiscent of a newsreel and this adds to the 'reality effect' within the film. Although made 21 years after the end of the Second World War, the film still tapped into prevalent social fears. The fear of invasion, common within wartime, was still in existence over 20 years later.

The conflicts associated with the film are many. On the most obvious level, the Nazi invaders are represented as a threat to the peace and security of Britain. On another level, they represent a threat to the moral fabric of British society. And on another, the Nazis are allegorical and represent the threat felt by many British individuals. We live on an island and have not been invaded for hundreds of years. Brownlow and Mollo's film is a reminder that invasion is always possible.

Case Study 8: *Bloody Sunday* (Greengrass, 2002)

Source: British Film Institute

Bloody Sunday, as has already been stated, tells the story of events that occurred in Londonderry on Sunday 30th January, 1972. At this point in history, Anglo-Irish relations were especially bad and the IRA had carried out a series of attacks. The film's story concentrates on a march against imprisonment without trial, which was organised by Protestant MP Ivan Cooper. The story is told over a period of 24 hours and presents the events leading up to, and including, the march. Thirteen people were killed in the clash between those marching and the British forces. The film takes its stance very clearly. The events are presented from the point of view of Cooper and those others who decided to march. Imprisonment without trial is clearly represented as a means for the British to not only control events in Northern Ireland, but also to arrest those about whom they only had the vaguest suspicions.

Scottish cinema

This particular FS3 topic asks you to discuss representation in Scottish films. This topic is not defined by a timeframe, so you will be able to draw your examples from a wider period. The main focus of the topic is how Scotland and Scottishness are represented in a selection of films. Your focus films for this section are *Local Hero* (Forsyth, 1983) or *Orphans* (Mullan, 1997).

As with all of the topics within Section A of the FS3 exam, you should consider some central questions and issues within your study of Scottish cinema. The issues most relevant to this topic are class, social deprivation, urban vs rural Scotland, gender and nation. You may identify other areas for discussion and you should feel confident to explore these, as well as the areas just mentioned. It would be possible for you to also include reference to films set in Scotland, but without the same kind of Scottish 'profile' as other, more pertinent examples. You could refer to *Braveheart*, for example, but you should not make a film such as this the focus of your answer.

Class in Scottish cinema

There are many possibilities for film examples within a discussion of class within the topic of Scottish cinema. Alongside the focus film *Orphans*, for example, which is set in a working-class context and explores the impact of a death on a family, you could consider *Shallow Grave* (Boyle, 1994), *Trainspotting* (Boyle, 1996) and *Ratcatcher* (Ramsay, 1999). *Shallow Grave* is set within an affluent middle-class world. The three characters who are the main focus of the narrative live in a large, stylishly decorated flat. Although they argue (and for some, eventually die) over money, they are not shown to experience economic hardship or urban deprivation. In *Trainspotting*, the drug addicts form their own underclass. They live in squalid flats and steal in order to sustain their habits. The glimpses the viewer gets of the families of Renton and the others, however, does point to the fact that these characters are in their new 'world', because they have opted out of their old one. *Ratcatcher*, on the other hand, is a film set on an anonymous housing estate. The characters in this film are poor. A dustmen's strike has made their already impoverished surroundings even more depressing. These are characters who are in stark contrast to those within the world of *Shallow Grave*.

Urban vs rural in Scottish cinema

The opposition between urban and rural is another connective theme between many of the films you might choose to study for this topic. *Local Hero,* for example, represents a rural idyll in the form of the village on the island to which Mac is sent. In this rural environment, a sense of community flourishes and the inhabitants of the village look after each other. It is the urban world of Houston, Texas that is to be escaped in this film. As we have seen in the previous section, both *Trainspotting* and *Ratcatcher* present an urban environment that is often squalid and uninviting. In Gillies McKinnon's 1996 film *Small Faces*, the urban world is no more inviting. The Glasgow setting of the film is overrun by rival gangs, vying for power. This is not a safe place for the young boy whose story the viewer is following.

Gender in Scottish cinema

The representation of gender within Scottish cinema is an equally interesting topic of study. *Local Hero*, *Ratcatcher*, *Trainspotting* and *Small Faces* all have a male character as the central focus, and in the case of *Ratcatcher* and *Small Faces*, this male character is a young boy. *Orphans* and *Shallow Grave* have both male and female central characters, but in both films it is the male characters who lose control when events take over. It is interesting that it is often the male characters within examples of Scottish cinema who are represented as most affected by economic deprivation, unemployment, death and dissatisfaction. *Ratcatcher*, however, could be said to provide a slightly different perspective. It is the central character's mother in this film who has to keep her family together during the dustmen's strike. It is only the mother of the boy who drowns whom we see grieving. Apart from young boys, and men in the army, men are mostly absent from the key events in this film.

The notion of 'Scottishness'

The notion of Scottishness, and what it is to be Scottish, should also be part of your debates. If in *Local Hero*, Scottishness equates with rural harmony and financial astuteness, then how is it defined within the other films we have looked at in this section? For Renton, in *Trainspotting*, 'Scotland is shite'. His is a nation of unemployment and financial hardship and, for him, being Scottish is not something to be recommended. Of course, his attitude is extreme and does not wholly echo that of the film's Scottish director. However, being

EXERCISE 5

Using the grid below, make notes on the use of key thematic areas in the films you are studying for this topic and the scenes that you think best exemplify your films' discussions of these areas:

	Representation of class	Representation of gender	Representation of the urban and the rural	Representation of Scotland and Scottishness
Film 1:				
Film 2:				
Film 3:				
Film 4:				

When you have completed your grid, make notes on what your identified scenes tell you about the messages and values that your film expresses.

Scottish in *Ratcatcher*, *Small Faces* and *Orphans* does seem to entail a degree of financial hardship. Whether this factor points towards a nationalist tendency in these films and highlights the plight of a nation previously legislated for by a government hundreds of miles away in London, is something you should debate.

Whatever films you choose for this topic, you should use the thematic groupings outlined above to help you formulate your responses within the exam.

Case Study 9: *Local Hero* (Forsyth, 1983)

Local Hero is the story of an American oil company's attempt to buy a Scottish village in order to build an oil refinery on the village site. Mac MacIntyre is the yuppie sent from Houston, Texas to the Scottish village in order to seal the deal. Houston is a city of economic affluence, but is also soulless and lonely for Mac. He lives alone in his apartment and spends his evenings ringing ex-girlfriends, just to hear another human voice. The Scottish village he is sent to buy is a direct contrast to this world. This rural idyll is pretty, full of nature and has a close-knit community. Mac, of course, quickly falls in love with the village. This film is structured around a series of oppositions: urban vs rural, community vs individualism, the modern world vs the traditional world. It creates an almost perfect view of rural Scotland, a place where it doesn't even seem to rain.

In *Local Hero*, however, the representation is not quite as simple as it first seems to be. The take-over bid by the Americans might initially seem to be brutish and invasive, but it soon becomes clear that the villagers want to sell and are already planning how to spend their money. This is a film in which those from diametrically opposing worlds seek what the other has.

Case Study 10: *Orphans* (Mullan, 1997)

Orphans tells the story of the Flynn family. The mother of the family has died and the four remaining children are now orphans. These children are adults, however, and the film's timeframe is of the 24 hours up to, during and after the mother's funeral. Each of the children deals with the death of the mother in a number of ways. Michael becomes aggressive in a pub and is stabbed. The oldest brother, Thomas, elects to remain with his mother's coffin until her funeral. John, the youngest brother, takes out his hurt by attempting to hunt down his brother's attacker. Their sister, Sheila, who uses a wheelchair, is eventually left alone in the Glasgow streets.

The film is set in a working-class environment and the characters they meet also contribute to the film's comments about class. The only affluent, middle-class family in the film is satirised and the husband is seen masturbating to pornography. The brothers in this film do not look after their disabled sister and instead, wander the Glasgow streets looking for a release for their grief.

Source: British Film Institute

Comedy

This is another potentially very broad topic and can be translated in many ways. The main issue to bear in mind if you study this topic, however, is that of intent and audience. What is the film you are studying attempting to say and to whom is it speaking? The focus films for the topic of comedy are *The Ladykillers* (Mackendrick, 1955) or *East is East* (O'Donnell, 1999).

In terms of your approach to this topic, there are three over-arching categories that you could use within your preparation. Try to group your film examples into those that:

- explore social and national stereotypes
- seek to challenge social assumptions
- create humorous scenarios through plot and circumstance.

Obviously, there will be some overlap with this sort of categorisation, but these three types of comedy could provide a useful organisational strategy within your notes. Remember that you will be analysing the way in which textual features help to create representation and how the film's attitudes relate to those that are held outside of it. You are not just evaluating whether or not you think a certain film is funny!

The issue of stereotyping

There are many examples of films that explore the issue of stereotyping and, of course, this exploration might be implicit or explicit. The film you are evaluating might also entrench stereotypes, rather than deconstruct and challenge them. The focus film *East is East* would provide a good example to start any discussion of the use of stereotypes and the representation of the Shah family might provide a useful reference point. This family is presented in a humorous way and their sensibilities are mocked, both by the other characters in the film and by the film itself. You could also bring the 'Carry On' films into a discussion of this area. These films employed a whole range of sexual, nation and gender-based stereotyping in their stories and could help you determine the audience's expectations of comedy in the 1960s and 1970s. Films such as *Carry on Doctor* and *Carry on Up The Khyber* presented extremely stereotypical depictions of men, women, homosexuals and foreigners, but were also incredibly successful at the box office. Whether these very obvious stereotypes were being offered up for challenge by these films, or whether the Carry On series tapped into common national attitudes, would prove an interesting topic of debate.

Social assumptions

East is East would also provide a very useful example of a film that might be said to challenge social assumptions. This film presents the viewer with two different constructions of the Asian community. First, there is the Khan family who live in a predominantly white neighbourhood. In this family, the mother is white and the father is Asian. Their children have been brought up in Britain. The children do not want to follow Asian traditions and in many scenes they challenge their father's authority.

The complexities of a life lived with dual cultural influences is presented in this film and is perhaps something that would challenge certain viewer's preconceptions. The second view of the Asian community comes when the Khan family visit Bradford. The clothes, food and traditions represented in these scenes would perhaps be closer to many viewer's expectations.

Gurinder Chadha's 2002 film *Bend it Like Beckham* also presents a side to the Asian community in Britain that might challenge commonly held perceptions. The central Asian family in this film still retain many traditional customs, but are also very much a part of the culture that goes on around them. This is, of course, most clearly expressed through the central character's obsession with football and David Beckham. She does not want to get married, but to go to university and carry on playing football. Chadha's film does poke fun at parts of the Asian community and comments on the tension between the traditions of Asian parents and the Westernised modernity of their children, but the satirical elements do not stereotype the Asian characters. Instead, they poke fun at *human* characteristics, regardless of race. This is a film in which the central character is female, plays football and is Asian – this kind of characterisation and narrative positioning seek to challenge many assumptions.

Situational humour

The films that have already been mentioned all create humour through plot and circumstance, but they also make points about gender and nationality. *The Full Monty* (Cattaneo, 1997) is another example of a film that uses circumstantial comedy and plot devices to create humour. This film is the story of a group of unemployed men in Sheffield, who eventually take up stripping to pay their bills. In two of the film's most humorous scenes, they are caught practising by the police and sent away by a couple of debt collectors while in their underwear. The narrative trajectory of this film is always towards the final striptease – in this way the plot promises a final pay off for the viewer's attention. The film is a comedy, but it also comments on the impact of unemployment on a male workforce.

In your answers, you should remember to discuss the textual devices used to create the particular representations discussed above in your chosen films. You should also remember to discuss how the comic elements of the film are being used to comment on particular issues.

EXERCISE 6

Make notes on three scenes from the films you have studied, that you think:

1. explore social and national stereotypes

2. seek to challenge social assumptions

3. create humorous scenarios through plot and circumstance.

When you have completed these notes, discuss with your partner why you chose these particular scenes.

Case Study 11: *East is East* (O'Donnell, 1999)

Source: British Film Institute

East is East is set in Salford in 1971 and focuses on an Asian family living in an otherwise white, working-class community. The film is at once a discussion of the position of an Asian family in Britain and the tensions that exist within that family. The Khans have six children, all of whom have different attitudes towards their father and the convictions that he holds. Near the beginning of the film, the eldest Khan child is seen escaping from an arranged marriage. He is subsequently found in London, working as a hairdresser. The other Khan children react to their father's expectations in varying ways. One pretends he is not Asian, another hides beneath his parka hood and another retreats into religion.

The Khan family are mostly accepted by their neighbours, except for one, who becomes the mouthpiece for the politician Enoch Powell's anti-immigration policies. The film does use situational comedy in order to engage the viewer, but also makes a point about the position of Asian families in British cities at this time in British history.

Case Study 12: *The Ladykillers* (Mackendrick, 1955)

This was one of the films produced by Ealing Studios and, as so often with an Ealing film, comes with the prefix, Ealing Comedy. Essentially a crime caper comedy, the story is of a group of criminals whose get-away is eventually foiled by the unwitting Katie Johnson. This is a film in which the comedy is generated via situations, as well as plot movement. The fact that it proved impossible for the gang to 'despatch with' Katie, does to some degree predict her role in their eventually foiled plan.

This film also holds up a mirror to Britain in 1955. It presents a Britain in which individuals might well turn to crime to alleviate their boredom or extract themselves from a problematic economic situation. The film might initially appear to be little more than a light comedy, but ultimately acts as a very clever satire on British institutions and a comment on the British psyche in 1955.

Approaching Section B: Close study

Both Sections A and B of the FS3 exam concentrate on analysing the messages and values apparent in films from British and Irish Cinema. Your understanding of representation and ideology will be essential for both parts of the exam. These are the essential common threads between Section A and Section B, but there are obviously differences, too. The first, and most obvious difference between the 'comparative study' and the 'single film close study' is that the close study is based on one film, rather than a group of texts. There are three other important distinctions of which you should be aware, and these are outlined below.

1. Text, representation and ideology.
   This section of the exam asks you to offer much more detailed reference to particular sections of your close study film. You might choose a question in the exam that asks you to concentrate on the opening of your film, its closing sequence or a sequence of importance within the film's narrative. For this type of response, your knowledge of micro and macro features, and how these features have been used to generate meaning, will be very important. The extension of your textual analysis into a consideration of representation and ideology will be an essential step within this type of preparation.

2. Context.
   Your preparation for the close study section of this exam should also include production information for the film. You might consider the companies behind the film's production and the individuals who were significant in its creation. Your chosen film might be part of a long-running franchise of films, and thus continue certain generic elements, or elements of style, that were established in previous examples. Your film might have been created by a team who have become synonymous with a certain type of film making. You might

focus on a film whose director is considered to have a particular, recognizable style of film-making. All of these issues will be relevant to your answers.

3. Critical and popular reception.
Study of the critical and popular reception of your film should also provide part of your preparatory work. The way in which the film was received by critics, and the potential impact of critical opinion on the viewing public, should make up an element of your debate. Popular opinion concerning the film, whether this be in the form of popular reviews or box office receipts, will also be relevant. Remember that you are also part of the film's audience and your own response to it is of equal importance.

This section of the FS3 chapter will be organised around these three important areas within your preparation and will draw on particular examples from the syllabus in order to illustrate how to approach each of the core areas of study.

Text, representation and ideology

This section of your notes should contain details of the way in which the textual features of your film have been used to create representation and the way in which these representational features interact with the ideologies that surround your film. Remember that an ideology is a commonly shared belief, and a dominant ideology is one that is most apparent within society at any one time. Ideologies can concern sexuality, gender, nation, class, ethnicity and age, so you will need to explore what your film text is saying about these areas and how the film's opinions relate to the social world around that film.

Always begin your study of representation with the features of the film text itself. As you know from your FS1 study, sound, editing, *mise-en-scène* and cinematography are used to relay information to the film viewer. You also know from your FS1 studies that meanings relating to a character's state of mind, a character's importance within the narrative, and the impact of attitudes expressed by a particular character can all be understood through the study of micro and macro elements. These are the skills that you use to begin your study of representation and ideology. You could even practise this skill by freeze-framing your film and analysing a still. The *mise-en-scène* and camera angles evident within this still will relay information about that character's importance within the film and their psychological state.

Once you have identified the important textual features, you should then move into a discussion of what these seem to suggest about the way in which key issues in the film are being discussed. Whether the issue is gender, sexuality, nation or power, you will be able to identify the film's attitudes through its use of textual elements. The next stage of your study will be to consider how the film's attitudes relate to the attitudes of the world outside the film. If your film takes a particular stance on homosexuality, for example, then do you think that this is shared by society, or is the film challenging widely-held notions?

The case studies below look at how particular issues are discussed in some of the focus films available for study. You should use these case studies as templates for the preparation of your own notes.

Case Study 13: Representations of gender in *Chicken Run* (Lord and Park, 2000)

Source: British Film Institute

Chickens in a chicken run are female: their function is to provide eggs. In this animated film, however, the female 'characters' have a much more significant role. They motivate events and eventually create their own means of escape. The chickens in this film represent a range of different female 'types'; they also occupy many of the roles in this film that would traditionally have been designated male. In the opening sequence of the film, Ginger, the most determined of the chickens, attempts to escape from the coop. She is captured and thrown into a coal hole. The parallels with the film's source text is clear. Ginger takes on the Steve McQueen role from the film *The Great Escape*.

The *mise-en-scène* of *Chicken Run* is extremely significant when looking at gender within this film. Although they live in a chicken shed and all have the same kind of perch to sit on, the chicken's costumes help determine their part within the gender debate. Some chickens knit, others wear pearl necklaces and neckerchiefs. They are very much presented to look like housewives of the 1940s or 1950s. They serve a function within the chicken coop and are repressed by the farmer and his wife. Mrs Tweedy is Gestapo-like in her attire and exhibits the brutality of which her husband is incapable. It is Mrs Tweedy who kills the first of the chickens, thus setting off the narrative trajectory towards escape.

Rocky, Mr Tweedy and Fowler provide the main male characters in this film. The only others are two 'spiv' mice who attempt to swindle the chickens. Rocky, the rooster, is revealed as a fraud by the chickens. Mr Tweedy is controlled by his wife and Fowler's attempts to keep the chickens in line prove impotent. Ultimately, however, the male and the female characters of the film work together in their escape.

As the film transposes the male-occupied roles of *The Great Escape* onto the female chickens, it does suggest that the prescribed gender roles of the 1940s are no longer relevant. However, it is not simply that the male characters in this film are incompetent and the female characters achieve, because Mrs Tweedy is the arch-villain of the piece. What the film does is to subtly deconstruct archaic notions of female powerlessness and male power. This could even be said to be a film about female liberation.

Case Study 14: Representations of the family in *Secrets and Lies* (Leigh, 1996)

Source: British Film Institute

The issue of family is central to the narrative of *Secrets and Lies*. The central motivation of the characters is towards finding or re-establishing a family. This is not a film in which the nuclear family exists. The character of Hortense, a young professional black woman, attempts to find her birth mother after her adoptive mother has died. She discovers that her real mother is a white, working-class woman, called Cynthia. Cynthia has another daughter, Roxanne, with whom she has a very troubled relationship, and a brother, Maurice, on whom she relies for both emotional and economic support.

Families in this film are troubled or broken. Maurice and his wife cannot have children and treat their niece Roxanne as if she were their surrogate child. Cynthia gave her daughter Hortense away at birth and did not even realise that she was black. Maurice and Cynthia live in very different worlds. His is financially affluent and he has a wife and a business. Cynthia struggles financially and works in a dead-end job. The film's narrative draws everything towards a barbecue scene in which Cynthia tells her family about Hortense.

The film uses many different scenes to articulate its attitudes to the family. Cynthia and Hortense's first meeting is a horribly tense occasion, in which the *mise-en-scène* is stark and the camera is positioned directly in front of the women sitting on the same side of the table. The information that Hortense delivers is as inescapable as the cinematography. What the film relays, through its representation of the family, is that in contemporary society the family unit can be constructed in many different ways. Although it is an extreme representation of familial dynamics, *Secrets and Lies* does seem to reflect the many different types of family in existence in Britain today.

EXERCISE 7

With a partner in your film class, choose one scene from the film you are studying for this section of the exam. Using the case studies above and your own knowledge of how representation is constructed, write notes on how this particular scene discussed certain key issues within the film as a whole and how the film relates to social opinions.

Context

As has been outlined in the section above, there are a number of key issues and areas of study that you should consider for this section. The first area concerns the production information surrounding your close study film. The companies behind your film's production might influence the eventual look of your film, but they will certainly be significant in relation to the potential exposure of that film and its breadth of release. Try to ascertain how much artistic freedom the director of your focus film had while the film was in its production stages and determine whether there were any other influences connected to production on this film.

Case Study 15: *Chicken Run* (Lord and Park, 2000)

Chicken Run was written and directed by Peter Lord and Nick Park. Made with 'stop motion' animation, the film was produced by Aardman Animations (GB), Pathe Pictures Ltd (GB) and Dreamworks SKG (USA). Aardman was set up by Nick Park and his team, and its involvement in production ensured a good degree of artistic freedom for the film-making team. Earlier successes for the Aardman team, including *Wallace & Gromit: The Wrong Trousers* (1993) and *Wallace & Gromit: A Close Shave* (1995) helped to ensure this creative control. Although Steven Spielberg's Dreamworks SKG was one of the companies behind production, the presence of this Hollywood giant did not seem to change the style or feel of Aardman's latest production. *Chicken Run* eventually took $17,500,000 in its opening weekend in the US and £3,850,000 in its opening weekend in Britain. It was both a financial and critical success.

The role of a film within a famous franchise is an important one. Any new film under an existing franchise 'banner' has to at once continue the success of any previous films and engage the audience with new elements. For a franchise film to be successful, it must be recognizable as part of the larger group of films, but also extend audiences' viewing pleasures. Similar to the way in which a successful genre can be sustained, a franchise film must offer both the expected and the unexpected to audiences. Once a franchise has become 'tired', or no longer socially relevant, it cannot be sustained. The relevance of a franchise study within this section of the exam is that it will provide you with information about both the textual elements of the film and the audience's expectations of that film.

Case Study 16: *Goldfinger* (Hamilton, 1964)

This film is part of one of the most famous franchises in cinema history: the James Bond films. Goldfinger was co-produced by Albert 'Cubby' Broccoli and Harry Saltzman. This partnership dissolved in 1976 and Broccoli alone went on to produce many more film within the Bond franchise, but it was the films he produced with Saltzman in the early 1960s (*Dr No*, *Goldfinger* and *Thunderball)* that established the Bond franchise. Based on the novels of Ian Fleming, the Bond films were pure escapism. The maverick government agent, who invariably saved the world from total destruction, became iconic. Although *Goldfinger* came very early in the Bond franchise series, audiences already had expectations. This film needed to have the exotic locations, beautiful women and high-tech gadgetry which had become part of viewer's expectations since *Dr No*. The continued identification of Bond with the actor Sean Connery was also part of the perpetuation of the Bond fantasy.

The significance of the director of your focus film will depend upon whether or not that director can be associated with particular stylistic signatures. You might find that the film you are studying is one of your director's first, in which case the identification of characteristic elements might be retrospective. This will still be relevant to your comments. If the film you

Case Study 17: *The Thirty-Nine Steps* (Hitchcock, 1935)

Source: British Film Institute

1934 was the year in which Alfred Hitchcock's international reputation as a master of suspense and the thriller genre really began to be established. In this year he made *The Man Who Knew Too Much*, which told the story of a British couple, touring through Switzerland, who become embroiled in intrigue. This film introduced viewers and critics to many of Hitchcock's characteristic suspense devices, including the implication of the ominous and sinister, beneath apparently safe exteriors. *The Thirty-Nine Steps* continued in the

performance from Clive Owen. It deserves to be seen. But how galling that we needed America to tell us about it.

Review of *Croupier,* by Philip Strick, *Sight & Sound,* July 1999

To see *Croupier* as more writer Paul Mayersberg's work than director Mike Hodges' is a powerful temptation. But as *Get Carter* reminds us (looking on reissue like a cross between *Alfie,* 1966, and *Bande à part,* 1964), Hodges is unfailingly professional in matching style to story. He sets up the context for his players with a discretion verging on anonymity and then, on a whim, takes time out for a striking detail (for example, in 1974's *The Terminal Man,* the silent invasion of white floor-tiles by bloodied water). Even so, given his special fluency with long shots, the confines of *Croupier* have cramped Hodges considerably: this is a basement-flat London, briefly glimpsed between forests of mirrors.

Reflections are integral to Mayersberg's scenario, as might be expected after the emphatic self-regarding theme of his *Eureka* script. Hodges' contribution is to fashion the casino as a glass cage of distortions, the eye constantly deceived by misshapen figures and rippled furniture, as unreliable as the occupants. Otherwise, he captures with a merciless accuracy the bedsit decor, the cramped kitchens and sparse sitting rooms, tiny arenas of emotional combat. Even when the scene shifts to a country mansion, the sense of entrapment is maintained, and the camera lingers on a copy of Géricault's painting *The Raft of the Medusa* in recognition of a similar predicament: despair, madness and an intolerable intimacy unite the drifting group of the near-dead. Where Hodges and Mayersberg also seem well attuned is in the isolation of their wheel-spinner, a recognisable fusion of the two Jacks – Carter and McCann from *Eureka* – who fell to earth in their separate ways. The croupier particularly resembles *Eureka*'s lost plutocrat in finding his plot of gold, a best-seller, and freezing into satisfied inaction. In fact, Mayersberg's reported starting point for *Croupier* was Kurosawa's *The Hidden Fortress* (1958), in which two peasants share a befuddled panic on the edges of a tumultuous history far beyond their comprehension.

In *Get Carter* the ruthless hitman uncovers a malevolent network for whom his personal vendetta is insignificant. Similarly, in *Croupier* the dealer is not so much crushed as anaesthetised when he learns he's simply been a card in somebody else's winning hand all along. His compensation, apart from a slightly dodgy new girlfriend, is the daily opportunity to indulge in the joyful exercise of numbers, a hobby lifted directly from the father-daughter relationship in *Eureka.* His 'mission' accomplished, he hails himself master of the game with the power "to make you lose". This dubious accomplishment is neatly celebrated by sweeping the camera (us), along with a pile of gambling chips, down a conclusive black hole.

Part of the intricacy of *Croupier* (very Mayersbergian) lies in the intermingling of 'fiction' and 'reality', portions of the story being disguised as the croupier's novel. Since all the characters are living their own fictions anyway, the flatly-rendered dialogue, spoken as if quoting a text, adds to the sense of a writer shuffling phrases and episodes until he finds the most suitable. At one point the on-screen Jack even corrects the off-screen Jake, who has been chipping in throughout the film with information and opinion. Such ironies aside, and despite earnest performances by all concerned, *Croupier* is an absorbing rather than an appealing exercise. As the croupier's partner observes on first reading: "There's no hope in it." But the misanthropist is dismissive: "It's the truth," he says.

EXERCISE 9

Your own response will provide an important element within your discussions of the critical and popular reception of the film you are studying. This exercise asks you to cohere your thoughts on the film and create a review.

In 1000 words or less, write a review of your single focus film. This review should be aimed at a particular film publication or newspaper and should include the following:

- details of the director's filmography
- details of any characteristic elements of style or theme of the director within this film
- information relating to franchise or genre features
- your thoughts on the acting and characterisation within the film
- details of key sequences and the messages and values they contain
- your overall opinion of the film.

Exemplar essay Section A

Question: How important is childhood and children in the films you have studied for Scottish cinema?

Children and the experience of childhood is a very important feature within the films I have studied for Scottish cinema. Children and their childhood experiences are often used as a filter, through which adult behaviours and the main issues of the films are relayed to the viewer. This essay will concentrate on three films in answering the essay question: *Orphans* (Mullan, 1997), *Ratcatcher* (Ramsay, 1999) and *Small Faces* (McKinnon,1996).

Orphans is the story of four adult children whose mother has died and who have to prepare for her funeral. The death has an enormous impact and sends each one off into the Glasgow night to deal with their responses to the death and their own particular problems. Thomas is the eldest of the children and he deals with his grief by attempting to keep vigil over his mother's coffin until her funeral the next day. Thomas has now been left as the 'head' of the family, but it quickly becomes apparent that he does not have the resources to look after the rest of his siblings. After his sister, Sheila, who uses a wheelchair, has crashed into a statue of the Virgin Mary in the church in which the funeral is to be held, smashing the statue, Thomas lets her go home on her own. Thomas thinks of himself as the most responsible of the children, but essentially he abandons the others.

The remaining two children, Michael and John, embark on their own dramatic journey after Michael is stabbed in a pub brawl. John attempts to take revenge, but Michael is intent on surviving until the morning with his stab wound until he can go to work and try to claim false compensation. His anxieties are clear. He is separated from his wife, hates his job, now has lost his mother and is attempting to escape his life. John's revenge attempt is thwarted, but it is the masculine pride of the attempt that is perhaps of most significance. All three of the male children in this film flee the reality of their mother's death. Their own sense of hopelessness becomes their dominant motivation as they attempt to find some kind of meaning. In this film the children are not young, but they present childish characteristics, all the same.

In Lynne Ramsay's *Ratcatcher*, childhood is an extremely vulnerable time. The game that results in a drowning at the beginning of the film introduces the film's bleak and hazardous tone. The central character of this film is a 12-year-old boy, who is haunted by the role he had in the death of his friend. He lives on an estate that is covered with rubbish due to a strike by refuse collectors. This boy dreams of escape and fantasises about a new estate, with pristine houses and green fields, to which he would like to escape. The children in this film have little to do except play with the rubbish: either this, or act as a sexual plaything for the local teenage boys, as does the girl whom the young boy befriends. The deprivation of the estate, and the economic impoverishment of those who live on it, has created a very troubled environment for the young people in this film. The effects of economic troubles are all the more evident when shown through the lives of the children.

The viewer's central guide through events in *Small Faces* is Lex, a young boy who becomes wrapped up in the gang-saturated world of Glasgow in the 1960s. Lex is fascinated by the characters who join these gangs and becomes a bystander at many of their 'events'. His initial sense that the gang members are powerful, glamorous individuals is shattered, however, when the gang wars affect his own family. Lex's brother is killed on an ice rink and the true nature of the gangs becomes apparent to Lex. As with the young boy in *Ratcatcher*, Lex acts as the viewer's eyes and ears for the film's events. At some points, as in the scene where Lex is taken to 'Tongland' by rival gang members, a point-of-view shot allows us to see events from Lex's standpoint. The 1960s are not 'swinging' in the Glasgow of this film and the barbarity beneath the surface is what both the viewer and Lex discover.

In these films, children and childhood provides a vehicle through which the real meaning of situations can be understood. Whether the viewer is made to experience events with the child, or to understand the issues of the film through the experiences of that child, these characters are extremely important. The role of 'child' in these films is fraught, whether you are an adult or not, and being a child within an urban context is full of potential dangers.

Assessment comments

This essay chooses highly appropriate examples to consider the issues raised in the essay question. Each of the films mentioned is explored in detail, with comments concerning narrative, textual features and representation clearly supported by textual reference. The candidate draws distinctions between the examples used, as well as identifying common features. A very clear and well-argued essay. Grade A.

Exemplar essay Section B

Question: To what extent does the opening sequence of your single focus film introduce the viewer to the film's messages and values?

The opening sequence to Kapur's film *Elizabeth* clearly introduces the viewer to the messages and values of this film. The viewer will probably already have some existing knowledge of Queen Elizabeth I and the events that occurred during her reign, but they might not have much knowledge of the events that led up to her taking the throne and the political context that surrounded this event. *Elizabeth* explores issues of power, nation, gender and religion and the opening sequence does much to introduce the viewer to these issues.

We are told in the opening sequence that the date is 1554 and that Queen Mary, a devout Catholic, is on the throne. Immediately, the viewer has a context in which to place the events to come. This date is only a few years before Elizabeth's ascendance to the throne, so Mary must be nearing the end of her reign. The significance of Mary's religion becomes evident when the viewer sees the first actual images from the film.

The non-diegetic soundtrack that opens this film is of sixteenth-century music. The historical context of the film is thus confirmed and the rising pitch of this music within the opening sequence also serves to imply a state of high drama and panic. When the viewer eventually sees the Protestant prisoners, it is clearly evident whose panic is implied by the music.

The opening credit sequence of the film does much to introduce the genre, tone and issues of the film. The dates and events that are shown through text during this sequence indicate the film's historical drama credentials. The dominant colour of the opening credit sequence is red, indicating both royal lineage and the blood that will spill during this film. This credit sequence also merges images of crosses within the red saturation, signifying both the significance of religion to this film and religion's associations with death and bloodshed. The last image that dissolves into shot during this sequence is of Elizabeth herself. The image is not of the actress Cate Blanchett, but of the real monarch. As this image appears, so does the name of the film. The viewer understands that this film is historical in genre, but also understands the importance of monarchy and power within its thematic discussions.

Once the credit sequence has disappeared, the film moves into real-life events. Red saturation of the opening sequence colouring is echoed in what we then see of events. The Catholicism of Mary, indicated in the opening credits, can now be understood to be so fervent as to be crushing of Protestantism. The credit sequence cuts to images of three Protestant prisoners having their hair brutally cut off. The knives used to do this are covered with blood and the viewer quickly understands that these individuals are going to their deaths. The power of the monarch and the dominance of their religious convictions is starkly apparent.

The prisoners are led out into a courtyard, to their deaths, and the viewer is positioned above them, as if looking down on events. This is an observational and powerless position to be in and it is clear that whatever the monarch dictates will happen, regardless of its barbarity. The Protestants appear very small, vulnerable and terrified in the next overhead shot as they are placed on a pyre, waiting to be burnt alive. The sequence then uses a series of mid-shots and close-ups to show both the terror of the prisoners and the anguished faces of the crowd around them. Their burning does not seem to be a popular decision, and so the power of the throne to order events, even if these are contrary to public opinion, is clear. The crowd attempts to help the Protestants and a frenzied series of mid-shots are used to illustrate the crowd's attempts to help the agonised prisoners die more quickly. The crowds are held back in their attempt and through the flames, the viewer can see a Catholic bishop surveying events impassively. The inhumanity of actions motivated entirely by religious difference seems all too clear.

The opening sequence ends with the frame filling up with frames, as the non-diegetic sound rises to a pitch of frenzy. The next cut is into near silence and whiteness.

The halls of power are calm, but what has happened in the opening sequence has been frantic and brutal. This opening sequence establishes religion, power, oppression, the monarchy and justice as key areas of debate within *Elizabeth*.

Assessment comments

A very clear and systematic answer, which moves confidently through the sequence, identifying textual characteristics and then evaluating these in terms of messages and values. There is excellent knowledge of film form and film language in this answer and a very good level of understanding of representational debate. Grade A.

Formal questions to consider: Section A

The war and its aftermath
1. How important is class within the films you have studied from this period?
2. How are Britain and the British public represented in the films you have studied for this topic?

Swinging Britain
1. To what extent is the idea of social revolution discussed in the films you have studied for this topic?
2. How are youth and age represented in the films you have studied?

Passions and repressions
1. What are the main tensions experienced by characters within the films you have studied for this topic?
2. Do the films you have studied represent different types of passion and repression?

Social and political conflict
1. To what extent are the conflicts personal or social in your focus films?
2. How important is gender within the films you have looked at for this topic?

Scottish cinema
1. How is Scotland and Scottishness represented in the films you have studied?
2. To what extent do you think masculinity is a common area of discussion within Scottish films?

Comedy

1. To what extent do you think the use of stereotypes is a common element within the films you have studied?

2. Do the films you have studied for this section attempt to challenge audience assumptions about particular issues?

Formal questions to consider: Section B

1. In what ways does the opening sequence of your film introduce the viewer to the messages and values of the film?

2. How important is a knowledge of the director and his/her work to an appreciation of a film?

3. From your knowledge of the critical and popular reception surrounding your film, discuss what the key issues in the film were for critics and for audiences.

Looking forward to the A2 year

Moving on to A2 Film Studies

The A2 year of your A level Film Studies introduces you to a variety of different films and film styles.

The film texts you covered in the FS1 and FS3 units were English-language films made in America, Britain or Ireland. The film industry study that you completed for the FS2 exam was also related to either the British or Hollywood systems.

The exams and coursework within the A2 year broaden your study of film considerably. The second year of A level Film Studies requires you to complete an individual research project and a piece of creative work. All of the skills and knowledge you gained during the AS year will be relevant to your A2 study and you should ensure that you make full use of them, and build on them.

The A2 year is divided into three units: FS4, FS5 and FS6. FS4 is a coursework unit and constitutes 40 per cent of your A2 grade. FS5 and FS6 are examined units and contribute 30 per cent each to your overall A2 score.

FS4: Making Meaning 2 is designed to test your research skills and ability to apply the film-related knowledge you have gained within a creative task. It presents two exciting challenges. The first is to choose a director, performer or studio and create a research project focusing on a question of your choice. The second part of the FS4 unit invites you to create an original short film, portfolio of film journalism or screenplay.

The FS5 exam focuses on World Cinema. It requires you to study an individual foreign language film *and* a film movement from another country. You may, within the first section of this exam, find yourself looking in detail at the films created in Japan between 1950 and 1970. Or, you might concentrate on Surrealist and Fantasy cinema. Whatever film movement you study, you will be extending your skills of textual analysis into a consideration of how particular film movements came about in different countries and why. The second part of this unit looks at a single film from World Cinema. Your knowledge of micro and macro features, and your knowledge of representation, will be essential for this section, but again, you will have opportunity to extend your understanding of film by considering the national context of your focus film and how this affected the style and content of the film.

FS6 brings all of your previous learning together in a consideration of a range of cinema-related, critical studies. By this point in the course, you will be a skilled film analyst, but this unit asks you to consider far more than just the films themselves. The FS6 exam focuses on critical approaches to film and asks you to evaluate how useful it is to study films using a framework of criticism.

Continuing your independent studies

As with the AS year, the more experience you have of film, the better your exam answers and coursework will be. You should aim to extend your knowledge beyond what you learn in the classroom by watching films similar in style to those shown by your teacher. Read film journalism in newspapers and magazines to extend your knowledge of texts and of critical approaches.

Your film diary

If you began a film diary at the beginning of your course (as suggested in the Introduction to this book), it will be very useful to continue with it during your A2 studies. Make notes on:

* the films you watch and the relevance they have to the A2 unit you are studying

* your own developing sense of the function of film and its relationship with its audience.

All of this background work will differentiate your coursework and exam answers from the others and will help ensure that you achieve the overall A level Film Studies grade you want.

Chapter 4

Film: Making Meaning 2 (FS4)

Overview of the FS4 Unit

You have to create two projects for the FS4 unit: one is a research-based task and the other is a creative project. The FS4 unit focuses on the relationship between those who create film texts and the film texts themselves. In essence, for the research project you are asked to consider how evident a film maker's particular style is across a range of their work and for the practical work you are asked to create a project that expresses your own style. There are no prescribed texts, individuals or production teams for this unit and you can make your choices from either mainstream or independent cinema. The FS4 unit will make up 40 per cent of your marks for A2 Film Studies and 20 per cent of your overall A level mark.

Skills required for Unit FS4

The FS4 unit is divided into two sections:

- the Auteur Research Project
- the Practical Application of Learning.

The two tasks have an equal allocation of marks – 50 each – and between them you are required to exhibit five core skills:

1. An ability to analyse the form, style and themes within films closely.
2. An ability to identify recurring features of form, style and theme across a range of films.
3. An ability to discuss how critical approaches, such as genre and authorship theory, can be used to assess film texts.
4. An ability to carry out a focused research task into films and their creators.
5. An ability to create practical work that shows understanding and consideration of the chosen medium – film journalism, screenwriting or film/video production.

These five skills are not completely new to you. Both the FS1 and FS3 units in your AS Film Studies asked you to consider how form, style and theme function within a film and you will have already, albeit implicitly, begun to notice recurring features within certain films. Your FS1 studies of genre also introduced you to a way of distinguishing one film from another, so you have already looked at how one critical approach can be used to assess films. The practical work you completed during FS1 will also be essential background for your projects within this unit.

Task 1: The Auteur Research Project

'Auteur' is the French word meaning author. For the purposes of this unit an auteur is an individual or a group who produces film texts with recognisable 'signatures', or characteristics. The individual or group can be associated within any national cinema, so you do not have to confine yourself to Hollywood, or British and Irish cinema. Your task for this section of the unit is to create a research title that considers the relationship between the auteur and the texts they create. For the purposes of this unit, the term auteur has three possible applications:

- the director as auteur
- the performer as auteur
- the producer or production team as auteur.

The director as auteur

If you choose to study a director, you will be considering whether or not that director has recognisable signatures (stylistic, formal or thematic) that can be identified across a number of that director's films. You might consider whether it is possible to identify an individual's signature within the collaborative film-making practice. You could concentrate on whether a particular director has brought their own signature to a particular genre. You would also have to evaluate whether it is useful to identify particular directors as auteurs, thus elevating them above the rest of the directing community.

You have thousands of directors to choose from for this type of auteur project, but it is essential that you choose a director of whom you have some prior knowledge. Try to choose someone whose films you have already seen and find interesting – someone who you already think might have a style that makes their films recognisable. You will have to choose a director who has made at least three films and it is advisable to choose a director who has made quite a few more than three, so that your potential frame of reference is broad enough. A certain amount of critical distance is required to create an effective project, so you should try not to choose a director about whom you might write a purely fan-motivated project. There are no prescribed directors for this project, but below are a few examples of directors who might make an interesting focus for your project:

- Tim Burton
- Jim Jarmusch
- Pedro Almodovar
- David Lynch

- Sally Potter
- Jane Campion
- John Woo
- Lars von Trier
- Howard Hawks
- David Cronenberg
- Kathryn Bigelow
- Billy Wilder
- Spike Lee
- Alfred Hitchcock.

The performer as auteur

If you choose to focus on a performer for your auteur project, then you will need to evaluate whether or not the performer brings their own particular style or signature to the films in which they star. Does the performer bring a recognisable element to films of particular genres? Is there a type of role, style of acting or interaction with other performers that could be said to be the significant recognisable element within the performer's films? Does the performer have any control over the production process of the films in which they star? You should try to choose a performer whose presence within a film can be said to be a defining element within that film. As with the director-based auteur project, there are literally thousands of performers on whom you could focus. Below is a list of some performers whose performances would lend themselves well to auteur scrutiny:

- Marlene Dietrich
- Cary Grant
- James Stewart
- Charlie Chaplin
- Robert de Niro
- Greta Garbo
- Marilyn Monroe
- Cate Blanchett
- Gong Li
- Jackie Chan.

The producer or production team as auteur

The third possibility for your auteur project is to study a producer, a production team or a studio and to consider whether there are consistent elements of style, form or theme within the films they have produced. You will need to choose a producer or a production team who have produced a body of work that has neither the signature of a director or performer, but seems to exhibit a set of characteristics connected with the production process. You could focus on Ealing Studios, for example, and assess whether there was any house style of production. You might consider whether Pixar films have signature elements, regardless of who is directing them. There are many possible avenues of enquiry for this type of project – you could also research into the circumstances that surrounded the production of a group of films. Were there any issues of historical context that affected film production? Who were the key personnel within the collaborative film-making process and what was their particular input?

Auteur theory: creating your auteur project title

As with any research project, a good title is crucial. For your auteur project, you should ensure that your title is small-scale and focused. Your project can be a maximum of 2000 words. This might seem like a lot – however, you will probably find that you have researched far more information than can be contained within this word limit. This is why you must have a clearly defined title for your project; one which has clear research limits. Your project title must also include a 'problematic' i.e. a question that focuses on a tension, a dynamic or a balance of input. Titles that are too broad, or that do not include a question to research, will not provide an adequate prompt for your project.

EXERCISE 1

In pairs, consider the two sets of possible auteur project titles below. First, decide on the set of questions you think are the most focused. Then identify the set of questions that include a 'problematic' and discuss with your partner what type of problematic is being used.

Set 1

- Has John Woo retained an auteur signature throughout his Hong Kong and Hollywood films?
- Has Kathryn Bigelow brought her own style to the action film genre?
- To what extent does the presence of Marlene Dietrich within a film shape that film's content and style?
- What influence do the directors of Pixar films have on the eventual products released?

Set 2

- What signatures can be found in the work of John Ford?
- What makes Guy Ritchie's gangster films different from those of other directors?

- What are the specific features of performance seen in the films of Jack Nicholson?
- How have Disney films developed over the years?

As you have probably already established, the first set of titles are those that would make for good auteur projects. The questions all have a precise focus and imply debate. The second set of titles are too vague. They offer questions, but assume an answer and do not offer a research focus.

When you have settled on a title for your project, your next task will be to choose your focus films. You should not focus on more than four or five films, as a wider focus would make your project too far-reaching and potentially vague. Make sure that the films you choose exhibit consistencies you can discuss. These consistencies might be thematic, stylistic or formal. If the auteur you are studying has a large filmography, you could define your focus films through era, or perhaps decade.

The elements of the auteur project: the catalogue and commentary

The syllabus states that this section of your research project must include:

'A collection of materials from a variety of sources, with a commentary on the materials listed in the catalogue' (500 words, excluding the catalogue).

Catalogue

A selection of materials concerning your chosen auteur, derived from a variety of sources e.g. the internet, books, magazines, TV programmes and DVD extras.

You will need to include at least ten different resources, chosen from the source types listed above.

For each of your resources, you will need to include (where applicable) details of the author, publisher, date, web address, date of transmission, distributor etc.

Commentary

The commentary is the section of your project in which you evaluate the resources you used. You will need to comment on:

- the influence of your sources on the title of your project and the films you have chosen for your focus
- the resources that were particularly useful in relation to your project title and what kinds of information you gained from that resource
- any resources that you found problematic or that were not particularly useful.

Case Study 1: Catalogue and commentary

Auteur Project Title: To what extent do 'Beat' Takeshi's widespread involvement in many facets of film-making and his highly individual style of direction define him as an auteur?

Catalogue and commentary

1. *Sight & Sound*, December 1997. 'The Harder Way' an interview with Takeshi Kitano.

2. The films of Takeshi Kitano on DVD: *Violent Cop, Hana-Bi, Brother*.

3. Review of *Violent Cop* from the unofficial Takeshi fansite, by Christopher Cameron. www.geomatics.kth.se/sjoberg/homepage/violentc.htm

4. Review of *Hana-Bi* by film critic Roger Ebert from: www.suntimes.com

5. Filmography information from the Internet Movie Database: www.imdb.com

6. Biographical information found on the Internet Movie Database.

7. Information on each of my focus films taken from links from the Internet Movie Database.

8. 27-minute documentary on the life and works of Kitano 'Beat' Takeshi 'A Scene by the Sea', taken from a DVD extra on the *Hana-Bi* DVD. Momentum Pictures.

The above selection of resources I managed to get hold of aided me a great deal, both in finding out specific information about Takeshi and his films, and also in understanding Takeshi Kitano as a member of the Japanese 'A' list of celebrities. Also, the biographical detail helped me to put into perspective the changes that have occurred in his films over his long career. I chose my three focus films as I had previously been alerted to the quality and originality of Takeshi's films by friends and by reviews in film magazines. The three films also span a decade and as such, provide the possibility for more informed comments concerning the changes in direction that Takeshi's cinematic style has taken over the years. Conversely, any similarity in films made such a long time apart would rule out time, or changing political context, as factors that have influenced the content and style of his films, and further highlight the input of the director himself as the main creative contributor.

Most of my research came from numerous internet sources, which may have worked to my disadvantage as this information cannot be controlled in any way and therefore must be regarded with a certain degree of scepticism as to its reliability. However, I managed to substantiate most of the information that these sources gave me with other (arguably) more reliable sources. The documentary: 'A Scene by the Sea' was one such source, which offered excellent confirmation of the internet sites. The IMDb was a particularly useful internet source, especially for institutional and biographical detail.

EXERCISE 2

With a partner, read through the case study on catalogue and commentary, above. What do you notice about:

- the range of source types?
- the range of resources?
- the evaluation of the source material?

Make a list of all of the elements of the case study that you consider makes it a good catalogue and commentary and any elements you think could be improved.

The presentation script

The syllabus states that your Research Project must include:

'The findings of the research, highlighting points of interest, in the form of an investigation script' (1000 words maximum, 40 per cent).

When you are writing this section, you will need to make sure that you include the following information:

1. An indication that you have knowledge of the breadth of your director/performer/ studio/production team's filmography (although you do not have to list every film). You could state the number of films made and the length of your director's career.

2. Identification of the three films you have chosen as your focus films and a discussion of *why* you chose these films.

3. Clear identification of the signature characteristics you think are evident in your director/ performer/studio/production team's films. These may be formal, stylistic or thematic.

4. Comment on the main institutional considerations connected with your director/ performer/studio/production team e.g. attitude of studio, budget issues or cast. Your director might have worked with the same actors or production crew across a number of films – this information would be relevant to your discussion. Your performer might regularly work for the same director or studio, and your studio or production team might be connected with a particular director.

5. A discussion of the reception of the films you have chosen. Critical reviews, box-office figures and fan reviews would be useful to your discussion.

6. Biographical information about your auteur that may have been influential on their films.

7. Discussions of influences on your chosen director e.g. other film makers, film movements, expectations or conventions of particular genres.

Your investigation script *must* include reference to the sources you identified in your catalogue. Make sure that you indicate the sources and resources that are related to the points you are making in this section of your project. As this section of your project is called a presentation script, it can be written in a way that could be presented. Rather than using an essay structure for your work, you might decide to create a series of bullet points, with explanatory notes. You might also like to create digital slides, which you could then annotate.

Case Study 2: Presentation script

Auteur Project title: With particular reference to the films produced in the period 1981–1988, how does Terry Gilliam construct his particular image of the fantastical and does this make him an auteur?

Presentation script

Terry Gilliam was born in Minneapolis in 1940. From a young age he was influenced by cartoons and animation, which have made him the actor, writer, animator and primarily director he is today. As a child, Gilliam enjoyed Disney's animated films, *Pinocchio* being a particular favourite. He was captivated by its dark, rich images, such as children turning into donkeys, and children in cages, and these images have had a lasting impact on his work. In The *Ten Best Animated Films of All Time* (item 2), Gilliam states: '. . . I notice that every film I have made features a scene with somebody in a cage – a trait I attribute to watching *Pinocchio*.' Later in his life, Gilliam continued to be influenced by the animation of the time. To his list of influential animated films, he adds Wladyslaw Starewicz's *The Mascot* (1934), Tex Avery's *Red Hot Riding Hood* (1943), Dave Fleischer's *Out of the Ink Well* (1938), Stan van der Beek's *Death Breath* (1964) and several others. Gilliam's maturation was coloured by each and every one, but in different ways – in these animations he saw Surrealism for the first time, as well as everything from the simplest animation puns, to the most breathtaking and extraordinary work, 'encompassing everything that Jan Svankmajer, Walerian Borowczyk and the Quay Brothers would do subsequently' (item 2). As well as these influences, Gilliam has always enjoyed drawing cartoons (item 5), as a way to impress and entertain people, and has persisted, despite being criticised for his preference for cartoons over paintings.

After graduating with a degree in political science, Gilliam worked as a writer/illustrator for magazines and advertising agencies. Later he moved to London, where he met the *Monty Python* team and worked as part of their team to create surreal animation, which would work alongside, or directly with, their sketches. By this point, it is clear that his vision of the fantastical was deeply rooted. The animation he created for the *Python* team was the culmination of all of the artistic skills and impressions he had accumulated over the years. In hindsight, even Gilliam himself finds it hard to see how he created such amazing images. In an interview as part of BBC2's *Monty Python*

Night (item 8), broadcast in 2001, he states: '. . . the guy who did it isn't me. I mean that it is somebody else who did it. I mean, I recognise some of me in it, but it's not, and I dunno how I thought of those things quite honestly. I look at them . . . and Jesus! How did my mind . . . what was my mind doing? How did I get to that point?' From this quotation, it is obvious that Gilliam's mind is constantly changing to encompass the new and exciting things he sees. After *Monty Python* disbanded in 1976, Gilliam continued to animate, but also went on to perform, write and direct.

The characteristics of Gilliam's fantastical auteur signature are:

- a fascination and focus on ordinary situations and flawed human lives, which are changed in some way by fantastical elements
- the reflection of Gilliam himself in one of the main characters
- a visual outpouring of all of the thoughts and ideas Gilliam has been collecting
- the use of animation and computer-generated special effects which are a clear link to Gilliam's influences over the years.

In 1981, Gilliam directed his second feature film, *Time Bandits* (item 15), which he also wrote and produced. Part of the purpose of this film was to procure enough money to make *Brazil* (1985), the screenplay on which he was already working. Finally, he co-wrote and directed *The Adventures of Baron Munchausen* in 1988. *Time Bandits* follows the story of Kevin, who is on an adventure with time-travelling little people, who want to use their time travel abilities to steal treasures from other periods of history. There are obvious links to other narratives, for example, the appearance of the little people through Kevin's wardrobe is not dissimilar to *The Lion, the Witch and the Wardrobe,* and there are close links to *The Wizard of Oz* as well. As Bob McCabe points out in an interview with Gilliam: '. . . the bandits are the munchkins, obviously, but also the supreme being as Oz, time as the yellow brick road and the dream structure of the movie . . .' (item 13, p.96). *Time Bandits* is essentially a retreat into childhood for Gilliam, a sentiment that he admits himself. He used small people in the film because he wanted it to be from Kevin's point of view. But there are other characteristics that are very true to Gilliam's personal vision of the fantastical. For example, when the small people push against Kevin's bedroom wall, the whole wall moves along and makes his room about three times as big. The time-travelling portholes also open in totally random places, and to add a touch of humour, the time travellers always fall out of the porthole onto the same couple. Although *Time Bandits* is aimed at a family audience, it does address some big issues, such as: 'Why does there have to be evil?' (item 13, p.90). Audience reception of the film in the UK was not very good. Despite good reviews, it failed to perform at the box-office, and never really reached its target audience, which was, of course, children. In the US, the film was much more successful.

Brazil is probably Gilliam's greatest film. It is set in the future, in an Orwellian society, in which pen pushers control everybody's lives: a strong comment on today's society. The film is a manifesto of Gilliam's darkest humour – Mrs Buttle is charged for the cost of the state, and for mistakenly arresting, interrogating and killing, Mr Buttle. This is a skill that Gilliam learned from Harvey Kurtzman – 'the ability to not merely sense and elaborate upon the grotesqueries of everyday life, but to never lose sight of the fact that the world and its people, even at their most malign, almost always remain hopelessly, unavoidably, human, and therefore are best looked upon with humour, rather than despair' (item 10, p.116). Gilliam says of his film: 'I have a theory about *Brazil*, in that it was a very difficult film for a pessimist to watch, but it was OK for an optimist to watch it. For a pessimist it just confirms his worst fears; an optimist could somehow find a grain of hope in the ending.' (item 11, pp. 3–4).

The sets in *Brazil* are an important and spectacular part of the film, and they truly reflect Gilliam's fantastical vision. The images of buildings with pipelines running through them can be seen in the animation he created for *Monty Python*, and the cityscape is in stark contrast to what the main character, Sam Lowry, dreams about. Dreams are a recurring theme in Gilliam's work. *Time Bandits* followed a dream structure, and dreams are very important in *Brazil*, because Lowry has his own idyllic fantasy in his head. At the very end of the film, he is saved by being able to retreat into his own dreamland. Overall, I think that *Brazil* is Gilliam's most surreal film, disturbingly so, because in some ways it is so close to reality. The film was very popular, despite being compared closely to Michael Radford's new version of *1984*, released just before *Brazil*.

The Adventures of Baron Munchausen is famous for its enormous and extravagant budget, and for the amount of problems Gilliam faced while filming in Italy and Spain. The film cost about $35 million to make; $10 million above the original budget. To add to the disruption caused by the financial wrangling between producers and distributors: '. . . costume shipments were trapped in a customs strike, animals and cast members were felled by illness, storms wrecked sets, and crew members were fired or fled in alarming numbers' (item 4, p. 2). It was purely Gilliam's will to make his film that eventually got it completed. The costumes and sets on *Munchausen* were spectacular and extravagant, adding to the fantastical screenplay Gilliam had crafted with the original *Munchausen* stories as its base. Again, Gilliam's auteur signature can be seen here – most memorably in the scene in which Venus mimics Botticelli's painting of Venus – a style of imagery and humour that was a regular feature within the *Monty Python* series.

Terry Gilliam's auteur signature is something he has crafted over a number of years, both consciously and subconsciously. His films are very personal to him – this is obvious from the amount of control he has over them, and the regular appearance of the same actors, such as Jonathon Pryce, Winston Dennis, and of course, several of his fellow

Pythons: John Cleese, Michael Palin and Eric Idle. Gilliam himself also appears in his narratives – he is Kevin, Sam Lowry and Baron Munchausen. He creates his own vision of the fantastical in all of his films by retaining enough control over them in order that he might express his dreams. His visions and dreams date back to the earliest influences he had as a child, and continue to change as he sees new ideas and images. Writer Jack Womack sums this process up perfectly: 'Gilliam has, through the years, developed his own view of existence so clearly, and so deftly, that to a degree greater than any other director, he is now able to create any kind of world, historical or imaginary, and make it absolutely believable and understandable to the audience.' (item 10, p. 114).

EXERCISE 3

Having read through the presentation script above, consider which pieces of information might be placed under the following headings:

1. Biographical
2. Textual
3. Contextual
4. Institutional

Do you consider the balance between these different types of information to be effective? Does this presentation script move systematically through the focus films and the points about them? Do you think that this is a good example of a presentation script?

The evaluation

The syllabus states that your Auteur Evaluation must include:

'A brief analysis of your own research methodology and brief critical reflection on the validity of an 'auteur' approach to your chosen subject' (500 words, 15 per cent).

You will need to include in this section:

1. A description of your research methodology i.e. how you found information and where you found particularly useful information.
2. An evaluation of your methodology. Was there information you found difficult to get hold of? Was your means of collecting information successful?
3. A summary of the factors that led you to identify your director/performer/studio/ production team as an auteur.

4. Your own thoughts on whether or not it is useful to identify certain individuals or groups as auteurs. Does it enhance our appreciation of their work, or limit it? Does auteur theory allow for productive analysis of directors/performers/studios/production teams and their work, or is it elitist?

Case Study 3: Evaluation

Project Title: Stanley Kubrick has worked within many different genres. Given the diversity of his filmography, to what extent can an individual auteur signature be identified across his work?

Evaluation

Before starting my research, I considered a number of film makers who I was interested in and admired. My first choice would have been Aronofsky, but decided against this director as the focus for my project because of his limited filmography. I am more interested in film technique and style than background and production information, so I designed a question that reflected my interests. With my question in mind, I searched through the resources I had gathered. I already owned copies of most of Kubrick's films, but used my college and local libraries to gather other sources. I did not find it difficult to find information on Kubrick due to the considerable academic and popular interest in his work. I had access to an archive of *Empire* magazines, which furnished me with more popularist reviews; and the Channel Four documentary, screened during a Kubrick season, offered me a particularly useful and more academic resource.

I have to admit that before I began this project, I already considered Stanley Kubrick to be an auteur. My research offered yet more substantiation for this view. The amount of control Kubrick had during the making of his films was considerable. His work displays a unique vision that brought new 'tones' to each of the genres he worked within. I was impressed by Kubrick's ability to produce an eclectic range of films, in varying film genres, which all expressed his particular signature. Is it elitist, however, to describe Kubrick (or any other director for that matter) as an auteur? I think the answer to this question lies in the definition of the term auteur. I consider an auteur to be a director who brings something of themselves to every project which they undertake and does not capitulate to external demands – someone who aims to achieve a unique vision. Using this definition, Stanley Kubrick definitely fits auteur criteria. I do not attribute a standard to the title of auteur. Bringing one's own signature to a film does not guarantee an amazing film product. It seems to me that what auteur theory enables critics and students of film to do is identify a style of film making, not a level of it.

EXERCISE 4

Read through the evaluation above. What does it say about:

1. Research procedures?
2. The usefulness of a critical framework, such as auteur theory?

Exemplar auteur project 1: Pedro Almodovar

Title: How far does Pedro Almodovar's treatment of controversial and challenging issues/themes establish him as a distinctive auteur?

Women on the Verge of a Nervous Breakdown.
Source: British Film Institute

Catalogue and commentary

1. Paul Julian Smith *Desire Unlimited: The cinema of Pedro Almodovar* (Verso, 2000).
2. Barry Jordan and Rikki Morgan-Tamosunas *Contemporary Spanish Cinema* (Manchester University Press, 1998).
3. Internet Movie Database www.imdb.com
4. Official Pedro Almodovar site at www.clubcultura.com/clubcine/clubcineastas/almodovar
5. Sony site for *All About my Mother*, including interview with Almodovar at www.sonypictures.com/classics/allaboutmymother
6. Review of *All About my Mother* at www.haro-online.com/movies/allaboutmymother
7. Online Guardian review of *Talk to Her* by Peter Bradshaw at www.guardianunlimited.co.uk/Critic_Review/Guardian_Film_of_the_Week
8. *The Radio Times Guide to Films* (BBC Worldwide Ltd, 2000).
9. *The Late Show* documentary on Pedro Almodovar (BBC Two, 1994).
10. DVDs of *All About My Mother, Women on the Verge of a Nervous Breakdown, Talk to Her, The Flower of My Secret* and *What Have I Done to Deserve This?*

I discovered that the most efficient and accessible way of finding out more about Almodovar and his films was through the internet. This was because much of the published work I found was in Spanish, and if Spanish language information was found on the internet, it could be easily translated. I also wanted to make sure that I took into account critical writing on Almodovar from within his own country, as this might give a more culturally-specific angle on his work and use of certain themes and images. Some of the internet information had to be double-checked, however, in order to ensure relevance and accuracy. I found *The Guardian* site of great use as it included reviews of Almodovar's films from different reviewers, often with differing opinions. It is evident from my research into the reviews of Almodovar's films that the critical reception of his films varies and this was one of the factors behind my decision to investigate his work. I chose Pedro Almodovar as my focus director primarily because of the perennial debates concerning his use of controversial themes and subject matter. I found the publications in my catalogue useful in determining signature characteristics of Almodovar's style. *Desire Unlimited*, in particular, helped me to establish stages in Almodovar's film-making career and to consider the social context of his work. The BBC Two documentary gave biographical detail, which was useful in my consideration of the influence of Almodovar's life and cinema experiences on his work. It also gave very useful detail concerning the impact of the Franco era on Almodovar and his role in *La Movida*, the post-Franco artistic movement. The tension between a director's life and the films they produce, and the way in which this tension manifests itself, is one of the factors that can help define an auteur, and this project will hopefully debate this tension within Almodovar's work. As well as studying my focus films (*All About My Mother*, *Women on the Edge of a Nervous Breakdown* and *Talk to Her*), I also watched Almodovar's earlier films, such as *The Flower of My Secret* and *What Have I done to Deserve This?*, in order to establish whether or not the same kinds of controversial subject matter are apparent in these and his later work. The sources within my catalogue were almost universal in their discussion of Almodovar as a director whose work is characterised by the use of controversial material and whose films are often received by audiences and critics in quite conflicting ways. This auteur study will focus on whether Almodovar's use of particular themes and images is intended to impart meaning and generate discussion, or whether its intention is merely to shock. The auteur status of Almodovar to a large extent hinges on whether there is an artistic integrity behind the willingness to shock.

Presentation script

In Item 8, Pedro Almodovar is described as the 'King of Kitsch'. This statement might give newcomers to Almodovar's films a taste of what to expect. His films have become famous for their quirky characters, intriguing plot twists and, most importantly, their original portrayal of controversial issues, such as sexuality, gender and violence. This factor alone might establish him as an auteur – a director who takes risks, challenges audiences and breaks from convention. Since Almodovar's first feature film *Pepi, Luci, Bom* (1980), he has continued to shock and challenge audiences with the direction of the 13 films that followed.

Almodovar emerged from an arts movement in Spain called '*La Movida*' (Item 9). After the death of General Franco, many Spanish artists became involved in this pop-cultural movement (Item 2). Francoism maintained a highly traditional perspective towards gender and sexuality and many restrictions were in place concerning how these values and ideas were expressed in the arts. Once this cultural and political oppression was lifted in Spain, Almodovar produced some of the most distinctive Spanish cinema since the work of Luis Bunuel (Item 3). Other directors, such as Carlos Saura and Jaime Chavarri, along with Almodovar, have become synonymous with post-Franco cinema. This was a new, explosive kind of cinema, focusing on subject matter that had previously been banned.

I chose to focus on three of Almodovar's films. *Women on the Edge of a Nervous Breakdown* (1988) was chosen not only because it is Almodovar's most successful film (Item 8), but also because it uses a filter of comedy to explore the issues of adultery and heartbreak. *All About My Mother* (1999) was chosen because it was supposedly the film that broke Almodovar into mainstream cinema. This film presents an array of different characters, some of whom are transsexual and two who have AIDS. *Talk to Her* (2002) explores rape, homosexuality and illness. These three films also represent women in very different ways. Almodovar's representation of women and presentation of his female characters has been much debated. His representation of sexual violence against women, in particular, has caused much controversy. Almodovar has used comedy as a means of presenting rape, for example. I decided not to focus on either *Kika* (1993) or *Tie Me Up, Tie Me Down!* (1989), which both include graphic scenes of sexual violence and employ comedy within their representation of rape. These two films received much criticism for their (apparently) flippant portrayal of sexual violence and I decided to focus on how controversial subject matter was used in Almodovar's more critically acclaimed work.

Almodovar tackles issues as part of the narrative and character development within his films. This contributes to the auteur signature within his work and can be seen in the themes he uses and also within the way in which he explores challenging subject matter. Almodovar's films often present scenarios in ways which provoke a conflicting response in the viewer. This can be seen in the way that rape is explored in *Talk to Her*, where Benigno rapes Alicia while she is in a coma. Peter Bradshaw, in *The Guardian* (Item 7) commented on the extraordinary way in which this was portrayed. He describes how initially feelings of sympathy arise for the victim and anger towards the rapist. Yet Almodovar manages to alter this initial response. The scene is drenched in

Mediterranean sun and 'cartoon-like hues' (Item 9) and the rape then seems to become part of Alicia and Begnigno's 'relationship'. Begnigno is presented as being alienated and lonely. Alicia hasn't *not* consented to sex, so is this really rape? The *mise-en-scène* and characterisation within this scene provide a means for the film to confuse the viewer and make them question their initial responses. As with many of Almodovar's films, intertextuality is used within this scene. *The Shrinking Lover*, a silent film in which a shrunken man has sex with his lover while she is sleeping, is referenced during the rape of Alicia. This comedic reference only serves to confuse the audience of *Talk to Her* further. Almodovar seems to be asking the viewer to question their own moral values, as well as those of Begnigno.

With *All About My Mother*, Almodovar presents women in many different roles. The central protagonist, Manuela, loses her teenage son when he is run down and killed by a car, and the movement of the film is towards her coming to terms with this loss. As well as her own, Manuela experiences the tragedies and losses of the other characters within the narrative. The potentially controversial component of this film is the use of transsexual characters and the comic filter Almodovar employs to discuss their plight. The character La Agrado's 'speech', for example, fuses comedy and pathos to discuss authenticity. Agrado's message is that the physical appearance of a gender does not necessarily render a person an 'authentic man' or an 'authentic woman'. 'She' presents a comic speech in which she details the cosmetic surgery she has had in order to approximate the female form, but indicates that authenticity consists of more than physical appearance, which, as she describes, can be bought. The meanings and ideas within Almodovar's scenes are often not what they initially seem. Agrado's call to look deeper than the physical surface is also a request from Almodovar that relates to the audience's reading of his films.

Almodovar's description of his use of comedy, *alta comedia* – high comedy (Item 1) – indicates that there is far more to his work than the desire to shock. *Alta comedia* is an exaggerated form of comedy, evident in many of Oscar Wilde's plays, such as *The Importance of Being Earnest,* and as such, it is characterised by anti-naturalism, where speech and performance are both very fast, and human ambitions and emotions are expressed apparently superficially. Almodovar's use of these elements within his films can make his treatment of powerful issues and themes seem trivial, yet the inherent pathos of many of his scenes is still retained, even heightened, by the comic surface. The witty banter and fast-paced repartee evident within *Women on the Verge of a Nervous Breakdown*, especially in Candela's dialogue, does not halt the sympathy the audience feels for the character. On the surface, the film conforms to the conventions of a comedy of manners, or an *alta comedia,* but the subject matter, which deals with the often crippling obsessions of the characters, their neuroses and anxieties, still remains poignant.

Almodovar's films have consistently dealt with controversial subject matter. They employ comedy to present the most difficult of issues and situations, but do not lack depth beneath the glossy and humorous surface. Whether the viewer agrees with the way in which Almodovar presents problematic material – in particular rape – or not, his films do engage the viewer in a dialogue with their own preconceptions and attitudes. Almodovar's work is always challenging. *Mise-en-scène* might conflict with character actions, characters might seem kitsch, but within all of this there is a demand for debate and thought. In this way, he is a true auteur.

Evaluation

Within my presentation script, I explored many of the factors I believe contribute to Almodovar's individual signature. The most useful sources of research material were probably Items 1 and 9. Item 1 gave me many ideas concerning how Almodovar's use of film form and style can be used to present controversial issues in a provocative way. Item 9 gave me background information concerning Almodovar's life in La Mancha and his role within *La Movida*. The internet provided many useful sites, especially those originating from Spain, which added a culturally-specific slant to the other debates I read on Almodovar's work. Given the fact that Almodovar came to the mainstream with *All About My Mother* in 1999, I wanted to evaluate how his films had been received in his own country prior to this date.

As my research project progressed, I grew increasingly convinced that Almodovar 'deserved' to have the title auteur. There are distinctive elements within his films that can be seen repeatedly: discussions of gender and sexuality; conflicts between *mise-en-scène*, dialogue and the action shown; and intertextual referencing. Almodovar challenges his audiences, and for this alone he should be designated an auteur. He uses film form and style with originality and seems to regard the film canvas as an ever-variable tool for the production of meaning. Almodovar's films always maintain a tension between the viewer's expectations regarding the representation of challenging subject matter and how that subject matter is actually presented. I am not convinced about the designation of the title 'auteur' to a director if what occurs is a hierarchy. Having a group of supposedly elite directors can create too high an expectation of their work. If the use of the word 'auteur' enables directors with distinguishable styles to be recognised and their work to gain further scrutiny, then I think it is a useful term to use. Almodovar has had much freedom in the production of his films. He is not tied to a studio and the artistic explosion of *La Movida* made originality possible, even mandatory. His work has progressed both technically and thematically, and his films have continually documented social attitudes and prejudices. If an auteur is a director who has contributed to wider social debates, by presenting issues in a way that demands that the viewer scrutinise their own attitudes, then Almodovar is indeed an auteur.

Assessment comments

The catalogue section of this project contains an excellent range of materials, derived from a good range of source types. The commentary clearly evaluates the usefulness and relevance of the resources to the candidate and indicates the resources that were of more, or less, use during the research process. The project title includes a clear problematic, which is then researched thoroughly during the presentation section of the project. The presentation section is sophisticated and challenging. Resources used are referenced well and there is clear evidence that the candidate has pursued the evaluation of resources and assessment of the project title's problematic in a diligent manner.

Information relating to biography, context and filmography is used in order to address the problematic and the candidate exhibits an excellent degree of understanding of the potential complexities and issues attached to an auteurist approach. The evaluation section confidently challenges the issue of the validity of employing a critical framework, such as auteur theory, to the evaluation of a director's work. The self-critique of the research process in the evaluation section is honest, reflective and intelligent. A well-written and thorough project. Grade 'A'.

Exemplar auteur project 2: David Cronenberg

Title: How far can the sci-fi/horror films of David Cronenberg in the 1970s and 1980s be described as the work of an individual auteur – taking into consideration the input of the large production team with whom he frequently worked?

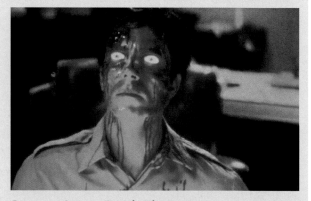

Scanners. Source: British Film Institute

Catalogue and commentary

1. Geoff Andrew *The Film Handbook* (Longman, 1989).

2. David Quinlan *Quinlan's Film Directors* (Batsford, 1999).

3. *Sight & Sound* Volume 9, Issue 4, April 1999.

4. Documentary: *Long Live the New Flesh* (Jillian Films, Canada/UK, 1987) Broadcast as part of Channel 4's *Eleventh Hour* scheduling.

5. The Internet Movie Database www.imdb.com

6. Films from the 1970s and 1980s off-air recordings: *Shivers, Scanners* and *Videodrome*.

7. David Cronenberg interview from *Mondo 2000*, uploaded onto a Cronenberg fan site: www.cronenberg.freeserve.co.uk/mond2000.htm

I found that this selection of sources helped me a great deal in finding out more about David Cronenberg – his work, influences and philosophy of film making. I chose the three films I focused on because the period of Cronenberg's work I am studying is regarded as his best. I chose *Videodrome* and *Scanners* because they were both made by the same production team; *Shivers* was chosen because it was Cronenberg's first non-student film and I wanted to see whether his distinctive style of film-making was apparent from the very beginning.

Cronenberg had, until recently, chosen to work outside of mainstream studios, using the backing of the Canadian Film Institute and sticking to his distinctive style of deadpan acting and cold *mise-en-scène*. I wanted to see if the films I have chosen differed from those made more recently in a much more mainstream context. Unfortunately, much of my research came from the internet, but I was able to find some books and extracts from magazines which were useful and gave some contextual background to Cronenberg's work. The documentary *Long Live the New Flesh* was extremely useful, as it charted Cronenberg's films chronologically and gave me valuable insight into the ideologies behind the images. The IMDb website was an invaluable resource, providing cast and crew listings, budget information, production background and a range of fan and official reviews.

Presentation script

The Internet Movie Database (Item 5) lists that between 1966 and 2002, Canadian David Cronenberg directed 19 films, a few of which were experimental shorts and a few horror works for television. In general, the films of David Cronenberg can be identified as horror, but with elements of science fiction deeply embedded within the horror themes, to create a very distinctive style of film that can be clearly identified as Cronenberg's. He writes and directs the majority of his films, with a few exceptions that are co-written or based on a pre-existing story. The films that are derived from novels or short stories are carefully chosen in order to be compatible with Cronenberg's style and themes. Stephen King's *The Dead Zone* and J.G. Ballard's *Crash* are two such stories. Cronenberg has also been criticised for trying to film the apparently unfilmable – his versions of *Crash* and *Naked Lunch* were greeted with mixed reviews.

What Cronenberg succeeds in portraying in his work are his recurring themes, such as his unique standpoint on the purpose of disease (Item 1), his philosophical views about the restrictions of the human body, the 'flesh', and the boundless possibilities of the mind – something which is often lost on critics who regard him as the 'Baron of Blood' (Item 5) and a pedlar of cheap violence. Not surprisingly, Cronenberg has a strong contempt for critics: 'Critics tend to do what only psychotics do . . . they confuse reality with illusion.' (Item 4).

The three films I have chosen are *Shivers (They Came from Within)* (1975), *Scanners* (1981) and *Videodrome* (1983). These three are often regarded as some of his best work and clearly illustrate his signature characteristics: the cold look and atmosphere of the *mise-en-scène*, the 'unhappy' ending of the main protagonist, themes of disease and control. *Scanners* and *Videodrome* have the same production team, although *Videodrome* had a higher budget and a much more polished look. *Scanners* was made with 4.1 million Canadian dollars and *Videodrome* with 5.9 million US dollars, over twice as much (Item 5). What is more significant than the amounts is that *Videodrome* was made with US money and signalled the moment when Cronenberg began to get interest from the US film industry. Despite the polished look of *Videodrome*, Cronenberg still manages to distort and disturb the familiar settings in which his films are set, with unflinching visuals designed to promote active thinking in the audience and shock them with unimaginable images. This provides one of the reasons why Cronenberg disagrees with censorship. He argues that the imagery he is showing cannot be implied, because it can not be imagined. How else could he portray the moment when Max Renn inserts a gun into his stomach, if he did not actually show it?

Shivers was Cronenberg's first film, other than his student shorts, and begins to show some of his trademark characteristics. Disease is represented in this film as phallic parasites that invade the human body, turn the host into a sex-crazed zombie and then spread to create a society based on 'free love', in which the usual social parameters do not exist. Cronenberg has a sympathetic viewpoint on disease: that it only does what it does to survive and thus should gain the same respect as the organism it is destroying (Item 1, confirmed in Item 4). *Shivers*, at its core, is an attack on the time in which it was made. Mindless orgies turn humans into blood-sucking parasites and what occurs is not a liberated society, but one in which basic human freedoms and choices are destroyed. The film can be read not only as a political comment, but also as an attack on critics and censors, who would not see beyond the sex and violence.

This political drive and the cold, emotionless *mise-en-scène* takes Cronenberg's work out of the typical horror film genre and establishes him as a director who has brought a distinct signature to a generic formula. Cronenberg's use of settings and light are reminiscent of horror films that precede his own, such as George A. Romero's *Night of the Living Dead* (1968). Often using dark backgrounds or shot a night, the light in Cronenberg's films is often extremely artificial. The neon strip lighting and halogen lamps used in *Shivers*, as well as the use of the apartment complex, creates an almost prison-like environment, in which the true horror of events is not lost through stylistics or glamorisation. His first proper film, *Shivers* was made for 179,000 Canadian dollars, so his cast was restricted to unknown Canadian actors, who Cronenberg acknowledges were in almost every other Canadian film at the time (Item 7). The lead actress in *Shivers* was Sue Helen Petrie and Cronenberg recalls how when she couldn't cry on demand, she demanded that she should be able to rub onions around her eyes and have Cronenberg slap her. That, Cronenberg states, was his entrance into the world of actresses and backs up his claim that it is not reality he is interested in, but illusion (Item 7).

What is interesting about *Scanners* and *Videodrome* is that they share almost exactly the same production team (Item 5). They share the same producer, Claude Heroux, and the same two executive producers, Pierre David and Victor Solnicki. The original score for both was by Howard Shore, the cinematographer was Mark Irwin, the editor was Ronald Sanders and the art direction was by Carol Spier. What is amazing is that despite having the same production team and being only two years apart in release, *Scanners* and *Videodrome* are two completely different films, but two which share the Cronenberg signature. The former is about telepathically powerful people, capable of killing with a thought, and the latter focuses on the media programming of viewers. *Scanners* tackles the issue of a minority group that is struggling to be accepted by a fearful community. They are perceived as diseased by the community around them, but this time, Cronenberg forces the viewer to empathise and sympathise with the stricken group, and to understand that the majority is not always right and naturally inclined to rule (Item 2). The graphic sequence in which a man's head explodes in front of a board of directors aptly demonstrates what real power is. *Videodrome* is more about Cronenberg's fascination with technology as an extension of the human body and includes graphic scenes, such as Max Renn's killing spree with a gun biologically grafted onto his body. The inclusion of Debby Harry, an icon of pop culture, also indicates Cronenberg's willingness to subvert audience expectations.

Cronenberg's signature use of the horror and sci-fi genres, his ideological stance on disease and society, and his insistence that the film audience challenges their own preconceptions, are all features evident within each of my chosen films. He is an auteur, because his films are distinguishable and unique. Cronenberg is an unusual film figure and enjoys telling the story of one of his friends going to see *Videodrome* and commenting: 'You know, some day, they are going to lock you up.' (Item 7).

Evaluation

I think that my presentation script succeeded in identifying key characteristics within David Cronenberg's films. I had wondered whether the use of the same production team on two of my focus films had contributed significantly to Cronenberg's signature and whether this would disallow him from being called an auteur. However, having studied *Scanners* and *Videodrome* in relation to *Shivers*, it is evident that regardless of production input, Cronenberg will always stamp his mark on any film he makes. Cronenberg does have creative control over his work, not least because he writes as well as directs.

I found the internet the most valuable resource for finding information, partly because of the many sites relating to Cronenberg, but also because publications I could not find were often critiqued on the web. The information on the internet can be unreliable, as it might be untrue, but all of the sources I used were cross-referenced with others and their validity proved. I was annoyed at not being able to find the book *Cronenberg on Cronenberg*, as this would have given some insights into Cronenberg's own responses to his work, which would have been extremely useful. However, the Channel 4 documentary, *Long Live the New Flesh* was an excellent alternative for this kind of information.

I think that Cronenberg can definitely be called an auteur. The term 'auteur' acknowledges the individuality of a director, and recognises their technical skill. Cronenberg has managed to alter his audience's preconceptions regarding the horror genre in particular, and I believe that this ability to make a genre one's own is a true indicator of auteur status. There are potential problems attached to the title 'auteur', however, and not just critical adulation. The individual auteur may well benefit from a cult following and a heightened level of respect, but studios might not feel that giving a big budget to a director who subverts audience expectations is financially prudent. Cronenberg has successfully moved from the sidelines to the mainstream and his films are still original.

Assessment comments

The catalogue section of this project demonstrates resourcefulness and excellent organisational skills. There is an excellent range of resources detailed. The commentary clearly evaluates the usefulness of the resources to the candidate and indicates clearly the resources that informed, and subsequently aided research of, the title of the project. The project title includes a clear problematic, which is then researched systematically throughout the presentation section of the project. The presentation section is articulate and challenging. Assumptions made about the work of the chosen director are addressed and challenged. Resources are well referenced and there is clear indication that a systematic pursuit of information has occurred in the project. Information related to biography, context and filmography is used in order to assess the project title and the candidate exhibits an excellent degree of understanding of the potential complexities and issues attached to an auteurist approach. The evaluation section shows a perceptive understanding of research procedures and addresses the issue of the validity of employing a critical framework, such as auteur theory, to the evaluation of a director's work. The self-critique of the research process in the evaluation section is frank, reflective and intelligent. An articulate and original project. Grade 'A'.

Exemplar auteur project 3: John Carpenter

Title: To what extent does John Carpenter's work retain an auteur signature, given the fact that he has worked both with larger studios and more independently?

The Thing. **Source: British Film Institute**

Catalogue and commentary

1. John Carpenter's first film *Dark Star* (1974), recorded from Channel 4.

2. John Carpenter's second film *Assault on Precinct 13* (1976) purchased on video.

3. *The Thing* (1982), John Carpenter's first studio film for Universal, purchased special edition DVD (including an audio commentary by John Carpenter and Kurt Russell).

4. *The Thing: Terror Takes Shape* (1998) documentary.

5. Outpost 31 '*The Ultimate The Thing Fan Site*' www.outpost31.com

6. The John Carpenter Website www.geocities.com/j_nada/carp/

7. The Official John Carpenter Website www.theofficialjohncarpenter.com

8. Pocket Essentials: *John Carpenter* by Michelle Le Blanc and Colin Odell.

9. Geoff Andrew *The Film Handbook* (Longman, 1989).

10. *David Quinlan's Film Directors* (Batsford, 1999).

11. *The Guardian's* television supplement film choice small article on *The Thing*.

12. *I Love 1976* segment and introduction to *Assault on Precinct 13* broadcast on BBC2 (2000).

13. Internet Movie Database www.imdb.com

14. Biography from Leonard Maltin's *Movie Encyclopaedia* (Plume) ISBN: 0452270588

15. *The Films of John Carpenter* John Kenneth Muir (McFarland & Company) ISBN: 0786407255

I feel that with all of the above information, I had a wide range of resources for my project, especially the period on which I was focusing. I was particularly interested in focusing on whether John Carpenter's style changed when he was given a big budget and how he was influenced by the B-movies he used to watch as a child. I was lucky because the books I found on John Carpenter were very comprehensive. One of my visits to the library led me to *The Films of John Carpenter* by John Kenneth Muir (item 15), a very in-depth evaluation of Carpenter's life and films, as well as the cheaper, less detailed, but still useful *Pocket Essentials: John Carpenter* by Michelle Le Blanc and Colin Odell (item 8). I found some good sources on the internet – however, I had to be sceptical about their validity. I was, however, more confident that I could trust the information on established sites like the IMDb and John Carpenter's official site. I also found some excellent information concerning film texts and production information on the John Carpenter website (item 6).

The DVD I purchased of *The Thing* had some extremely useful extras, such as directorial comment on the film and production information, including a two-hour documentary about the characters and the process of the film's production. Sadly, the DVD versions of *Assault on Precinct 13* and *Dark Star* do not contain this kind of institutional and textual information and were, therefore, not particularly useful for my project. The signature characteristics of Carpenter's work, which I shall outline in the presentation section of this project, were also discussed in many of the publications and websites I used as resources, and Carpenter's shift from an independent to a mainstream context was also commented on in some detail. The films I have chosen span eight years of the director's cinematic output and include examples of independent and mainstream ventures. I chose this range in order to see whether an auteur signature can extend into a more mainstream context and whether Carpenter managed to retain artistic control when confronted by big studios and big budgets.

Presentation script

Carpenter started off making independent and student films, but was inevitably picked up by Hollywood. He did make a brief return to independent features in the late 1980s, with *Prince of Darkness* (1987) and *They Live* (1988) (item 15), but then followed them up with a dismal Chevy Chase vehicle *Memoirs of an Invisible Man* (1992). I think that this is indicative of Carpenter's output as a whole. He was initially an auteur – writing, directing and producing his projects and these movies were typically very original – but later on in his career, he started to work more for the studios, making films from other people's scripts, under the control of others. This, I would argue, caused his material to decline.

The typical stylistic characteristics of a John Carpenter film are:

- Use of dark *mise-en-scène*.
- 'Zombie-like' antagonists – the mute Michael Myers in *Halloween* (1978) is an excellent example. This is common in a number of B-movies, such as Hammer's take on the Frankenstein story, Howard Hawks' vegetable killer in *The Thing from Another World* (1951) and the radioactive mutants of *The Day the World Ended*.
- The use of self-composed soundtracks. In the earlier part of his career they were usually also self-performed.

- Male leads are typically portrayed as anti-heroes, Snake Plissken in *Escape from New York* (1981) is a great example, as is Macready from *The Thing*. Both characters were played by Kurt Russell, whom Carpenter has worked with in a number of his films. This is in contrast to many of the B-movies that influenced Carpenter as, in these, heroes were typically wholesome, 'all-American' types.

- A presentation of empty spaces as full, and full spaces as empty.

- The themes of isolation and boredom crop up in a number of Carpenter's films. Both of these themes were common in the films of Carpenter's hero, Howard Hawks.

The three films I have chosen come from the first half of Carpenter's career. They are his first feature film *Dark Star* (1974) (actually a student short film that was later expanded), then his second feature *Assault on Precinct 13* (1976) and finally, his first major studio film, *The Thing* (1982). It is significant that *The Thing* could be considered different from the first two focus films, because it is a mainstream studio (Universal) film and had a mainstream budget – $10 million. Although it is influenced by a prior film and story (items 3, 4 & 5), Carpenter's version is self-consciously influenced by the McCarthy Communist 'witch hunts' and subsequent paranoia. The film is also regarded as an AIDS allegory, although the disease was not widely known of at the time (item 4). There is quite a time gap between my second and third focus film, and in this gap Carpenter made *Halloween* (1978), *The Fog* (1980) and *Escape from New York* (1981). I believe, however, that the films I have chosen share important stylistic and thematic characteristics, which make them representative of an auteur signature.

One of the consistent features across my chosen films is that they all feature ordinary people forced into extraordinary or life-threatening situations. The astronauts of *Dark Star*, for example, are not heroes, but ordinary people. This is exemplified within Dan O'Bannon's Pinback and the video diary sequence explaining his true background: 'I am not the real Sergeant Pinback, I am fuel maintenance technician Bill Frugge. I DO NOT BELONG ON THIS MISSION!!' *The Thing* is in part a remake of the 1951 film *The Thing from Another World*, directed by Christian L. Nyby and produced by Howard Hawks, though it is more a retelling of the original source material *Who Goes There?* by Joseph W Campbell (items 3, 4, 6, & 7). It features a group of researchers, doctors, scientists and even a chef, forced into fighting a shape-shifting alien menace. *Assault on Precinct 13* (also, almost a retelling of another Howard Hawks film *Rio Bravo*, starring John Wayne), does feature police officers, who the viewer might normally expect to be heroes, but it also features convicts, a telephone operator and a traumatised civilian, who are all forced to band together. This is something of a consistent feature within the films of Howard Hawks, who Carpenter has cited as a direct influence (item 13 & 15). My chosen films also feature protagonists confined within one particular environment: a space ship; a police station; and an Antarctic Research station; who are forced to contend with the boredom of confinement – as shown by Boiler's gun in *Dark Star* and Macready's chess computer in *The Thing*, for example.

Despite a number of productions for the studios, Carpenter's motto is: 'Make your own film' (item 7) and this could be why nearly all of the full titles for his films feature his name *John Carpenter's . . .* This could be an exercise in branding or promotion, but I prefer to read it as John Carpenter asserting himself and his signature style. This attribution of his films has led to arguments with the studios over his high-profile, money-driven films. There have even been projects that have never been finished, or even started, because of such quarrels, including a sequel to *Escape from New York* (after the frankly dire *Escape from L.A.*, however, this is probably not a bad thing). Carpenter first learned the necessity of keeping control of a film during the making of a college short, which he co-wrote, entitled *The Resurrection of Bronco Billy*. This short film won an Academy Award, but Carpenter and company were refused royalties after the University of California insisted that it was their property (item 13). Subsequently, on a number of his earlier films, Carpenter insisted on almost total control: he wrote, directed, produced, edited (and even composed and performed on most soundtracks) on the earlier, and arguably the best, films.

Since the early 1980s, he has been entrusted with a number of high-profile and high-budget features, but sadly, most of these have been flops at the box office. A lot of Carpenter's work has been well received by audiences and critics alike, but this is not always reflected in box-office receipts. His 1984 film *Starman* was nominated for an Academy Award and had its own cult following, but did not reap huge box-office rewards. *The Thing*, however, was a commercial and critical disaster (items 3, 4, 5 & 11), but was loved by the few who actually saw it. Retrospectively, however, critics have changed their minds about *The Thing*, often citing it as one of Carpenter's best films and one of the scariest films of the 1980s. It was released on the same weekend as Spielberg's *ET*, which could only have stalled its box-office takings. *The Thing* did manage to recoup its initial budget, but this has occurred through video and DVD sales, TV release and cult screenings. It also managed, eventually, to gain the critical respect it deserved (item 4). It is interesting to point out that for a number of years *Halloween* was the highest-grossing independent film ever (items 7, 8, 13 & 15).

John Carpenter was born in 1948 and was brought up on a diet of science fiction comics, films and stories from the 1950s and 1960s. He was particularly fond of the horror 'creature features', such as *Them!, The Forbidden Planet* and Hawks' version of *The Thing*. As with many film makers, his love of film inspired him to make his own and he began on his own 8 mm camera. Carpenter then went on to make films at the University of California film school where, with Dan O'Bannon, who later went on to write Ridley Scott's *Alien* (item 8), he made the film *Dark Star* as a short coursework project. This was later expanded to feature length for the relatively small sum of $60,000. Shortly after this, Carpenter was approached by an investor and given $100,000 to make a film about whatever he wanted. Inspired by Hawks' *Rio Bravo*, Carpenter decided to make an urban Western, set in the modern day. The result was *Assault on Precinct 13*. Carpenter's love of the horror and science fiction genres led him to make some truly classic movies, but his frustration with what in his opinion is a slow and bureaucratic studio system led him to try to be involved with his productions at every stage.

Evaluation

I went to libraries, bookshops and websites for my research and also to my own video and DVD collection for video materials. Some very useful information came from the internet: there are a number of John Carpenter websites and many are comprehensive. One of my best sources of information was John Carpenter himself. I used his official website for information, as well as DVD audio commentaries. I managed to find some excellent biographies of Carpenter, too. I was hoping to find some interviews with him in my copies of *Sight & Sound* magazine, but was disappointed to find very little. This might, however, have something to do with this magazine's own canon of directors?

I was fairly successful in getting information for my project, but was surprised to be so saturated with information regarding *The Thing*. It would have been useful to have a much more balanced reference to his work. I was especially disappointed to find that the DVDs of *Dark Star* and *Assault on Precinct 13* had virtually no extras, whereas the special edition of *The Thing* was brimming with extra, extremely useful, information. I think that audio commentaries or institutional information would have enhanced these two DVDs. By looking for information on John Carpenter in libraries, I found some very useful information, which was easily accessible and easy to evaluate. I found that on the internet, you have to be that much more scrupulous with information. Many of the sites I used had to be cross-referenced in order to ensure the validity and authenticity of the information. I do not assume that print texts are always valid and authentic, however, it is far easier to ascertain the source and publisher of a book, than it is an internet site.

I think that it is fair to call Carpenter an auteur, but I do register that this is less true within some of his later projects. His insistence on taking near total control of his projects is what leads me to believe that he is an auteur, and when he does this, his works seems to benefit. In the part of his career on which I was focusing, Carpenter was still in full control and had only just started work for the studios. I believe that this is his best period. I also think that the prefacing of his film titles with his name is Carpenter's way of sealing his individualism and, by extension, his auteur status.

I enjoyed researching this project as John Carpenter is among my favourite directors and *Dark Star* is one of the most intriguing and subtly powerful films I have seen.

I do believe that there was a shift away from originality and auteurism for Carpenter that resulted in some mediocre films. However, I do not believe that this detracts from his auteur credentials. With enough financial pressure and generic parameters, would any director be able to retain a consistent auteur signature?

Assessment comments

The catalogue section of this project contains an excellent range of materials, derived from a good range of source types. The commentary clearly evaluates the usefulness of the resources to the candidate and indicates the resources that informed, and subsequently aided research of, the title of the project. The project title includes a clear problematic, which is then researched systematically throughout the presentation section of the project. The presentation section is confident and insightful. Resources are well referenced and there is clear indication that a systematic pursuit of information has occurred in the project. Information relating to biography, context and filmography is used in order to address the project title and the candidate exhibits an excellent degree of understanding of the potential complexities and issues attached to an auteurist approach. The evaluation section addresses the issue of the validity of employing a critical framework, such as auteur theory, to the evaluation of a director's work. The self-critique of the research process in the evaluation section is honest, reflective and intelligent. An articulate and thorough project. Grade 'A'.

Task 2: Practical Application of Learning

There are three possible tasks to choose from under the title 'Practical Application of Learning':

- film/video production
- film journalism
- screenwriting.

Whatever task you complete, it will make up 50 per cent of the FS4 overall mark. Alongside your piece of practical work, you will also need to submit two pieces of writing. One should outline the aims and rationale of your intended project and one should present an evaluation of the finished product. Each of these pieces of writing must be a maximum of 500 words. The three options for practical work in this unit allow you to draw on your previous learning. Your understanding of film language and film form, gained in your study for the FS1 unit, will help you consider issues of appropriate style, structure and content. Your work on audience for the FS2 unit should prompt you to consider the audience (their expectations and potential consumption pleasures) for your practical work.

Film/video production

If your centre is able to provide you with equipment, you may find yourself creating a short film. As well as the other written elements you need to complete, the film/video production option requires you to create a 200-word synopsis, as well as a short film of between three and five minutes. The syllabus prescribes a maximum group size of four for this project and you should not exceed this number. As with any piece of practical work, planning and organisation are essential for an effective final product.

Short films differ from feature films in significant ways. You have a maximum of five minutes for this film project and you must design your film accordingly. It will not be possible, for example, to construct a complex and lengthy narrative within this time restriction. Your locations will be limited to those you can access reasonably easily. You will not be able to reproduce extravagant pyrotechnics or computer-generated imagery (CGI). The best types of film project are those that have clear limits, in terms of scale and technique. The syllabus does not specify a genre for this task and you could choose any. Be careful, however, as if your short film is a genre piece, you will need to make sure that you can present the conventions of that genre effectively. Some of the very best short films are those centred on a scenario, rather than a whole narrative. The 'What if?' question is often a very useful one. What if a door led onto something unexpected? What if surreal events ensued out of an everyday action? What if we could all hear each others' thoughts? A simple premise can be made dynamic by thwarting audience expectations and presenting unexpected consequences to events. Your teacher will no doubt show you examples of short films as a prompt for your own work. Consider how these are structured, the stylistic techniques they use and the type of story they tell.

EXERCISE 5

In your group, work carefully through each of the stages below, reading the guidance notes at each stage in order to ensure that you produce an effective short film.

Brainstorming of ideas

Your film-making task is a collaborative exercise and as such you may find that your eventual film includes ideas from each member of the group. Ask yourselves the following questions and make notes on the discussions you have regarding the answers:

1. What is the central premise of the story?

2. How many central characters are there? Who are they? What are their backgrounds and states of mind? Who would play them?

3. Who would be the target audience for this kind of film? What are their expectations?

4. Is the film a genre piece? If so, what are the generic conventions that can be used in the film?

5. In what time period is the film set?

6. What kind of location would be appropriate in order to create this time period? Does the group have easy access to the locations discussed?

7. What kinds of props would be necessary for this short film? Does the group have access to these kinds of props?

8. Is non-diegetic sound going to be used? If so, what kinds of tracks would be appropriate? Is diegetic sound important? If so, what kinds of diegetic sound, and how would these be generated?

9. Are there key features of cinematography that would help present the ideas and events within the film?

10. Is the type of editing to be used important? If so, what edit types would be most appropriate?

Synopsis writing

When your group has finished brainstorming ideas, a synopsis can be written. A synopsis is a condensed statement or outline. This synopsis is an outline of your ideas for your short film. It is not a 'blow by blow' account of all of the elements of your film, just a summary of the main features. Try to identify the elements of your film that you think would be of most interest to the potential audience. Is there a key event or mystery at the heart of your film? How is/are the main character(s) portrayed and what is it about them that might be engaging for the viewer? In what time is your film set? Does it have recognisable generic elements? Does it have a twist or a revelation at the end? (Look back at Chapter 1, Exercise 15 if you have any doubt as to the structure or content of a typical synopsis.)

Storyboarding

You may have submitted an original storyboard for your FS1 coursework in the AS year of the course, which means that you may already have experience of the requirements of this aid to film making. The FS1 chapter in this book gives thorough guidance on how to create a storyboard and the structural and content considerations that you need to remember. Storyboards are an essential part of the preparation for making a film as they act as a guide to filming. At the end of this section some examples of storyboards for students' short films have been reproduced and you should use them as a guide to creating your own. Remember that storyboards need to include the following information:

- camera angle
- camera distance
- camera movement

- character movement
- sound
- edit type
- genre elements
- narrative information i.e. a brief statement of what is happening in each frame.

You will need to produce a comprehensive storyboard for your short film. Make copies so that each member of your group can monitor what is being shot at the filming stage.

Shot lists

Shot lists provide a systematic and chronological guide to filming. They are an essential tool in the organisation of filming. Although changes may be made to the shot list when actual filming occurs, shot lists provide an essential framework for filming while on location. Your group will need to decide on what type of shot is needed, as well as how long the shot lasts and what is being filmed. Use headings such as the ones in the table below to create your shot list.

Camera angle	Camera movement	Camera distance	Shot duration	What is in the frame?

Filming

It may sound obvious, but the factor that will make or break your project is organisation. At this stage in the project, you will have created your synopsis, storyboard and shot list. You must remember to take the storyboard and shot list on location while your group is filming. As you know from your experience of watching films, the camera should function as an invisible and almost imperceptible observer of events.

You need to consider the following questions very carefully when you are setting up your shots:

1. Where is the light source? If your light source is behind your subject, they are going to be in shadow. Is this the effect you want?
2. Is the framing accurate? Are the elements you see in the frame the elements you want? You should be careful not to allow extraneous objects to creep into the frame. By the same token, make absolutely sure that the frame composition is good. Are the characters or objects you are filming in the right section of the frame to create the meaning you desire?

3. Have you filmed all of the cut-away and cut-in shots you require? It is always best practice to shoot slightly more than you want and discard extra shots at the edit stage, than find yourself without enough footage.

4. Is the camera head still? There is nothing worse than reviewing footage and finding that your shots wobble. If possible, you should always use a tripod for static shots, or if a tripod is not available, rest your elbows on something static while taking the shot.

At the end of your filming, check the footage you have taken against your storyboard and shot list to make absolutely sure that all of the footage you need has been filmed. Then watch the footage again and discuss with your group whether or not it generates the kinds of meaning that you want. If any of the shots are out of focus, badly framed, badly lit, wobbly, or make no sense, then re-film them!

Editing

You will probably be using a digital editing program to edit your footage and this will have a facility for you to name or identify the shots you have filmed. It is very important to label each of the shots you have in order to make the editing process simple.

The first stage of any editing process should be to create a rough edit of material. For a rough edit all you will need to do is place the shots in the order you want them to be. This should be done before any edit types are inserted, as it will allow you to gain a sense of the overall movement of your short film. The next stage of editing is to decide on edit types and any effects you think are appropriate for your shots. Remember that transitions other than straight cuts (i.e. dissolves and wipes) tend to affect meaning. Your editing decisions should be made with the generation of appropriate meaning in mind and not with the aim of 'wowing' your viewer with elaborate effects. You are not making a music video, but a short film. The same principle should apply to the use of special effects. A sepia wash might look effective, but if your short film is contemporary or futuristic, an effect that implies history and age is not appropriate.

When you and your group are happy with the short film you have created, you should present it for feedback from the rest of your Film Studies class. You could ask your audience what they think of the technical elements of the film, any generic elements, the characterisation, the story and whether it makes an effective short film. This feedback will help when you are writing your self-evaluation, so you should make some notes on what other members of your group think of your work.

Film journalism

This option for the second part of your FS4 unit offers quite a lot of scope for the types of writing you could do. There is more to film journalism than writing reviews – your portfolio of pieces will include between two and four different types of writing. The pieces in your portfolio should have no more than 2000 words in total. If you limit your choice of imaginary publication to those such as broadsheet newspapers and *Sight & Sound* magazine, this option could appear very difficult and intimidating. Try to broaden your choice. Film journalism does not just exist in print form. You might decide to write a fan piece for the internet, for example, or a profile of a performer or director for their website. Whatever type of film journalism you choose and whatever publication you decide it should be read in, there are three key considerations that you should remember.

1. Style of language and address.
   Whether you are writing for a student magazine, a mainstream film magazine, an internet site or a newspaper, you should study the style of language carefully before commencing writing. In order to make your piece of film journalism as authentic as possible, you will need to consider the questions below:

   - How formal is the style of writing?
   - Does the piece of film journalism use film terminology?
   - Is the reader directly addressed (as 'you') by the writer?
   - Are the sentences that are used complex? Is a lot of information given, in sentences with lots of clauses?

2. Target readership.
   Before you begin writing it is absolutely essential that you correctly identify who is going to read your piece of film journalism. Approximately how old are they? What are their interests? What kind of film viewing experience can you assume they have? Why are they reading the piece? Is it for information? For advice on future viewing? To broaden their knowledge of film? To be challenged in their assumptions regarding a particular aspect of film? All of these questions will need to be answered, for your film journalism to be effective.

3. Content type.
   You will be creating between two and four pieces of film journalism, each with different content types. What is included in a review will be different from the content of an article. An interview requires different information to a profile. Your first decision will be related to the focus of your piece of writing. Are you going to concentrate on a genre of film, an individual film, a director, a performer or a studio? Your next decisions should use the following questions as guidance.

   - What is the frame of cinematic reference needed for your chosen piece? How many films will you need to refer to? Are they mainstream or independent productions?
   - Is it necessary to give information regarding a director's filmography?
   - Is it necessary to include details of film plot-lines?
   - Are details of actors' earlier films required?
   - Is it necessary to provide an argument or discussion topic around the film, director or performer you are discussing?

   All of these questions should be considered carefully before you begin writing.

The decision about what types of film journalism you include in your portfolio should only be made after thorough research. Read as many different types of film journalism as you can find in order to make informed choices. To help you, below are descriptions of three types of film journalism available to you:

Reviews

Reviews are probably the most recognisable form of film journalism and exist in many different contexts. They invariably follow quite a systematic structure in order to relay the necessary information to the reader. Obviously, the publication in which the review appears has an impact on the language and content type of the review, but as a guideline, the structure of a review is as follows:

1. Background information on the reviewed film. This could take the form of a comment concerning where the film fits (or doesn't) into the director's filmography, detail of any original source for the film or any controversy surrounding the film and its release.

2. Comment on the writer's response to key elements of the film. These could include key scenes, key performances or key stylistic features.

3. A summary of the good and/or bad points of the reviewed film and a recommendation or rejection of it.

Discursive articles

These are the kinds of article that tend to take a standpoint about an aspect of film and present arguments around a central point. They might focus on a moment in cinema history, a film movement, a genre or an aspect of the film industry. Discursive articles present an argument, which is then systematically substantiated by the presentation of evidence. The best of this type of article challenges the reader's assumptions about an aspect of film and involves the reader in a discussion.

Interviews

As a prompt for an imaginary interview, you could use the information you collected during your auteur project. You may have studied a director, performer or studio and could use any one of these as the background source for an interview. Obviously, if your auteur project concerned a studio, then you will have to select an individual from that studio as your subject. You might decide to base your interview on one film from your chosen individual, or you could create an interview that functions as a retrospective of that individual's work. You could use the details collected for your auteur project concerning your subject's background; their viewing experience; their philosophy of film making; and signature characteristics, in order to ensure an authentic feel to their responses.

EXERCISE 6

Work through the exercises below to prepare for and write your articles:

1. Choose up to four different real pieces of film journalism and make notes for each in a grid similar to the one below.

	Target reader profile	Key language features	Key content features	Type of publication
Piece 1				
Piece 2				
Piece 3				

2. Using the notes on article types and appropriate content above, draft your pieces of film journalism.

3. Ask two or three of your classmates to read through your drafts and comment on the language, content and target audience.

4. Using the feedback you receive from your classmates, finalise your portfolio of film journalism pieces.

Screenwriting

If you completed the screenplay task for the practical component of your FS1 coursework, you will already have a very good idea about how to plan and create an effective screenplay. This task does differ from your AS task, however, and you should make yourself aware of the differences. As well as the aims and rationale and self-evaluation sections (500 words each), you will be required to complete a synopsis (200 words) and a screenplay (1800 words). Your screenplay could be for a sequence from a complete feature film (as described in the synopsis), or for a complete short film. As an A2 project, your screenplay will need to demonstrate a higher degree of knowledge application than the screenplay you may have completed for your AS course. Your micro and macro knowledge will still be essential for this project, as will your knowledge of film audiences, but you could also consider the knowledge you gained during the writing of your auteur project in your screenplay. You may have studied a director whose use of cinematography, *mise-en-scène*, sound or editing caught your attention. Your chosen auteur subject may have worked within a particular film movement or style that you want to use as an influence for your work for this unit.

As with all of the practical tasks, it is essential that you plan your screenplay thoroughly before you begin writing.

EXERCISE 7

Consider the questions below before you begin writing (the first questions are very similar to those printed within the FS1 section of this book. The last questions contain new elements to consider).

1. What is the genre of your screenplay? What generic conventions of that genre are you going to use in your practical work? Are the generic conventions going to be used literally or will they be subverted?

2. If the screenplay is for a sequence from a film, where does the sequence appear in the overall narrative of your film? How is it evident that the sequence is from the exposition, development, complication, climax or resolution segment of the narrative?

3. Who are the characters seen in this scene? What do they look like? How do they feel? How do they interact with one another? How can the future audience for this film understand character state of mind or motivation from the elements included in the screenplay?

4. Where is the scene set? How does the location and setting of the scene help to convey information to the film's potential audience? How is the scene lit? What meanings does the lighting help generate? Do the elements of set or location contribute towards the viewers' understanding of the genre of the film or its position within a film movement?

5. Are there any props evident in your scene? Are they significant to the film audience's understanding of character, genre, themes or narrative? How will these props be presented to the audience – through cut-ins, cut-aways or via another cinematic device?

6. What sound is evident in the sequence? Is there non-diegetic sound? If so, what type? Is there dialogue? How is the dialogue delivered? What kind of information is being conveyed by what is said? Is there other diegetic sound? How does this help to convey meaning?

7. What kinds of camera angle, movement and distance are used? What information does the cinematography you have chosen help generate? Is the meaning relayed literal, obscured or somehow contradictory to the audience's expectations?

8. What edit types will be used? Are these consistent with the mood, atmosphere and narrative information created within the sequence?

9. Who would be the audience for a film created from this screenplay? What would their expectations be of the kind of film you are creating?

10. What comments could be made about the cinematic, political or aesthetic choices evident within the ideas you have for your screenplay? Does it appear to have been influenced by your experience of cinema, by styles of film making that are evident today, or by the political climate in which the screenplay is being created?

Make sure that you have clear answers to these questions before you begin writing.

The layout of your screenplay is also very important and you will need to be fully aware of the industry standard for screenplay presentation. Try to read through a few industry screenplays before you begin setting out your work. You should ask the questions above about the industry screenplay to find out what devices are being used to create different kinds of meaning. You will notice that, in terms of layout, they invariably:

- present directorial information, such as descriptions of settings, in *italics*
- use abbreviations such as EXT (exterior) and INT (interior) to locate the action and CU (close-up), LS (long shot) to denote shot distances
- place the name of the character speaking either on the left-hand side of the page or in the middle of the page
- indent the speech of the characters, to fully differentiate it from the directions that are included.

If this is the first time you have created a screenplay, look back at the examples, advice and exercises in the FS1 chapter of this book, before you begin your work.

The written work
Aims and rationale

The aims and rationale section of your project allows you 500 words to explain the stylistic, thematic and formal choices you have made for your written work. Ideally, you should write this before you begin the practical work, as it provides an indication of intent, not a retrospective analysis. The aims and rationale section should include an identification of the target audience you assume for your practical work and a discussion of the expectations the target audience would have for the film, article or screenplay you have created.

You will also need to explain why you have chosen to use certain stylistic and formal features in your practical work and what impact you assume they will have on the audience for the piece. Are there generic conventions that you plan to employ or exploit within your practical work? Were there any other influences on your choices? The aims and rationale should give a clear indication of the thought processes behind your practical work.

Self-evaluation

This piece of writing should be completed after you have finished the practical work. You have 500 words in which to evaluate your finished product clearly. You will need to consider how successful the stylistic and formal elements of your piece are and whether or not you think the meanings generated were those you intended. Consider also whether or not you consider your practical work meets the needs of the target audience you identified in the aims and rationale. The feedback you received from your classmates could act as a useful prompt for some of the questions you might have regarding your finished practical work.

Exemplar practical application project 1: Film/video making (written component)

Sporadic Recollections: Synopsis

The film begins with a man waking up in a field, with his clothes neatly folded next to him. He has a 'bar code' on his back. He then gets up and walks off. He stumbles into the Public Record Office. The bureaucracy the man is faced with sends him on a chase around the offices on a search for the right forms to find out exactly who he is. In exasperation, he sits down and fishes a surreal object out of his pocket. The object has an address label hanging from it. This triggers a sudden memory of a party where everybody knows him, but he is jolted out of this memory when the object drops from his hand. He walks out of the Public Record Office towards the address and potential freedom. Upon reaching the door, he is shot by the occupant of the house. The film ends with another man waking up in a field, with his clothes neatly folded next to him. He gets up and walks off.

Aims and rationale

Our film is generically Surrealist, being more fragmented and disturbing than realist film. It leaves more for the viewer to interpret, despite it having meaning to us as creators. While solutions are given, they serve to open up more questions. The film is intended to be a strong comment on the control that bureaucracy holds over us in everyday life and how it is very hard, impossible even, to break away from it. It also explores the controversy of identity – that while we are supposedly free, people are given numbers and filed away in the archives of institutions such as the Public Record Office, police stations and prison systems. Even in more everyday pursuits, such as shopping, we are identified by an ID number, sort code or account number.

In creating this piece, we were influenced by the work of Terry Gilliam and David Lynch, among others. Lynch has created superb pieces of contemporary Surrealism in the form of *Blue Velvet*, and more specifically *Lost Highway*, and often uses a narrative 'loop' within his films to create a feeling that you are stuck there, infinitely going round in circles. Similarly, Luis Bunuel, creator of *Un Chien Andalou*, used this technique in *That Obscure Object of Desire*. Our film is quite strongly influenced by Terry Gilliam's *Brazil*, which in its turn was influenced by George Orwell's *1984*, which explores what would happen under bureaucratic totalitarian control where 'pen-pushers' control your entire life.

We have illustrated the frustration of being one in a sea of people who have no control over their lives. To achieve this, we have placed the protagonist in a situation where nobody knows him and he knows nobody. He is alone and extremely vulnerable. This is accentuated by the fact that he is outside and completely naked at the start of the film. To represent the oppression of bureaucracy we have used the example of excessive amounts of paperwork and the ludicrous scenario of a man having to visit numerous government offices just to find out his own identity. We have also used faceless 'pen-pushers' who appear only as a hand with a pen or a mouth with a voice.

The film will be shot in black and white. Framing will be non-conformist, as with many Surrealist films. This also helps to represent the nature of bureaucracy, because only parts of the bureaucrats are shown. They are shadowy, not fully drawn humans. The editing will be more fragmented than in realist cinema in order to disturb the viewer and accentuate the man's frustration, as he is sent on a wild goose chase to fill in multiple forms. The most realist and stable section of the film will be the flashback, which is intended to be comforting to the man and also to the viewer. In contrast, the fastest and least stable section of editing is towards the very end, when the occupant of the house opens the door and shoots the man. This will be shot from the man's point of view and the murderer will only be seen for a second. The sound of gunshot will continue after the cut to where the second man wakes up naked.

Self-evaluation

We set out to make a Surrealist film and despite being restricted by the limitations of time and equipment, I think we have succeeded in achieving what we aimed to. Generically, *Sporadic Recollections* is surreal, and therefore polysemic: several members of our audience came up with different, independent readings of the film. These included that of the central protagonist being in fact dead. The film is fragmented and quite disturbing – characteristics of the surreal genre. The non-diegetic sound contributes to the feeling of discomfort and evokes a certain empathy with the character. I was also particularly pleased with how the flashback sequence worked out in terms of sound, *mise-en-scène* and editing. The sudden silence, in contrast with the discordant music, after the protagonist's mad chase around the building, creates a sense of unease and tension. The *mise-en-scène* also contributes to the atmosphere as it is bland, institutional and unfamiliar. The editing is slow and in stark contrast to the previous scene, giving the audience a chance to draw breath and ponder. The framing here functions to marginalise the man, making him look small and insignificant. Similarly, the extreme long shot at the start has a similar effect, and in addition causes a sense of ambiguity – he is alone, in an open field and yet he is trapped. As the camera moves in, the audience can see why – the man has been labelled with a barcode. The opening sequence effectively sets up the conflict of freedom and confinement, which the film explores, and makes a strong comment on the labelling of human beings by bureaucracy.

As well as the opening sequence, I especially liked the '106' sequence. The shooting location was superbly contemporary – similar to some of the locations of David Lynch's films, such as *Lost Highway*. Although we were shooting in black and white, the colours here were fantastic and the hole in the wall presented an opportunity for some very interesting shots. The editing is also particularly good where it cuts from a shot of the man walking down the drive to a shot of him arriving, filmed through the hole in the wall. The framing and the graphic matches of doorbell and hole in the wall add to the sense that this is an interlinked, circular narrative. Our use of black and white produced a superb atmosphere throughout the film. The shades of grey and the contrast of black and white help to create the bleakness of bureaucracy and illustrate the man's struggle to be released from it. From the audience's point of view it also makes the film more perplexing and intriguing.

In terms of narrative structure, the film also worked out well. In the planning stages, most of our ideas had the length and complexity of feature films, but we were eventually able to extract the basic elements and adapt them for the short film. *Sporadic Recollections* is only four minutes long, but does contain a whole narrative. By introducing a loop, or circular structure, to the narrative, we created an enigmatic ending. Overall, I am very pleased with our film. It has a surreal, Kafkaesque feel to it and produced the desired effect on our audience.

Assessment comments

This is a highly effective short film, which uses the conventions of Surrealism to excellent cinematic effect. The cinematography of the piece displays flair and innovation and the editing works to generate meaning and affect the audience in exactly the ways outlined in the aims and rationale. There is a very high degree of personal authorship evident in the work and it makes its ideological point with flair. The written sections of this project are articulate and show excellent knowledge of other relevant films. Grade 'A'.

Exemplar practical application project 2: Film journalism

Aims and rationale

I am going to complete written tasks for three different publications in order to create a diverse portfolio of materials, with each piece aimed at a different audience. There are many different kinds of writing which could come under the heading 'film journalism', but I am going to complete a preview, feature article and review, for *Premiere* magazine, *Total Film* magazine and *The Guardian/Observer* newspapers respectively.

Premiere magazine is a mainstream film publication. Its target market is relatively broad so the style of its articles is mostly populist. The language of the pieces written for *Premiere* is quite simple and does not include many specific pieces of film-related terminology, as they would be difficult for the target reader to comprehend. *Premiere* is a magazine for consumers who like film, but do not necessarily study it. The types of films included are usually mainstream and have a broad target audience. Thus, any impenetrable language would be alienating for the average *Premiere* reader. The type of address used in this magazine is often direct, implying a similarity of cinematic taste and expectation between the writer of the piece and the reader. The 'Preview' section in *Premiere* is designed to make the audience aware of films for future release and tantalise them with detail. These pieces often include a reference to the director's previous work and a brief indication of the key elements of the film. As *Premiere*'s readership is younger than a publication such as *The Guardian*, the information contained in the Preview section does not include complex critiques or references to stylistics or context, which would not be in the target reader's frame of reference.

Total Film has a slightly different target audience than *Premiere* magazine. The style of writing is a little more dense and the magazine includes features that discuss more complex features of film. If the target audience for *Premiere* is mostly the teen market, then *Total Film* caters for late teens and those film consumers in their twenties. The films reviewed in *Total Film* range outside the mainstream and can include reference to the kind of cinematic detail that is absent from the writing in *Premiere* and the like. I have chosen to write a feature for this publication that discusses a genre of film and questions its intent and impact. The language of the piece is more mature and challenging than the preview piece, in order to try and prompt the reader into questioning their own expectations and responses to genres of film.

I think I will find *The Guardian/Observer* review the most difficult piece to write. If I could actually write like Philip French, then I think a future career would be guaranteed! The target readership of *The Guardian/Observer* newspaper is adult. The film section of this newspaper also seems to cater for readers who have a pre-existing knowledge of film and an awareness of not only film-related terminology, but film

Early cinema was predominantly frequented by the working classes, whose budgets could only stretch to the nickel it cost to visit a 'nickelodeon'. Theatre has become a mostly middle-class excursion. Prohibitive ticket prices and the inveterate snobbery around a theatre visit seem to exclude working-class audiences. The theatre stage is a more immediate space, where suspension of disbelief is paramount in order to allow the audience to transport themselves to the locations represented. The proscenium arch of the theatre defines the space in which the action is set. Films do not have such restrictions. They are often shot on location and the evocation necessary in theatre is less necessary when the audience literally sees the hills or city or sea. Both forms, however, seek to engage the audience in a journey of discovery, whether it be into character psychology, ideological stance or historical event. It is subject matter that is for the most part transferred between film and theatre, and not technique. *Chitty Chitty Bang Bang* has become a highly successful West End production. Baz Luhrman's *Romeo + Juliet* did wonders for the Year 9 SATS students who found Shakespeare's play dull and impenetrable. These examples transfer the content and not the means. The former film ably generates the feel of the Baron's kingdom through complex stage mechanics and the latter cleverly transfers teenage angst from Verona to a contemporary American city. It is this rare technical transfer that embues Sam Mendes' *American Beauty* with such poignancy and power.

Earlier in his career, Mendes was a theatre director. His 'training' was at the Donmar Warehouse theatre. Productions such as *The Blue Room* and *Cabaret* were met with huge critical acclaim and his future as 'the next Peter Hall' was heralded. This seems a strange platform to launch into film making, but this was the trajectory on which Mendes was headed. With Spielberg as executive, and by all accounts a very nurturing executive producer, Conrad Hall, as the exceptionally experienced cinematographer, and Alan Ball as the accomplished scriptwriter, Mendes had a rich source of advice from which to draw. He also had the raw courage to turn his theatrical hand to the cinematic.

American Beauty stars Kevin Spacey as Lester Burnham and Annette Bening as his wife Carolyn. Their family is completed by Thora Birch, as daughter Jane. Lester's voice-over informs us after the first minute or so of the film that a year later 'I will be dead'. This revelation has a dual effect. The audience at once realises the direction in which the narrative is headed and also begins to hear Lester's narration as from beyond the grave. The potential danger of a revealed ending and the exploded enigma that can result from this is instantly avoided by our immediate intimate view of Lester's world. We see him asleep, get up, masturbate in the shower and stumble towards the stifling mundanity of his day. Lester has seemingly given up on life – maybe a suicide is implied. Shakespeare's *Romeo and Juliet* tells us of the events in the play in its Prologue and the audience still remains attentive because the manner of events unfolding is extraordinary. *American Beauty* might begin with a revelation, but its manner of unfolding is equally as gripping.

These are characters who are amazingly varied and complex. As is necessary in directing one of the great works of the theatre, this film explores all of its characters and not just the main protagonists. The power of a great story, either on stage or screen, lies in its ability to sustain the interest of the audience, and subsidiary plot lines are an essential element within that audience engagement. They underpin the central events and create threads that are ultimately joined. *American Beauty* is Lester's story. We understand this from his presentation as narrative guide, albeit a subjective one. The narrative propels us towards a discovery of how and why Lester ends up dead. The film is also a story about the family around him, who both contribute to his malaise and ultimately provide him with his solace. Mendes' skill is to present both the experiences of Carolyn and Jane as creating both independent psychological reality and mirrors up to Lester's state of mind. We are presented with stage-like sets on which Carolyn and Jane pursue what they think will make them happy. Carolyn's most poignant scene ends with her having not made a house sale, her pristine exterior in tatters, standing in front of the blinds within an empty room. Mendes' theatrical background comes to the fore here. The camera is static. The audiences watches Carolyn's breakdown without being allowed to turn away. The window she stands in front of acts as a kind of proscenium arch, framing her lonely tears and holding them within the audience's gaze.

There are many instances within *American Beauty* where the audience seems locked into an auditorium-like position by the camera and where the characters are held within an acting space. The office cubicle in which Lester works restrains him, but at the same time liberates the meanings around him. The Fitz family are framed together, on the sofa, watching the viewing choice of the father, Colonel Fitz. The camera again is static and they are offered to the audience for, what becomes uncomfortable, scrutiny. Mendes does not move his camera for the sake of cinematic dynamism, he leaves it to watch his characters and unearth their secrets. This is a highly original piece of film-making, which explores the myths that underpin affluent suburban American culture. As the tag-line for the film suggests, you should indeed 'look closer'.

Self-evaluation

Looking back at the three pieces of film journalism I created for this task, I do think that they have distinct and distinguishable styles. My aim was to write three different types of article for three different types of audience, and I feel that I have managed this successfully.

The aim of the 'preview' was to provide the most relevant and engaging details of the plot for *The Village*, without giving away the film's 'secret'. I think that this piece manages to present tantalising details of the future release and at the same time provide the target reader with details of the director's other works, which they may have seen and enjoyed. The style of writing is suitably simplistic and quite informal, which would be involving and not threatening to the teen market at whom *Premiere* is targeted. The feedback I received in class regarding this section of my project indicated that the preview was a successful mix of background information and prompt to see the film.

The article for *Total Film* magazine, although aimed at a slightly older target audience who would have more background knowledge of film, was still written with the informality of that publication. This magazine has a similar relationship with its target readership to *Premiere*, in that it seeks to involve the reader in a mutually comprehensible discussion. *Total Film* articles refer to films the reader would probably have seen, but offer a slightly different reading of them. They are not as challenging or film literate as those written for *The Guardian* or the *Observer*, but still have the capacity to make the reader think. From the feedback I received from my classmates, I think that this piece successfully involves the target readership and leaves them with an interesting question regarding their expectations of genre.

I was initially very concerned about writing a piece in the style of a newspaper such as *The Guardian/Observer*, but once I had settled on my premise for the review I felt much more confident. I think that this piece does offer a different route into the film *American Beauty* than the target readership might have initially expected. I also think that the type of reader of these newspapers is probably also a theatre-goer and would be intrigued by a review that asks them to consider their expectations of theatre and cinema together. I feel that the language of this piece suits the more formal style of these newspapers and assumes a knowledge in the target reader that publications such as *Premiere* and *Total Film* cannot necessarily assume. My classmates found this a very well-written review and commented on how the originality of argument would be very interesting for *The Guardian/Observer*'s target readership.

Assessment comments

This is a very mature portfolio of work. There has obviously been thorough study of the publications referenced and the style of language used for articles. The candidate identifies the target audiences for the three pieces accurately and explores their expectations with confidence. There is an assured grasp of the conventions of film journalism and the content type necessary for these three different styles of writing. The portfolio offers pieces that are not merely review form, but also those that are more discursive in style. A confident collection of pieces, that indicate excellent understanding of target audience and publication style. Grade 'A'.

Exemplar practical application project 3: Screenwriting

Shadow Of Fear: Synopsis

It's 1929 in downtown Chicago. It's a time and place overrun by gangsters and crooked cops. The film opens with Detective Harry Tipper, an old 'has-been' cop explaining to his friend, Detective Jake Fenton, that he has stumbled upon some information that he wishes he hadn't. Harry explains that Connacelli (a powerful Mafia boss) has 'wasted' three of his best men trying to gain the information that he knows Harry has got. Before Harry is brutally murdered by Connacelli's henchmen on his way home, he passes on the information to Jake, who then takes on the task of finding out what this information means and why Harry was killed for it. At Harry's funeral, Jake meets Susie Warrington, a reporter on the *Chicago Times* who is investigating stories of alcohol smuggling in and out of the city. After being told that the case is closed by the Chief of Police, Jake continues trying to avenge Harry's death, despite the obstacles he faces. He becomes involved with Victoria Easy, one of Connacelli's favourite girls, and it appears she has her own reasons for wanting to share information with Jake. Despite constant pressure from the police department and the Mayor's office to leave the case alone, Jake and Susie's investigation begins to uncover a vast web of bootlegging, prostitution and murder. It all comes to a climax in one of Connacelli's warehouses, where Jake, Susie and the few men they can trust become involved in a huge gun fight with Connacelli's men. Connacelli escapes to the roof, where he is confronted by Jake and killed. Susie exposes the Mayor and the Chief of Police as Connacelli's partners and they are later shamed in the papers and dismissed.

Aims and rationale

The genre of this film is certainly a Hollywood thriller. However, I also want it to have the feel of an old 'classic' gangster movie, which would have perhaps starred James Cagney or Humphrey Bogart. It is, of course, important to include some of the more contemporary elements of a modern thriller as well, in order to engage today's audiences. To achieve this, the film needs to combine the techniques of modern film making, as well as utilising those from the period of classic gangster films. For example, the opening sequence of the film introduces two stereotypical 1930s detectives and a scene reminiscent of the British thriller, *The Third Man*. The dialogue must be straight to the point and somewhat predictable and corny. The opening sequence should be set in a smokey cafe, with some real 1920s jazz music to help create atmosphere. The scene in which the character of Harry is being followed should use shadows to evoke the tension at the heart of the thriller genre.

The colour of the film is very important, as most of the classic thrillers were made in black and white. However, it is important to take into account a modern audience's expectation of colour. To get around this problem, the film should tone down most

217

of the colours and use mainly natural light, such as street lights or light beaming through windows. This natural light should provide some degree of familiarity and meet expectation for modern audiences who expect some colour and brightness, but having a duller tone to the colours used in the *mise-en-scène* should evoke a period style. A perfect example of this is *Road to Perdition*, which retains an older, classic look, while still using colour. Hopefully, the appeal of this film will be of seeing one of the viewer's favourite old classics, but one with the budget and capabilities of a modern Hollywood blockbuster. The action sequences should be spectacular and realistic.

The narrative must also appeal to audiences by making sure that there are enough characters and subplots to keep them interested. There will be a love interest and a variety of characters with different motives. A good example of a thriller that utilises a number of characters and differing motivations is *L.A. Confidential*, which offers the story from the perspective of three different detectives, each unravelling a different aspect of the plot. The aim of this story is to combine the modern day thriller blockbuster, with a great story and psychologically intriguing characters, within a classic old movie style.

Screenplay: Opening sequence

Scene 1

It's way back in 1929, a time when entire towns were run by the Mob and there is hardly a straight cop left on the force. We are outside a small Italian restaurant downtown and it's early in the morning . . . real early, about one or two o'clock. It's dark, cold and there is hardly anyone around.

We open with an establishing shot outside the restaurant, as a slow piano intro comes in. The music is typical 1920s jazz. We cut to a close-up of a cup of coffee. It's black and we see a hand enter the shot and pick up a small, silver teaspoon. The hand then stirs it around a couple of times, taps the spoon against the edge of the cup, places the spoon back down on the saucer and then picks up the coffee to take a mouthful. We then cut to see the man drinking the coffee. His face looks old and weathered and he looks very anxious. He is dressed in a grey suit and hat and has a small moustache. Let's just say he has the word 'cop' written all over him. His name is detective Harry Tipper. He quickly turns his head and gives a look over his shoulder. We then cut to a shot of another character standing by a chair, on the other side of the table. We cannot see his face, but we hear his voice say, 'Good evening, Harry.' His voice has a thick Irish accent and the tone of his voice is firm, yet curious. His name is Detective Jake Fenton, a young Irish cop who we assume is here to meet Harry. Even when he sits down, the audience cannot see his face clearly. Some suspicion and tension are retained for the audience. We can see his clothes and hear his voice clearly, however. He is quite a scruffy young man, dressed in a white shirt, black tie and hat. The fact that he obviously knows Harry suggests that he is also a cop. The two are now sat down at a table in the corner of the restaurant and begin their conversation. The camera is positioned over Harry's shoulder, focused on Jake slouching over the table, looking tired.

Jake: How's it goin' Harry? Better be good news, getting me out at this time in the morning.

Harry: How's your Molly doin'?

Jake is tired and wants to get to the point. Harry seems to be trying to avoid the topic, but Jake is having none of it.

Jake: You didn't bring me down here to talk about Molly! The least you can do is get me a coffee.

Harry instantly raises his hand, clicks his fingers and a waitress places a cup of coffee in front of Jake.

Jake: Thank you! Now, what you got for me and no bull! You look shiftier than Stazione at a police convention!

Harry realises that Jake wants to get straight to the point and isn't going to mess around.

Harry: You Irish really are grumpy!

Jake: Harry!!

Jake gives a small smile, as he knows his pressure on Harry has worked and he is going to get straight to the point. At this point, the camera switches to directly over Jake's shoulder, focusing on a very nervous Harry.

Harry: It's this last case I'm workin' on. I came across some information I wish I hadn't. You know this whole homicide thing?

Jake: Uh huh.

Harry: Well, it's bigger than that.

Jake: How big?

Harry: Connacelli wasted three of his best men for the information I have and I think he knows I've got it.

The camera cuts to an overhead shot, looking directly down on Jake and his coffee.

Jake: You want my advice, Harry? Find a hole and hide in it! What's this got to do with me anyway?

In this shot, the camera is looking down and focusing on Jake's cup of black coffee, perhaps symbolic of the dark hole Harry needs to hide in. Next the camera cuts back to over Jake's shoulder, as Harry gets to the point.

Harry: I need you to hold onto some information for me, that's all! If I go down with it, the whole city will go up in flames!

We cut to a shot directly level with the table, with the camera positioned next to Harry. We see Harry hand Jake the information over the table. Jake accepts it, but somewhat reluctantly. He places his hand on the information and replies:

Jake: I should have stayed in bed!

Then we see Harry ready to leave the restaurant. He says 'wish me luck!' and we see Jake salute him goodbye. Jake then mutters the words 'see you later, Harry.'

Scene 2

We move outside, onto the cold, dark streets of downtown Chicago. The camera then cuts to a new character named Louie 'Bignose' Baggio (one of Connacelli's boys). He sparks up a cigarette and looks around carefully, eyes fixed like an eagle waiting for its prey. The action then cuts to Harry, making his way home. We see Harry as he crosses the river over a small footbridge and we can tell that he is anxious through his facial expressions. He pauses to lean on the side of the bridge and look out over the river. There is no-one around and the only movement is a few ripples on the river. After a brief moment, Harry continues to walk over the bridge, towards the camera. He keeps looking over his shoulder to see if he is being followed. Suddenly, we see a close-up of the expression on his face change from anxiousness to one of fear, as if he has seen a ghost.

We cut to see Louie, leaning casually against a lamppost, his eyes fixed on Harry. He is dressed in a suit and hat, with glasses, and his facial expression is serious. As Harry sees Louie, we cut to a full shot of him walking past. Harry is central frame and Louie is leaning on the lamppost at the far right of that frame. Harry walks past cautiously and gives a nervous, glancing look back over his shoulder, before trying to hasten away. We cut to a close-up, at a low angle, at Louie's feet, as he drops his cigarette and stamps it out. At this point, it is made very clear that he is a gangster by his 'spats'.

We then cut to a full shot, looking down a long, old street. Harry is walking swiftly towards the camera, constantly looking over his shoulder. Not far behind him is Louie. The lighting is dim and against the old stone houses we can see the shadows of the two characters. Harry turns a corner sharply and looks behind him, then speeds up to try and lose his follower. However, Louie is also quick to turn the same corner and it is clear that he is only just behind Harry. We cut to a long shot of Harry, walking away from the camera. A close-up is then seen of Louie, who seems to have an evil look on his face, as if he knows that Harry is not going to get away. We then rejoin Harry as he attempts to get home. He now believes that he is no longer being followed, but gives one more glance over his shoulder as he turns the corner, just to make sure. The camera then cuts to the other side of the corner. Harry stops suddenly in front of the camera. His face drops and he takes a deep breath and mutters the words, 'Mr Connacelli, what a pleasant surprise.'

It is then revealed just who Harry is talking to. In front of Harry, there is a group of five men, standing in front of cars. The headlights of the cars light up the street. The men are all dressed in dark hats and suits, and with the exception of one of them, they are all holding 'Tommy' guns. The four men holding guns all aim and fire, emptying whole magazines. The other man remains still, watching. We assume this man is Connacelli. After the gunfire has stopped, the scene fades to black.

Self-evaluation

The inspiration for this film came from a number of different gangster films, such as *Road to Perdition* and *The Untouchables*. I particularly liked the *mise-en-scène* in *Road to Perdition*, especially the costumes and the lighting. Nearly all of the characters are wearing dark two-piece suits and hats. I think that the lighting used in this film evokes the feel of a black and white film, even though the film is in colour, and I find this impressive. The film uses mostly natural light, from street lamps or windows, to give a realistic feel to it. The use of light to cast evocative shadows was also something I used – this can be seen in the scene where Harry and Louie are walking down the street and both of their shadows are enlarged against the houses.

The character of Harry was partly inspired by characters within both *The Untouchables* and *Lethal Weapon 4*. From viewing the characters played by Danny Glover and Sean Connery, I was inspired to create an old-fashioned, straight cop. However, as with Sean Connery's character in *The Untouchables*, he is murdered by the villains. As for the look of the second scene, in which Harry is being followed by Louie 'Bignose' Baggio, I was inspired by Carol Reed's *The Third Man*, which made use of shadows and unusual cinematography around the old streets of Vienna. Reed's film is also a thriller and I was influenced by how he used the conventions of that genre. Some of the more stylised shots in the first scene are there for a reason. For example, the high-angle shot looking down on Jake and his cup of coffee is meant to represent the dark hole that Harry needs to crawl into and hide in.

Another shot that is deliberately composed to generate meaning is the table-level shot of Harry passing across his information to Jake. The reason for this camera positioning is to make the envelope look much bigger, in order to emphasise the importance of this information. I made Jake Fenton Irish, in order to try and generate a sense of the period in which the film is set. There were a significant number of Irish immigrants arriving on the American East Coast during that period. As for the choice of names, I took inspiration from a computer game, *Timesplitters 2*, which is set in the 1920s, an Italian restaurant called Stazione and an Italian footballer, Baggio. I tried to include a number of elements in the film that would be recognisable and attractive to modern, Hollywood-literate, audiences. These included the 'love interest', Susie Warrington, the huge explosion that destroys Jake's house, and the highly choreographed, dramatic, climactic gunfight.

▣Assessment comments

This is a very accomplished piece of practical work. The synopsis provides an engaging and thoughtful outline of the original film. The aims and rationale illustrate a clear understanding of the requirements of the genre used and the student's desire to place the film within an older cinematic context. The screenplay evidences a confident and assured grasp of cinematic form and technique. The sequence functions very well as an opening sequence, establishing character, setting and narrative momentum. The self-evaluation acknowledges influences and describes the individual voice that has been added to the gangster film form. A confident, stylish and imaginative piece of work. Grade 'A'.

Chapter 5

Studies in World Cinema (FS5)

Overview of the FS5 Unit

This unit has been specifically designed in order to offer the opportunity to study forms of cinema that are very different to those that you have studied earlier in this course. The focus is World Cinema – both Section A and Section B include films and film movements from a range of historical periods and countries. Unit FS5 requires you to look at the film text and its form, as well as institutional and historical conditions that affected film production. You will need to consider why the films focused on in this topic were made and what technical, ideological and aesthetic factors contributed to their production.

The FS5 exam is one and a half hours long. You will need to answer one question from Section A and one from Section B. The mark distribution for this exam is slightly unevenly weighted: there are 30 marks available for Section A and 20 for Section B. You should use the time available within the exam accordingly, with 50 minutes for your Section A answer and 40 for your Section B answer.

Skills required for Unit FS5

This unit asks you primarily to identify and analyse the characteristic features of different kinds of cinema. There are three other key skills that you should be aware of when preparing for the FS5 exam:

1. The ability to recognise the significant ways in which the forms of the films you study are similar to, and different from, those found in mainstream, Hollywood-style, films.

2. The ability to place the films you study within a wider context of the developments and changes that have occurred within film history.

3. The ability to present a personal voice when analysing films from World Cinema and reflect on the challenges these types of films may present to your viewing.

Approaching Section A: Film styles and movements

Section A is the topic-based section of the FS5 exam. For each of the five topics, two focus films have been identified and you must make sure that you comment on one of these films in your answer. Alongside the discussion of your focus film, you will need to include analysis of at least two other relevant films (one of these could be the other focus film identified for your topic, if you choose). The core of your discussions for the topic you are studying should be debate about what makes the films distinctive. Their distinctiveness should be debated in terms of style and theme. The circumstances of the films' production – their historical, political and institutional context – will also constitute an important part of your analysis. There will be two questions about your chosen topic to select from in the exam.

German and Soviet cinemas in the 1920s

The study of this topic requires that you look at film products within these two countries from the 'mature silent' period. The focus of study should be how films during this period from both Germany and Russia construct stories and create psychological realities. It may seem that these two countries had very different film industries and film products: German film-making was synonymous with the Expressionist movement and Soviet film became linked inextricably with the theory and practice of montage. However, for the purposes of this topic you should be looking for connections, rather than differences. The films you study may be linked stylistically, thematically or ideologically.

There are two focus films for this section: *Nosferatu* (Murnau, 1922) and *Strike* (Eisenstein, 1924). You must study one of them, but you could use both within your research. Alongside Murnau's Expressionist classic *Nosferatu* you might look at other examples from German cinema at the time, such as Weine's *The Cabinet of Dr Caligari* or Lang's *Metropolis*. As well as Eisenstein's *Strike*, there are many other films from this period in Russian cinema that would make fascinating study, such as Vertov's *Man with a Movie Camera* or Eisenstein's *Battleship Potemkin*.

German cinema in the 1920s

Before about 1910, early German cinema was not afforded much critical standing. The films shown in the *ladenkino* (the German version of the nickelodeon), were watched mainly by working-class or unemployed people, so the middle-class establishment of critics and intellectuals did not consider that cinema was of much artistic merit. It was not until the work of Oskar Messter, and his establishment of a studio in Berlin, that film began to receive more critical status. Messter's films had more serious content than the films that had gone before. They were also more technically sophisticated. Also, in 1910, a film movement began, based on the idea of the *Autorenfilm*. This was a style of film-making that advocated using more serious themes and more innovative style within cinema. Films such as *Der Student von Prag* (directed by Stellan Rye in 1913) began to appear on German cinema screens and these acted as stylistic precursors to the work of the German Expressionists. Rye's film follows the experiences of a young student who sells his soul to the devil. The film has atmospheric lighting and a metaphysical theme. Cinematic devices evoke psychological realities. All of these factors would be seen again in the Expressionist films of the 1920s.

During the First World War, Germany was, of course, cut off from France, Britain and America. The films shown in German cinemas at that time were either from Scandinavia or 'home-grown' German products. The German film industry had to be more productive at this point in order to fill the gaps left by the French, American and British film products that were not available to German audiences. Scandinavian films at this point in cinematic history were often highly atmospheric and utilised *mise-en-scène* to promote psychological states. This was to be a significant influence on the later, German Expressionist films.

Das Cabinet Des Dr Caligari (Weine, 1919) is the most useful place to start any study of German cinema in the period. It provides a fascinating study of the birth of a new type of cinema in Germany. The original story for the film differs from that eventually seen in cinemas – this, in itself, is highly significant. In the original version, Caligari's travelling fair has come to the town of Holstenwall and a series of brutal murders is uncovered. A student, Francis, discovers that the killings have been perpetrated by Caligari's assistant Cesare, under the instruction and influence of Caligari himself. Cesare is kept in the cabinet of the film's title and only released in order to carry out Caligari's evil plans. The idea of an authority figure abusing his power to carry out brutalities had clear political associations in post-war Germany. The version of the story that finally appeared on cinema screens was narrated by Francis from an asylum for the insane, and it is eventually revealed that Dr Caligari is a quite benevolent person, who runs the asylum. The changes authorised by the studio behind Weine's film – Decla Bioskop – exchanged a political thrust within the film's story for a discourse on the nature of paranoia and psychological breakdown. Whether it was felt that the original story's political comment would be insensitive so close to the end of the war, or whether the change was made in order to promote audience engagement, is something you will need to debate if you study this film.

In terms of the style of *Das Cabinet Des Dr Caligari*, there are clear expressionist elements. Expressionist artists, such as Walter Rohrig, were drafted in by Weine to create the sets for the film, and the disturbing *mise-en-scène* that was created was very different from films that had gone before. Francis' disturbed state of mind is clearly mirrored in the jagged shapes and spatial distortions evident in the film's sets. The characters within the film exist within a world of sharp, angular shapes and ominous shadowing. They exist within a clearly Expressionist environment. It is the troubled nature of the soul that is narrated in this film – what the viewer sees is the psychological instability of Francis transferred into the arena of the film's action. Thematically, *Das Cabinet* does refer back to the metaphysical and psychological struggles of the student in Rye's influential film of 1913, *Der Student von Prag,* mentioned earlier. *Stylistically*, Weine's piece has clear Expressionist credentials. Any study that includes this film, however, would need to evaluate whether, ideologically, it has links with other German cinema from this period and with films from Russia that were made at this time.

Case Study 1: *Nosferatu* (Murnau, 1922)

Nosferatu's secondary title is '*a symphony of horrors*' and this provides an interesting starting place for an analysis of the film. Murnau's 1922 classic utilises a wide range of cinematic techniques, all employed to unsettle the audience. As with a symphony, it melds many different elements to create a powerful overall effect. The film derives its story from Bram Stoker's novel *Dracula*, although this influence was never credited. *Nosferatu* was mostly shot on location in central Europe, by cinematographer Fritz Wagner, and uses its locations powerfully. The expression of mood and atmosphere are central to the German Expressionist movement. Murnau's film evokes the horror of the vampire and his attacks through evocative use of lighting. *Nosferatu* does not use expressionistic sets, as in *Caligari*, but instead employs cinematography and lighting to generate atmosphere and impact. The vampire is often lit in order to cast his shadow over the film – figuratively and literally. He is often shot from below to create a sense of power and menace. The vampire's movement is slow, often jerky, created through the use of 'stop motion' photography. His otherness is clear, as is his seductive power.

If the changes in the story of *Das Cabinet Des Dr Caligari* render the film stylistically expressionistic, but not ideologically so, it will be important for you to discuss whether this is the same for *Nosferatu*. The protagonists within Gothic tales – vampires, werewolves and monsters – can be read as threatening to the bourgeois sensibilities and politics of the characters, and the society, that these creatures attack. *Nosferatu*'s pursuit of the Harker couple is threatening not just to them individually, but also to the social politics which they represent. There is a sexual undercurrent to the vampire that challenges both the propriety of the couple and the society in which they live. *Nosferatu* is the outsider, the marginalised individual, who does not live by the same code as others and is therefore a threat to the status quo.

EXERCISE 1

Imagine that you have been asked to create a poster publicising the re-release of *Nosferatu*. With a partner, either draw or describe in words what this poster would look like. Your task is to use expressionist elements in order to engage and interest a new audience for Murnau's film.

Soviet cinema in the 1920s

Before 1917, the film industry in Russia was not at all established. Unlike in Britain and America, where early cinema products were seen mainly by working-class people, poverty in Russia meant that the working classes could not afford to go to the cinema. The Russians who did have money did not see cinema as a valid art form and found it a very poor substitute for the theatre. Following the Communist revolution in 1917, the landscape of Russian cinema began to change.

Dziga Vertov was a leading participant in the development of early Russian cinema. He began working within the documentary form and, even at this stage within his career, was experimenting with the inclusion of subliminal images and very dramatic reconstructions of historical events. Vertov's work was very pro-Soviet and he gained backing from the Soviet Cinema Committee. Vertov, and a group of other young documentary makers, established a group calling themselves 'Kinoki' (Cinema eyes). They published a manifesto calling for an end to what they called an 'impotence' in cinema at that time. The group's manifesto described an alternative to this impotent cinema. Film should, according to them, be a tool for presenting a version of real events via expressive and dynamic style. The most famous of Vertov's films is perhaps *The Man With the Movie Camera* (1929), which incorporates the principles of his manifesto. This is a film about the film-making process. It shows the making of a film, while at the same time it is a film about film making. There is a reflexivity in this that was incredibly innovative and could even be said to predict the reflexivity of post-modern film making at the end of the twentieth century. Vertov uses split-screen effects and superimposition in *The Man With the Movie Camera*, in an attempt to create a dynamic and engaging sense of real events.

The films of Sergei Eisenstein are extremely significant within the study of Soviet cinema in the 1920s. Eisenstein was a Marxist intellectual who sought to transfer his politics into the structures of film making, as well as the content of film. In 1923, Eisenstein published a manifesto that proposed the use of a 'montage of attractions' within cinema. He advocated the use of many images, edited together quickly and powerfully, to create a point or message. The montage of attractions principle of film making did not follow the linear/continuity narrative form of Hollywood cinema, but sought to create impact, and generate the reality of events, through the dynamic juxtaposition of images.

Case Study 2: *Strike* (Sergei Eisenstein, 1924)

Strike was Eisenstein's directorial debut. Eisenstein intended it to be the first in a series of films narrating the rise of the Communist party, but, in the end, it was the only film of the series to be released. The film was designed to be an attack on the bourgeois as it existed in politics and also in film making. The story of the film concerns a plan by the workers to strike and the attempts of the authorities to impede the strike by placing pro-authority spies within the ranks of the workers. The strike is eventually stopped by savage and brutal means and many of the workers are killed.

In terms of its political message, *Strike* is clear. Authority in the hands of the bourgeois is misused and abused. The workers, or proletariat, have few rights and when they attempt to extend them, they are crushed. The film presents a justification of the Communist Party's rise to power and presents Communism as pro-worker and pro-proletariat rights. This message is incorporated in the narrative of the film through various means. There is no one hero in the narrative, the workers are a collective. In this way, the individualism of the bourgeoisie is rejected. The slaughter of the workers at the end of

Source: British Film Institute

the film is cut against scenes from an animal slaughterhouse. The message is clear. The masses are dehumanised under bourgeois authority.

Stylistically, the film employs innovative technical strategies in order to get its message across. Shots collide within montage sequences, rejecting narrative continuity in favour of impact and effect. Eisenstein uses dissolves in order to relay meaning and shows the discord of events through the juxtaposition of images – the slaughter sequence being the most dramatic example of this. Eisenstein wanted his film to be both stylistically revolutionary and reflective of the Russian revolution itself. *Strike* narrates an event that justifies the coming to power of the Communist party. It also acts as a seminal moment in the development of the use of montage in Soviet cinema.

Your task, if you study this topic, will be to consider the events that occurred in the cinema of both Germany and Russia during the 1920s, and identify similarities and differences. You should look at the social and political backdrops that existed in these countries during the twenties and consider how this affected the films that were produced. Are there political, stylistic or thematic links between films made in these two countries? Is there a commonality of response in both German and Soviet cinema to Hollywood structures and film content?

EXERCISE 2

With a partner, choose one sequence from *Strike*. Prepare notes for a presentation you will give to the rest of your class in your next Film Studies lesson. Your notes should include details of:

1. The particular stylistic elements of your sequence.

2. The thematic and ideological discussions apparent within your sequence.

3. The impact you think the sequence would have on both a contemporary cinema audience and the audience who would have seen the film at the time of its release.

Neo-realism in Italy and beyond

The 'beyond' part of the title for this topic is included in order to indicate that neo-realism is not in itself fixed as part of Italian cinema history, but has occurred in many different cinema cultures. Although this section of the chapter will concentrate on Italian neo-realism, it is possible to extend your study beyond the 1940s and 1950s in Italy, to encompass other neo-realist trends – in India or Latin America, for example. There are two focus films stipulated for this topic. One is De Sica's 1948 film *Bicycle Thieves* and the other is Olmi's 1978 film *The Tree of Wooden Clogs*.

As with other film movements, Italian neo-realism began with a call to create a type of cinema that was different from what had gone before – to create films that were stylistically and ideologically different from the films that had become the mainstay of Italian cinema. In 1943, the critic Umberto Barbaro wrote an article that demanded a style of film making that would be authentic and stylistically innovative, and reflect the lives of ordinary people. It was Barbaro who first used the phrase neo-realism, in his idea of what should come about.

Italian cinema, under the direction of Mussolini and his Department of Culture, had tended towards the epic. The films produced under the Fascist regime were often extremely sentimentalised and on a grand scale. The Italian Fascist intent of aligning Italy at that time with the Roman Empire (thus deriving quasi-Imperial status) was clear in these films. This myth-building was something the neo-realists wanted to replace with a cinema that reflected actual social conditions and real social concerns. When Mussolini and the Fascists were overthrown at the end of the Second World War, this change became possible.

The directors who took advantage of the post-Fascist freedom in Italian cinema were not new to directing. Unlike the French new wave or Surrealist directors, these were film makers who had already proved themselves, both critically and at the box-office. The likes of Visconti and Rossellini already had artistic reputations and they were able to use these in order to get their new films into circulation. These pre-existing reputations could do little to rebuild some of the studios that had been destroyed in the war, however, and the necessity to shoot on location became one of the hallmarks of the neo-realist movement.

The neo-realists' drive to represent real life, rather than a fictional and over-dramatised version of it, was an essential part of their philosophy of film making. The financial predicament of the Italian post-war film industry also meant that film stock was at a premium and directors would often use different types of film or lower quality types of film, because of the restrictions on availability. The often grainy film stock used in neo-realist films of this period did not contradict the aim of the neo-realists, however, but served to contribute to it. The grainy look added to the documentary feel of these films.

The neo-realist directors often used non-actors in their work and this also contributed to a feeling of 'real' events being depicted. Without the recognition factor that occurs when a well-known actor appears on screen, viewers were more likely to believe in the reality of what they were seeing. Improvisation of acting and dialogue also became a signature characteristic of the neo-realist movement and again this contributed a realistic feel to the films. The move away from standard narrative forms, as described by Barbaro in his 1943 article, was evident in the structuring of narratives within the neo-realists' films. Events often seemed to collide, rather than seamlessly move from one into another. The continuity principles of Hollywood cinema were challenged or rejected through the inclusion of scenes of seemingly disparate events.

In terms of the politics of neo-realism in Italy in the 1940s and 1950s, the reaction to, and rejection of, Fascism and the restrictions it imposed on cinema, are clear. The neo-realists' drive for cinema to reflect the real life of the Italian masses does have similarities to the politics of cinema proposed by those directors within the Soviet Montage movement, in that it requires cinema to act as the voice of the people, rather than those authorities who control them. The neo-realists demanded freedom from aesthetic, political and technical control. They wanted a cinema that would give voice to Italy's youth – its future, rather than its past.

A very good place to begin your study would be with Luchino Visconti's 1942 film, *Ossessione* (*Obsession*). The film is based on the novel *The Postman Always Rings Twice* by James M. Cain (there are also two American films adapted from this novel). The story is of an obsessive love affair, which ends in the murder of the husband of the woman involved in the affair. The film was shot on location and dealt with the passions of two working-class people. It is starkly shot, avoids stylisation and represents the affair through innovative cinematic techniques.

The principles of the neo-realist movement are perhaps most vividly evident within Roberto Rossellini's 1945 film *Roma, Citta Aperta* (*Rome, Open City*). This film is set during the time of the 'opening up' of Rome after the fascist regime has crumbled. It offers a backdrop of historical reality and uses this to tell the story of resistance to the Fascist regime and the Resistance movement in Italy at that time. What is so innovative about the film is the way in which these historical happenings are told through a filter of life on the streets of Rome. Rossellini uses a series of everyday, often unconnected, events to deliver comments on the war and those who fought against it. The film uses low-quality film stock to evoke a documentary feel to the events that are depicted.

Case Study 3: *Bicycle Thieves* (de Sica, 1948)

Vittorio de Sica's work was also of great significance within the Italian neo-realist movement. His 1946 film *Sciuscia* (*Shoe Shine*) related the story of the destruction of innocence under Fascist-controlled Rome and used grainy film stock in order to generate an effect of bleak reality.

His most famous work, however, and one of the focus films within this topic, was *Ladri di Biciclette* (*Bicycle Thieves*, 1948). The story of the film evokes the economic hardship within post-war Italy. An unemployed man pawns the family's sheets in order to buy a bicycle, so that he can get to new employment. The bicycle is then stolen and the man and his son scour the streets of Rome in an attempt to find the bicycle and the thieves. The story is anti-epic. On one level, it is a poignant tale of hardship. It is also, of course, a comment on the social conditions and political context of the time in Rome. Unemployment was rife and the working classes were in a state of despair. The culpability for the man's predicament lies with the Fascists, whose war had destroyed hope and economic security for many working-class people.

Bicycle Thieves was very well received by the critics. It won the 1949 Academy Award for Best Foreign Language film and was lauded in many countries. In terms of representation, political stance and story type, the film is a very typical neo-realist piece. Technically, it employs many of the 'conventions' of the neo-realist movement. It includes events that seem to collide, rather than move fluidly from one to another. It incorporates seemingly random events, such as the protagonist's meeting with a group of priests. It uses non-actors – the film's main protagonist was played by a factory worker, coached by de Sica. *Bicycle Thieves* is at once a moving story of the effects of poverty on one family and a comment on the effects of war on the everyday lives of individuals.

EXERCISE 3

Watch the opening sequence of *Bicycle Thieves* again. Make detailed notes on the way in which this sequence:

- establishes the mood and atmosphere of the film
- introduces the viewer to the ideological concerns of the film
- indicates the neo-realist style of the film.

Case Study 4: *The Tree of Wooden Clogs* (Olmi, 1978)

Ermanno Olmi's 1978 film *The Tree of Wooden Clogs* won both the *Palme D'Or* and the Ecumenical Jury prize at the Cannes Film Festival in the year of its release. The film's narrative stretches over a twelve-month period and follows the lives of three peasant families, all of whom work on an estate. The film's dialogue and events centres around the members of these families and the relationships both within the families and between the different families. Olmi drew on his own experiences as a child within a peasant family for this film.

As this film was made much later than many of the other examples of neo-realism you may have chosen to study, it will be necessary to look carefully at whether or not you consider *The Tree of Wooden Clogs* to be stylistically and thematically consistent with films made within the standard chronological span of Italian neo-realism. Many elements of this film hark back to neo-realist principles of film making. Olmi used non-actors for his film – peasants from the region in which he shot it. The sound for the film was recorded at the same time as the images and to promote the authenticity of the regional setting, the language spoken in the film is Bergamesque, not Italian.

The thematic concerns of *The Tree of Wooden Clogs* also echo those of 1940s and 1950s neo-realist pieces. It reflects a particular social condition and articulates specific social concerns. The almost feudal relationship between the peasants and the landowner in Olmi's film represents an attack on an extremely traditional and imbalanced economic and social dynamic. What this film does not share with the likes of *Bicycle Thieves* and *Rome, Open City* is a post-Fascist context and Fascist target.

EXERCISE 4

With a partner, make two lists of notes. The first list should include textual evidence for the ways in which *The Tree of Wooden Clogs* is similar to the 1940s and 1950s Italian neo-realist films you have studied. The second list should describe how it differs.

When you have completed both lists, discuss with your partner whether or not you think neo-realism is a movement that extended beyond the period of the 1940s and the 1950s.

Japanese cinema: 1950–1970

The director who is probably most synonymous with Japanese cinema of this period is Akira Kurosawa. This topic area gives plenty of scope for the study of this director. However, one important thing to remember is that it will not be enough in the exam to limit your analysis to Kurosawa and his films. Your focus for the topic of Japanese cinema should be the varying genres and styles of film evident with the twenty-year period of the topic's title. As with all of the FS5 Section A topic areas, there are two possible focus films. You could study one, or both. Kurosawa's 1950 film, *Rashomon*, provides one of the focus studies and Suzuki's 1966 film, *Tokyo Drifter*, provides the other.

From the early Japanese films of the 1920s, there have been two dominant genres seen in Japanese cinemas: *jidai geki* and *gendai geki*. *Jidai geki* films are period pieces. They are set before 1868, the year the feudal system was abolished in Japan. *Jidai geki* films usually include Samurai warriors, ghosts or supernatural elements, sword fights and historical romances. These films often represent a fictionalised notion of Japan's past. *Gendai geki* films are set in contemporary time. They represent contemporary life in Japan. The *gendai geki* genre includes *shomin geki* films, which represent and deconstruct middle-class life in Japan.

Case Study 5: *Rashomon* (Kurosawa, 1950)

Source: British Film Institute

Rashomon was made at the very beginning of the identified time period of this topic's title. It is set in twelfth-century Japan and is structured around four separate narratives, each giving a version of the event at the heart of the film's narrative. The film offers a fascinating discussion of the nature of truth, more specifically of the subjective nature of truth. The story of *Rashomon* offers a complex set of perspectives and subjective readings. The film begins with three people who are sheltering from the rain beneath the Rashomon Gate (in Kyoto). A woodcutter and a priest tell the third person a story. The woodcutter presents a tale of finding a nobleman dead in a forest. The man has been stabbed, but his knife is missing. The priest tells the third person that he had seen the nobleman and his wife travelling before the murder. Both the priest and the woodcutter have just come from the police station, where they have been giving statements. They tell the third person that at the police station, a bandit had been captured who confessed to the killing. They then relate the bandit's account and at this point within the film, the levels of truth have already become complicated. The bandit had told of his desire for the nobleman's wife and his rape of her. His story then reveals that she had then forced her husband and the bandit into a dual, which her husband had lost.

The next account of events is that of the wife. Still being related by the priest and the woodcutter, these accounts of events are already at second or third hand. The wife's story is that after the rape her husband rejected her, because he deemed her virtue to have been easily lost. She had fainted with grief and awoken to find her husband dead next to her.

The final version of events is again related by the priest and the woodcutter and is apparently that of the nobleman, relayed through a medium. The dead man's version paints another different picture of events. After her rape, his wife had begged the bandit to take her away with him. Because of the shame he felt, the nobleman had then committed suicide. The final narration comes from the woodcutter, who then admits that he was actually an eyewitness to the events. His account is that there was no dagger, but the nobleman was killed by a sword thrust. The fight between the nobleman and the bandit had been motivated by the woman. The men did not want to fight and the nobleman's death was almost an accident. At this point in the film, the woodcutter's account is presented as if it were the objective truth. It is only when the stranger who is listening to all of these conflicting accounts suggests that there might be no dagger because the woodcutter had stolen it, that the truth is then again in question.

Rashomon presents an intricate and complex narrative, in which conflicting truths are presented to other characters and to the audience of the film. Reality is not fixed – the truth lies somewhere in the collision between all of the versions of events that are presented. Kurosawa's film was extremely influential on many other film movements because of its technical skill, but also because of its discussions of perspective and objectivity. The film deals with the nature of memory and the influences that shape remembered events. Technically, *Rashomon* is extremely impressive. It includes complicated tracking shots and point-of-view shots that position the viewer inside the individual perspectives of the differing narratives. *Rashomon* was critically acclaimed, winning the Golden Lion at the Venice Film Festival during its first year of release. It is an example of the *jidai geki* genre, which Kurosawa worked with many times in his career. The settings, time period, fight scenes and representation of Japan it employs are all characteristic of this genre.

As has already been stated in this section, Kurosawa was not the only great director working in Japan during the period from 1950 to 1970. Kenji Mizoguchi was acclaimed as an auteur by the French *Cahiers du Cinema* critics and won much praise for his cinematic artistry. His 1952 film *The Life of Oharu* won the international director's prize at the 1952 Venice Film Festival. The film is set in seventeenth-century Kyoto and provides another example of the *jidai geki* genre. The film focuses on the life of a prostitute and through the presentation of her tale, Mizoguchi comments on life in Japan under the feudal system. His 1953 film *Ugetsu* is also a *jidai geki* piece. It is set during the feudal wars in Japan in the sixteenth century and focuses on two young men who leave their wives to go off in search of fame and fortune. They eventually discover that what they had left behind was more valuable than what they were searching for. The film includes the historicised romance and supernatural elements that are typical of the *jidai geki* genre.

Yasujiro Ozu is another important director in the history of Japanese cinema. Unlike Kurosawa or Mizoguchi, Ozu worked mostly within the *shomin geki* genre. His films reflected contemporary social concerns in Japan. Ozu's films concentrated on narratives concerning how lower-middle-class people attempted to deal with the social, cultural and economic constraints they faced. His cinematography is very different from that of Kurosawa's. The complex and lengthy tracking shots found in Kurosawa's work are not evident in Ozu's. Instead, the camera is much more static, even remaining in rooms when characters have left. Ozu's use of this 'off-screen' space was a significant, stylistic element in his work. Both *Tokyo Story* (1953) and *Tokyo Twilight* (1957) were very successful films for Ozu.

Japanese cinema of the 1960s contained films that many critics attributed to a new wave in Japanese film-making. Directors such as Hiroshi Teshigahara, Seijun Suzuki and Shohei Imamura began making contemporary films that dealt with young members of Japanese society and the effects on Japan of rapid industrialisation. This period of Japanese film history saw a new genre develop – *seishun eiga* or 'youth film', which seemed to capture the anxieties of Japanese youth in a rapidly changing society.

Case Study 6: *Tokyo Drifter* (Suzuki, 1966)

Seijun Suzuki's 1966 film *Tokyo Drifter* focuses on the character of Tetsuya, a young *yakuza* (member of the Japanese mafia). Tetsuya attempts to pursue a legitimate career, but this attempt is thwarted and he is then pursued across Japan. The scenarios in which he finds himself, the confrontations he has and the vivid sets in which the action takes place provide the main ingredients of this film. Suzuki's film explores and presents a Japanese underworld, full of assassins, gangsters and hitmen.

The visual elements of Suzuki's film indicate its Japanese 'new wave' credentials. The colouring of the film is often abstract and always vivid. Tetsuya's blue suit, for example, is an incongruous outfit for a man who is trying to escape notice. His journey takes him through snowbound and dimly lit environments and it is this extreme of *mise-en-scène* that helped mark the film as part of a new era of Japanese cinema. The action and fight sequences are many and often seem incongruous, but they define *Tokyo Drifter* as very much a film for a youth audience.

The incongruous moments in the film, the events that often seem irrelevant and the lurid colour palette Suzuki uses create an almost surreal atmosphere for this *yakuza* story. The film moves through varying sets, rather than realistic locations. It intersperses humour with the violent exchanges and presents a recognisably modern world, unlike that presented by Kurosawa and his contemporaries. Thematically, the film is concerned with issues of gangland violence and the difficulties that Japan's youth confront within this type of society. It articulates a tension within 1960s Japanese youth culture, but also presents events in a visually dynamic way, designed to attract youth audiences of this period.

EXERCISE 5

1. Use magazines or the internet to find two critical reviews of the focus film you have studied for this section. Read through both of the reviews carefully and make notes on their main points.

2. In your Film Studies class, discuss what the reviews you chose said about your focus film and what your own responses were to the film.

Cinematic new waves

This is a slightly unusual topic within the FS5 exam, because it has three sub-sections you can choose from:

- the French new wave (1958 to 1965)
- East Asian new wave cinema
- a comparative study from different new waves.

There is a guiding question across all three of these sub-sections, however, which is: 'What is a "new wave"?'. Your task will be to consider whether there are any historical, technical and/or thematic considerations that link the films you are discussing within the sub-section you have chosen. The two focus films for this section are *A Bout de Souffle* (Godard, 1959) and *Chungking Express* (Wong Kar-Wai, 1994). Obviously, each of the sub-sections lends itself to the study of one or both of these focus films. For example, for the comparative study sub-section, both of the focus films could be used.

The French new wave 1958–1965

Post-war films in France tended to be literary adaptations, which focused on story and dialogue in order to create linear narratives. The French *Nouvelle Vague* (new wave) held itself in opposition to this type of cinema – Francois Truffaut's rejection of *'La tradition de la qualité'* referred to this type of film making – one in which technique was unobtrusive and technical devices were employed to aid the viewer's suspension of disbelief. The origins of the *Nouvelle Vague* in French film-making can be found in the magazine *Cahiers du Cinema*. This publication was devoted to articles concerning film and film making. *Cahiers* was founded in 1951 by Andre Bazin and quickly became the forum for many young writers interested in film, among the most famous being Francois Truffaut, Jean-Luc Godard, Claude Chabrol and Eric Rohmer. All of these writers were cinema enthusiasts, whose viewing experiences had encompassed a variety of film texts from traditional French cinema, to Hollywood, to German Expressionism and beyond. The *Cinematheque Francaise*, which has an enormous archive of films from around the world, was a regular haunt of these writers.

This eclectic experience was to greatly influence the criticism, and later the film making, of these directors and others.

The *Cahiers du Cinema* critics focused on two major principles in their writing. First, that cinema should never be a solely intellectual experience, that it should engage the audience's emotions equally. This engagement tended to focus on an evocative use of *mise-en-scène*, but also included the use of other technical devices, too. Second, that films should include a sense of personal authorship. As you will have seen in your studies for the FS4 unit, '*La Politique des Auteurs*', or Auteurism, highlighted the need for the identification of the director's signature within their work. It was Truffaut's 1954 essay: 'Une certaine tendence du cinema Francais' ('A certain tendency in French cinema') which not only attacked the '*tradition de la qualite*' mentioned above, but also called for '*La Politique des Auteurs*'. A film, according to Truffaut and the other French new wave critics, should be a personal, artistic expression; one that includes individual signatures from the director. The *Cahiers* critics did not merely identify the need for personal signatures within films, they also named directors whose work they thought exhibited signature characteristics. The likes of Howard Hawks, Alfred Hitchcock and Orson Welles, as well as French directors and directors from many other countries, were therefore deemed to be auteurs.

In terms of the actual film making of the French new wave directors, theory did eventually become reality, with Truffaut's 1957 film *Les Mistons*. Although this was a short film, it did mark the beginning of a significant change in French cinema products. 1959 was an incredibly significant year for the French new wave and three films were made in that year that sealed the artistic status of this new film movement. Truffaut's *Les Quatre-cent Coups* (*The 400 Blows*) won the best direction prize at the Cannes Film Festival in 1959 and proved both a critical and commercial success. Resnais' *Hiroshima, Mon Amour* was also a big commercial and critical success and Godard's *A Bout de Souffle* helped consolidate the critical reputation of the French new wave.

Contrary to some opinion, the French new wave did not collapse after 1959 and many more, extremely fascinating, films were made after this date that you could include in your study of this topic. Truffaut's *Tirez sur le Pianiste* (*Shoot the Pianist*, 1960) and *Jules et Jim* (1961) would make very useful references in your exam essay. Godard's 1961 film *Une Femme est une Femme* and Resnais' film of the same year, *L'Annee Derniere a Marienbad*, would also lend themselves to much useful comment on the French new wave.

There are a number of characteristics, both institutional and technical, that are shared by French new wave films and these will become an essential part of your discussions. As has been already stated, the French new wave directors were cinephiles. They had absorbed many different styles of cinema from many different countries and this eclecticism can be seen in the films they produced. *A Bout de Souffle*, for example, employs conventions of the gangster genre in order to construct its story. The films were made with low budgets and a tight shooting schedule, in response to both budgetary considerations and a desire to present a more edgy style of cinema. Editing did not follow continuity rules and many of the French new wave films employ edit types such as jump cuts in order to make the mechanics of the film-making process obvious to viewers. Naturalistic lighting and locations are also a characteristic within the films of the French new wave and serve to mark a difference between these films and the studio-based products that the new wave directors rejected. The use of on-location sound recording is also evident and its function is twofold: to render scenes more immediate and again to create a viewing situation in which the technique behind the film is visible to the viewer. Hand-held cameras were also used in the shooting of some scenes and again this provides a jerky effect that signals the mechanics of the film to its audience. There is a strong reflexive tendency within French new wave films,

Case Study 7: *A Bout de Souffle* (Godard, 1959)

Source: British Film Institute

Jean-Luc Godard's 1959 film *A Bout de Souffle* has become an iconic product of the French new wave. It has been both critically and commercially successful for decades and remains one of the most famous products of the French new wave era. It was shot on location and made with a tiny budget of $90,000. As has already been stated, the film utilises the gangster genre, but reworks the conventions of that genre to focus on the relationship between the gangster and his American girlfriend, rather than the relationships between different gangsters.

A Bout de Souffle is extremely characteristic of the *Cahiers du Cinema* philosophies and contains many of the technical devices used in other French new wave products. The film is shot on location and uses these outdoor locations to frame the chaotic and dynamic action of the film. Jean-Paul Belmondo's protagonist is neither hero nor villain, thus not allowing the film's audience to have a clear response to him. There are innovative sequences, shot using a hand-held camera, in which shots seem to collide and the viewer is disorientated. The sound recording in the film is naturalistic and on location. Belmondo's character often seems to mumble – again the viewer's clear interpretation of events is thwarted. The film utilises jump cuts to break with linear, continuity narrative traditions. Many different types of disorientation occur within Godard's film: the use of seemingly disjointed shots, disorientating shifts in location and perplexing shifts from close-ups to long shots. All of these technical devices help to create a very different type of viewing experience to that which the *Cahiers* directors challenged.

in that they at the same time tell a story and present the technique of the storytelling process to the viewer.

East Asian new wave cinema

If you attempt to encounter and evaluate all of the possible 'new waves' in all of the East Asian countries, you will find this a very difficult topic to pin down. Your first decision should be the particular country on which you are going to focus. Bearing in mind that the focus film for this section is *Chungking Express*, the simplest route with this topic might be to decide on Hong Kong cinema.

As a country of almost diametrically opposed national characteristics, Hong Kong is fascinating. At the time *Chungking Express* was made, Hong Kong was under British sovereignty. In 1997, however, it reverted to Chinese control. In 1994, the 'personality' of Hong Kong was Western, but with a Cantonese-speaking population. It was geographically attached to mainland China, but functioned as a thriving contemporary metropolis. The tensions at the core of this tiny modern nation, about to be reabsorbed by its powerful, Mandarin-speaking neighbour, were clear. Hong Kong cinemas were full of Hollywood products. Businesses in Hong Kong were more global than Chinese, and European and American influences could be seen in everything from fashion to television programmes. It was not that Hong Kong wanted to hide its East Asian-ness, but that it was a place distinctly different from its Communist neighbour.

The cinema of Hong Kong had always been a melting pot of influences, with Cantonese folk tales and martial arts films providing much of its indigenous cinema. Those films which became known as examples of the Hong Kong new wave, did not so much reject the cinema that had gone before but steer Hong Kong cinema in a new direction. By the late 1970s, Western audiences had begun to become aware of Hong Kong cinema. If these audiences' first introduction to the cinema of Hong Kong had been via Bruce Lee films, it was the films of the late 1970s, such as Tsui Hark's *The Butterfly Murders* and Ann Hui's *The Secret* (both made in 1979) that presented Hong Kong cinema as far more than just martial arts films.

With a new, global audience for its films, the Hong Kong film industry entered the 1980s with an opportunity not just for wider critical acclaim, but also for increased commercial success. John Woo's 1989 film *The Killer*, for example, introduced him to a global audience as an innovative action film maker. By the 1990s, the Hong Kong film industry was known to a much more global audience. The many action films made during the late 1980s and 1990s became the most conspicuous product of the Hong Kong film industry. It was at this stage during Hong Kong's film-making history, that what is often called the 'second stage' of the Hong Kong new wave came about. If the first stage had produced films such as *The Butterfly Murders* and *The Secret,* this second stage saw Stanley Kwan's *Actress* (1993) and Wong Kar-Wai's *Chungking Express* (1994).

Case Study 8: *Chungking Express* (Wong Kar-Wai, 1994)

Source: British Film Institute

Chungking Express is quite an unusual film, even within the context of other examples from the Hong Kong new wave. Visually and stylistically the film is extremely striking and is structured around two strangely interlocking narratives. Two men, 'Cop 223' and 'Cop 663', are the main characters within the two narratives. Both of the policemen experience rejection by the end of the film and the two narratives are more than merely thematically linked. Both, for example, frequent the 'Midnight Express' fast food restaurant and both have contact with the character Faye who works there.

The stylistic elements of *Chungking Express* are perhaps the most striking thing about the film. It uses hand-held camera, jump cuts and slow motion to create a film reminiscent of those of the French new wave. The main characters in Wong Kar-Wai's film also have the kind of disappointment with the world that is common in the films of Godard and his contemporaries. *Chungking Express* is not just a film of unexpected cinematic technique, however, and Cop 223's obsession with tins of pineapple adds yet another unusual element.

Chungking Express is very different from the action genre pieces that were so common in Hong Kong cinema up to that point. It has a visual and stylistic dynamism, but the malaise of its central characters runs counter to the physical activity of action protagonists. The character of the 'woman in the blond wig' is a smuggler, who shoots one of her fellow criminals, but this crime is left undiscovered and unpunished; a plot element that would be unheard of within a generic action title. The characterisation, storyline and style of *Chungking Express* all seem to articulate a state of high anxiety and impermanence. Considering the fact that the handover of Hong Kong to China was only three years away when this film was made, it is not surprising that Wong Kar-Wai's film seems saturated with disillusionment and trepidation.

Comparative study

The comparative study option within the cinematic new waves section asks that you use different examples of new wave cinema in order to consider what constitutes a new wave. You could use the previous two national new waves (French and East Asian) in order to consider this question, but equally, you might range outside of the specified national new waves to discuss whether it is possible to find historical, technical or thematic consistencies. One important issue to remember, however, is that the focus films for this section are still *A Bout de Souffle* and *Chungking Express* and you must make sure that one of these films provides at least part of your discussion.

It would be very easy to become lost in a study of the varied examples of new wave cinemas, but the simplest way of remaining in touch with the required focus of this section is to constantly keep in mind particular criteria for assessing the films you choose. Ask yourself the same questions about each of your films. These questions should be based on the more general issues of historical, technical and thematic considerations. The exercise at the end of this section provides a list of the kinds of questions that would be useful in your search for similarities between your chosen texts.

You have a wide range of new wave cinemas to choose from. You might, for example, consider the films produced after the demise of General Franco in Spain in 1975. You could look at Pedro Almodovar's earlier work, such as *Pepi, Luci, Bom and Other Girls on the Heap* (1978) and consider how it functions as a challenge to the repressive sanctions imposed on film and other art forms under Franco's Fascist government. You could include analysis of *La Movida*, the artistic movement that sprang up after the Fascists lost power, and discuss the place of Almodovar within this movement.

An analysis of the Danish Dogma 95 movement would also provide a fascinating discussion of new wave cinema. Begun by Lars von Trier and Thomas Vinterberg, Dogma 95 films are created around ten basic principles of film making. These include shooting on hand-held cameras, using only natural lighting and real settings and sound that has been recorded at the same time as the images of the film. Von Trier's 1999 film *The Idiots* would provide a fascinating subject for this topic, as would Vinterberg's *Celebration* (1999).

Whatever films you choose for the comparative study, remember that for this topic the interaction between text and subtext is particularly important. Consider the impact of historical events on the films you have chosen. Does your film articulate a response to these events? Consider the films that were being produced in that country before the film you have chosen – does your film act as a challenge to the structure and content of the earlier films? Ultimately, you will need to decide whether or not you think that the films you are studying are part of a new wave of national film making and give fully substantiated reasons for your decision.

Surrealist and fantasy cinema

Unlike many of the other topics within the FS5 exam, the topic of 'Surrealism and Fantasy' does not have national or historical boundaries attached to it. Surrealist and fantasy films have in common a rejection of standard (Hollywood) narrative structuring, but they differ in several ways. One way of distinguishing between the two styles of cinema is to consider

EXERCISE 6

With a partner, discuss the following questions in relation to the examples of new wave cinema you have chosen:

1. When was each of the films made? Did any significant political or social events happen around the time of the film's production?

2. Did the director of your film experience any significant restrictions, either during the period before the film was made or during the period of production?

3. Were there any technical restrictions or, conversely, new developments in film-making technology that affected the production of the film?

4. Are there any stylistic features of the film that seem to distinguish it from other films made during the same period?

5. What seem to be the thematic pre-occupations of the film? Do these pre-occupations seem to act as a challenge to any dominant social or political attitudes at the time the film was made?

6. How was the film received by critics and audiences at the time of its release? Did responses to the film acknowledge any differences between it and films that had gone before? Was the film discussed at the time as an example of a new wave in cinema in that country?

intention and impact. Traditionally, at least, Surrealist films include an attack on the bourgeois and bourgeois values. Fantasy cinema, in the most part, presents itself as visual spectacle rather than ideological comment. This is, of course, a very basic distinction and the rest of this section will consider the differences between the two film movements in more detail.

The two focus films for this section are *The Phantom of Liberty* (Bunuel, 1974) and *Alice* (Svankmajer, 1988). As with any of the FS5 topics, you must use one of these films in your discussions, but you may choose to use both. In order to debate what constitutes a Surrealist or a fantasy film, however, you should make sure that your essay includes references other than just the focus film(s). It is not enough, for example, just to concentrate on the films of Luis Bunuel, as this would not give enough depth or range to your answers. You could consider Cocteau's *Orphee*, for example, or Jeunet's *Delicatessen*. You could also consider whether Surrealist or fantasy films exist in today's cinema and include Lynch's *Lost Highway* or *Mulholland Drive* in your discussions.

Surrealist cinema

Surrealist cinema is essentially provocative, visually and politically. The antecedents of Surrealism can be found in art, but cinema provided an excellent medium to present disturbing images. Cinema audiences were also accustomed (although cinema was still young and audiences did not have a huge history of viewing) to stories being told clearly and unenigmatically. Therefore, for the Surrealists of the 1920s and 1930s, part of the impact of their films was derived from a stark difference to what had appeared on the cinema screen before. The critics and directors who were drawn to a Surrealist ethic in film making at that time were largely those who were searching for an alternative to Hollywood mainstream products and the structures they used. In France, for example, where a more Impressionist style of cinema was common, Surrealist directors wanted to challenge this kind of style. They saw it as regressive and harking back to nineteenth-century forms of art.

André Breton's 1924 Surrealist Manifesto had called for a new form of cinema – one that could bring together 'two apparently contradictory states of dream and reality into a sort of absolute reality, or surreality'. Breton and his fellow Surrealists realised the mass appeal of cinema and saw the cinema canvas as a way of addressing a mass audience. Their idea was that the bourgeois institutions and politics that were being challenged in Surrealist films would also be at odds with the politics of the mass audience. Breton's manifesto of Surrealism saw cinema as a place where everyday situations could be imbued with extraordinary qualities – that the combination of the visual and the aural found in cinema could be used to liberate subconscious meaning. What the viewer was consciously seeing and hearing, and what they were subconsciously understanding, was the dynamic the Surrealists hoped to exploit. The relationship between the objective and the subjective was also key to the Surrealist movement. The notion of an objective reality i.e. one that exists in the collective consciousness, was part of the Surrealist debate. Because these films offered representations of dreams and the workings of the subconscious, they considered the realities that exist for every individual i.e. subjective reality. The experiences that are often considered beyond language and any fixed description, were those that the Surrealists attempted to show visually in their films. The shifting nature of understanding and perception was depicted through the disparate and, often disturbing, images in Surrealist films. For Surrealists, the relationship between a film and its viewer was interactive and liberating. If meaning was not fixed by traditional cinematic structures, then the audience could extract a subjective meaning of their own.

Whether the Surrealist films you have chosen to study are French, Spanish or from another nation, your task will be to attempt to find commonality. Are there conventions to Surrealism, or is this in itself a contradiction? There are connections, and these can be most easily expressed in a series of thematic couplings: desire and death, perception and reality, conscious and subconscious, and the bourgeoisie and the masses. The means by which these pairings are presented in a Surrealist film may differ, but when you assess whether or not a film can be classed as Surrealist, you should look for evidence of such pairings.

As stated at the beginning of this section, you should not only look outside of national boundaries, but also those of chronology. Consider whether you think that Surrealism, in its true form, survived beyond the 1920s and 1930s, or whether it has continued into more contemporary cinema. For example, *Lost Highway*, David Lynch's 1997 film, involves a protagonist whose consciousness seems to split, so that he becomes two separate characters. Fred Madison 'becomes' Pete Dayton after experiencing what Lynch has called a 'psychogenic fugue'. He splits his personality in order to attempt to understand why he has murdered his wife. The narrative of the film is fractured and does not follow strict linear lines. The debate concerning objective and subjective reality is clearly narrated through Fred's (subconscious) attempts to understand the events that occur. Is it possible, therefore, that *Lost Highway* is a Surrealist film, even though it omits the bourgeoisie attack which is central to early Surrealism?

Case Study 9: Bunuel's *The Phantom of Liberty* (1974)

Source: British Film Institute

Luis Bunuel's 1974 film is constructed around a series of nominally connected episodes. As with other examples of Surrealism, it flouts conventional narrative constructions and instead offers individual sequences which are linked thematically, visually and politically rather than by narrative sense. The twelve distinctive sections of the film have residual elements of the section that has gone before, but do not together create a traditionally cohesive narrative. The events in the Napoleonic wars of the first section, for example, are then revealed as part of a history book, being read by a nanny. The nanny is then seen to be working for a bourgeois family, the father of which is then shown to be suffering from bizarre dreams. Each episode springs from an element of the previous one. Ultimately, it is coincidence that connects the twelve parts of the film.

True to the Surrealist 'philosophy' of film making, *The Phantom of Liberty* offers an attack on repressive social, religious and political codes. The institutions represented within the film are undermined by the events and imagery of the piece. Policemen and schoolteachers cannot find a missing girl. Monks are seen playing cards and using religious artefacts for bets. In one of the most humorous and surreal sequences, the army are seen hunting foxes with tanks. The judicial system is incompetent and allows the release of a murderer. The bourgeois father's dreams are presented as a product of a decadent and self-absorbed lifestyle.

Bunuel uses extremely dark and controversial themes in his film to indicate the hypocrisy of the characters and institutions he targets. *The Phantom of Liberty* employs incest, sado-masochism and fetishism to strip away the veneer of what it criticises. The film also uses devices such as dreamscapes, flashbacks and wipes in order to promote its surreal effect. Viewers of this film are denied the security of standard narrative patterns and identifiable imagery. Instead, they are presented with a visual discussion of Karl Marx's phrase 'the phantom of liberty'. Bunuel's film is not a piece of communist dialectic, however, and should not be approached as such. The phrase from Marx functions to introduce a challenge to accepted notions of freedom. *The Phantom of Liberty* is a film that presents social, political and religious codes as ultimately repressive and contrary to the true freedom of the individual.

EXERCISE 7

With a partner, read the following quotation from André Breton's Surrealist Manifesto:

'Perhaps the imagination is on the verge of recovering its rights. If the depths of our minds conceal strange forces capable of augmenting or conquering those on the surface, it is in our greatest interest to capture them.'

Using textual references from the films you have studied for this topic, discuss whether or not you think that the Surrealist films you have studied gave cinematic 'life' to Breton's statement.

Fantasy cinema

As has already been stated in the introduction to this section, the line between Surrealist and fantasy cinema is often very blurred. Distinguishing between the two by means of an evaluation of ideological intent is, however, perhaps the simplest means. Fantasy cinema might contain what appear to be surreal (with a small 's') elements, but it does not have the same political motivation. Fantasy cinema does not replicate the attack on bourgeois society that is seen in the films of Bunuel and his Surrealist contemporaries. Any surreal imagery in fantasy films functions primarily to promote a sense of the fantastical and to enthral the viewer with visual spectacle.

Alongside the problem of distinguishing between Surrealist and fantasy cinema, is the issue of the application of the term 'fantasy' to so many films. The *Star Wars* films have fantastical storylines, as does the *Lord of the Rings* trilogy, however, they do not contain the kind of fantasy sequences that would make them suitable study texts for this topic. You need, therefore, to be very careful in your choice of texts if you choose this topic.

The safest way to approach fantasy cinema is to concentrate on those films which contain the kind of imagery that could be deemed to have a deliberate fantasy element and those that have been designed to engage the viewer through striking, fantastical visuals. The work of French director Jean-Pierre Jeunet, for example, would make for fascinating discussion. *City of Lost Children*, for example, creates a visual arena in which the rational seems to have been rejected, where dreams and the imagination reign. The mad scientist of the film, Krank, cannot dream, so seeks to steal the dreams of the children he abducts. The film includes a fantastical cityscape and characters straight out of a nightmare, such as Irvin, 'the talking brain'. This film centres on the quest of One and Miette to find One's abducted brother, Denree. It is not a film about politics, but one in which the imagination and the ability to dream is presented as essential to life. Jeunet's *Amelie* is also a film in which reality seems to have come adrift and fantasy is the norm. Amelie's heart is seen pounding in her chest and she dissolves to water when confronted with Nino. The viewer is presented with Amelie's fantasy and the fairlytale credentials of the film are clear. The fantastical imagery has been created to draw the viewer further towards Amelie's world; not to make an ideological point.

The work of Terry Gilliam could also provide an interesting case study of fantasy cinema. The plastic surgery sequences in *Brazil*, the fantastical locations of *Time Bandits* or the antics of *Baron Munchausen* would all be worthy of study for this topic. Of course, a study of fantasy cinema could include study of earlier examples of the genre and these could very productively be used in comparison to more recent examples. For example, Georges Méliès *A Trip to the Moon* provides an early example of fantastical scenarios and visually striking imagery. The animated content of Méliès' 1902 film provided an original viewing event for audiences at the time. Jean Cocteau's fantasy pieces, such as *La Belle et La Bete,* could also provide very useful study and an interesting comparison to modern fantasy cinema. *La Belle*'s *mise-en-scène*, for example, evokes the dream-like world in which the fairy story can be played out.

Whatever films you choose to study under the title 'fantasy cinema', make sure that you offer textual evidence for the points you make, as well as well as comments on narrative and audience reponse. Remember that fantasy films do not have to include real action and, indeed, the focus film for fantasy cinema is a piece of pure animation.

Case Study 10: *Alice* (Svankmajer, 1988)

It is extremely fitting that Svankmajer used Lewis Carroll's tale of fantastical scenarios and childhood nightmares as the basis for his animated film. Carroll's *Alice in Wonderland* presents a world in which reality is not fixed and dreamscapes become the norm. Svankmajer's *Alice* takes these visualised anxieties further. It begins with the line: 'Now you will see a film for children. Perhaps.' So it is clear from the beginning of this film that the fears and dreads that are visualised are not solely those of childhood imagination.

Source: British Film Institute

Svankmajer takes the viewer on a journey into Alice's dreams. These dreams are populated by the characters of Lewis Carroll's story, but in Svankmajer's version these characters are even more bizarre. The white rabbit's watch is pulled straight out of its chest, rather than its pocket, which at once reminds the viewer of the original story and also presents this version as much stranger. Alice's experiences echo those of Carroll's character, but they are more frightening and Alice seems to be in a much more threatened position in Svankmajer's story.

As a piece of fantasy cinema, *Alice's* credentials are clear. Svankmajer plays with the viewer's expectations of *mise-en-scène* to create a hyper-real world in which anything could happen. The character of Alice is at sea in her dreams and experiences the kind of frightening journey in which the safety of a predictable reality is absent. Images of drawers and desks are a significant feature of the film, mirroring the rabbit holes of Lewis Carroll's story, but here they are even more looming and ominous. Svankmajer uses these images to suggest the potential for entrapment or obliteration of the self – a common nightmare anxiety. The non-diegetic sound of the film further instils a sense of the sinister within Alice's dreams. Hers is a fight back to consciousness.

EXERCISE 8

1. Working in a small group and using all of the information above concerning fantasy cinema, create a synopsis and list of cinematic ideas for a new, original fantasy film. Make sure that you take into account the stylistic and the thematic elements of a fantasy film.

2. Read your finished synopsis to the rest of your Film Studies class. Your class should then decide on one synopsis that could form the basis of the next great piece of fantasy cinema.

Exemplar essay: Section A

Title: To what extent do you consider the films you have studied for the Surrealist and Fantasy topic to be motivated by distinct political and social views?

Without a framework of political and social views, the Surrealist films I have studied would appear merely a random collection of abstract images. The political stance of early Surrealist directors, such as Bunuel, is what gave coherence and intent to their work. It is the strong sense of messages and values in the films I studied that gave meaning to the meaningless images these films incorporated.

Throughout his career, Luis Bunuel was committed to social and political change. His contempt for (what he held to be) hypocritical views of the bourgeoisie, is apparent in many of his films. In *The Phantom of Liberty*, for example, Bunuel reveals the hypocrisy of the upper-middle-class family through their sacking of the maid for allowing a stranger to show their daughter 'rude' pictures, only to then be seen looking at the pictures and becoming aroused. Bunuel further entrenches the sense of hypocrisy by then revealing the pictures to be of famous landmarks.

Bunuel's *That Obscure Object of Desire* also articulates his challenge to what he considers to be social repression. In a society that represses the individual's natural desire, through oppressive religious, social and moral codes, unnatural desire can come to the surface. *L'Age d'Or* incorporates the same kind of demand for freedom of expression and the same kind of warning about the perils of repressed desire. A man's desire of a woman is denied and his response is to imagine the woman on the toilet! For Bunuel, the repression of the individual by hypocritical institutions, such as the church and the government, is directly responsible for perversions.

More contemporary examples of Surrealist film, however, do not seem to articulate the same kind of social and political concerns. David Lynch is a director who regularly incorporates surreal imagery and surreal sequences in his work, but he also uses these images on an artistic, rather than a political level. *Lost Highway*, for example, centres around the character of Fred, who 'becomes' Pete during a 'psychogenic fugue'. The incident is surreal and yet the intention of it is not political. Lynch presents to his audience a situation in which the committing of a murder, and the psychological breakdown which led to that murder, have caused a character's mind to split in two. This is more a discussion of a psychological condition than a condemnation of institutions.

In order to be politically and socially motivated, a director needs a context to work against. In Bunuel's time, the class system and the ensuing social double standards provided a clear target. In a more contemporary world, Surrealism has become more of an artistic, than a political choice.

Assessment comment

This is a very clearly written essay, which considers both sides of the argument. There is clear evidence of detailed textual understanding and the textual examples given are used appropriately. The essay is confident in its argument and clearly structured. The candidate shifts comment to a more contemporary film with ease and uses this section of the analysis to consider a distinction between Surrealism 'then and now'. Grade 'A'.

Formal questions to consider

German and Soviet cinema in the 1920s

1. To what extent do you think examples of both German and Soviet cinema use 'expressionist' elements to relay meaning to their audiences?

2. To what extent do you consider the films you have studied for this topic to be an artistic reaction to the cinema which had gone before?

Neo-realism in Italy and beyond

1. Using detailed reference to the films you have studied for this topic, discuss whether or not you consider the 1940s as the true period of Italian neo-realism.

2. Do you consider the motivation behind examples of Italian neo-realist cinema to be primarily artistic or political?

Japanese cinema: 1950–1970

1. To what extent do you consider genre classification useful in your assessment and analysis of Japanese cinema during this period?

2. How are youth and age represented in the examples you have chosen from Japanese cinema 1950–1970?

Cinematic new waves

1. Is it possible to identify consistent features of new wave cinema across examples from different nations?

2. From your study of particular examples of new wave cinema, what do you think are the main motivating factors in the emergence of a cinematic new wave?

Surrealist and fantasy cinema

1. How important is the representation of the sub-conscious within the films you have studied for this topic?

2. To what extent do you consider the films you have studied for this topic to be an artistic reaction to mainstream forms of cinema?

Approaching Section B – Close study: Contemporary world cinema

This section of the FS5 exam asks you to focus on one film example from contemporary world cinema. The focus of your preparation for this part of the exam will be the close textual features of your chosen film i.e. the way in which micro and macro features create meaning and response. Obviously, your answers will have to extend past the essays you did for FS1. For example, you should consider carefully how thematic and representational features are generated through the use of textual elements. The context of your film will also be relevant to your study. You should look at auteur-related elements and identify any key signature characteristics that are evident in your focus film. You might also be able to locate your film within a film movement and this will be of significance in your answers. The social, political and historical context of your film will also need to be identified and you should consider these factors as potentially having influence on the style, structure and content of your film.

In the exam, there will be a choice of three questions, of which you should answer one. There are two generic questions in Section B that you could answer if you have studied any of the focus films. It also includes a question that is specifically related to one individual film.

You will have already gained many of the necessary skills for this section of the FS5 unit from your exam preparation for FS3: British and Irish Cinema. Your ability to consider text and context will be absolutely relevant for this exam. The difference, of course, is that in the FS5 exam you will be focusing on world cinema and will have to discuss films that have a potentially very different target audience, content type and context of production. This section of this chapter will focus less on the films themselves and more on the skills needed to produce a successful exam answer. The examples and case studies used to illustrate points made are drawn from the list of close study films available for Section B.

Discussing text and representation

The skill of using close textual detail to inform a discussion of the representational aspects of a text is one that you will have used for your FS3: British and Irish Cinema exam. Representation is constructed through textual elements and informed by the context of a film's production. You will need to give detailed consideration to the way in which cinematography, *mise-en-scène*, sound and editing function to create representational meaning within your chosen film. Consider what the film seems to be saying about gender, race, nationality, age and sexuality. These messages will have been relayed to the film's audience via textual choices. Once you have identified what you consider to be the film's main representational depictions, you will need to discuss what the nature of these is. Are the groups represented within your text presented in a way that seems to conform to the dominant social attitudes of the time in which the film was made, or do they seem to challenge dominant ideologies?

EXERCISE 9

Choose a scene from your focus film. First, identify the particular features of cinematography, *mise-en-scène*, sound and cinematography that seem to be attached to particular characters or groups of characters. Then make notes on the way in which the textual features within your scene seem to be guiding the viewer towards a particular response to the character or group. Finally, try to make notes on the relationship between the attitudes expressed about particular groups in your chosen scene and what you understand to be dominant social attitudes. Does the scene seem to be reinforcing these dominant social opinions, or challenging them?

Case Study 11: Opening sequence of *Real Women Have Curves* (Cardoso, 2002)

Source: British Film Institute

Patricia Cardoso's 2002 film is set in Los Angeles. The central character, Anna, is a young woman of Latin descent, who wants to go to college, but finds herself forced into working in her sister's sewing factory. The film opens with the sound of an old woman singing in Spanish. Although the sound might appear to be non-diegetic, it is in fact diegetic – the identity of the singer is revealed later in the opening sequence. The audience immediately infers that the setting of the film will at least partially be in a Spanish-speaking neighbourhood. The opening image is a mid-shot of Anna, cleaning the windows of her family home. She is framed, in mid-shot, by the window and the audience first sees her through the glass. Anna is young, in her late teens, and obviously has the curves of the film's title. Her body language and expression imply that she is not happy in her task. Anna's framing through the window implies an observational standpoint for the audience and assumes that she will be the focus of the film's narrative.

Anna is then called by her sister to go and see their mother. The *mise-en-scène* of Anna's mother's bedroom is predominantly floral and chintz. The room is stereotypically 'feminine' in tone and it becomes obvious, from the subsequent conversation that Anna has with her mother, that this room is an arena for the mother's self-indulgence and manipulation of her family. Anna's mother is in bed, feigning illness. Anna, her sister and their grandfather stand around the bed as if viewing a performance that has been re-enacted many times. Anna's mother states that Anna will 'have to make breakfast for the men' thereby indicating to the viewer the nature of the gender roles in the family and the fact that Anna's mother seeks to perpetuate them. The tension between Anna's desire to experience her last day at high school and her mother's refusal to see Anna's education as a priority are clearly evident here. *Real Women Have Curves* discusses the nature of gender expectations and the significance of these expectations within a Spanish/American community. Anna's struggle in the film will be that of a young, Americanised, Latin woman attempting to find her place within a world of tensions.

Anna refuses to make breakfast for the men and the camera then follows her out of the front door. The camera is hand-held at this point and again takes an observational stance on her life. The viewer then sees Anna's journey to school and, as the journey goes on, begins to understand the cultural contradictions within Anna's world. She begins her journey in 'downtown' Los Angeles. Anna's neighbourhood is not poor, but is more modest than the environment in which she goes to school. The *mise-en-scène* of the first part of her journey shows signs for Spanish restaurants and has Spanish music as its non-diegetic backdrop. Anna is then seen on a bus and is again framed next to a window. This window is grimy and it is difficult to see outside, which acts to contrast with the much more pristine windows of the second bus she takes, which is going towards Beverly Hills. This obscuring of a view on the first bus becomes emblematic of the difficulty Anna has of getting her viewpoint heard at home. When Anna's bus draws up at her school, the stark contrast between what she has come from, and where she has gone to, becomes starkly evident. The school is a large, redbrick building. When we cut to Anna in her classroom, we see that her background is obviously different from that of those around her. The representations of culture and nationality in this opening sequence set the tone for the rest of the film. In a conversation between Anna and her teacher about going to college, it becomes evident that the reason she will not be going is to do with her family. Los Angeles, in this film, is divided into different geographical areas, which have individual cultural and economic profiles. Anna's family seem to adhere to a traditional value system, in which family members (literally) work together to support their extended family members. Gender roles are quite fixed in this world and the expectation is that a young woman will give up her studies and begin work, not continue into higher education. Clearly, these hurdles are what Anna will have to overcome during the film's narrative.

Discussing social, political and ideological context

This area of investigation and preparation does not have to be as daunting as it may initially seem. As you already know from your AS and A2 studies, a film is a product not merely of its director, cast and crew. The look and content of a film are also influenced by audience expectations and the ideas that were circulating at the time the film was produced. Your focus film was made at a particular point in history and in a particular national (and social) context. Consider what the film seems to be indicating about the politics and social opinions that surrounded its production. The discussions of social and political issues might be explicit, delivered through the dialogue of certain characters, but they might also be implicitly delivered through the construction of character, the *mise-en-scène*, the narrative pattern and even the cinematography.

If a particular political event occurred at the time of the film's production, the film may comment on it. A particular attitude towards a social group might also be apparent in your film text. This section of your preparation will probably overlap with the notes you have made on representation, but you should extend your comments beyond the representation of social groups to the representation and discussion of social issues and ideological standpoints. You might decide that your film challenges opinions held by the majority of society, or you might find that it supports a social attitude. Remember, of course, to make notes on your own responses to the messages that are apparent in your film. You may have sympathy with the standpoints that are being taken, or your own thoughts and ideas may be diametrically opposed to those of the film text. The dialogue between the messages of your chosen film and your own attitudes is an important aspect of your discussions in the exam.

EXERCISE 10

1. Make a list of all of the questions your focus film seems to be asking. These might be questions about events, social groups, political stances or social assumptions.

2. Make notes on what you consider to be the film text's answers to these questions.

3. With a partner, discuss what your own responses are to the questions and answers that you have identified.

Case Study 12: Pedro Almodovar's
All About my Mother (1999)

Source: British Film Institute

Pedro Almodovar began his film-making career during the post-Franco period. Spain had spent 25 years under Franco's military dictatorship, which repressed much of the cultural and intellectual life. Following Franco's death in 1975, the country underwent rapid social and cultural change. Almodovar was instrumental in forming a cultural movement known as '*la Movida*' centred around the Spanish capital Madrid. *La Movida* sought to portray and celebrate the new freedoms that were possible in Spanish life and art. Almodovar's early work presented sex and sexuality in all of their potential manifestations, reflecting the backlash against the artistic repression of the Franco era, and articulated a rejection of the politics and cinematic aesthetics that had gone before.

All About my Mother was made 24 years after Franco's death and around 20 years after Almodovar's first cinematic discussions, so this film had no need to counter a recent repressive regime. What it does do, however, is present Spain at the end of the twentieth century.

All About my Mother is a film that asks and answers many questions. It questions the nature of sexual identity, the definition of the family and the relationship between genders. For the most part, the film does not ask its questions explicitly, but through character construction and scenarios. The film reverses the positions of stereotypically centralised groups and those who usually occupy the margins of a film's narrative. The transsexual Lola provides the motivation for the narrative's central search; the film's other transsexual character, Agrado, becomes a central figure within the reconstructed family of Manuela. The positioning of Lola and Agrado articulates the film's attitude to them. Neither is judged for their transgender identity. Lola's main crimes in the narrative are those of emotional abandonment and infecting Sister Rosa with the HIV virus. Agrado may draw attention to her transgender status through her 'speech' to the theatre audience, but she is not denigrated or rejected for this. The film asks us to judge people by their actions, not their surface, sexual characteristics. Even on this basis, Lola is not wholly damned by the film, instead, she is presented as a pitiable character.

The nature of the family is another focal concern of *All About my Mother*. Contemporary Spain (like any other contemporary European country) has many different manifestations of the family unit. Nuclear families exist, but so do families with one parent, families with adopted members and families made up of friends, rather than blood relatives. Within a period of social history where the stereotypical family unit is no longer the most common, Almodovar's film offers alternatives. Manuela becomes a surrogate parent to Sister Rosa and the 'kindness of strangers' that occurs between Manuela, Huma, Sister Rosa and Agrado is shown to be as strong as any family bond.

If this film challenges the viewer to reject stereotypical notions of the family, gender and sexual identity, it also does the same with AIDS. The narrative suggests that Lola has become HIV-positive through intravenous drug use and not sexual contact. The film's tragic events also indicate the indiscriminate nature of the disease. Sister Rosa is a Catholic Nun, but becomes infected. She is not promiscuous, a drug user or homosexual – the groups most commonly shown in film as being infected.

Almodovar's film functions as a challenge to certain stereotypical social attitudes. It does so, however, through its own very original means. It does not adopt a crusading or angry stance with regard to the issues it discusses, but allows the viewer to encounter its opinions through the process of the narrative.

Discussing auteur implications

Although you are not involved in an auteur study for this exam, there might be auteur-related implications to be identified within your focus film. It will be worth seeing some of the other films created by the director of your chosen film, to assess whether any signature characteristics are evident within these and your focus film. Look out for stylistic and thematic signatures that might be evident across your director's work. These signatures may also have an implication in terms of national cinema – the thematic considerations that are evident could relate to the country in which the film was produced.

Case Study 13 : *Beau Travail* (Claire Denis, 1998)

Desire is violence, by Chris Darke, *Sight & Sound* July 2000

Claire Denis' uniquely sensual films are hard to see in the UK. Chris Darke talks to her about watching men from the margins.

Are the films of Claire Denis French cinema's best-kept secret? It certainly seems so in the UK. While her work is regularly praised at film festivals around the world, her last film to be distributed here was her Cameroon-set debut *Chocolat* in 1988. None of her subsequent films has made more than a festival appearance until now, yet she remains highly regarded. Denis describes herself as '*une fille d'Afrique*' (a daughter of Africa): born in Paris in 1948, she was two months old when her family moved to Africa and until the age of 14 she lived in a number of countries during the dying years of French colonialism and the coming of African independence. When we met in Paris in March to talk about her most recent film, *Beau Travail*, it became clear her childhood is still a key influence.

Chocolat was the fictionalised account of Denis' experiences as a young girl told from the perspective of a woman named France who returns as an adult to her childhood home in post-colonial Cameroon. Denis' second feature *S'en fout la mort* (*No Fear, No Die*, 1990) opens with a quote from Chester Himes: 'All men, whatever their race, colour or origins, are capable of anything and everything.' The statement resonates across Denis' subsequent cinematic forays into extreme physicality, rendered with an increasing attention to the sensual details of flesh, the body and the borderline between desire and violence. In *S'en fout la mort* the underworlds of illegal cock-fighting and French immigrants overlap and feed off each other in a portrait of exploitation and barely buried desires that find shape in the savage ritual. Denis' controversial 1993 film *J'ai pas sommeil* (*I Can't Sleep*) was based on the notorious case of Thierry Paulin, a serial killer who murdered 21 elderly women in Paris between 1984 and 1987. Denis' film is as much about the anonymity that the murderer, a prostitute, drug-dealer and drag artist played by non-professional Richard Courcet, was able to maintain within a fluid demi-monde of drifters and immigrants as it is about his crimes. While the social canvas of Denis' films has tended to depict uneasy micro-communities of underbelly-dwellers, her filmic style has increasingly moved away from a traditional French realism towards more elliptical, poetic and sensual structures. *U.S. Go Home* (1994) and *Nenette et Boni* (1996) indicated that she was developing a startlingly singular style – cinema as an aching reverie of sweat and flesh – that reaches its most refined expression in her most recent work.

Beau Travail is Denis' sixth feature but only the second in which she has revisited the territory of her childhood. Freely inspired by the work of the 19th-century American writer Herman Melville, in particular the novella *Billy Budd*, and filmed in the former French colony on the north-east coast of Africa that since 1977 has been the Republic of Djibouti, *Beau Travail* immerses the viewer in the world of the French Foreign Legion as seen from the perspective of Galoup (Denis Lavant), a legionnaire devoted to his CO Bruno Forestier (Michel Subor). The names Forestier/Subor will be familiar to Godard aficionados; the actor played a character of the same name in Godard's 1960 film *Le Petit Soldat* whom Denis has revisited some 40 years later. Galoup's devotion to duty and the life of the legion is tested by the arrival of new recruit Gilles Sentain (Grégoire Colin) whose selfless heroism Galoup sees as a threat to his authority. A war of nerves ensues, culminating in Sentain's near death in the desert and Galoup's court-martial. But this synopsis doesn't begin to do justice to the way Denis tells her story of hothouse emotions igniting under African skies. Since *Nenette et Boni* (which also featured Colin) she has developed an extraordinarily sensuous style of film-making whose impact derives from its combination of music (*Beau Travail* mixes dance music and Benjamin Britten's opera of *Billy Budd*), editing rhythms and the cinematography of her long-time collaborator Agnès Godard.

No one else in France is making films like Denis' and the combination of the release of *Beau Travail* and a complete retrospective of her work at the National Film Theatre provides the opportunity to catch up with her development. When we met in Paris Denis was hung-over, having just wrapped the shoot of her next film, starring Vincent Gallo, the night before. Small, wiry and, after a couple of aspirins, alert and forthcoming, she told me how a daughter of Africa found a new home in cinema.

Chris Darke: What made you want to make films?
Claire Denis: I was absolutely unfit for anything else. Cinema appeared to be a territory where I could survive. In *Beau Travail* Galoup says he's 'unfit for civilian life'. Well, when I came to France after having lived in Africa I felt I was unfit for life! The directors working then who interested me were Godard, Besson, Antonioni and, later, Fellini. But I was just a spectator – I didn't imagine that I would one day make a film.

Did you have a classical French cinephile background?
Not classical because I'm not French but a daughter of Africa. I grew up in Africa where there were no cinemas so I discovered cinema late, at 14 or 15 years old, all at once and indiscriminately. Cinephilia, in the classic sense of the Cinémathèque and *Cahiers du cinéma*, was something I came to much later, perhaps when I was 25 years old.

You say you're not French but a daughter of Africa . . .
It's a bit romantic. I feel like a bit of a foreigner, but I know I'm French. When I was very young I regretted this, I wanted to be anything but French.

Your childhood in Africa must have given you another perspective on France.
Yes, because I came to live here reluctantly. I was already nostalgic for another world. Usually, when one is an adolescent, the feeling is that life is just beginning. I felt I'd already finished one life and was mourning it heavily.

Was this feeling shared by your parents?
I think so, though we never talked about it. It wasn't that we regretted decolonisation – we weren't *pieds noirs* [French people born in the colonies]. Politically, my father was a supporter of African independence. However, for my mother there was a feeling of a lost world that she'd never find in France. It was something to do with the plastic beauty of the landscape, the immensity of it and the sense of being slightly apart

257

from the world. We weren't Africans, we were blond Africans so we were slightly transient people. I think I liked that.

'Beau Travail' is your second film set in the former French colonies. But what attracted you to Herman Melville?

I always thought of Herman Melville as a brother in the sense of sharing his feelings of sadness, nostalgia and disappointment, the sense of having lost something. For me, Africa is like the seas Melville missed so much.

You worked as an assistant to Jacques Rivette. Did you learn much from his methods?

Rivette has principles rather than methods and these are less his own than those of the directors he admired: Renoir and Rossellini. Perhaps these principles have to do with duration, sequence-shooting, rewriting during the shooting and never considering the screenplay as complete.

When you shoot a film is there already a highly refined screenplay?

Yes. I need to write a well-worked-out screenplay but I also need to be able to modify it, to separate myself from it during the shoot. I'm not proud of this – it's not a method I'd recommend. But it's my own way of being adventurous and for me a shoot has to be an adventure. If it's too comfortable I feel it's not cinema. There has to be an element of risk.

Are there other ways of attaining this?

Yes. With the camera. I hate it if it's all worked out in advance. Sometimes when I write the screenplay with my collaborator I'll have certain shot breakdowns in my head but I can never think of them as final. I need to remake them in the shooting, which lends that element of risk. It's the same when I'm shooting sequence shots – I don't shoot cutaways or coverage. It's idiotic, but it's my way of feeling alive in the filming.

Since 'Nenette et Boni' there's been a real sensuality to your work as well as great attention to the rhythms of the film. Do you have an idea of the feelings you want the spectator to experience?

I want to share what's troubling me, to convey that to others. If there wasn't this slightly insane desire to share things that are fleeting I think I'd change jobs, write books or plays. No other artform is as simultaneously trivial, vulgar and sublime as cinema. The film industry lives for the idea of profit, so how can one have an approach that's as egotistical as wanting to share with an audience something that's an intuition, a fragment? Yet real cinema is a way of transforming the technical and industrial material and making the sublime coincide with it. And I think sensuality is the key. Cinema cannot exist except through eroticism. The position of the spectator is like a kind of amorous passivity and hence is highly erotic.

Often in your films there's a fascination with watching men fighting or working.
I like writing stories about men not because I want to dominate them but because
I like to observe and imagine them. A man is a different world and this masculinity
interests me. French cinema is so full of talk – I couldn't care less about these people
talking about their lives. Godard said that in cinema there are women and guns and
I agree completely. That's to say, there's sex and violence. Cinema functions
through these even if one is highly intellectual. And Melville functions on exactly
the same elements.

**But in 'Beau Travail' the violence and love between the men are expressed as
camaraderie rather than through sex.**
Sex between characters doesn't interest me. What's important is the sexual charge that
passes between the actors and the spectators. Filming sex scenes is very difficult. There
must be violence for there to be desire, I think – and that's what's so beautiful about
Oshima's films. I expect if I went into analysis I'd be found to be abnormal – I think
sexuality isn't gentle, nor is desire. Desire is violence.

**Often in your films ritual is a way of blocking or diverting this desire, as in the
cock-fighting in 'S'en fout la mort' or the choreography of the legionnaires in
'Beau Travail'.**
What interests me is often what precedes the sexual act – which, despite everything, has
very few variations. One can't really film sex unless one pretends or one works with
actors who specialise in it. Ritual is interesting because it's a way of expressing the
sexuality of bodies outside the sexual act itself.

Why did you decide to treat the legionnaires' movements in a stylised way?
I was working from the real movements of their training. In Melville's sailor stories
there are descriptions of sailors climbing up and down the rigging and it's like a dance.
And I found that to translate what Melville was writing about dance worked better than
dialogue.

**In the last scene Galoup dances frenziedly in a nightclub – it's half solipsistic, half
abandoned.**
In an early draft of the screenplay the dance fell before the scene where he takes the
revolver, contemplating suicide. But when I was editing I put the dance at the end
because I wanted to give the sense that Galoup could escape himself. When we shot this
scene in Djibouti I knew after the first take it was going to go at the end of the film. So
on the second take I knew he had to leave the nightclub and I'd have my ending.

The dialogue is quite spare – it almost has the form of a prose poem.
We wrote two screenplays. The first was called 'Galoup's Notebook', which was a diary,
his memoirs. From that we started to construct the film as its counterpoint.

So the images work as a counterpoint to this text?

Exactly. But the voiceover is a third text I wrote from my memory of Godard's *Le Petit Soldat*. In *Le Petit Soldat* Michel Subor's character has deserted from the French army – he's killed a member of the FLN [the Algerian anti-colonialist Front de Libération Nationale] in Geneva – so it seemed logical he should resurface in the Foreign Legion. I didn't want to take the character's name from *Le Petit Soldat* - Bruno Forestier – and emphasise it, so I used the bracelet he wore in Godard's film. It's more than a homage because it's one of my favourite films and Michel Subor is one of my favourite actors.

You seem to have a group of people who are close collaborators: Jean-Pol Fargeau as co-screenwriter; Agnès Godard as director of photography.

Chocolat was shot by another DP and Agnès Godard did the framing. *S'en fout la mort*, also. But she became a DP with me. I'd say it's a very Godardian ideal, a team or small group with whom you can share everything as companions. It's very idealistic. When you nourish one another it can work, but it's like being in a couple. It can be very frustrating always working with the same people but it gives you a lot of security that allows you to explore.

Do you write with certain faces in mind?

The first faces that interested me were Isaach de Bankolé and Alex Descas. At first I preferred black faces. Vincent Gallo is an old face for me – the first time I shot him was 10 years ago in a short I made in New York called *Keep it for Yourself*. He was also in *Nenette et Boni* and *U.S. Go Home*. These faces are strong, and beauty pisses me off. They have inspiring personalities – like Denis Lavant or Subor in *Le Petit Soldat*. If I'd been making films in the 60s I'd have made films with Subor.

There's a sense in your last two films of the development of an almost abstract film-poetry.

I had a collection of Melville's poems at the editing desk when I was working on *Beau Travail*. The screenplay was also written in a poetic manner inspired by Melville. It can be very hard at times to find the right musical rhythm for the editing. But duration isn't something one finds at the editing stage, it's something that's arrived at during the shooting which the editing must respect. When shooting I get goosebumps because of the passage of time and I have to trust that. But I must say that for me it's not very difficult: I'm a lazy, passive person who has always adored waiting, watching and listening. Outside of film-making I'm not especially active, I'm like a sponge.

You can't say to yourself 'I want to make an abstract film' – it's a bit dumb as a working method. But to try to capture someone's memories, Galoup's for example, to ask why he misses the Legion and Djibouti and to want to convey this cinematically inevitably becomes a little abstract. I think it's easier for me as someone who's marginal and isolated; I don't have a studio behind me telling me what not to do. But if I'd set out to make *Beau Travail* as a consciously anti-narrative film I would have failed – I don't think one consciously marginalises oneself, it just happens. European cinema is saturated by a form of storytelling that's almost televisual and American cinema remains, in plastic terms, very strong. Think of *Dead Man* and *Ghost Dog*. But there's also Hsiao-Hsien Hou and Ming-Liang Tsai in Taiwan, the young Kurosawa in Japan – these are people I feel very close to. I don't feel at all marginal in their company.

How do you relate to the new generation of French women directors?
I played a role in Letitia Masson's first film *En avoir (ou pas)*. She was one of the first of the young film makers to write to me saying they liked what I did. Letitia told me that she thought of me as her "godmother", which was very touching. Noémie Lvovsky, too, considers me like an elder sister. But do I feel close to them? Yes and no. That's to say I'm touched by their comments but I don't like all their films.

Do you think your marginality has to do with the fact that you're a woman making films in France?
No. I don't think I make the sort of films which have the characteristic traits of French cinema, which is to say a lot of dialogue and a very social focus. Some suggest my marginality has to do with the fact that my films have a lot of marginal characters in them. But I don't think so. I think it's more that I don't express myself like mainstream French directors. But being marginalised is a way of being slightly protected – I'm doing my own thing with no one interfering and that suits me. *Beau Travail* didn't cost a lot to make and though the film I finished shooting last night cost twice as much again that's not to do with me. Rather, since *Buffalo '66* Vincent Gallo costs a lot and shooting in Paris is expensive.

Was the new film shot entirely in Paris?
Yes. It's called *Trouble Every Day*. There's a lot of English in it because Vincent speaks in English. There's also a young American actress called Tricia Vessey, who was in Jarmusch's *Ghost Dog*. It also has Béatrice Dalle and Alex Descas, pretty much the family I've worked with before. It should be ready by autumn and I'm impatient to see how it'll turn out.

Discussing audience reception
The most straightforward kind of audience reception you can evaluate is that of the other members of your Film Studies class, who are also studying the film. The internet will also give you access to a wealth of audience comment and review. One issue to remember, however, is that your focus film is an example of world cinema, and as such will have been first seen in the country of its origin. The way in which the film was received when it was first shown will

EXERCISE 11

After reading the interview with Claire Denis above from *Sight & Sound* magazine, answer the questions that follow.

1. What does Claire Denis say about what has influenced her attitudes to film making and the types of film she makes? To what extent has Claire Denis' own life informed the style and content of the films she makes?

2. To what extent is Claire Denis' film making a collaborative process?

3. What specific comments in the interview are made by Denis about *Beau Travail*?

4. What does Denis say about the position of female French filmmakers within the film industry?

5. From the information you have gleaned from the interview, do you think that Claire Denis has specific signature characteristics that she incorporates into her films?

be of relevance to your background preparation. Box-office figures will be significant and again, you could use the internet to provide you with figures from the country of the film's release and with those of its global release. You might also be able to find reviews from the film's country of origin on the internet, which can be automatically translated.

Once you have gathered together box-office figures and audience comments, you should make notes on the countries in which the film was most successful and on the features of the film about which there are most comments. Use the exercise below to gather and assess audience response information about your focus film.

EXERCISE 12

1. Ask your classmates the following questions about your focus film:

   - What was your favourite scene of the film and why?

   - What did the film tell you about the country in which it was set?

   - What would you consider to be the main messages of the film? How did you relate and respond to these messages?

   - What do you know of the film's director? Could you sense any signature characteristics within this film and others (by the same director) you know about?

- Did you feel that the film showed any genre characteristics?
- Did you feel that the film was accessible to you, given the fact that its frame of reference related to a different country?

When you have answers from two or three members of your group, make notes on the similarities and differences between the responses you received.

2. Use an internet site, such as the Internet Movie Database (www.imdb.com) to collect examples of audience responses to your focus film. Try to find responses which have come from other countries as well as from Britain. Use the questions below to analyse the responses you find.

- What were the different scenes identified in the comments? What was it about these scenes that the viewer particularly enjoyed or disliked?
- What did the comments say about the story of the film? Was the subject matter something the viewer could relate to?
- What was said about the stylistic elements of the film?
- Was the director mentioned, and if so, what comments were made about the director's style of film making and their other films?
- Do the viewer comments tell you anything about the target audience for the film?

3. When you have completed the questions in 1 and 2, compare and contrast the notes you have made.

Case Study 14: *Show Me Love* (Moodysson, 1998)

Source: British Film Institute

Below are three user comments about *Show Me Love*, adapted from those found on the Internet Movie Database.

1. Date: 4 September 2004. Canadian IMDb user.
   A friend of mine read about this movie on a website and told me I had to see it. Three weeks later she had ordered it from a website. When I looked at the cover, I thought: 'it's not even in English'. I watched it the first time, because I was forced. I watched

it every night after work for the next month and a half. I watched until I didn't need to read the subtitles anymore. I thought the story was so real, and the acting . . . it was like watching a documentary about two young girls falling in love. Being a lesbian myself, you'd think the kiss in the car would be my favourite part, but it wasn't. It was the part where Elin and her sister Jessica have the argument in the park. I could really feel how confused Elin was and how much she just wanted to be able to let it all out. This movie is a must-see.

2. Date: 21 April 2004. Swedish IMDb user.
I can only join in all of the praise about this film. *Show Me Love* captures what it is like to be a teenager in a very pure and non-*American Pie* kind of way. You don't have to be a lesbian or even female to relate to this. The story is wonderful and the two main characters are amazingly well portrayed by Rebecka Liljedahl [sic] and Alexandra Dahlstrom. Director Lukas Moodysson has had more recent success with both *Tillsammans* and *Lilja 4ever*. *Show Me Love* is a must-own for any serious film fanatic, but also a must for anyone who has ever been a teenager.

3. Date: 9 December 2003. French IMDb user.
I know this film would have been different if extreme film makers, such as Harmony Korine or Larry Clark had been involved. This film is great, because it is neither gross (like many other films about teenagers) or extreme. Moodysson's film shows a special sensibility and respect for its young protagonists and what they are feeling. This film is about the isolation many people feel at this age. If you appreciate the kind of film that is gentle, but still makes a point, you should watch *Show Me Love*.

Discussing critical reception

It is important when you consider the critical reception of your focus film that you cover a range of reviews and critics' opinions. You might find that the majority of critics agree on their response to the film, but you might also find that there are wildly differing opinions. You do not have to restrict your review search to those written in English – it is possible to locate foreign language reviews (especially on the internet) and have them automatically translated. When making notes on the critical responses to your chosen film, try to identify the following kinds of information:

- the features of style that are discussed
- the thematic elements that are discussed
- information concerning the director and their other work
- the context of the film's release, in terms of institutional issues or information
- any comments concerning the social/ ideological context in which the film was released.

EXERCISE 13

Use the internet or magazines to find two reviews of your close study film. Read them through carefully and note down the overall response of the critic to the film, any comment on the director's other work or signature characteristics, any contextual information included in the review and any key scenes and stylistic features mentioned.

Alongside the notes you have made about the critic's response to your focus film, make notes on your response to the film. Do you agree with the critic's point of view? Are there any elements of the text or its context that you think the critic either hasn't considered, or hasn't considered carefully enough? Now use your notes in response to the reviews you chose to create your own review. Remember that reviews follow a standard structure. The three stages of a review are outlined below to help you:

1. Background information on the reviewed film. This could take the form of a comment concerning where the film fits (or doesn't) into the director's filmography, details of any original source for the film, or any controversy surrounding the film and its release.

2. Comment on the writer's response to key elements of the film. These could include key scenes, key performances, or key stylistic features.

3. A summary of the good and/or bad points of the reviewed film and a recommendation, or rejection, of it.

When you have completed your review, ask someone who has not seen the film to read it and comment on whether your review would encourage them to see the film, or not.

Case Study 15: *La Haine* (Kassovitz, 1995)

Below are two reviews of Kassovitz's film *La Haine*.

Review of *Hate* (*La Haine*) by Roger Ebert, Chicago Sun-Times, 19 April 1996

'Society is like a man falling off a building. As he passes each floor, he calls out, 'So far, so good!' (Story quoted in *Hate*.)

Mathieu Kassovitz is a 29-year-old French director who in his first two films has probed the wound of alienation among France's young outsiders. His new film 'Hate' tells the story of three young men – an Arab, an African and a Jew – who spend an aimless day in a sterile Paris suburb, as social turmoil swirls around them and they eventually get into a confrontation with the police.

If France is the man falling off the building, they are the sidewalk.

In Kassovitz's first film, 'Cafe au Lait' (1994), he told the story of a young woman from the Caribbean who summons her two boyfriends – one African, one Jewish – to announce that she is pregnant. That film, inspired by Spike Lee's 'She's Gotta Have It,' was more of a comedy, but with 'Hate', also about characters who are not ethnically French, he has painted a much darker vision.

In America, where for all of our problems, we are long accustomed to being a melting pot, it is hard to realize how monolithic most European nations have been – especially France, where Frenchness is almost a cult, and a political leader like Jean-Marie Le Pen can roll up alarming vote totals with his anti-Semitic, anti-immigrant diatribes. The French neo-Nazi right wing lurks in the shadows of 'Hate,' providing it with an unspoken subtext for its French audiences. (Imagine how a moviegoer from Mars would misread a film like 'Driving Miss Daisy' if he knew nothing about Southern segregation.) The three heroes of 'Hate' are Vinz (Vincent Cassel), Jewish, working class; Hubert (Hubert Koundé), from Africa, a boxer, more mature than his friends, and Saïd (Saïd Taghmaoui), from North Africa, more light-hearted than his friends. That they hang out with one another reflects the fact that in France, friendships are as likely to be based on class as race.

These characters inhabit a world where much of the cultural furniture has been imported from America. They use words like 'homeboy'. Vinz gives Saïd a 'killer haircut, like in New York.' Vinz does a De Niro imitation ('Who you talkin' to?'). There's break-dancing in the movie. Perhaps they like U.S. culture because it is not French, and they do not feel very French, either.

During the course of less than 24 hours, they move aimlessly through their suburb and take a brief trip to Paris. They have run-ins with the cops, who try to clear them off a rooftop hangout that has become such a youth center, it even has its own hot dog stand. They move on the periphery of riots that have started after the police shooting of an Arab youth. When his younger sister's school is burned down, Vinz's Jewish grandmother warns, 'You start out like that, you'll end up not going to temple.' What underlies everything they do is the inescapable fact that they have nothing to do. They have no jobs, no prospects, no serious hopes of economic independence, no money, few ways to amuse themselves except by hanging out. They are not bad kids, not criminals, not particularly violent (the boxer is the least violent), but they have been singled out by age, ethnicity and appearance as probable troublemakers. Treated that way by the police, they respond – almost whether they want to or not. As a filmmaker, Kassovitz has grown since his first film. His black-and-white cinematography camera is alert, filling the frame with meaning his characters are not aware of. Many French films place their characters in such picturesque settings – Paris, Nice – that it is easy to see them as more colorful than real. But the concrete suburbs where Kassovitz sets his film (the same sterile settings that were home to Eric Rohmer's cosmically different 'Boyfriends and Girlfriends' in 1987) give back nothing. These are empty vistas of space – architectural deserts – that flaunt their hostility to the three young men, as if they were designed to provide no cover. The film's ending is more or less predictable and inevitable, but effective all the same. The film is not about its ending. It is not about the landing, but about the fall. 'Hate' is, I suppose, a Generation X film, whatever that means, but more mature and insightful than the American Gen X movies. In America, we cling to the notion that we have choice, and so if our Gen X heroes are alienated from society, it is their choice – it's their 'lifestyle'. In France, Kassovitz says, it is society that has made the choice.

Review of *Hate* (*La Haine*) by Stella Papamichael, www.bbc.co.uk/film 4/8/04

It's been labelled French cinema's answer to *Boyz N The Hood*, but *La Haine* (*Hate*) has a flavour all of its own. Writer-director Mathieu Kassovitz butts European urbanity up against American street style as kids clash with cops in suburban Paris. The result is an explosion of scathing social commentary and dynamic storytelling. Delving into the generational, racial, and class divides of his native France, Kassovitz offers a fearless – if unreservedly pessimistic – attack on the frontlines of power.

During a riot in the outskirts of Paris, police beat an Arab teenager (Abdel Ahmed Ghili) into a coma, fuelling a fire of hatred inside Vinz (Vincent Cassel) – a Jew who swears to 'whack' a cop if the boy dies. It's left to Vinz's cohorts, the jocular Saïd (Saïd Taghmaoui) – also Arab – and subdued African boxer Hubert (Hubert Koundé) to talk him out of his bloody plan as they embark on a loafing odyssey from the immigrant neighbourhoods to the big city. Still, the time bomb keeps ticking.

Counting down 24 hours, Kassovitz never gives the illusion of a happy ending. This is a fatalistic account of society's decline and it's plainly one-sided – the only cop who shows sympathy for the 'troubled youth' is ineffective among an army of bigots and bullies. Evidently Kassovitz sees things in black and white, which might explain his choice of a striking monochrome print.

But it's the conviction and bold invention with which Kassovitz tells the tale that makes it utterly compelling. Despite a meditative pace, there are shades of Scorsese in his kinetic camera moves, and in a scene lifted straight from *Taxi Driver* where Vinz poses in the mirror with a gun, snarling, 'You talkin' to me?'

Playing Vinz, Cassel radiates with a blistering intensity throughout, while Koundé offsets him with a cool self-assurance. Taghmaoui also turns in an outstanding performance, offering comic relief to balance the otherwise unbearable tension. Superbly acted and brilliantly executed, *La Haine* will tear through you like a bullet.

Exemplar essay: Section B

Title: How is gender represented in your chosen close study film?

Pedro Almodovar's 1999 Oscar-winning film is not just *All About my Mother*, it is also all about gender. The discussion of what constitutes gender provides one of the central concerns of the film. What it is to be female or male is central to the characters of this film and provides some of the crucial tensions of the narrative. In *All About my Mother* the stereotypes attached to gender are presented and deconstructed.

The female characters in Almodovar's film are central within the narrative. The 'mother' of the film's title is Manuela, whose son's death prompts her to go in search of her past. Manuela has been a single parent throughout the 17 years of her son Esteban's life. She has been a strong and positive influence in her son's life and represents the struggle that some women face when the father of their child is absent. The intertextual reference to Tenessee Williams' play *A Streetcar Named Desire* offers a parallel with Manuela's own struggle. She played the character of Stella, opposite her husband playing Kowalski, and life mirrored art when Manuela escaped from her own insufferable relationship. As the viewer discovers, the gender roles within Manuela's marriage were skewed. Her husband bought himself breasts and dressed as a woman, but still remained the kind of controlling and uncompromising husband who prompts women to flee. The maternal qualities of Manuela extends beyond her own son, to Sister Rosa and ultimately to Sister Rosa's own child. The film suggests that for women, being maternal is an intrinsic part of their gender identity. The narrative of the film is structured around key scenes of female interaction, with the absences of the story provided by male characters.

Women in *All About my Mother* are mostly resourceful and resilient. They compensate for the lack within the male characters. Sister Rosa and her mother have an absent male in their family. Rosa's father has an illness that has destroyed his memory and he therefore cannot function as a support to the women. He is not represented as a negative character, but as one who has to be supported as if he were a child. Mario, the actor who plays Stanley Kowalski in *A Streetcar Named Desire*, requests oral sex from Agrado in one of the film's many comic scenes and although the viewer fears that the brutishness of his stage character mirrors Mario's own, he is still not wholly criticised by the film and is seen supporting Agrado when 'she' delivers her speech in the theatre.

The male characters of *All About my Mother* may not be emotionally competent, and they are absent or problematic, but they are not damned by the film's narrative. Even Lola (formerly known as Esteban, father of Manuela's son, also called Esteban) is not constructed as abhorrent when the viewer finally meets 'her'. The narrative trajectory has been towards the finding of this character. Lola's culpability is widespread.

'She' was a promiscuous and hypocritical husband to Manuela, 'she' stole from Agrado, made Sister Rosa pregnant and passed on to her the HIV virus. However, Manuela's son Esteban's search was for this character; and Manuela even takes Sister Rosa's baby to see his 'father'. In this scene, Lola is not dressed as a cliched transvestite. 'She' is given equal and symmetrical frame space with Manuela and the audience cannot help but feel sympathy for this character who cries when 'she' sees the photograph of 'her' son.

Esteban's death is the prompt for Manuela's return to Barcelona, Esteban's father, Lola, provides the object of Manuela's search and Sister Rosa's son, also called Esteban, provides Manuela with hope and the narrative with a potential future. If part of what constitutes femaleness in this film is a powerful drive to be maternal, part of what it is to be male is to provide an absence for the female characters to fill. One of the most telling scenes in Almodovar's film relating to the question of gender is Agrado's speech. Agrado is a pre-operative transsexual, like Lola. What is particularly interesting about Agrado, however, is her awareness that surgery might approximate femaleness, but it does not necessarily guarantee authenticity. Agrado's speech in the theatre discusses this contradiction. 'She' describes 'her' plastic surgery and presents questions about authenticity. A woman, says Agrado, is not just made up of her primary sexual characteristics. Agrado's speech does not fully answer the question of what a woman 'is', but the film does offer a possible answer. A composite of Manuela, Sister Rosa and Huma would provide a woman who can face tragedy and difficulty with strength, who can reach out to others who need help and who is kind. Agrado is not without these positive characteristics and the film seems to suggest one key aspect of gender: it is not the outward appearance of gender that is important to gender identity. In fact, as long as an individual is a good person, they are 'authentic'. Gender can be approximated through surgery, but kindness can't.

Assessment comments

This essay shows very good understanding of both the focus film and the demands of the essay question. The candidate establishes a response to the question and argues systematically, using very well-chosen textual examples to substantiate the points made. This answer also exhibits a high level of general Film Studies knowledge and key film concepts are discussed with confidence. Grade 'A'.

Formal questions to consider

The following questions are of the generic type and could be used to analyse any of the FS5 Part B focus films:

1. To what extent do you think your chosen film challenges audiences' preconceptions about particular social groups?

2. What do you consider to be the most distinctive visual features of your chosen film?

3. To what extent do you think an understanding of the director's other work would allow the viewer a greater understanding of your chosen film?

4. Have the critical reviews you have read about your chosen film confirmed or challenged your own reading of the film?

5. Do you think it is necessary to locate your chosen film within its social and political context in order to appreciate it fully?

Chapter 6

Critical Studies (FS6)

Overview of the FS6 Unit

This unit constitutes the final unit of your A level Film Studies course. It is a synoptic unit, which means that all of the skills you have learnt during your course can be used to answer questions within this exam. Content knowledge you have gained from the other units in your Film Studies A level may also be relevant for your Critical Studies answers.

The FS6 exam is two hours long. It is divided into three sections: Sections A, B and C. Each of the three sections has four topic areas within it, and there is a question on each topic. You need to answer three questions, one from each of the three sections. The mark distribution for this exam is slightly unevenly weighted: there are 20 marks available for Section A and 15 each for Sections B and C.

Each section has a heading that explains how the four topic areas in that section are connected. The heading will also give you an indication of which previous units of the Film Studies A level you can draw on for your answers. You may find that there are films you have studied for one of the sections in the exam that seem to be relevant to other sections. You can mention the same film in different sections of your FS6 exam, but you should not use the same film as a main focus in more than one section.

Outline of Sections A, B and C

Section A: The Film Text and Spectator: Specialist studies

This section of the exam concentrates on the relationship between film and its audience. The topics in this section ask you to consider how the film spectator responds to the film text. You should draw on everything you have learnt (from your FS1 studies onwards) about how the use of cinematic devices and codes can be used to generate meaning and how the audience receives this meaning. The topic areas in Section A are:

- Early cinema before 1917
- Documentary
- Experimental film making
- Shocking cinema.

Section B: Producers and Audiences: Issues and debates

This section refers directly back to your AS studies on producers and audiences. The focus of this topic is the industry of film, and the organisations and institutions within that industry. The topic areas for this section focus on the producers of film, rather than film texts:

- Regulation and censorship
- The dominance of Hollywood and indigenous film production
- Independent film and its audience
- Fandom – and its significance to the film industry.

Section C: Meanings and Values: Critical approaches

Your studies for British and Irish Cinema for the AS FS3 unit were subtitled 'Messages and Values' and this section is an extension to the AS unit. For Section C, you are asked to consider different critical approaches/frameworks and assess their usefulness in the reading of film texts. The topic areas for this section are:

- Genre and authorship studies
- Performance studies
- Film interpretation and social/cultural studies
- Gendered film studies.

Your teacher will probably have chosen the topic to be studied in each section for you, and you will probably find that the three topics that they have chosen have links. For example: Shocking cinema (in Section A); Regulation and censorship (in Section B); and Gendered film studies (in Section C) have clear links and similarities. A film that has had a shocking impact on its audience, may have caused censorship debate and also have been the focus of feminist film criticism. Studying topic areas that have links is a productive way of approaching the exam, but you must ensure that the focus and tone of each of your answers is in line with the section heading. For example, a film studied for both the Shocking cinema and Censorship and regulation topics should be considered in terms of audience impact for Section A, and in terms of institutional impact (e.g. BBFC response) for Section B.

Skills required for the FS6 unit

As a synoptic unit, the FS6 exam draws together all of the skills you have learnt during your two-year A level Film Studies course. There are three key skills that have been identified for this exam and you should keep them in mind when preparing for it.

1. The ability to reflect critically on key Film Studies concepts and critical approaches used in the analysis of film texts.
2. The ability to bring learning from other Film Studies units into the discussion of critical approaches to film.

3. The ability to articulate an original and personal response to the critical studies analysed within the FS6 exam.

Section A: The Film Text and Spectator: Specialist studies

Early cinema before 1917

There is a specific reason why this particular topic area has a cut-off point of 1917 – 1917 saw the advent of full-length feature films. Between 1895 and 1917, cinema was in its infancy and it is this 32-year span that will be your focus. The beginnings of cinema were an incredibly exciting time, with major developments in cinema-related technologies and significant shifts in audience viewing practices.

For any of the topics you study under Section A of the Critical Studies exam, it is essential that you remember the *title* of this section. 'The film text and spectator' is the focus of Section A – you are asked to consider the relationship between what is viewed and those who view it. The dynamic between film and its audience is a constantly developing one. Your study of 'Early cinema' should focus on the experience of film-viewing before 1917, and how the particular relationship between moving images and their audience came about.

As well as looking at specific films for this topic, there are also some essential areas you will need to study. The questions that you should consider are:

1. What kinds of images were shown in early cinema?

2. Did early cinema involve narrative storytelling techniques?

3. Who went to the cinema before 1917? Did early audiences have a specific class, gender or age profile?

4. Where did early audiences view films?

5. Why did early audiences go to 'cinemas'? Was cinema-going escapist, or socially galvanising?

6. Did early films have an ideological impact on early audiences? Were the producers of early films offering messages and values via the images they included?

Your consideration of the questions set out above will need to be rooted in specific dates and film examples. During the period from 1895 to 1917, there were many important shifts and developments that you will need to consider. These developments did not only occur in the United States, but also in Europe, and you should ensure that your research covers these, too.

Early cinema technology

Before 1895, there was no such thing as a 'cinema'. Viewing moving images was a solitary experience. The Kinetoscope allowed an individual viewer to watch a series of images on a strip of film. The Kinetoscopes were just a novelty, however, and it was not until 1895, with the emergence of the Panoptican projector and, very soon afterwards, other kinds of projector, that the cinema experience we know today began to come into existence. The Panoptican and its like made it possible for more than one person at a time to view a series of moving images projected onto a screen or wall. It was at this point in the history of cinema that film became a collective viewing experience and the practice of watching projected images with a group of people came into existence.

Thomas Edison's company was the leading proponent of early cinema in the US and was behind many of the developments in cinema-related technologies at the time. Edison's assistant, W.K.C. Dickson, had developed a camera that made short 35 mm films in 1893, and it was Edison, in the US, who attempted the first example of a cinema monopoly. With the advent of projectors, the potential revenue from cinema-going audiences became apparent. Shops and small businesses began turning their premises into small projection facilities. These were called 'Nickelodeons' (because the admission price was a nickel) and were at first mostly frequented by working-class people. Very soon, however, small exhibition contexts were placed within middle-class areas of cities in order to maximise potential profits.

In an attempt to secure revenue from the thousands of Nickelodeons that were being set up all over the United States, the Edison Company joined forces with another major film technology developed at the time, Biograph, to form the Moving Pictures Patent Company (MPPC). The MPPC's aim was to licence technologies used within the Nickelodeons, thereby generating revenue from film screenings. During the first ten years of the twentieth century, film audience figures grew to tens of millions and the MPPC saw huge profits. By 1910, the MPPC had its own film distribution company – The General Film Company – and looked set to become the dominant force in the American film market. The American Department of Justice, however, ordered the MPPC to divide up into smaller offshoots, thereby impeding a potential monopoly.

In Europe, the Lumière Brothers were at the forefront of early cinema. In December 1895, in Paris, they held a grand screening of moving images projected onto a screen. The Lumière Brothers had developed their own camera and projection technologies, and were as significant as the likes of Edison in the birth of cinema. Their first films were of ordinary people in parks, on beaches or even leaving work. Their films differed significantly from those produced by Edison, whose films included images of contemporary celebrities (actors, sports stars etc.) performing for the camera. Edison's films, therefore, provided a very different type of experience for cinema-goers, than those of the Lumière Brothers; offering escapism in the form of celebrity displays that presented images detached from the average cinema-goer's experience. The latter offering images which reflected the actuality of many viewers' lives. One element which linked both the Edison and the Lumière styles of film, however, was the use of a rudimentary form of narrative. Cause and effect was apparent in both films, often in comic scenes where an action has a consequence and a reaction.

As well as Edison and the Lumière Brothers, there were other extremely significant people within early cinema. Perhaps the most famous of these was Georges Méliès. Méliès' films began in the Lumière mode, with scenes of everyday events. As with the films of Edison and the Lumière Brothers, Méliès' first films showed individual scenes, often taken in one shot with a static camera. His later work began to show significant differences, most notably in his use of fantasy elements. He brought the fantastical into early cinema and evolved the cinema-goer's experience still further. Rather than an experience of escape through celebrity performance or a mirroring of real-life occurrences, Méliès took cinema into the realms of dreams and fantasy.

Early film examples

1. 1895 *La Sortie des Usines Lumière*
   The first Lumière Brothers film, depicting factory workers leaving the factory for the day.

2. 1902 *Le Voyage dans la Lune*
   Possibly Méliès' best known film, featuring a fantasy trip to the moon. Méliès used models and superimposed images in order to generate the fantasy and comic elements of this film.

Le Voyage dans la Lune. **Source: British Film Institute**

3. 1903 *The Great Train Robbery*
   Directed by Edwin S. Porter, for the Edison Company, this was one of the first films to attempt continuity editing and narrative form. The film includes a series of events that takes the audience from a position of safety, through discomfort and then to an eventual resolution.

4. 1905 *Rescued by Rover*
   An example of early British film, this was directed by Levin Fitzhamon, and echoed the crime-related, continuity-edited, narrative of *The Great Train Robbery*.

Rescued by Rover. **Source: BFI Films: Stills, Posters and Designs**

5. 1915 *Birth of a Nation*
   Directed by D. W. Griffith, this film used complex narrative devices and innovative cinematic techniques. It has caused major controversy, because of its racist images and narrative elements.

EXERCISE 1

With a partner, look at the images from examples of early cinema above. Discuss what these stills indicate about the technologies used to create the films, the style of the film-making and the subject matter of these films.

Developments in cinema 1895–1917

The developments in cinema during the period 1895–1917 were many and various. The kinds of camera and projection equipment we know today were invented; and cinematic techniques such as continuity editing, cross-cutting and shot-reverse-shot began to become a more common mechanism for telling a story.

For the audience, the practice of watching film became a more complicated and involved process. Merely seeing a set of moving images depicting a physical movement, or small set piece, began to develop into an experience of watching a relatively complex piece of narrative. Audiences during this period began to be presented with stories that carried messages and values – that they could either relate to or reject. The ideological impact of cinema began with the appearance of these stories, and your evaluation of early cinema should include discussion of the intention behind and the reception of the images seen in early films. It will not be enough to describe the process of technology development in your answer for this topic. You will also need to discuss how cinematic devices, representation and narrative type were used to convey meaning and ideological standpoint. Films during this period of cinema development included representations of gender, race, religion and nationality. You will need to consider how these representations were constructed, what they relayed in terms of meaning and how they were received by the cinema-going audience.

Case Study 1: *Birth of a Nation* (D.W. Griffith, 1915)

The original idea for *Birth of a Nation* came from a play, *The Clansman*, adapted by clergyman Thomas E. Dixon Jnr from his own novel. The film relates the story of a Confederate soldier, following his return home to South Carolina after the Civil War in America. The soldier returns to what he perceives as a home town ravished by 'Blacks' and his response is to become a Ku Klux Klan organiser. This subject matter is, of course, deeply problematic. The soldier and his 'struggles' are the narrative focus of the piece and his allegiance to the Klan is offered as a necessary response to events. Both Dixon's novel and his play are essentially racist in ideological position and Griffith's film retained this stance. His romanticised notion of the American South, and his belief that the essence of what was truly American was under threat at this time by Blacks,

Source: British Film Institute

meant that Griffith 'read' Dixon's play as 'the romantic struggle of heroic man', rather than a piece of racist diatribe.

Griffith extended the chronological breadth of Dixon's play to include the years just before the Civil War and the Civil War itself. The epic nature of the chronology that Griffith created for his film is echoed in the film's budget: it cost $110,000 to make – at this point in cinema history a staggeringly large amount of money to spend on the production of a film. Griffith invested a lot of his own capital into the film, which only serves to confirm the very personal nature of the project. As a piece of cinema, *Birth of a Nation* was innovative and spectacular. It included thousands of different shot set-ups, sophisticated cross-editing and a complex musical score. (Developed by Griffith, with composer Joseph Carl Breil, it included music by Wagner, Verdi and a number of traditional American folk songs.) The dramatic and dynamic tension between the images on the screen and the music served to create an epic and original feel to the film. The film has a lengthy and, for the time, very complex narrative, which presents and connects many events and locations. It uses cut-ins to promote the symbolic potential of objects and advances the cause-and-effect narrative dynamic. The film's cinematic innovativeness and technical acumen do not justify its content, but the visual experience amazed and engaged audiences.

In 1915, *Birth of a Nation* was the longest and most expensive film ever to have been made. Although it subsequently became extremely successful, the path of the film into cinemas was not a smooth one. Because of its length and budget costs, the film did not get distribution immediately. Griffith, along with a group of others who trusted that the film would be a success, had to set up the Epoch Production Company in order to distribute the film. The film went on to make tens of millions of dollars at the box-office, but initial responses from the film industry were not positive enough to secure an outside distributor. The film was premiered in 1915 (at this point called *The Clansman,* after the play on which it was based). It was not until the first public performance of the film, slightly later in 1915, that the title *Birth of a Nation* came into existence. Whether this title was more emotive, or whether it was created in order to distinguish the film from the play, is a matter of debate. The film opened to huge critical acclaim and commercial success. Critics were in raptures over the technical innovations and stylistic advances that the film offered. At this point, critics seemed to overlook the problematic subject matter and ideology of Griffith's work. It was not until the NAACP (National Association of the Advancement of Coloured People) brought pressure to bear, that some public discussion of the film's racist content began. The end result of the NAACP's pressure was that some of the most racist scenes within the film were cut, notably those in which the black characters sexually assault white females.

The public debate concerning the film's content was further fuelled by historians and academics who took issue with the erroneous representation of events in the film and the representation of blacks within the southern states at that time. The film's first screenings in several states in America were met with protests and on some occasions, riots. There was a shift in response to the film, resulting in President Woodrow Wilson issuing a statement, which, although confirming his original statement of wonder at the film's technical brilliance, also included comment on the deeply 'problematic images' found in the film. Griffith's response to the snowballing criticism was to rail against what he saw as the censorship of cinema. Whether the director was overtly racist or not has been the focus of much speculation. He certainly had a very romanticised notion of the history of the time. His film is a distortion of history and presents racist representations. Whether the label 'racist' should be used or not about the director is something you can debate, having seen the film. What is not in debate, however, is that after the film was released, there was a resurgence of Klu Klux Klan activity and a swelling of its membership.

Documentary

As one of the options under Section A of the FS6 exam, the topic of documentary should be approached with a focus of 'text and spectator'. Your studies should concentrate on how documentary attempts to construct the 'real'; and the strategies used in documentaries to make the 'real' engaging to the audience. There is a historical dimension to this topic and some study of how conventions of reality construction have changed over the years will be important within your preparation. You could look at two contrasting styles of documentary film making from two historical periods and consider what influences have caused changes in documentary conventions.

Early documentary film making

In 1926, John Grierson (one of the most famous proponents of British documentary film making) first used the term 'documentary'. Grierson was describing the 1926 film *Moana*, directed by Robert Flaherty, and described documentary as 'the creative treatment of actuality'. His description identifies two key features of the documentary film – that it should be reality-based, but presented in a dynamic and engaging way. The process of documentary film making within this early description is of piecing together 'fragments of reality' to make an involving whole. Grierson also identified the purpose of early documentary, which was to 'inform, instruct and educate'. These are lofty claims for any film form, and you will need to consider not just whether subsequent documentaries continued to 'inform, instruct and educate', but whether this is an accurate description of their function at all. Also, there is an implication concerning a documentary's audience implied in Grierson's description – that the viewer is passive and brings little to the dynamic between themselves and the film.

What John Grierson identified as the mode and purpose of the documentary has, of course, been challenged over subsequent years. For example, during the 1940s, British director Lindsay Anderson, and other members of the Free British Cinema movement, called for a freer type of documentary that did not construct class-based hierarchies. These film makers criticised the tendency in early documentaries to have a middle-class voice-over commenting on the lives of working-class people. The Free British Cinema movement resented the ideological implications of a reader with 'received pronunciation' delivering comments on the hardships of working people. You should consider what kind of relationship is being constructed between the film makers and their subjects in the documentaries you study.

There is an inherent tension at the core of documentary film making. The drive and purpose is towards constructing the real, but there has to be enough creative/stylistic artifice involved in order to allow the documentary to catch the viewer's attention. There are many important questions you should ask yourself if studying this topic. Should documentaries have narratives, which are structurally engaging but do not necessarily represent the real sequence of events at the core of the documentary? Does auteurism exist within documentary film making and does the style or presence of the director unduly affect the reception of the film? You might also consider how representation functions within a documentary and ask yourself about the ideological thrust behind what is presented on the screen. Do you think that a documentary should be entertaining, or is this contradictory to the basic principles of the form? To what extent are re-enacted events made more dramatic in order to generate excitement and tension for the audience? Does the presence of the camera significantly alter the events being filmed and undermine the attempt to capture reality? These are all essential questions and you should consider them carefully when you are watching examples of the documentary form.

Types of documentary
The genre of documentary, as with many other genres, has many sub-divisions. You should remember to consider the type of documentary you are studying, as well as the strategies it uses to generate a reality effect. For ease of recognition, the four terms that can be used to describe the four main categories of documentary are:

- exposition
- observation
- interaction and
- reflexive.

An exposition style of documentary will usually have a narrator to explain the events being presented to the viewer. This style is often used with the type of documentary that includes images the viewer may not have seen before. Science-based documentaries, such as those about wildlife, often have a narrator to explain what is happening or what viewers are seeing. Documentaries without any type of narrator are of an observational style. They seem to merely present events and images and leave it up to the viewer to explain what is seen to themselves. Of course, it has to be remembered that even observational documentaries are constructed through camerawork and editing, so they may not necessarily be as 'untainted' as they initially appear to be. Interactive documentaries position the interviewer in front of the camera, either interviewing a subject or interacting with the events that are being presented. Journalistic pieces of investigative reporting often use an interactive element. Reflexive documentary style, as with any other reflexive form, reveals the mechanics of the documentary film-making process at the same time as it presents events.

Alongside the style of the individual documentary you are studying, there are other important factors to consider. What, for example, is the social or historical context of the documentary and how does this context affect what is being presented? What was the technology available to the film maker at the time the documentary was made and how does this influence the type of material included within the film? These questions, as well as the question of the cinematic techniques used to construct reality, are essential within your analytical process.

As has already been stated at the beginning of this section, one productive means of study would be to compare documentaries from different periods of history and comment on their similarities and differences. You might, for example, choose a documentary by the early documentary maker Robert Flaherty and analyse it alongside later examples. Flaherty was an American who had a passion for exploration. His early work was mostly concerned with indigenous populations, such as the American Indians. His 1922 film *Nanook of the North* documented the lives and struggles of an Eskimo and his family. The film gained huge critical and commercial success. A retrospective reading of the film might point to a mythologising and romanticising of Flaherty's subject matter, but at the time it was very successful. Flaherty went on to make *Moana* (1926) (about which Grierson first used the term documentary), *The Twenty Four Dollar Island* (1927), *Elephant Boy* (1937) and *Louisiana Story* (1948).

Humphrey Jennings is another key individual in the development of the documentary form and his work differed greatly from Flaherty's. Jennings was a Marxist poet and painter, who was also very interested in the Surrealist movement of the 1920s. As a Marxist, Jennings tried to counter the class-based observations that he identified in the work of Grierson and others. Jennings made documentaries for the Mass Observation Unit, which had been set up by left-wing intellectuals to document the lives of ordinary British people. Unlike the kind of documentary he found class-bound, Jennings' work for the Mass Observation Unit presented accounts of working-class life from the mouths of the working-class people themselves. The style of Jennings' work also differs from that of other film makers. His interest in Surrealism sometimes crept into the documentary form and his poetry and painting background tended to give a more artistic feel to his work. Jennings' work included *Locomotive* (1935), *Penny Journey* (1938), *Fires Were Started* (1943) and *Family Portrait* (1950).

There are many other periods of documentary film making that would make for an extremely worthwhile study. The *Kino-Pravda* (Film Truth) works of the Russian director Dziga Vertov would make an excellent topic of study. You might also look at the films generated by the Nazi propaganda machine. A study of Leni Riefenstahl's 1935 film *Triumph of the Will*, which records the 1934 Nazi Nuremberg rally, would provide a fascinating discussion of the role of ideology within documentary film making. Today's documentary film makers have the advantage of digital technologies, such as camera and editing software, which has certainly had an impact on what can be recorded. Your study of documentaries might compare an historical example of documentary film making with a contemporary example. You might look at the work of Michael Moore and consider how *Roger and Me, Bowling for Columbine* or *Fahrenheit 9/11* differ from, or are similar to, earlier examples of the documentary genre. Below is a case study of a modern documentary film that would provide a useful study in combination with an earlier one:

Case Study 2: *Touching the Void* (Kevin MacDonald, 2003)

Source: British Film Institute

Kevin MacDonald's documentary *Touching the Void* won a BAFTA and an Evening Standard award. It received universal critical and audience acclaim. The documentary is based on the true events that occurred during a climbing trip in Peru, in 1985. One of the climbers on the trip, Joe Simpson, subsequently wrote a book about the events and this provides the basis for the events depicted in the film.

In order to present the story of two climbers who attempted to ascend the previously unclimbed West face of the *Siula Grande* mountain in Peru, and nearly perished, dramatic reconstructions were essential. The realism of this documentary is, therefore, to a large degree, reinforced by the locations represented. MacDonald filmed on a real glacier in order to approximate the arena of Joe Simpson's and Simon Yates' ordeal. The documentary is of an exposition style, with both Simpson and Yates used as narrators for the events. They are seen in a studio, offering comment and recollection to the viewer. Of course, their presence creates an interesting effect, because it becomes obvious from the beginning of the documentary that they both survived. They substantiate the authenticity of events through their narration, but it has to be remembered that the truth of their telling is subjective, as is always the case when people draw on memory.

The reconstructed scenes within this documentary are powerful, and are rendered even more dramatic by the narrator's comments concerning their states of mind at key moments. This mixing of reconstruction and narration presents a powerfully emotive version of events. There is a narrative structure to *Touching the Void* and this structure, in many ways, echoes what the audience for the documentary would expect from a feature film. The calm and hopeful expectation of the first scenes is quickly shattered – what comes next is escalating tension, only broken when the two climbers are reunited at their base camp.

Touching the Void was made in 2003 when computer-generated imagery (CGI) would have been an easy device for manufacturing the film's dramatic sequences. However, the film does not rely on CGI, preferring instead to use real locations and stunts. Perhaps the audience's awareness of CGI technologies and their ability to spot CGI elements, rendered its use counter to the reality effect MacDonald was attempting to produce. The cinematography works to create drama, however, and the mixing of extreme long shots, close-ups of harrowed faces and point-of-view shots presenting the full horrors of the climbers' predicaments, functions to create extreme tension for the audience. Editing also functions to punctuate the reconstructed event scenes with the climbers' commentaries and to delay the moments when the audience's tension is released.

EXERCISE 2

With a partner, use the internet, film magazines and other pieces of film journalism to research the critical and audience reception of Michael Moore's documentary *Fahrenheit 9/11* (2004). Use your notes in a discussion concerning the role and impact of contemporary documentary.

Experimental film making

This topic involves the study of films that fall outside of any of the other categories used within this unit. It extends beyond a consideration of independent cinema and encompasses those films that are explicitly experimental in style and content. The title 'experimental cinema' is broad and can include films designated as 'avant-garde'. Your study of this topic might even extend into the study of film 'installation' work.

What is an experimental film?

An experimental film does not conform to traditional notions of film style and film content. It might use technologies in an original and unusual way to create images that run counter to what audiences would expect to see in a standard piece of cinema. You should choose case studies for this section that create an experience for the film viewer that is different from the viewer's usual expectations of cinema. Typically, an experimental film can be said to take an anti-establishment position and this could be in terms of style, structure or content. The rejection of tradition within experimental film making is a key factor, and the case studies you choose should offer some form of comment on the cinematic norms that had gone before.

There are many possible avenues of study for this topic and many types of film that could be labelled as 'experimental'. Do not forget that your FS5 studies could be very useful for this topic. For example, the Surrealists employed experimental techniques, and positioned their films as very clearly counter to traditional notions of film making. You could also bring in your study of German Expressionism and Soviet Cinema, and consider the ways in which directors, such as Vertov, Murnau and Eisenstein created film experiences that were very different from those that audiences had previously experienced. The use of montage techniques within Soviet cinema, for example, was incredibly experimental for the time and introduced audiences to a new type of cinema experience. If your chosen topic of study for Section A of the FS5 paper was Cinematic new waves, you could transfer some of these film examples to a discussion of experimental cinema. At the time, the hand-held camera techniques, real locations and subjective sound used by the French new wave directors, for example, was viewed as experimental.

The question of historical context is an important one within this section. What was experimental in the 1920s for example, would not be today. It will be important for you to discuss the relative impact of films you have studied from different eras within cinema history and to consider why these particular types of experimentation came about. One important question you will need to ask yourself is that of the ideological 'profile' of experimental cinema. Does a type of film making that seeks to extend the boundaries of film-making technique and style, have an ideological element? If experimental films 'attack' traditions of narrative structuring, content type and cinematic technique, do they also attack the ideological stance of the films they are rejecting? If your case studies include Surrealist pieces, such as *L' Age d'Or* and *The Phantom of Liberty*, then the answer to this question is 'yes'. Bourgeois values and social repression were explicit targets. If your case studies include contemporary video installation work, then the answer might be different.

You do not have to confine your studies to FS5 subject areas and contemporary pieces of experimental cinema, however, and there is a wealth of other cinema that would provide equally fruitful study. You might consider American experimental film work – the films that came out of Andy Warhol's 'Factory', for example. *Women in Revolt* (1972) and *L'Amour* (1973), directed by Warhol, could provide interesting topics of study, as could the Warhol-produced *Flesh* (1968) and *Trash* (1970). You might also analyse the films of American director Stan Brakhage. Also a film theorist and critic, Brakhage sought to present an alternative film experience in films, such as *Sirius Remembered* (1959) and *Hell Spit Flexion* (1983).

Whatever films you choose to study, remember that your aim is to attempt to describe two aspects:

- the elements of style and structure that you consider to be experimental, and
- the impact this different type of cinema experience had on people who viewed the film.

EXERCISE 3

Create a description of cinematic ideas for your own, original, piece of experimental film making. Your notes should include your plans for:

- technologies to be used
- specific characteristics of cinematography
- editing techniques
- sound elements
- *mise-en-scène*
- content type.

Case Study 3: Maya Deren (1917–1961)

Maya Deren was born in Russia, but emigrated to the US with her family, when she was a child. Although only 44 when she died, Deren had made a significant contribution to experimental cinema. Deren's first film *Meshes in the Afternoon* (1943) has since become one of the most famous examples of experimental film making. This film rejected the formal structures of film making, characterisation and narrative in order to create 18 minutes of striking images in which the boundaries between dream and reality seem to have been permanently blurred. The time frame of the film, along with its merging of dream and reality, and avoidance of standard narrative structuring, make *Meshes in the Afternoon* a striking example of experimental film making.

Shocking cinema

The question on shocking cinema is concerned with the interaction of a film with its audience. The focus of your answer should be the implicit or explicit strategies a film utilises to elicit a response from the viewer. The FS6 exam is a synoptic unit – this means that you could draw from your understanding and knowledge of any part of your Film Studies A level when constructing your answer. You learned how to evaluate the impact of the micro and macro elements of film in your FS1 studies and this knowledge should be used to assess how the stylistic elements of a film can be used for shocking impact. The work you did for FS2: Producers and Audiences will be invaluable when considering any financial motivation for the inclusion of shocking elements within a film. FS3: British and Irish Cinema afforded you the skills to discuss messages and values. The ability to distinguish between implicit and explicit messages and values within a film will be crucial to your assessment of 'shocking' material. Your FS4 Auteur study may have alerted you to how particular directors use cinematography, editing, sound or *mise-en-scène* to engage an audience's response and the FS5 unit on World Cinema may have opened your eyes to texts from other nations which tap into different cultural pre-occupations. The point is that you already have the framework of knowledge needed in order to encounter this question in an informed and articulate manner. Don't waste all of this background knowledge by allowing yourself to offer an essay that merely discusses your own seeming unshockability!

The best responses to shocking cinema questions are those in which the candidate considers both the technical and structural features of a film, and how they are used to elicit various types of shock. It is not only explicit sex and graphic violence which may cause a viewer to retreat from a film. It might be the viewer's sensibilities concerning race, sexuality, religion or politics that are offended. The Collins English Dictionary defines the word shock in four ways:

1. 'To experience, or cause to experience, extreme horror, disgust or surprise.'

2. 'To cause a state of shock in a person.'

3. 'To cause to come into violent contact.'

4. 'Something which causes a sudden and violent disturbance in the emotions.'

These definitions do not identify a cause. They do not attribute shock to any particular stimulus. In fact, what shocks us can be totally subjective. Your task in the exam is not to build a hierarchy of shock, with violence at the top, sexually explicit material a close second and politically, racially and religiously induced shocks at the bottom. Your task is to assess how different types of shock can be constructed in a film text and the possible impact that this might have on the spectator.

Consider the use of the non-diegetic voice-over from the character Alex, in Stanley Kubrick's *A Clockwork Orange* (1971). In the first 30 minutes of the film, Alex commits rape and murder. He is violent and remorseless, but he is also our narrative guide. As such, our usual response would be to view him as, at least to some degree, reliable in his narration of events. Narrators only allow us to see what they want us to see, but they are not traditionally morally reprehensible. Alex joins the likes of Patrick Bateman in Brett Easton Ellis' novel *American Psycho*, and Humbert Humbert in Vladimir Nabokov's novel *Lolita*, as a narrator whose version of events is saturated with his own self-justification and self-delusion. In terms of the shock factor of Alex's narration, perhaps it lies within our willingness to trust him and our responses to his lightness of tone and seeming naivety. Kubrick did not choose an actor with big baby-blue eyes for nothing. Malcolm McDowell plays Alex as half precocious child, half pathological criminal, and it is this duality that infects the voice-over and causes the viewer to be shocked at their own sympathy, even identification, with a character such as Alex.

William Friedkin's 1973 film *The Exorcist* is also a film in which the shock elements have to be carefully considered. Unlike *A Clockwork Orange*, *The Exorcist* employs special effects in order to create some of the more shocking scenes. A contemporary viewer may thus consider the film's scenes of Regan's facial disfigurement, projectile vomiting and head spinning as unrealistic and therefore not shocking. A good essay that uses this film as a reference would consider the shift in responses caused by our recent exposure to CGI-created horror and discuss how the advances in animation and prosthetics affect our responses to body-related horror effects. It would be wrong to describe the 1973 audience of *The Exorcist* as overly susceptible to shock, but it would be right to consider how the technology surrounding cinema has had an impact on both audience expectations and responses.

The function of representation in film texts is another area that can be considered when evaluating a film's 'shocking' impact. D.W. Griffith's 1915 film *The Birth of a Nation*, based on the Reverend Thomas Dixon Jnr's novel *The Clansman*, was technically innovative and impressively epic in its construction of narrative. Viewers in 1915 would have been presented with a film that utilised some of the most advanced cinematic methods of its time. However, Griffith's film and Dixon's novel share an ideological thrust that is deeply shocking – they are unapologetically racist. The Klu Klux Klan, the organisation that advocated white supremacy and murdered blacks, is presented positively, even gloriously. As a piece of cinematic art, *The Birth of a Nation* pushes the boundaries of cinema forward, but as a political document it is shocking even today. Your studies might include this kind of film, where the technical art of the piece is at odds with its troubling content, and if you have studied a similar film, there is an important question which you will need to consider. Given the fact that audiences are often impressed by technical innovation, does their potential shock become tempered by the 'wow factor' of groundbreaking elements?

The cultural or cult status of a film could also become a part of your debates concerning shocking cinema. The 'mythology' surrounding certain films and their content can provoke a 'must see' response in the viewer. Films banned from video release under the 1984 Video Recordings Act subsequently became the subject of frenzied speculation. What was it in *SS Extermination Camp*, *Cannibal Holocaust* and *Driller Killer* that had caused all the furore? The tendency of legislative measures to increase viewer interest in certain films is one area you could discuss in your essay. Do laws contribute to these films being attributed a cult status? Do the kinds of films banned after the 1984 act mirror social sensibilities, or moral panics? Your answer for the shocking cinema question should not focus on context and institution (these debates would be appropriate for a Section B censorship question). However, a discussion of how certain films may have been deemed more shocking than others because they tapped into prevalent social fears could act as a part of your debate. If audiences are 'told' that a film is shocking, because it has been banned or withdrawn from circulation, how does this affect their personal responses to the content of the film?

Whether you were shocked by the almost cartoon sequence which tells the back-story of Malory's abuse by her father in *Natural Born Killers* (Oliver Stone), the scenes of Jews being herded towards the gas chambers in *Schindler's List* (Steven Spielberg), the pathological behaviour of the character of Frank in *Blue Velvet* (David Lynch) or the scene in which Bambi's mother dies in *Bambi* (Disney), your essay will be as valid as any other candidate's as long as you consider some fundamental questions:

1. What are the different types of shock a viewer can experience when watching a film?

2. What are the stylistic, narrative and representational devices being used to elicit a response from the audience?

3. Is the film using these devices with an explicit or implicit intent to shock?

4. How does the viewer respond to the shock that has been caused?

5. To what extent is cinema a more or less effective vehicle for shock than any other medium?

Your response to the last of these questions could provide an interesting conclusion to your shocking cinema answer. Consider whether or not you think that film is a medium capable of generating a shocked response in its audience. The audio/visual experience of seeing a film in a cinema, for example, is very different from seeing that film on television. Is the immersion experience of viewing a film in the dark, on a big screen, with other audience members' responses echoing around you, a context in which you might be more, or less, shocked?

EXERCISE 4

In a small group, make a list of all of the different types of shock you think can be experienced by a film viewer. Then, for each of these types of shock, list two film or scene examples, which you could then use as references within an essay for this topic.

Case Study 4: *A Clockwork Orange* (Stanley Kubrick, 1971)

The reception of Kubrick's 1971 film is well documented. The film was given an 'X' certificate by the British Board of Film Classification and passed for general release. After the film's release, however, various elements of the press began to attack the film, accusing it of inciting copycat-style crimes. There were allegations that rapes and murders had been carried out by individuals who had been heavily influenced by

287

Source: British Film Institute

the film. As a response to the growing condemnation of his film, Kubrick withdrew *A Clockwork Orange* from circulation in Britain in 1974. The film was still available in other countries, but was not to be seen on screens in Britain until after the director's death in 1999.

Any study of *A Clockwork Orange* within the Shocking Cinema topic of the FS6 exam will need to consider both the impact on audiences the film had in 1971 and the impact that it has today. The level of graphic violence, which viewers today see regularly in mainstream films, might seem to render the depiction of the actions of Alex and his Droogs relatively mild. However, *A Clockwork Orange* has a much more complex message than many contemporary Hollywood action products and its impact is established via much more complex stylistic means. The film is based on Anthony Burgess' novel of the same name, and both Kubrick and Burgess have described the story as one concerning the need for free will. Alex initially has free will, but uses it for violent ends. He rapes and murders, because at this point in the film he has the freedom to do what he wants. The premise of the film – that free will should be the right of even those who abuse it – could in itself be shocking to those who are sympathetic to the kind of totalitarian regime that eventually sends Alex for his 'treatment'.

A Clockwork Orange forces the viewer to identify with the lead Droog, Alex. His narration (and therefore version of events) provides the voiceover and this narrative guide is often presented as charming and cheeky, as well as violent and sadistic. Alex is our unreliable narrator and by the time we see him in the Ludovico clinic, undergoing aversion therapy, a degree of sympathy for, and identification with him has been established in the mind of the viewer. One of the types of shock established by the film might well be that the viewer's point of reference and object of sympathy is in fact also a rapist and killer. The film creates this identification with Alex by representing the other characters in the film as far worse than him. These characters are either perverse (the truant officer), mad (the writer) or hypocritical (the politician). Even the cat lady, whom Alex murders, is represented as a collector of pretentious artworks. None of the subsidiary characters seem completely innocent and this in itself provides an interesting problematic within the film. Is it because the viewer 'sees' events through the narration of Alex that this characterisation occurs, or is it that the film lacks sympathy even for its victims?

Stylistically, *A Clockwork Orange* is innovative and engaging. Kubrick's use of slow motion, emotive soundtrack and hand-held camera create a dynamic and stylised arena in which events are played out. Does this render the viewer immune to the shocking content of the film, or heighten it? There are textual examples either way for this debate. Alex's revenge on Dim, by the canal, is shot in slow motion with a rousing orchestral score, which seems to render Alex's actions, if not justifiable, then certainly visually engaging. However, Alex's rendition of *Singing in the Rain* as he attacks the writer and his wife establishes another level to the horror of the scene and confirms his inability to have any sympathy for his victims.

A Clockwork Orange provides a fascinating text to study under the heading of Shocking Cinema. It promotes an anti-totalitarian standpoint, but does so via a complex use of cinematic techniques and a disturbing positioning of the film's audience. If you study this film, you will need to make sure that you consider both the ideological thrust of the piece, as well as the textual devices used in order to relay that message.

Section B: Producers and Audiences: Issues and debates

Regulation and censorship

One of the fundamental questions you will need to ask yourself if you are studying this topic is: Who is censorship for? Is the censorship of film designed to protect audiences from exposure to certain images, and if so, who decides what is to be censored, and what rationale do these individuals have for the censorship decisions they make? These are questions you should answer by making sure that you understand the changes and developments that have occurred in censorship history.

The first film ever to be banned was *Cheese Mites* (1897), directed by Charles Orban. The film showed microscopic images of the effects of mites on a piece of cheese. As innocuous as this might appear to us today, these images upset the British Cheese Federation, who felt that the film could deter people from eating cheese. The pressure that the BBFC brought to bear eventually persuaded Orban to withdraw his film and it was banned from public release. Early films were viewed in Picture Palaces and early film stock was highly flammable. In 1909, with the Cinematograph Act, the government gave local councils the power to oversee safety standards within cinemas. This ruling was quickly extended to include the power to ban films a local council considered inappropriate.

It was not until 1913 that the early incarnation of the British Board of Film Classification came into existence. The film industry felt that the overseeing of film should not be left up to local councils and created the British Board of Film Censors, whose role was to assess films for public consumption. As this now meant that the film industry was responsible for assessing its own products, some critics saw the BBFC as having a clash of interests. At this point in cinema history, there were two main criteria of 'taboo' for the BBFC: representations of Christ, and nudity. These focal concerns were to change significantly over the course of the BBFC's history. It is interesting to note at this point, however, the differences between the treatment of theatre and film productions. Plays were treated much more leniently than films, because of their different audiences. Plays were predominantly watched by the middle classes and film by the working classes. The history of censorship in many ways offers a reflection of the class system in Britain and attitudes to it. Why was it that middle-class audiences were deemed sensitive and intelligent enough to view certain material and to distinguish effectively between fact and fiction, whereas working-class audiences were seen as impressionable and easily inflamed?

The BBFC's attitude to many significant examples of early cinema acts to exemplify the different attitudes that were held concerning different classes. Eisenstein's 1926 film *Battleship Potemkin* was banned from mainstream release because of its revolutionary subject matter, but was screened at the Film Society, whose members were middle-class intellectuals. Were the BBFC afraid that Eisenstein's classic would incite civil unrest? F.W. Murnau's expressionist work, *Nosferatu*, was also denied mainstream release because its subject matter was considered by the BBFC to be too disturbing for the masses. Any film that presented revolutionary subject matter or was considered inflammatory of the masses was considered unsuitable for wide release.

Horror films have been very significant to the history of censorship. Although *Nosferatu* was banned and later works of American horror films were considered vapid and lacking in artistic integrity, it is the latter, very commercial examples of the genre that forced a shift in BBFC thinking. The 1930s saw a wave of Gothic-inspired horror films, such as *Frankenstein* and *Dracula*, coming over from America. The BBFC saw little artistic merit in these films and feared the effect they would have on mass audiences. However, these films were incredibly successful at the box-office and the BBFC could not ignore the financial benefits of their release. Eventually, the BBFC created an 'H' certificate, especially for horror, in order to warn potential audiences of their content. The power of economics had overcome some of the BBFC's prejudices about certain genres of film.

The Second World War marked a very significant shift in what could be shown on the cinema screen. Before 1939, the BBFC had echoed the government's attitude of appeasement towards Nazi Germany, by not allowing films that represented Nazism as problematic to be screened. Once the war broke out and attempts at appeasement had come to an end, the cinema began to exhibit films that showed some of the horrors inflicted during the war. The Pathé News reels of the time, which included horrific images of concentration camps, also acted to open up the constraints on what could be shown on film. After the war was over and more information concerning what had gone on in the extermination camps came to light, film makers began to express their responses to the war in extremely graphic films. The public had seen these images anyway, in Pathé News reels, so it would have been ridiculous to censor their inclusion in feature films. One very significant film in the discourse on Nazi Germany was Alain Resnais' 1955 film *Night and Fog*. This film included horrendous documentary footage of Auschwitz and what the Allied Forces found there after the Nazis had been overcome. The BBFC did make small cuts, but allowed the film general release, with an 'X' certificate.

The 1950s saw some relaxation of censorship, especially films destined for art-house cinema, but the BBFC did not show the same degree of latitude to mainstream films. The question of who was going to see the film and how they would be affected still continued. Laslo Benedek's 1954 film *The Wild One* was banned because of its portrait of rebellious youths, and was not given a certificate for the next 15 years. Films deemed by the board as potentially inciting to the working classes were routinely denied certificates at this time and the fears that were expressed during the BBFC's assessment of *Battleship Potemkin* persisted.

At the beginning of the 1960s, the BBFC had a new Chief Censor, John Trevellyan, and were working within a social climate that was becoming much more liberated. There were significant shifts in BBFC decisions during this time and one important example of this was Basil Dearden's 1961 film *Victim*, which documented social prejudices towards homosexuality (the homosexual act, at the time the film was made, was still illegal in Britain). *Victim* did not contain explicit images, but its content was new to cinema screens and the fact that the film was passed marked a response to the times by the BBFC.

The early 1970s, and 1971–72 in particular, were extremely important years within the history of censorship. Stephen Murphy took over as the BBFC's Chief Censor and several films were released that caused much controversy. Sexual violence became a focal concern of the BBFC. Ken Russell's 1971 film *The Devils* caused much debate, with its depiction of masturbating nuns and graphic scenes of torture. The film was passed, with cuts, but a campaign by the Festival of Light, a religious organisation, and various sectors of the press, led to numerous town councils banning the film. Regardless of obtaining a BBFC certificate, town councils still had the power to ban a film. Sam Peckinpah's 1971 film *Straw Dogs* also came in for much debate. Scenes of sexual assault, especially a rape scene that appears to become consensual, were the focus of debate. Stephen Murphy advised cuts to the film before its release, in what was an unprecedented move from a BBFC Chief Censor. Stanley Kubrick's *A Clockwork Orange* (1971) was passed by the BBFC with an 'X' certificate, but was then withdrawn by the director after a press-inspired moral panic concerning the film. It was Bernardo Bertolucci's 1972 film *Last Tango in Paris*, however, which was to highlight a significant issue around film censorship. The film was passed by the Board, with some cuts, and released. However, a private prosecution was brought against the film for obscenity, which eventually failed because it was found that the Obscene Publications Act did not cover film. It was not until the 1977 Criminal Law Act that film came under the jurisdiction of the Obscene Publications Act and could therefore be held liable if images were deemed obscene.

The next important stage in the history of censorship was the advent of video. Prior to 1984, video did not come under the control of the BBFC. Distributors could release almost any material on VHS and distribute it. Sam Raimi's 1981 horror film, The *Evil Dead*, for example, was one film that did incredibly well on video in the years before 1984. After much pressure from both individuals and groups, and as part of their 'Victorian values' promise, the Conservative government passed the 1984 Video Recordings Act, which ordered that all films on video had to be submitted to the BBFC prior to release. The pressure had come because of so-called 'video nasties', which had been blamed for numerous copycat offences in the early 1980s. After 1984, titles such as *S.S. Extermination Camp*, *Cannibal Holocaust* and *Driller Killer* were taken out of circulation. Films on VHS were often more heavily cut than those exhibited at the cinema and this was primarily due to the impossibility of monitoring who would watch the film in a home context.

The 1990s saw the BBFC continue with the very lucrative job of assessing film on video for release. The decade also saw some very long debates over the release of certain films. The release in Britain of Oliver Stone's 1994 film *Natural Born Killers* was held up by debate within the BBFC. The film was eventually released, but due to the violent content of Stone's film, including scenes of sexual violence, the video release did not happen until many years after the cinema release of the film. As has already been indicated, the differences between classification for cinema and video release provide an important area of debate within the topic of censorship. Films on video are often more heavily cut (or in extreme cases the transfer from film to video is denied) because of the more open viewing context of video.

At the end of the twentieth century, the BBFC were more concerned with representations of sexual assault, drug taking and imitable violence, than with the focus on blasphemy and nudity that had begun the history of film censorship in the early years of the century. Sexually explicit material was passed for cinema release, but scenes of sexual violence were still cut. Virginie Despentes and Coralie Trinh Thi's film, *Baise-Moi* (2000), for example, shows actual sexual encounters which were not cut, but a graphic rape scene had some seconds removed. The BBFC today is a very different organisation than its original 1913 incarnation. Below is a case study that outlines the criteria and concerns of the BBFC today.

Case Study 5: The British Board of Film Classification today

The British Board of Film Classification, or BBFC, is an independent organisation. It is non-governmental and generates revenue from the fees it charges for the classification of films, DVDs, videos and digital games. It is the job of the BBFC to assign categories (U, Uc, PG, 12, 12A, 15, 18 or R18) or to recommend cuts. There are specific criteria that the BBFC examiners use in order make assessments, but, in addition, 'general principles' are used by all examiners in their evaluations. These include:

- comparing present with previous classification cases in order to maintain consistency of classification

- consideration of audience – examiners will consider who the film/game is aimed at and who is likely to see it
- consideration of the context of images shown – examiners will consider the intention of the whole film etc. and its messages, rather than take images in isolation
- legislation that might be relevant to some images.

These general principles act as a framework within which other, more specific, criteria are used to evaluate whether or not a film/game should receive a classification or which classification should be given. These specific areas of focus concern violence, language, sex and drugs. In terms of language, each of the Board's classification categories has its own stipulations on the type of language that is appropriate. For U certificates, infrequent use of very mild bad language is all that is acceptable. For a 12 classification, a film/game can only use very strong language (such as 'fuck') rarely, and it has to be completely justified by context. In real terms, a 12 film will only be allowed one use of the word 'fuck' and this must be absolutely justified by the context in which it is said. In a 15 film, frequent use of strong language is acceptable, but verbal sexual abuse is not. Within an 18 film, there are no constraints on language, even sexually abusive language.

In terms of the BBFC's assessment of sex on screen, there are, again, specific guidelines. Extended scenes of simulated sex always gain the film an 18 certificate. Any glamorisation of sexual assault will invite potential cuts within that scene, as will scenes in which rape is seemingly enjoyed by the victim. There are other factors used by the BBFC examiners in order to assess scenes of sexual activity – these include: identification of whether the sex is part of a relationship or is casual, how much nudity is involved in the sexual encounter, whether or not the scene is necessary within the film's narrative, or if it is gratuitous, and how the sexual contact is shot i.e. the number of close-ups, slow motion sequences etc. All of these factors will be considered in the classification of a film with scenes of sexual activity.

The issue of representations of violence on screen has always been a contentious one. As has been indicated in the previous paragraph, representations of sexual violence are always treated with caution and often cut if the rape or assault is shot in a way that might excite viewers. The BBFCs current guidelines on the assessment of violent content include specific questions that examiners must consider when assessing a film. Whether or not the violent scene is necessary to plot development, or gratuitous, is one such area for examiners to consider. The viewer's response to the violent actions shown is also of utmost importance. Does the viewer identify with the aggressor or the victim? Is the violence shown exciting? Whether or not the violence is sadistic is also significant, as is the film's overall attitude to the violence it contains.

The representation of drug taking and a film's stance in relation to drugs, is another high priority area within the BBFC's assessment of particular films. If a scene seems to be instructive of drug-taking procedures, or to represent the effects of drug taking as being glamorous or without consequence to the individual, it will be taken into account. The type of drug used within a film will also affect the assessment of that film.

The criteria of the BBFC have evolved and changed over the many years of the Board's existence and it is important to consider the factors that have contributed to these changes. Legislation has been an important factor within the changing of both the BBFC's remit and its criteria. The most relevant acts to the BBFC's work have been:

- *The Cinematograph Films (Animals) Act 1937* - the passing of this act made it illegal to show scenes in which actual cruelty to animals occurs.

- *The Obscene Publications Act 1959* – this act deems it illegal to show images (or a whole film) that have 'a tendency to deprave and corrupt' a significant number of those who view it.

- *The Protection of Children Act 1978* – under this act it became illegal to show indecent images of a child (under 16).

- *The Video Recordings Act 1984* – this act brought video under the remit of the BBFC and required producers seeking to distribute films on video to submit work to the BBFC for classification.

There may well be films that you have studied under Section A of this unit that are highly relevant to the topic of regulation and censorship. It is possible to use the same film as a reference in both sections, but with one important proviso. Section B is not a text-driven component in the exam – the focus is 'Producers and Audiences'. Thus it is the institutional considerations around a film and the response of audiences to the film's release that are of a higher focus than the film text itself. You might be asked in the exam to consider the evolution or developments in regulation and censorship, to consider the social and ideological factors that have motivated changes in censorship criteria and the legislation surrounding it. You might be asked to examine a particular point in censorship history and consider what factors at that point in history affected the regulation and censorship of film. You might even be asked to consider the different types of regulation and censorship that exist within different countries. Use of textual examples will be essential, but they should always be discussed in the wider context of how they have been affected by the institutions and organisations who regulate or censor, and the social/ideological context in which these institutions or organisations operate.

EXERCISE 5

Using the BBFC's internet site, make a note of all of the current issues and pieces of legislation that are currently relevant to this organisation. You should also make notes of any contentious films that are being processed.

The dominance of Hollywood and indigenous film production

You should try not to work on the assumption in this topic that Hollywood is a kind of monster that destroys everything in its path. This would be too literal, and too reductive, to allow any real debate. There are two questions, however, that would provide very interesting discussions within your exam essays and these are:

1. What is the role of an indigenous film industry?

2. Is it possible for this indigenous industry to grow within a context of Hollywood's economic dominance?

In order to approach this topic properly, the first thing you should do is to make sure that you understand the term 'indigenous'. In terms of this topic within the FS6 exam, indigenous can be defined as relating to an individual country. More specifically, the topic asks you to consider the role of a nation's own film industry in relation to that of Hollywood. As with many of the other topics for this exam, your previous studies can be drawn on for specific content. Your FS2 studies, particularly those relating to the Hollywood film industry and the British film industry, will be especially relevant here. You might extend your frame of reference to include other indigenous film industries, such as Bollywood, but should remember that your main aim should be to answer the two focus questions for this section.

In terms of the generic question of the role and importance of an indigenous film industry, your discussions will need to evaluate the cultural and ideological significance of nation-specific film producing. Given the fact that the majority of films exhibited in British cinemas, for example, are from Hollywood, is it important for the British film industry to produce films that have more cultural relevance and ideological significance for British audiences? The answer to this question of British cinema, and indeed the answer to this question related to any other national cinema, will take you into a consideration of the role of cinema in representing a nation and that nation's issues. The political climate of a nation at any one time in history, the social issues that the country is experiencing, and the dominance of particular attitudes, can all be reflected in the films produced in that country. As you will have seen in your previous studies, the ideological content of a film might be explicit or implicit. A film might consciously debate particular social issues, or it might reflect those issues via its treatment of particular social groups. If, therefore, it is the role of national cinema to mirror the social and ideological climate of a country at any one time, this might not be an individual film's intent.

It will be your task in this topic, therefore, to identify what you think the general role of a national film industry is, and how this interacts with the Hollywood industry. It is not as clear cut as stating that what indigenous film production is, Hollywood is not – you should attempt to formulate your own attitudes towards what indigenous film industry products should do.

EXERCISE 6

With a partner, discuss the statements below relating to the role of indigenous film industries.

1. National film products should articulate current social debates.

2. Indigenous film industry products should discuss the economic situation of that country.

3. Films produced by an indigenous film industry should represent and discuss key points within that nation's history.

4. National film examples should, either explicitly or implicitly, debate dominant social ideologies.

Your answers to these questions will provide you with both a definition and a 'stance' within your exam essays.

The question of whether it is possible for indigenous film industries to flourish within a global film context, dominated by Hollywood and multi-national companies, is the second important consideration for this topic. The answer to this question should consider production, distribution and exhibition issues, and will need to include specific economic examples. You will need to consider the issue of film funding within your answer and describe the issues related to the generation of film investment within your indigenous industry. Is there, for example, government funding available? In terms of distribution, consider the position of major US distributors, such as UIP and Twentieth Century Fox, within your indigenous market. What kind of percentage share do they have, as opposed to that of other distributors? You should also consider the number of films released in your indigenous market from the US and compare that with the numbers of films which originated in other countries. The case study below offers a template of the kinds of information you need to include in each of these answers.

Case Study 6: The British film market

In 2003, the top ten box-office successes in British cinemas were:

- *Finding Nemo*
- *The Lord of the Rings: The Return of the King*
- *The Matrix: Reloaded*
- *Love, Actually*
- *Pirates of the Caribbean*
- *The Lord of the Rings: The Two Towers*
- *Bruce Almighty*
- *X-Men 2*
- *Calendar Girls*
- *Johnny English.*

With the exception of perhaps *Calendar Girls,* these are all films that have been either produced by Hollywood, or have been made specifically with an eye on the American market. In 2003:

- 55 per cent of all films released in the UK were from America
- 31.5 per cent were from Europe
- 7.5 per cent from Asia
- 2 per cent from Australasia
- 1 per cent from Africa
- 3 per cent were intercontinental co-productions.

These figures are very telling. Over half of all of the films released and exhibited in British cinemas in this year were from the US. Films produced by the British film industry made up a section of the percentage of films from Europe. One of the reasons for this high percentage of Hollywood products is the dominance of US distributors globally. The market share of film distribution in 2003 was as follows:

- Buena Vista International   26.6 per cent
- UIP   22.5 per cent
- Entertainment Film Distributors   14.5 per cent
- Warner Bros.   10.4 per cent
- Columbia TriStar   9.8 per cent
- Twentieth Century Fox   8.8 per cent
- Pathé   1.9 per cent

- Icon Film Distribution   0.7 per cent
- Others   3.7 per cent

The difficult economic route for British films is clear. Given the dominance of Hollywood products on cinema screens and the market share of US distributors, even getting British films shown is difficult. Of course, this then means that funding is more difficult to achieve. Unfortunately, the British film industry still experiences something of a vicious circle.

Independent film and its audience

This topic should not be confused with the previous one, concerning indigenous film production. Independent films are not necessarily indigenous and vice versa. This topic concentrates on the nature of independence within cinema and what criteria have to be met in order for a film to be considered independent. The second area of focus for this topic is the nature of the audience for independent film. Who are they? What are their expectations of cinema? Why are they particularly drawn to independent film?

In order to try to formulate a definition of independent cinema, it is useful to keep certain key areas in mind: production, distribution, exhibition and technology. If a film is financed by a multi-national company, it is debatable whether it can be said to be independent. However, as we have seen, many examples of indigenous films have difficulty raising finances, so a problematic economic 'birth' is not necessarily a factor within a definition of independent cinema. One way of using the issue of financing within the identification of independent cinema, might be to ask *why* the film might have had difficulty in securing financing. If the answer is based purely on an associated controversy or a lack of confidence in the film's quality, then it is doubtful whether the film in question can be said to be independent. If the problem of securing funding is connected with the film's anti-establishment content, or experimental style, then it is more appropriate that this film be designated 'independent'.

Often, independent cinema is defined as that which lies outside the mainstream, including films that have an avant-garde style, or an ideological positioning that runs counter to that which is dominant. Independent films do not have to be experimental in style, but they may use techniques that are not common within mainstream film making. If a film has had a difficult time gaining financing, it might also have trouble securing a distributor, if the distributor that producers approach usually deals with more standard types of films. Of course, if the path to distribution is littered with hurdles, exhibition will also be problematic.

So far, our definition of what is an independent film has highlighted the problem of funding, issues of content and style, and the potential difficulties of widescale exhibition. It would be a mistake at this stage, however, to assume that the word 'independent' is synonymous with the word 'problem'. There are distributors, such as Optimum Releasing in Britain, who regularly distribute independent film and there are avenues of financing, such as the Arts Council of Britain, who have specific amounts of funding for non-mainstream films. The dominance of Hollywood, and its associated distribution and exhibition machinery, does cause problems for independent films, however, but this is in no way the end of the story.

As has already been stated, style and content are two important factors in the distinction between mainstream and independent cinema and the advent of digital film technologies has had a significant impact in this area. Budget has been acknowledged as an issue for independent cinema, so the developments within film technologies that are cheaper, but of comparable quality, are incredibly significant for independent film. Both Lars Von Trier's *The Idiots* and Mike Figgis' *Time Code,* for example, were filmed entirely on digital cameras. The light weight of these cameras, and the effects that can be applied to footage in digital editing programs, mean that the stylistic innovations often associated with independent cinema can now be executed relatively cheaply.

For the independent film audience, the key issues are connected with the questions of 'where?' and 'why?'. The end result of the potential hurdles faced by an independent film in securing financing, distribution and exhibition, and the nature of the style and content of many independent films, means that the context of release for independent films is often the art-house cinema. It would also be worth investigating whether any of the films you have identified as independent have been premiered at any of the more independent film festivals, such as Sundance. Why audiences watch independent films is a more complex question. One answer might be because the structure and style of this type of film offers an alternative to the Hollywood mainstream experience. Another interpretation might include the ideological

EXERCISE 7

Look through the programme of your nearest arts cinema and make a note of two or three films that are to be released soon. For each of these films, prepare notes under the following headings (the most accessible source of information for this task is the internet):

- budget and investors
- distributor and marketing campaign type
- number of screens for exhibition
- use of new technologies in the film
- content – does the film have any particular ideological point to make?
- audience reception of the film
- box-office.

positioning of independent cinema. Films that offer a challenge to dominant notions of gender, class, nationality and sexuality, are often 'enjoyed' most by those who wish to question ideological standpoint and debate social issues.

Case Study 7: *The Blair Witch Project* (Myrick and Sánchez, 1999)

Made for $35,000, *The Blair Witch* project went on to make $1,000,000 at the box-office. The film was made with financing from the directors' own pockets and investment from other individuals. Distributed ultimately by Artisan, *The Blair Witch* team began their distribution campaign with what has gone down in history as one of the most successful internet teaser sites ever. The site presented itself as authentic and created such 'word of mouth' on the internet, that the release of the film was eagerly anticipated. The film was shot entirely on digital cameras and edited on digital software, and it was both the hand-held camerawork and the grainy nature of some of the footage which helped to generate the film's distinctive style.

Audiences flocked to see the film, which seemed to both extend the boundaries of the horror genre and combine horror with documentary effects. Although not particularly challenging ideologically, the film's shooting style and use of digital technologies do make it an alternative experience to mainstream horror products. The marketing of the film continued the blurring of reality and fiction that had been introduced through the film's website. Posters for the film showed the female character's eye, transfixed by something terrifying outside of the shot. This marketing campaign did not highlight the stars, special effects or huge action sequences of a film – instead, it promoted the new experience of horror that the film promised to deliver. As a film with a low budget, an original style of cinematography, a reliance on digital cameras and a non-resolved ending, *The Blair Witch Project* makes a very good example of an independent film.

Fandom – and its significance to the film industry

One of the best resources for your work on this section of the FS6 exam will be your notes from your FS2 exam preparation. The work that you completed and the case studies you compiled for FS2 will be very useful when approaching the topic of 'fandom'. Your FS2 exam will have posed many questions connected with the film industry, including those concerning the relationship between the film consumer and the industry that creates film products. This section asks you to expand on these FS2 considerations and to include your own experiences as a film consumer in your answers.

An interesting area to consider first is the nature of fans and fandom. What constitutes a fan? You will need to consider who this person is, before moving on to consider their relationship with the film industry. The questions to ask when distinguishing a fan from an ordinary film viewer are listed below.

1. Does this person visit websites for particular genres of films, directors or stars on a regular basis?

2. Will this person go to see a film regardless of pre-release adverse criticism, because it is in a particular genre or has a particular star or director?

3. Does this person take part in extra-viewing activities related to their chosen fan pre-occupation, such as conferences, being part of a crowd at a premiere or contributing to a website?

Issues relating to fandom

The central issue of this topic might be said to be control. Is it the film industry that dictates the products that are released, or is it members of the film audience, who often have specific expectations of particular films. Your FS1 studies brought up the issue of genre and its importance to both the film industry and the film spectator. These dynamics could provide the basis for extended study in the FS6 exam. If audiences have conscious or unconscious knowledge of the conventions which they expect to be apparent within a particular genre of film, then are genre products released to cater for this need? You might argue that the proliferation of certain genre releases at certain times in cinema history dictates the films available to audiences and caters solely for a specific group of fans of a specific genre. This argument would indicate a controlling of fan consumption and an attempt by the industry to create new fans of the genres that are proving to be the most lucrative at the box-office. The alternative argument to this is that by releasing 'clumps' of disaster movies, slasher films or films inspired by comic books, the film industry is responding to a prevalent audience 'taste' for particular genres of film.

Another important issue to consider is the impact of marketing and publicity on film fans. Saturation marketing techniques that bombard film audiences with posters, trailers, tie-ins and press coverage could be said to create demand, rather than respond to it. The same applies to star-related fandom. You should consider the point at which an actor becomes a star and the role of the industry in sustaining the actor's star status. In today's film world, stars are not taken from 'stables', in which they were groomed for star billing; they usually rise up through a number of films until there has been enough exposure to make them part of audience word of mouth. Is it a foregone conclusion, therefore, that with enough film and press exposure any actor can become a star and thus generate a body of fans?

The role of fan-related literature is another area you will need to consider in your discussions of this topic. Fanzines and fansites on the internet provide a very useful gauge of the current level of interest in certain types of films, stars and even directors. The internet, especially, has provided a global forum for fan debate and this global forum could be read in two ways. It could be said that a vast number of sites and a high volume of positive comment about a film or star might prompt the film industry to release films that cater for this expressed need.

On the other hand, if internet fan-based discussion comes post-release, then it could provide momentum for a film's continued appeal.

Your task for this topic will be to highlight the main areas of debate around this topic and use your own film consumer experience to substantiate your responses. Can there be such a thing as fan autonomy, whereby the fan of a particular genre, director or star is directly catered for by the films released into cinemas? Is it the case that the fan is in fact constructed by distribution and marketing devices, in order to provide a consistent consumer for film industry products? Or is the relationship between the fan and the film industry mutually influencing? Make sure that you formulate your own responses to these questions during your preparation for this topic.

EXERCISE 8

Using the internet, make a note of as many fansites as you can find. For each of the sites describe the content and breadth of fan contribution. When you have completed these notes, also note down whether you think the site was created before or after the release of a particular film. How do the notes you have made inform your discussions about the nature of the relationship between the film industry and film fans?

Case Study 8: Genre, fans and the industry

In recent years, films inspired by comic books have become some of the most successful films at the box-office. Cinemas around the world have exhibited *Spiderman*, *Spiderman 2*, *Hulk*, *Daredevil* and the *Batman* series. These films were all 'inspired' by established comic books and all had existing fan bases. For the film industry, however, a pre-existing audience is in fact a double-edged sword. In this case, on the one hand, people who enjoyed the comic books might have been relied on to go and see the film, on the other hand, the expectations they had may mean they were critical of the film versions. What the film industry had to do with the comic book films was to include enough of the original elements of these comic book tales to encourage the existing fan base, and at the same time, employ enough special effects and big action sequences to attract a new audience.

There is no clear cut answer to the question of how much influence the fans of this type of film had on the films that were eventually released. There are two potential audiences – the fan of the comic strip and the fan of the big budget, blockbuster spectacular. In the case of *Spiderman* both of these fan groups were satisfied. Peter Parker still had the naivety and skills of the original Spiderman character for the comic book fans, but he also managed the kind of spectacular action sequences that would satisfy fans of the summer blockbuster. The sheer number of films inspired by comic books that came out in close succession also demands two potential readings. For the industry, one success justified further huge investment. For the consumer, the promise of the recognisable and the original (usually CGI-generated) was enough to make them go back to the cinemas for more. It has to be remembered, also, that the fans of these films were not wholly drawn from the ranks of those who had enjoyed the original comic books. Many young audience members were not only engaged by the films themselves, but the promise of superhero outfits, games, toys and plastic characters with their fast food.

Section C. Meanings and Values: Critical approaches

Genre and authorship studies

This topic draws directly on your FS1 Macro and FS4 Auteur study knowledge. As with any of the questions for the FS6 exam, the focus of this topic will be to assess how useful the application of genre and authorship study is to film, and to consider whether using a critical framework such as these allows more information to be gained from the text.

Genre studies

As you will have realised from your FS1 Macro studies, genre has a function for both the producer of a film and the consumer of that film. For the film industry, genre provides a means by which films can be classified for marketing and publicity purposes. Genres are 'born' when elements of a pre-existing, financially successful, film are transferred to other films. Obviously, these conventions are modified to some degree, to retain audience interest, but they come to function as a template for future films. In this way, the film industry seeks to replicate box-office success and to secure financial return on a film. This combination of the 'same and yet different' also functions to secure audience recognition and engagement. Whether consciously or unconsciously, viewers associate particular conventions with particular types of film and expect to see the conventions they expect. This gives viewing satisfaction, but has to be combined with a novel or different presentation of conventions so that the viewer feels that they are watching a 'new' film. Genre classification is ultimately a means by which a film can be identified for both the audience and the film industry. Your evaluation of genre studies should extend beyond this, however, and consider what the study of a genre can tell us. Genres and generic conventions are not fixed. They are fluid – responding to external factors, such as the historical, social and ideological context of the genre film. Once you have discussed the usefulness of identifying different genres, you should also analyse the factors in play at the time a particular film was produced that affected the way in which generic elements were used.

There are many important questions you will need to ask of yourself in your preparation for this topic – you should remember to treat genre studies as a critical framework that you can question and assess. Consider whether or not you think an auteur signature is possible within the making of a genre film. You may decide that originality and predictability of generic format are mutually exclusive, or you might find directors who seem to bring an individual signature to the genre pieces they create. You should also consider the reasons why genre criticism emerged and whether it came about in response to auteur criticism, which highlights the work of the director rather than the generic elements of a film.

Genre criticism moved film criticism away from a focus on the auteur. Even the French publication, *Cahiers du Cinema*, which had elevated the auteur to such a high degree, began to publish articles on genre theory in the 1960s and early 1970s. Andre Bazin, a central figure within the *Cahiers* critics' writing on auteurism, wrote 'The Evolution of the Western' during this period in order to assess the impact of genre rather than auteur. If auteur theory sought to uncover a director's repeated signature characteristics within a film, genre theory concentrated on how analysis of genre components could liberate meanings concerning the social ideologies that surrounded the making of a particular film. Genre becomes, in this instance, the framework for a film. What overlays that framework, in terms of the particular presentation of genre characteristics, is indicative of the social context of a film and the dominant ideologies that were apparent at that time. Genre theory thus seeks to identify similarities and differences, both of which are influenced by a film's context.

Bazin and the film critic Robert Warshaw used the Western genre as a basis to discuss genre systems. This early genre theory focused on the way in which generic elements become subconsciously recognisable to the viewer and therefore to function as an organising system for audiences and as a means by which films can be recognised. In the 1980s, genre criticism began to expand its remit to include discussion of films as cultural products. If generic conventions are repeated across a group of films and these conventions are affected by the cultural and ideological context in which these films were made, then genre study could provide a useful means by which dominant ideologies could be understood. Genre study therefore became a means of understanding how issues such as race, gender, age and nationality were viewed at the time a film was produced. The ways in which American Indians have been represented within the Western over the years, for example, clearly narrates the shifting attitudes of audiences to this group of people. You should remember, then, that genre has a textual, contextual and institutional significance. It is not static and can be used as a barometer of social ideas. When attempting an understanding of a film text, consider whether a genre studies perspective might be a useful tool.

Authorship studies

You have already considered auteur theory during your FS4 studies and probably have already formulated an opinion as to how useful auteur identification is. For this topic, the focus is the framework of auteur criticism, rather than its application to specific individuals and their work. In contrast to genre studies, auteur theory holds that the director is the primary creative force behind their film; that it is the repeated use of individual signature characteristics that distinguishes a group of films from any other, rather than the genre connections between those films.

Auteur study first became widely noted in *Cahiers du Cinema*, the French publication mentioned in the earlier section on genre. Before writing about genre and the Western, Andre Bazin and his fellow *Cahiers* critics focused on the importance of the director within the style of a film. In 1954, Francois Truffaut's essay 'Une certaine tendence du cinema Francais' ('A certain tendency in French cinema') cohered the *Cahiers* critics' thinking, criticising traditional French film making and calling for a cinema of auteurs. The *Cahiers* critics then wrote a series of articles which identified those directors they viewed as original and significant. This list included the likes of Alfred Hitchcock, but excluded directors such as John Huston. The subjectivity implied by this list is something you will need to consider carefully.

Auteur theory did not just remain in France. Andrew Sarris' essay 'Notes on the Auteur theory in 1962' effectively brought auteur theory to America and defended the process of 'ranking' directors. Sarris translated auteur theory into three governing criteria, which could be used to assess a director's potential auteur status. You should analyse these criteria carefully and decide whether you think they provide an effective framework for criticism:

1. An auteur has to be technically competent and cannot merely leave the technical production of a film to others.

2. The auteur will include within their work certain repeated signatures. These might be stylistic, thematic or ideological.

3. The auteur's own personality and tendencies will become evident within the films they make. This might be conscious or unconscious.

Your evaluation of auteur theory should challenge the ideas of the *Cahiers* critics and the criteria identified by Sarris. In your discussions, you should also challenge the notion of a single creative vision behind a film by considering the impact of other key personnel (cinematographers, editors, composers and screenwriters), the studio behind the film and the technology available to the auteur. If, for example, a director utilises CGI (computer generated imagery) within their work, is the film still entirely a product of that director's vision or have the individuals who created the CGI elements had an impact on the overall work?

Your consideration of auteur study should include answers to all of the questions outlined above. You might decide that an auteur approach to films liberates different kinds of meanings than genre study, but meanings that can be of equal importance. You might, on the other hand, conclude that analysis based purely on one individual restricts the potential meanings of a text.

Case Study 9: Genre study of Wes Craven's *Scream* (1996)

The horror genre includes many sub-divisions (or sub-genres): slasher films, psychological horror and gothic horror cinema. Sub-genres and hybrid forms (films that merge more than one film genre) take conventions and utilise them in a way that may be amended, subverted or self-consciously commented upon. Wes Craven's *Scream* provides an example of the slasher format, but also offers a commentary on the construction and consumption of the horror film.

The classic conventions of the horror film include: the 'final girl', a frightening place, brooding or ominous *mise-en-scène*, narratives that move from equilibrium to disturbance and back to a new equilibrium (although according to Structuralist critic Todorov, this deep structure is evident in all stories), a monster/monstrous human, themes of death and destruction, iconography such as knives and masks, and a disorientation or disturbance of the audience. In *Scream*, these conventions are employed literally and at the same time, self-consciously. The dialogue of the film includes detailed descriptions of the mechanics and effects of the horror film.

Sydney (played by Neve Campbell) fulfils the role of the final girl. The characters around her are picked off one by one, and she is left at the end of the film having to confront the killers. This confrontation allows her to discover the true identities of the killers and find out the truth about her own mother's murder. The final girl re-establishes order by confronting her own past traumas and fears.

In *Scream*, the frightening place is not a gothic castle or an isolated house, but the family home. From the first killing of Casey Becker in her middle-class suburban home, we realise that the place we would normally consider to be safe is, in fact, a place of danger. Part of the threat and fear generated in this film is concerned with the invasion of the familial and domestic. These killers attack in the home, thus making the invasion that much more intimate.

The opening scene of Casey Becker's killing also provides examples of the ominous *mise-en-scène* characteristic of a horror film. She moves around a house lit by lamps that provide pockets of light and shadow. The darkened spaces are frightening for Casey and also for the viewer, because they provide places for a killer to hide. The lack of illumination in the scene is both literal and symbolic: neither we nor Casey know what lurks in the darkness. The mist over the swimming pool, which we see when Casey looks out of the window, also provides an example of disorientating *mise-en-scène*.

In terms of narrative, *Scream* follows the equilibrium-disturbance-new equilibrium pattern of most horror films. The peace of the small town is broken by the killing of Casey and chaos ensues as other characters become victims. The mid-section of the film charts the successive killings and the inability of the local police to solve the crime. It is only with the final confrontation scene that peace is reinstated. This equilibrium, however, is of a wiser and more cynical type.

The monsters in *Scream* are, of course, the killers who bring chaos and death into the world of the film. What is interesting about Wes Craven's version of this convention, however, is that they are not damaged victims who kill because of their own pain. These are bored teenagers with little or no motive (at one point in the film a character comments on the horror genre, proclaiming: 'This is the millennium. Motives are incidental.') and for many viewers this is a far more frightening creation. Death and destruction are what is inflicted upon the world of the film by the killers, but in *Scream* we are made to look further into this theme. Within a media-saturated environment, where we are bombarded with images of death and pain, are we becoming desensitised to the reality of killing? Sydney lives with the horror of her mother's murder and as a character shows us the reality of what is seen on the screen, but those around her seem not to understand the impact of killing fully (until of course they become the killers' next victim). Through the character of Gayle Weathers (the news reporter), Craven debates this point; Gayle has written a sensationalist book about the man she thinks killed Sydney's mother. For many of the characters in the film, murder provides either a book deal or part of the horror film genre and has ceased to be seen as a real threat.

Scream includes many classic icons of horror. We see knives and a mask in the opening sequence and these are used throughout the film to signify the killers. Knives are intimate and violent weapons. The killer must attack from close quarters and often stabs many times, heightening the fear and pain of the victim. *Psycho, Halloween* and *Nightmare on Elm Street* all include the use of knives, with the first two films also including disguises or masks. Horror films use disguise as a means of disorientating the viewer and obscuring the killer's identity until the end of the film.

As has already been mentioned, the position of the audience is important to the effectiveness of the horror genre. Often, we are 'placed' within a scene – *Scream* includes many scenes in which we are positioned as Casey Becker or Sydney, waiting for the attack. Subjective (or point-of-view) camerawork forces us to enter a scene of a film and experience the character's fear. The dangerous situations we are sometimes forced to experience make the pleasure of the film's final peace and safety even more palpable.

Horror films often have a knowledgeable audience who are aware of horror conventions and have certain expectations of the genre. *Scream* acknowledges that its audience will have seen previous horror films. It invites us to comment on the predictability of the genre and at the same time offers us a new, self-conscious, but none the less frightening, example of the horror film.

Ultimately, the application of genre study to Wes Craven's film does liberate meaning. The film acknowledges its debt to the horror genre and its sub-genre, the slasher film, by creating thrills and chills, while at the same time offering a discussion of that genre. Identifying and discussing the generic codes used in this film allows for an interesting study of the changing nature of slasher films and the changing contexts in which slashers have been made.

EXERCISE 9

Using the case study above as a template, choose a genre film and write an analysis of how the generic elements of that film have been used. What is the impact of this use on the film viewer?

Performance studies

You may come to this topic of study feeling that it follows on from your FS2 studies of the nature of the 'star'. Your preparation for the FS2 exam component on stars will be relevant here, but performance studies extend the evaluation of the star into the arena of physical performance. Whereas in your FS2 preparation you would have sought to make a distinction between actors and those who have been constructed as stars, this FS6 topic focuses on the way in which the physical performance of an actor can be 'read' by the film spectator.

The style and movement of a physical performance not only demands a response from the viewer to the individual who is performing, it also has an impact on the film as a whole. The meanings that can be generated through an individual performance are legion. You should consider the ways in which elements of a performance are translated into meaning by the viewer. Probably the easiest place to begin your discussions of this topic is with a question. What is the function of performance for the film spectator? The first possible answer to this question involves 'suspension of disbelief'. This is the process by which a film spectator 'forgets' the context in which the film is being shown, and the fact that events are fictional and have been squeezed into an artificial time frame. Performance is of central importance within this process. For characterisation to be believed and suspension of disbelief to take place, the actor has to physically perform an authentic version of the character, as well as deliver that character's lines. Performances that do not seem to suggest the psychological, as well as the physical, reality of the character will stop the viewer from believing the fiction.

Physical transformation

This process can even be affected by the look of the character. The actor needs, to a greater or lesser degree, to transform into the character. This process might include prosthetics; it will include hair and make-up, but it also needs to involve an adoption of body language and body movement that the viewer will read as authentic. Charlize Theron's performance of the central character in *Monster* (2003), for example, required prosthetics, body padding and authentic costume, but equally importantly, it required Theron to perform the heavy, nervous movement of the central character. Even with a perfect visual transformation, the viewer's belief in Theron's character would have been shattered if the actress had moved with the grace she normally has.

You do not have to involve yourself with complicated discussions of semiotics in order to provide a successful exam answer for this topic. However, some reference to the meanings signified by different elements of performance would be of use. You should consider the list of elements below when evaluating the importance and impact of a particular performance:

1. Voice: accent, intonation, pitch.
2. Facial movement and facial gesture.
3. Body idiosyncrasies: particular movements created for that character.
4. Physical presence in the cinematic space: how much room does this character take up?
5. Body movement: walking, running, dancing etc.

Any one of these elements of performance can produce meaning concerning the character's state of mind, their emotional response to another character, or their importance within the narrative as a whole. All of them act as signifiers of meaning and all of them have a potential impact on the viewer. They might encourage an empathetic response, a desirous response or a revulsion.

Viewer expectations

There is another aspect of performance that will be important for you to discuss – the expectations of the viewer of the cinematic experience. The performances we see that seem to promise escape for the viewer into a more exciting world need to help register that excitement. The role of performance within a blockbuster, for example, is quite specific. Audiences do not want to be reminded of the mundane or the ordinary, they expect to be transported into an arena in which things are possible. This expectation can be deconstructed in a number of ways. Action heroes need to be active, for example, they must present a physique and a performance that makes the viewer believe they are capable of great physical feats. Love interests need to be either physically beautiful or present attractive characteristics. The villain in a big budget film must not be completely indistinguishable from the good characters.

In order to create a comprehensive answer under this heading you will need to consider all of these different issues. Whether you write about stars or actors in your answers, remember to consider them in terms of the meanings generated by their performance, the effect this performance has on the rest of the film, and the relationship between that performance and the cinema audience.

EXERCISE 10

Choose an example of a performance from both a mainstream and an independent film. Using the criteria outlined in this section, make notes on the similarities and differences between these two performances.

Case Study 10: Dustin Hoffman's performance in *Rain Man* (Levinson, 1988)

This was a performance for which Dustin Hoffman won a Best Actor Oscar. The story of the film centres around two brothers: Charlie and Raymond Babbit. Charlie is a self-absorbed man who seeks to use his autistic savant brother in order to win him money at the Las Vegas casino tables. The relationship is initially fraught, but as is expected from a mainstream film, Charlie is eventually transformed by the relationship he has with his older brother.

In terms of performance, Dustin Hoffman's role was by far the most difficult. Tom Cruise, as Charlie, acted as the handsome, self-obsessed younger brother, but in many ways this role predominantly was there to provide a physical and emotional contrast to Raymond. As with any performance of a disabled character, the potential for stereotyping and offence had to be considered within the performance. The vulnerability of the character of Raymond was created through both the contrast with the character of Charlie and Hoffman's physical presence itself. Hoffman is shorter than Cruise and far less athletic in physique. This immediately suggested that it should be the younger brother looking after the older one. Hoffman's shuffling walk also contributed to the impression that this was a character who was not confident in the world.

The story required Charlie to take Raymond out of his usual environment and place him in scenarios that he would, at least initially, find threatening. The order and repetition required by an autistic person was represented in the film by Raymond's need to have certain food for his meals and to watch particular TV programmes at set times of day. If the security of repetition is broken for an autistic person they may become extremely distressed – this was represented by Hoffman through a series of incidents in which he began to smack his own head and become physically disorientated.

Raymond's voice was also central to the audience's understanding of his character. His tendency to repeat words said to him and the soft, low voice in which he spoke confirmed for the audience that this was a character who was childlike, vulnerable and very different from his louder, brash brother. To create the necessary suspension of disbelief that would allow viewers to believe that an actor whom they had seen many times before, could fully occupy the role of an autistic savant, Dustin Hoffman had to at once appear vulnerable within the film and also be registered as the focus of it. An early scene, in which both the viewer and Charlie Babbit realise that Raymond is in fact a savant (he knows immediately how many toothpicks have been dropped on the floor) establishes Hoffman's character as the governing interest in the film's narrative.

Film interpretation and social/cultural studies

Although the title of this topic might initially appear daunting, it does in fact pick up on many of the skills and some of the content analysis you have done before. The main focus of this section is an exploration of the relationship between text and context. In other words, you are being asked to discuss how the messages and values you identify within a film might help you understand the world from which the film comes. Your key area of consideration will be what can be understood about the social and political attitudes that surrounded a film's production.

Key areas to consider

You have met this kind of study before and both your FS3 and FS5 preparation can be used within this topic. What can be added to this are your own observations and evaluations that have been generated by your film viewing experiences outside of the classroom. You should not forget the analytical skills you gained during the FS3 and FS5 units when discussing this topic area – your understanding of representation and messages and values will be extremely important. Make sure that you consider the four key components of representation discussion in your essays:

1. An analysis of how micro and macro elements help construct the way in which certain individuals and groups are represented.

2. A discussion of what the particular presentation of groups and individuals seems to suggest about the film text's attitude to them.

3. The relationship between this attitude of the text and the dominant attitudes that were present at the time of the film's production.

4. Your own response to the attitudes present in both the film and the film's context.

You will need to consider whether or not the relationship between the opinions and attitudes expressed in your case study films conflict with or confirm those which surround the film.

As with any of the topics within Section C for the FS6 exam, it will also be important to discuss whether or not you think this kind of analysis is useful and productive. Does an understanding of a film's context make the viewing experience more complete, or does it over-complicate the experience for the viewer?

As with your earlier studies, there are many representational areas that it would be possible to discuss and therefore many social attitudes that you could evaluate. Issues of class, race, gender, age and nationality can be explored through many of the film examples you have already studied. You could look back to your FS3 notes and extend your evaluation of the relationship between the representation of Scotland in films such as *Trainspotting* and *Ratcatcher*, and then investigate whether or not these representations seem to echo dominant social attitudes. Or, you might consider the way in which the working man was presented in examples from Soviet cinema and consider whether this representation tapped into dominant social thought.

You might decide to look at other examples from your own viewing experience, and discuss what ideological understanding can be gained from analysis of the relationship between film text and film context. There are many recent examples of films, which although not present within your FS3 and FS5 studies, would provide very useful debate. Mel Gibson's *The Passion of the Christ*, for example, includes very specific representations of Christ, the Jewish elders and the Romans. The film has spawned much debate and a consideration of whether or not this film mirrors dominant social attitudes to these groups, and to Christ, could provide a fascinating case study.

EXERCISE 11

With a partner, choose a scene from one of your case study films. Then, using the four stages of representational analysis set out earlier, make detailed notes on the construction of representation, the attitudes of the film, the relationship between the film's attitudes and those around it, and your own thoughts on the debates you identify.

Case Study 11: The introduction of Jim and Jim in *American Beauty* (Mendes, 1999)

American Beauty deconstructs notions of the American Dream. All of its main characters live in a world of affluent suburbs and economic choice. The houses are large, they have white picket fences, and the costumes and cars of the characters also confirm the context of the film as middle-class America. The central character, Lester Burnham, lives next door to a gay couple, both of whom are called Jim. Their introduction into the story of *American Beauty* is highly significant in their representation.

During the opening sequence of the film, Lester Burnham's wife Carolyn is seen in their front garden tending to her perfect roses. Lester watches out of the window as one of the Jims approaches Carolyn to ask her advice about growing roses. He is dressed very smartly, is obviously a professional and is presented very clearly as part of the American Dream. The Jims live in a large, perfectly presented house, they are both professional men and they are a gay couple. Aside from Lester's introduction of them, 'that's Jim and that's his partner, also called Jim', the Burnham family never refer to the couple's sexuality. The Jims are seen in scenes later in the film helping Lester to get fit. They are not only happy and wealthy, but they are also healthy and kind: all of which contributes to their representation in this film as a perfect couple, who are perfect neighbours, who live a perfect American life.

There is only one character in this film who is presented as homophobic – Colonel Fitz, who lives on the other side of the Burnhams. His attitude, however, is criticised by the film and presented as entirely outdated and offensive. Of course, the last scenes of the film reveal why this character is so homophobic: he is in fact gay, but has repressed his feelings and transformed them into a masking bigotry.

The *mise-en-scène* surrounding the two Jims, their dialogue and the attitudes of the majority of the other characters, suggests that their presence in this film is important because they contribute to a debate about the nature of the American Dream – not because the film discusses being gay. The stance of the film is clear. However, it is debatable whether their representation in this film is consistent with that of all America.

Gendered film studies

For many students, this topic can seem extremely daunting. The extraordinary amount of gender-related criticism available and the complexity of the language often used in this criticism is indeed quite off-putting. However, this topic does not demand that you wade through volumes of feminist and gender-related debate. The focus in the gendered film studies topic is not film theory, but audience response. You do not have to be able to quote vast tracts of critical debate in order to formulate a successful essay in the exam. What you need to be able to do is show understanding of the basic issues of gender-related perspectives and use this understanding to assess film examples. These examples can have been directed by either male or female directors. You could examine mainstream or independent film examples. Whatever film text you choose to examine, your basic question is the same: does applying a framework of criticism such as a gender-related perspective allow greater appreciation of a film text?

There are particular key terms and ideas with which you should make yourself familiar and you will need to use these in your pieces of analysis. These terms should act as a framework for your assessment of film and your evaluation of the usefulness of a gendered analysis of film texts:

- representation
- the 'male gaze' and objectification
- exhibition
- gendered genres
- gender and race.

Representation

As representation is a key concept of Film Studies, you already have discussed it in depth. In the context of this particular topic, discussions of representation should focus on how textual elements have been used to construct particular representations of gender. As a filter through which dominant ideological positions can be understood, representational analysis will be a key feature in your evaluations of how the film text relates to its social context. You should begin any analysis of representation by identifying how stylistic devices have been used in your chosen film to construct a character (or group of characters). Consider how features of *mise-en-scène*, cinematography, sound and editing have been used to imply a particular attitude towards this character or group. Once this stage of analysis has been completed, you should consider how the attitude or position implied by the character's construction relates to any debates external to the film. It is this interaction between the representation used in the film text and the dominant attitudes of the social context in which the film was produced that will fuel your discussions. You will need to consider carefully whether or not you think the representation of gender offered by the film challenges, or reinforces, dominant social ideologies. Your film might deconstruct stereotypes through its particular representations, or it might present confirmation of them.

One interesting way in which to analyse gender representation is through a genre-based approach. Given the fact that genres evolve and the presentation of genre conventions is affected by dominant social ideologies, a study that chronologically traces the representation of gender within a specific genre can reveal much about changing social attitudes. Try the exercise below, in order to assess how genre developments can reveal shifting social attitudes to gender.

EXERCISE 12

The grid below includes a chronological list of horror films. It also includes a series of headings that you should use in your analysis of these films. Watch as many of the films (or sections of the films) listed as you can. For each, make notes under the headings on the grid.

When you have made your notes, discuss what you think the different representations of female characters indicates about the gender-related social attitudes that existed at the times the films were made.

	Narrative significance of female characters	Significant micro elements used with female characters	Attitudes of male characters to female characters	Social attitudes challenged or reinforced by representation
Nosferatu (1922)				
The Mummy (1959)				
Psycho (1960)				
Dracula: Prince of Darkness (1966)				
Halloween (1978)				
Alien (1979)				
Scream (1996)				
The Blair Witch Project (1999)				

The 'male gaze' and objectification

This is a phrase originated by Laura Mulvey in her 1975 essay 'Visual Pleasure and Narrative Cinema'. You do not, however, need to read the whole of Mulvey's essay in order to understand and effectively use the idea. The concept of a 'male gaze' is based on the assumption that traditional narrative cinema is structured around a series of looks; characters looking at each other and the audience looking at the characters. According to Mulvey, the look is controlled by male characters within the film and the male members of the audience. Female characters are more looked at than looking. In this dynamic, the female characters become the objects of the gaze of not only the male characters, but also the male members of the cinema audience. The female characters are thus excluded from this dynamic, because the male characters within a film are not constructed as objects of a gaze. Mulvey attaches the Freudian term 'scopophilia', to the male gaze and thus defines the look as at least sexual and at its extreme, perverse. According to Mulvey's theory, a further level of male empowerment and gaze control comes from the economic context of (especially) Hollywood products. The male-dominated Hollywood film industry constructs objectified female characters in order to cater for male audiences.

In a consideration of whether or not you think the films you have chosen as case studies construct a male gaze, you should substantiate your comments with specific textual details. Does the cinematography used in your film position the female characters as objects of the gaze? Are the female bodies in your film fragmented through close-ups of the female form? Are point-of-view shots constructed as sexually motivated? You could even consider films that are explicitly about 'looking' and the perverse extreme of the male gaze. Michael Powell's controversial 1960 film *Peeping Tom*, for example, which tells the story of a serial killer obsessed with filming his female victims and then watching the footage, would provide a fascinating study. Whether Powell's film ultimately condemns its killer or makes the viewer complicit in his perverse desires would make an interesting question for debate.

Another interesting avenue of discussion under the heading 'male gaze' would be to attempt to find examples of films in which the cinematography constructs male characters as the object of a gaze or films in which there is equal objectification of both male and female characters. Sally Potter's 1992 film *Orlando* could provide one such case study. As a character whose life spans several centuries, and both genders, Orlando is seen desiring male and female characters. In one of her historical incarnations, the now female Orlando meets the character of Shelmerdine. These two characters not only discuss gender identity and express opinions about gender roles that are contrary to those dominant in their historical context, they are also both shot with a series of lingering close-ups and point-of-view shots. Shelmerdine and Orlando are both presented as objects of desire – male *and* female viewers are given the opportunity to desire them.

Exhibition

Characters within a film who invite objectification and a desirous gaze 'exhibit' themselves. They perform for the other characters and for the cinema audience, demanding that they be viewed. Exhibition has traditionally been the preserve of female film characters, in an attempt to get both male characters and male audience members to notice them. The exhibiting female character might be dancing, singing, walking or moving in any other way that demands notice. As an act that seems to be of the characters own volition i.e. it is not forced, this type of exhibition might initially appear to indicate female control. However, it is the desired result of the exhibition that needs to be evaluated: if the object of the exercise is male attention, then power does not really rest with the female character. Grace Kelly's character in Hitchcock's *Rear Window,* for example, presents her body and her name to

James Stewart's character while she walks around his apartment, turning on lamps. We understand very clearly in this scene that this kind of deliberate exhibition is the only way the female character can secure the male character's attention. You should consider whether the female characters in your chosen films seek to secure the male gaze by performing or exhibiting. They might not be dancing, singing or taking off their clothes, but they might be 'performing' for male characters and viewers all the same.

Whether male characters in films exhibit in the same way is an interesting question and you might add in to your discussions examples of film sequences in which the 'performance' is male. Gene Kelly's dance routine in *Singing in the Rain* certainly secures audience attention, but is the motivation behind the performance concerned with encouraging female desire? The narrative trajectory of *The Full Monty* is towards the final strip routine and the naked men are presented in front of a mostly female crowd. The motivation of this explicit piece of exhibition, however, has been defined very clearly from the beginning of the film. These men strip for financial security and a reinstatement of their self-belief. Demi Moore's strip routines in *Striptease* are apparently also motivated by financial need. Whether or not the sequences from these two films are comparable, or whether the latter, through both *mise-en-scène* and cinematography, constructs the strip as predominantly titillating for a male audience, would provide an interesting case study debate.

Gendered genres

The question of whether particular genres of film have a gender bias is an interesting one. In the section on representation, the changing representation of women within particular genres was discussed, but the genre debate can be taken further into a consideration of whether particular genres are targeted at either male or female audiences. Yvonne Tasker is a film critic who has written extensively on the relationship between gender and genre. She has identified particular genres that have traditionally been the preserve of male audiences and questions whether they are being reshaped for a wider (and of course, more profitable) cinema audience. Tasker has focused on the action genre to discuss this particular debate and this genre does indeed generate some interesting questions.

Traditionally, the action hero is male and a maverick, and exhibits the kind of physical prowess that makes him ultimately triumphant against any odds. Since *Aliens* (1986), however, there have been examples of action films and action hybrids that have featured a female lead. *Terminator 2* (1991) and *The Long Kiss Goodnight* (1996), for example, are both action films in which the physical prowess of the central female character are highlighted. The female leads in these films wear the regulation action costume, a white vest, they handle firearms with confidence and dispatch enemies without a qualm. These women are not, however, wholly without the kind of female characteristics that would make them acceptable to male-dominated action audiences. In *Terminator 2* and *The Long Kiss Goodnight,* the female characters have children, and in *Aliens*, Ripley has a surrogate child. This, according to Yvonne Tasker, is the narrative compromise that makes the centralising of the female in the action genre acceptable.

Your case studies of gender and genre could extend beyond the action genre into others that have traditionally presented male orientated narratives and centralised male characters. You might consider the reworking of the road movie genre within Ridley Scott's *Thelma and Louise* or the Western with the female gunslinger, *The Quick and the Dead* (Sam Raimi). Whether these films do little more than provide a novelty within an established genre would be an interesting topic of debate. Another possible avenue for analysis within the area of gender and genre would be those films that have been designated 'chick flicks' by their publicity. Films that are explicitly targeted at a female audience and are marketed as if they can be grouped as a kind of genre could provide interesting examples of study. Romantic comedies, which are traditionally targeted at a female audience, would provide further fruitful study. You could consider whether films such as *Miss Congeniality, Bridget Jones' Diary, You've Got Mail* and *Two Weeks Notice* actually do present and discuss the kind of female-related issues their marketing seems to promise. Ultimately, your question on gender and genre should be whether or not genre is gender specific and what impact this has on cinema audiences.

Gender and race

One of the most recent additions to the gender and film debate has been that of gender and race. Feminist film critics, such as bell hooks and Tania Modleski have written extensively on the representation of black female characters and their representation. The issues of race and representation could provide you with a very interesting topic of debate, especially given the omission of this area of debate from much of early gender-related writing. As with all of the sub-sections within the gendered perspectives topic, an approach based on case study is the most straightforward. It is not necessary to confine yourself to non-white directors or female directors – an evaluation of films from male and female, ethnic and white directors could produce very interesting comments. You might look at Steven Spielberg's *The Color Purple*, for example, and assess whether or not it presents an authentic narrative of black female oppression or a packaged, stylised version. Forest Whitaker's *Waiting to Exhale*, which presents the lives of four African-American women, whose challenges are less financial than relationship orientated, could also make for an interesting case study. The films of Gurinda Chadha, which include *Bhaji on the Beach* and *Bend it Like Beckham*, and centralise the Asian woman's experience in Britain, would also make for interesting study.

Whatever films you choose to focus on, you will need to evaluate whether or not an authentic female experience is being presented to audiences and what particular circumstances of non-white female characters are being articulated by the film. Consider the intent of the films you have chosen. Do they document, challenge or entrench attitudes to women from ethnic minority groups? If the characters you are studying live within an adoptive culture, what is the relationship between this culture and the women who have moved into it?

Case Study 12: Is romantic comedy a genre for women?

When you have made your notes, discuss what you think the different representations of female characters indicates about the gender-related social attitudes that existed at the times the films were made. As a genre of film that has traditionally been designated 'female', an analysis of romantic comedy provides much interesting debate. This case study will ask a series of questions about romantic comedy from a gendered perspectives position, in order to assess whether this genre is indeed for women. There may be a central female character in a romantic comedy, and her experiences might also be central to the narrative, but do these films make a feminist point or merely entrench conservative standpoints on gender?

The first question that needs to be asked of this genre concerns objectification and exhibition. Are female characters in romantic comedies objectified within the narrative and do they perform or exhibit themselves for male affirmation? If objectification is constructed through cinematography, then the use of point-of-view shots and bodily fragmentation will help to establish an answer. Post-transformation, Sandra Bullock's character in *Miss Congeniality* is seen walking towards the camera, in slow motion. The viewer's vantage point is the same as the character played by Benjamin Bratt. We are encouraged to be as impressed by her recreation as he is. The first visual introduction the viewer gets to Julia Roberts' character in *Pretty Woman*, is through a series of shots of her torso. The viewer does not in fact see her face until two or three minutes into her introduction.

The second question concerns the relationship between the film text and the female spectator. If romantic comedy is a genre for contemporary female audiences, then viewer's might expect to see a lesser degree of compromise or sacrifice on the part of female characters. Contemporary audiences might expect the narrative trajectory of a film to avoid the subsuming of the female character into a male-dominated dynamic. A much more conservative and traditional narrative trajectory still seems to exist, however, and whether the character is a lawyer who gives up her principles for her relationship (*Two Weeks Notice*), or a bookshop owner who falls for the man who has put her out of business (*You've Got Mail*), it is the male character's life and expectations that seem to be dominant in the end.

The third question that can be asked of the romantic comedy genre concerns the issue of female experience. The resolution sequence of a romantic comedy traditionally has a relationship or a marriage. Although contemporary romantic comedies do not always end with marriage, they do end with a relationship, which is presented as the goal of the female character. *Bridget Jones' Diary* narrates the character's obsession with finding a relationship, even the slightly less traditionally structured *My Best Friend's Wedding* sees Julia Roberts' character literally chasing the object of her affection.

As a means of assessing romantic comedies, the central ideas of a gendered perspective approach prove very telling. Neither film language or film narrative construct the female characters in these films as particularly empowered. What comes across most strongly is that even within an environment of more progressive attitudes to women, rom coms maintain their particular conservative stance.

Exemplar essay 1: Section A

Question: Is a film more likely to shock viewers through its content, or the way in which this content is presented?

To a certain extent, the nature of shock is subjective. Different viewers will have different attitudes, viewing expectations and levels of sensitivity. A film might have content that is shocking for one viewer, and use a visual style that shocks another. Making a distinction between the content and the style of a film is problematic, however, and it is usually a combination of the two that has the most affect.

There have been examples in cinema history of films that have such cinematic originality, that their shocking content seems to have become almost acceptable. D.W. Griffiths' 1915 film *Birth of a Nation*, for example, was technically innovative and in many ways furthered cinematic developments. It was, however, explicitly racist in content, something the viewing public did not seem to mind or even register, as they flocked to see the film in their tens of thousands. It might be argued that the film has only been read as racist retrospectively, but campaigns at the time the film was shown and a retraction of praise by President Woodrow Wilson prove that it was known that the content was extremely problematic.

Surrealist cinema provides another interesting topic of debate for this question. With incredibly shocking imagery, such as the eye slitting sequence in Bunuel's *Un Chien Andalou*, these films also rejected classic patterns of narrative and explicitly criticised middle-class values. The seemingly unconnected series of images that many Surrealist films contained, the lack of formal narrative and attacks on social institutions, such as the church, the military and the police, all contributed to their shocking impact. For Surrealist cinema, especially, image and content were inextricable.

Stanley Kubrick's 1971 classic, *A Clockwork Orange*, also provides an interesting example within this debate. The shocking visual elements include Alex's torture scenes, the phallic masks of the droogs and the horrific images of the captured writer's wife prior to her rape. All of these visual elements have the potential to shock. What Kubrick's film also does, however, is engage the viewer through dynamic and original visuals. The swirling hand-held camera effect of Alex's teasing and murder of the Cat Lady and the stylish slow motion of the droogs' walk near the canal, are more engaging than shocking. The way in which many of the events are visually presented could be said to detract from their potential shock effect.

Visual dexterity seems to have been an important element within Oliver Stone's creation of *Natural Born Killers*. Stone employs different types of film stock, animated effects and montages of imagery in order to tell the story of mass murderers Mickey and Malory Knox. The style used to present their story is slick. What viewers must ask themselves, however, is whether or not this type of visual demands an engagement with and attraction for the main characters, which is inappropriate given the horrific violence of which they are capable.

Whether a film shows images of mutilation and carnage through stylish visual effects, or more literally and brutally, both have the capacity to shock the viewer. Unfortunately, however, within a period in cinema history in which ever more dazzling stylistic devices are being employed within films, there is a potential for the shock effect of content to be overshadowed by the 'wow factor' of the way in which the content is presented.

Assessment comments

This essay engages very confidently with the essay title. It offers appropriate film examples and has chosen these examples from different periods within cinema history in order to make different points. There is an obvious assurance in this candidate's writing and the issues contained within the essay title are fully explored. Confident and accurate work. Grade A.

Exemplar essay 2: Section B

Question: With reference to a key point within censorship history, discuss some of the key issues that influenced censorship decisions at that time.

Film censorship is an evolving entity. At its best it can ensure the safe passage to cinema screens of relevant and challenging films, but at its worst it can either 'butcher' film texts or place films within a certification category that will make it impossible for the people who should be watching the film to see it. The early 1970s in Britain was a particularly fraught time in censorship history and many issues concerning the BBFC and the viewing public came to the fore.

The first two years of the 1970s saw a major change in the running of the BBFC. Stephen Murphy took over as the BBFC's Chief Censor and with his new position,

She also inherited a number of very contentious films. The role of town councils within the regulation of film also came into the limelight during this period. The first film to encounter the influence of town councils was Ken Russell's 1971 film *The Devils*. The BBFC censors had debated long and hard over this film. It contained graphic depictions of violence and contained controversial images, such as masturbating nuns. Eventually, however, the film was passed by the BBFC, with an X certificate. Cuts had been made to some of the more sadistically violent scenes, but the nudity had remained, as had the anti-religious element. This film's release sparked a campaign by the Christian pressure group, The Festival of Light, who claimed that the film was blasphemous and should be banned. The BBFC did not withdraw the film from circulation, but many town councils banned it from their local cinema screens. The message to the public was clear: a BBFC certificate was only the first stage of a film's release. A film might not remain in cinemas long, if town councils bowed to public pressure.

Stanley Kubrick's *A Clockwork Orange* was also of great significance within the censorship debate. The film included scenes of rape and murder. It also presented these events from the point of view of the film's corrupt protagonist, Alex. Kubrick's film was, however, as much a condemnation of the institutions who punished Alex, as a condemnation of the character himself. It was deemed fit for cinema screens by the BBFC and passed with an X certificate. As with *The Devils*, however, this was not the end of the story for *A Clockwork Orange*. Stories of so-called 'copycat' crimes began to hit the press and Kubrick received death threats. It was not the town councils who banned the film this time, however, but Kubrick himself who withdrew his film from circulation. The film was not shown again in Britain until after the director's death in 1999.

In 1972, debate and outrage over a film eventually caused legislation to be amended. Bernardo Bertolucci's film *Last Tango in Paris* was passed by the BBFC, with some cuts, and released into cinemas. A tale of the sexual affair between two people, this film attracted the attention of not just The Festival of Light, but also a retired man who brought about a private prosecution of the film, claiming that it depicted a real affair between the two main actors, Marlon Brando and Maria Shriver. This private prosecution sought to prosecute the film under the Obscene Publications Act, but it was not until the case had begun that lawyers discovered that the Act did not cover film. *Last Tango in Paris* escaped prosecution, but its case did prompt others to call for an Act that could cover film. In 1977, the Criminal Law Act brought film into the Obscene Publications Act.

Whether censorship came in the form of cuts from the BBFC, town council rulings or self-imposed withdrawing from distribution, the films released within the first two years of the 1970s did come in for much debate and criticism. The events in the first part of this decade do highlight a number of important issues regarding censorship and regulation at this point in history, however. The BBFC did not have the last word in censorship and their decisions could be overthrown by town councils or a film's director. The case of *Last Tango in Paris* also highlights an interesting fact. Up until 1977, the legislation on offer did not have jurisdiction over film. Legislation had not kept up with the changes and developments in film content.

Assessment comments

This is a very detailed response, which discusses a particular point in regulation and censorship history very confidently. The candidate has avoided merely describing events within this period and has extended factual detail into a discussion of the nature of censorship itself. The essay engages with the issue of 'who censors?' clearly and competently and uses the case studies identified to consider the varying influences on censorship decisions. This essay shows excellent historical knowledge, as well as a firm grasp of relevant debates. Grade A.

Exemplar essay 3: Section C

Question: With reference to specific case studies, discuss the value of using a critical framework, such as gendered perspectives.

Critical frameworks of any description are often a double-edged sword. They have the potential to 'liberate' more meanings from a film text; however, they also have the capacity to render the film being analysed somewhat two-dimensional and seemingly important on only a few levels. What they can be relied upon to do is to produce some interesting information about a film text, just not all of it. A gendered perspective-driven study can encourage very useful debates concerning the representation of gender and the importance of gender issues within cinema today. Analysis of the particular type of representation attached to a character or group of characters, and the place of debates concerning gender roles and gender identity within a film, can be indicative of not just the attitudes of the film itself, but of social attitudes around that film.

The key areas of analysis within any gendered perspectives analysis are objectification, exhibition and the 'male gaze'. This essay will consider how these terms can be used in the gender-related analysis of *Fargo* (Coen Brothers, 1996) and *The Hours* (Stephen Daldry, 2003). The Coen Brothers film has a central female character: Chief Marge Gunderson. Marge is not just a central character, she is the detective in the film who unravels events and eventually arrests the criminal. The Coens' film is a generic mix of thriller and black comedy, with the character of Marge playing a significant role within both genres. In terms of the thriller narrative, it is Marge who stops the chaos that has ensued from the committed crime. It is she who re-establishes law, order and tranquility to the world of the film. These are usually tasks put aside for the male character within the thriller genre. In terms of the black comedy elements, the scene in which Marge meets her old school friend Mike, has to ward off his advances and then hears that his wife has died (this is subsequently shown to be a lie), is one of the best black comedy moments in the film. Frances McDormand's Marge, therefore, is not marginalised within the film's narrative, neither is she relegated to a supporting role.

In terms of objectification, exhibition and the male gaze, Marge is a very unusual character. She is heavily pregnant throughout the film, the freezing weather means that she is invariable swaddled in clothing and when we do see her in a dress, it is the voluminous pregnancy kind. Marge is the Chief of Police in her area. She has both rank and intellectual superiority over the men who work for her. She is not presented as an object of desire for any of the male characters. Even with her husband Norm, Marge is seen is the object of his care and love, rather than his desire. This is not to say that the Gunderson's relationship is being presented as cold, but the heavy pregnancy and the multiple murder case are obviously priorities for Marge. If Marge exhibits anything in this film, it is her capability, not her body.

Within Stephen Daldry's *The Hours*, female characters again play central roles within the film's narrative. The characters played by Nicole Kidman, Meryl Streep and Julianne Moore provide the focus of the film and the filters through which the film's main issues are discussed. As with Marge in *Fargo*, their *mise-en-scène* disallows objectification. One character is pregnant, one dresses in shapeless clothes and one is in a gay relationship with a woman who no longer seems to see her as desirable. The function of these three women in the narrative is to articulate the film's central concerns of time and memory. The events they experience are tragic and poignant, and these events revolve around them, rather than around the relationships they have with male characters.

With both *The Hours* and *Fargo*, there is an absence of the kind of fragmenting cinematography that is associated with the construction of a male gaze. They are also characters with whom the female audience members can identify. The pivotal position of the female characters in these films, and the lack of objectifying micro elements, serves to present them as the focus, rather than the object of these films. Ultimately, a gendered perspectives framework allows important meanings to be discovered in these film texts.

Assessment comments

This candidate exhibits a confident grasp of both the chosen case study films and the critical framework applied to them. *The Hours* and *Fargo* are discussed with assurance, and the points made by the candidate are clearly substantiated with textual reference. The candidate's understanding of film form and of representational issues are clear within this very systematic argument. Grade A.

Formal questions to consider

Early cinema before 1917

1. To what extent does the experience of contemporary cinema audiences differ from that of early cinema-goers?

2. What impact did social and political issues have on the products of early cinema?

Documentary

1. Is there a marked difference between the way audiences view documentary and fiction films?

2. Is it possible to identify consistent cinematic conventions within documentary films?

Experimental film making

1. What do you consider to be the main challenges to audiences when viewing experimental films?

2. Are the experimental elements of the films you have studied predominantly visual?

Shocking cinema

1. Is it the subject matter of the films you have studied or the way in which this subject matter is visually presented, that is most shocking for cinema audiences?

2. To what extent are images of graphic violence and explicit sex the most shocking for cinema audiences?

Regulation and censorship

1. What do you consider to be the main motivating factors behind changes in cinema regulation and censorship?

2. With reference to a particular period within cinema history and specific case study examples, discuss the relationship between film regulation and dominant social opinions.

The dominance of Hollywood and indigenous film production

1. What do you consider to be the main economic differences between Hollywood and a specific example of an indigenous film industry?

2. With reference to specific case studies, consider whether or not it is possible for indigenous film industry products to gain global exposure.

Independent film and its audience

1. Is independent film stylistically or financially different from mainstream film?

2. How useful is it to group different film examples under the heading of 'independent'?

Fandom – and its significance to the film industry

1. What influence do film fans have on the film products we see in cinemas?

2. How important are new technologies in the creation of fans for particular films?

Genre and authorship studies

1. Do critical frameworks, such as genre and authorship studies, allow for a greater understanding of film texts?

2. With reference to case studies, consider the strengths and weaknesses of either a genre or authorship studies approach to analysing film.

Performance studies

1. Using reference to particular performers, consider whether an analysis based on performance studies adds to the viewer's appreciation of film texts.

2. Is it possible to separate the performer from their performance? Refer to specific case studies of performers in your answer.

Film interpretation and social/cultural studies

1. Does the consideration of a film's messages and values detract from or add to the viewer's appreciation of a film?

2. With reference to particular case studies, discuss the ways in which evaluation of the ideological impact of film affects the viewing experience.

Gendered film studies

1. Using specific case studies in your response, consider the ways in which an analysis of gender has allowed you a greater appreciation of film texts.

2. With reference to at least two films, discuss the ways in which a gendered film studies perspective has changed your reading of a film.

Glossary

A

above-the-line costs: the costs of a film before shooting begins, including those for locations, screenwriters, directors and actors.

aerial shot: a camera shot taken from an overhead position. Often used as an establishing shot or within an action sequence.

ambient sound: the normal sound that already exists within a particular scene or location.

animation: the process by which inanimate objects are made to look as if they move. Animation might be 'stop motion' or computer generated.

artificial light: a source of light created by lighting equipment, rather than from natural sources.

audience: people who watch a film.

auteur: a French word meaning author. Used to refer to a director whose work contains characteristic elements.

B

BBFC (The British Board of Film Classification): the organisation that allocates certificates to films in Britain.

back lighting: the type of lighting that comes from behind a character.

back story: information given in a script that outlines details about a character's life, but is not shown in the film.

behind-the-scenes footage: information about the making of a film, often found within DVD extras.

below-the-line costs: the costs of a film after shooting has begun. These costs include those for locations, costumes etc.

billing: the placement of an actor's name on publicity material, such as posters. The position of a name on a poster will indicate the status of an actor.

blockbuster: a term used to describe big budget Hollywood films.

blue screen/green screen: a process in which action is shot in front of a blue or green screen. This action is then overlaid onto either a real or computer-generated background.

Bollywood: the Indian film industry.

box-office: a term used to describe the amount of money generated by a film after its cinema release.

C

Cahiers du Cinema: the French film criticism magazine, begun in 1951 by Andre Bazin.

camera angle: the position of the camera in relation to the subject of a shot. The camera might be above, below or at eye level with what is being filmed.

canted framing: a camera angle that makes what is shot appear to be skewed or tilted.

censorship: the process by which a film is deemed to be fit or unfit for audience viewing.

CGI (Computer-generated imagery): images that have been generated on computer software and then added to a film.

character theme: the element of a soundtrack which becomes associated with a particular character in a film.

chiaroscuro lighting: a type of highly contrasting lighting, which gives deep shadows and bright highlights.

cinematographer: the person responsible for camerawork and lighting on a film.

cliff-hanger: the end of a scene or a film that does not give a sense of resolution to the film's audience .

continuity editing: the most common type of editing, which aims to create a sense of reality and time moving forward.

contrapuntal sound: a soundtrack, the tone and feel of which seems to be at odds with the images being shown.

convention: a frequently used element which becomes standard in a group of films.

credits: the information at the beginning and the end of a film, which gives details of cast, crew, producers and distributors.

cult film: a film that might not have had box-office success at the time of its release, but over time has generated a loyal following.

cutaways: shots of objects or people which are not part of the main scene, but have relevance to it.

cut-in shot: a shot of a small element within a scene, which is shown because it is of importance.

D

deep focus: a type of camerawork that shows action near and far away from the camera with equal clarity.

denouement: the moment in a film when all of the secrets and enigmas of the narrative are revealed to the audience.

diegesis: the story of a film.

diegetic sound: sound that can be heard by the characters within a scene.

disequilibrium: the period of instability and insecurity within a film's narrative.

distribution: the marketing, promotion and placement of a film in particular cinemas.

dolly: a platform on wheels, on which a camera can be placed and then moved around.

E

editing: the stage in the film-making process in which sound and images are organised into an overall narrative.

enigma: the question or mystery that is posed within a film's narrative.

equilibrium: a state of peace and calm, which often exists at the beginning of a film's narrative.

exhibition: refers to the showing of a film to audiences on cinema screens.

eyeline match: a type of edit which cuts from one character to what that character has been looking at.

F

feature film: a full length film shown at the cinema.

fill light: a type of light used to lessen the impact of harsh shadows that may be thrown by other lights used.

film form: a term used to describe the shape or structure of a film.

final cut: the final version of a film after all of the sound and image editing has been completed.

flashback: a scene or moment in a film in which the audience is shown an event that happened earlier in the film's narrative.

flash forward: a scene or moment in a film in which potential future events are shown to the film audience.

framing: the selection of elements such as characters, setting and iconography that appear within a shot.

freeze frame: the effect of seemingly stopping a film in order to focus on one event or element.

G

genre: a system of film identification, in which films that have the same elements are grouped together.

graphic match: an edit effect in which two different objects of the same shape are dissolved from one into the other.

gross: the amount of money a film makes at the box-office before expenses have been deducted.

H

high concept: a term used to describe big budget films, which have spectacular sequences and high production values.

high-key lighting: a type of lighting that creates balanced lighting within a scene and emphasises bright colours.

hype: the interest and excitement generated about a film that is about to be released.

I

iconography: the objects within a film that are used to evoke particular meanings.

institutions: the companies or organisations that play a role within the film-making process.

intertextuality: reference within a film to another film, media product, work of literature or piece of artwork.

J

jump cut: a type of edit that seems to jump from one image to another, without attempting to sustain continuity.

juxtaposition: the placement of two (often unconnected) images or scenes on either side of an edit to create an effect.

K

key light: the brightest light source used within a scene.

L

linear narrative: a style of storytelling in which events happen chronologically.

low-key lighting: a type of lighting that creates a dim or underlit scene.

M

mainstream cinema: a term used to describe films which are made for a wide or mass audience.

marketing: the process by which a film is advertised to potential audiences.

master shot: a shot which contains all of the action in a particular sequence.

merchandising: products which are sold on the back of a film release, such as toys and clothes.

mise-en-scène: a French term, which literally means 'put into the frame'.

mogul: a word used to describe the extremely powerful individuals who ran studios during the 'Golden Age' of the Hollywood Studio System (1930–1948).

montage editing: the editing together of seemingly unconnected images.

multiplex: a cinema complex which has a large number of screens and shows mostly mainstream film products.

N

narrative: a term used to describe the way in which a story is told.

national cinema: the film industry and film products within a particular country.

non-diegetic sound: sound that does not exist within the story of the film, but is put onto the film in post-production, such as the soundtrack and voice-overs.

O

overhead shot: a type of camera shot in which the camera is positioned above the character, action or object being filmed.

P

package: a portfolio of information put together by a film producer in order to entice investors to back a film. Often contains information about key cast members and key scenes in the film.

panning: the horizontal movement of a camera from left to right or vice versa.

parallel editing: a type of editing in which events within two locations are cut together, in order to imply a connection between the two sets of events.

pitch: the short description of a film, which includes key elements of characterisation and plot, which is used to ignite interest in a film-making project.

POV (point-of-view) shot: a shot that positions the viewer as if they were a particular character.

post-production: the stage of the film-making process, in which editing and special effects work is completed.

pre-production: the period within the film-making process, before filming begins, in which the producer of the film will organise both personnel and finances.

prequel: a film which is set chronologically before another film which has already been released.

producer: the individual who secures financing for a film and organises details of the locations, cast and crew.

projection: the process of transferring a film from celluloid or digital tape onto a cinema screen.

pyrotechnics: special effects within a film which involve fire, fireworks or explosions.

R

reaction shot: a shot that shows the reaction of a character either to an event or to another character.

remake: a film that has the same title and storyline of a previous film and echoes the original closely.

representation: the way in which a particular individual or group are presented within a film and the attitudes which this presentation suggests.

rough cut: the first edit of a film, which might do little more than organise shots taken into an order.

S

screenplay: the written details of a film's dialogue, camera work, lighting and settings. Used during the filming process.

sequel: a film in which story and character seem to echo a film that has already been released.

sets: artificially constructed locations for a film.

setting: the place in which the story (or parts of the story) take place.

sleeper: a film that does not initially appear to be a success at the box-office, but eventually proves to be very successful.

sound: the elements within a film that can be heard, rather than seen.

soundbridge: sound that extends from one scene to another, over an edit.

sound effects: sounds that are added to a film during the post-production stage.

sound track: the music added to a film in the post-production stage.

split screen: the separating of the screen into two parts, each of which holds images attached to a different story.

stop motion animation: the process of shooting models one frame at a time and then editing these frames together to create animation.

storyboard: a series of, often hand-drawn, pictures, that outline what

needs to be shot in a particular scene.

synergy: the release of two products, such as a film and a song from that film's soundtrack, at the same time, to create mutually beneficial publicity for the two products.

synopsis: a brief description of the main characters and events used within a film.

T

teaser trailer: a trailer that includes only a few 'titbits' from a forthcoming film, used to generate initial interest.

tie-in: a promotional product associated with a particular film, which is often given away with fast food.

trailer: a series of short extracts edited together to provide an advert for a forthcoming film. Contains more information than a 'teaser trailer'.

U

underlighting: a lighting effect where the main source of light within a scene comes from below a character. This is often used to make a character appear frightening.

V

vertical integration: a situation in which one company owns the means to produce, distribute and exhibit films.

voice-over: a commentary from one individual or character, which explains the events being presented to the film viewer.

W

whip pan: an extremely fast horizontal camera movement.

wipe: an edit type in which one image seems to push another off the screen.

Bibliography

General Film Books

Cook, David A., 1996, *A History of Narrative Film*, W.W. Norton and Company

Nelmes, J. (ed.), 2003, *An Introduction to Film Studies*, Routledge

Tasker, Y. (ed.), 2002, *Fifty Contemporary Filmmakers*, Routledge

Bordwell, D., and Thompson K.,1990, *Film Art: An Introduction*, McGraw-Hill

Bordwell, D., and Thompson K.,1994, *Film History: An Introduction*, McGraw-Hill

Hill, J., and Church Gibson, P. (eds.), 2000, *Film Studies: Critical Approaches*, Oxford University Press

Nelmes, J. (ed.), 2003, *Introduction to Film Studies*, Routledge

Haywood, S., 1996, *Key Concepts in Cinema Studies*, Routledge

Cook, P., and Mieke Bernink, M. (eds.),1999, *The Cinema Book*, British Film Institute

Hill, J., and Church Gibson, P. (eds.), 1998, *The Oxford Guide to Film Studies*, Oxford University Press

Websites

www.aint-it-cool-news.com
Useful for popular reviews.

www.bfi.org.uk
Information about the BFI's resources and reviews/articles from *Sight and Sound* magazine.

www.cinema-sites.com
Includes listings for many useful specialist film sites.

www.documentaryfilms.net
Listings for useful documentary film sites.

www.entertainmentlink.co.uk
Contains many useful links to film sites and sites concerning stars and directors.

www.filmeducation.org
Information on particular films and film concepts.

http://film.guardian.co.uk
Reviews and articles on films, directors and stars.

www.imdb.com
Institutional information of all kinds on thousands of film titles. Biographical information on directors and stars. An exceptionally useful site.

www.ukscreen.co.uk
Useful information concerning the British film industry.

Magazines

Sight & Sound

Empire

Total Film

Premiere

Media Magazine (published by the English and Media Centre, www.englishandmedia.co.uk)

Index